MR. DOOLEY
ON IVRYTHING AND IVRYBODY

by

Finley Peter Dunne

Selected and with an Introduction by
ROBERT HUTCHINSON

DOVER PUBLICATIONS, INC.
NEW YORK

This new Dover edition, first published in 1963, is a selection from the following editions of works by Finley Peter Dunne:

Mr. Dooley in Peace and in War, Small, Maynard & Company, 1898.
Mr. Dooley in the Hearts of His Countrymen, Small, Maynard & Company, 1899.
Mr. Dooley's Philosophy, R. H. Russell, 1900.
Mr. Dooley's Opinions, R. H. Russell, 1901.
Observations by Mr. Dooley, R. H. Russell, 1902.
Dissertations by Mr. Dooley, Harper & Brothers, 1906.

Robert Hutchinson selected the essays and wrote an Introduction for this Dover edition.

International Standard Book Number: 0-486-20626-2

Library of Congress Catalog Card Number: 63-2652

Manufactured in the United States of America

Dover Publications, Inc.
180 Varick Street
New York 14, N.Y.

INTRODUCTION

Finley Peter Dunne, one of America's great humorists, was born in Chicago on July 10, 1867, the son of middle-class Irish parents. His father was a carpenter, devoutly Catholic; his mother an invalid who shared with her seven children her great love of literature. The boy was considered bright at home but unpromising at school: he graduated last in his class of fifty at West Division High School and went to work for the Chicago *Telegram* as an office boy. Four years later, at the age of twenty-one, he astounded everyone by becoming, in Horatio Alger style, city editor of the Chicago *Times*. Four years after that, in 1892, he was placed in charge of the editorial page of the Chicago *Evening Post*. Success seemed to be at hand: Dunne wanted to become a great publisher and write editorials that would mold public opinion.

His success was to come in a different form. Impressed with the brilliant strokes of humor that crept into Dunne's copy, Cornelius McAuliff, managing editor of the *Post*, suggested that Dunne write a series of weekly humorous articles for the *Post's* new Sunday edition. The articles would be unsigned, and Dunne would be paid ten dollars apiece for them. Dunne agreed to try; and on December 4, 1892, the Post carried a purported dialogue between "Colonel McNeery" (actually James McGarry, who kept a respectable public house on Dearborn Street) and John J. McKenna, a small-time Chicago politician. More articles followed, and interest in the series grew. When McGarry became concerned about the notoriety he and his bar were receiving, "Colonel McNeery" was allowed to return to Ireland; and on October 7, 1893, Mr. Martin Dooley, Roscommon Irishman, bachelor, and one of the great characters in American literature, made his first public appearance behind the bar of the small saloon he ran on "Ar-rchey Road" (Archer Avenue), center of Chicago's poor Irish population. Hennessy, the great listener, came along in 1896.

From the first the series was acclaimed by Chicago readers as something completely new. There had been cracker-box philosophers before—Dakota farmers and Tennessee mountaineers —but never a city man, and never one so knowing and so sophisticated as Mr. Dooley. Dunne's own onetime reservations about dialect humor were forgotten in the popular clamor for more of Mr. Dooley's colorful speech. And Dunne was not long in seeing that the series offered, through the person of Mr. Dooley, a perfect opportunity to speak out against the corruption and hypocrisy so apparent at all levels of Chicago life during the 1890's. Through Dooley he could name corrupt Council members, through Dooley attack aldermen like Bathhouse John Coughlin and promoters like Charles T. Yerkes. And because Mr. Dooley was so funny and meant only half of what he said, no one, not even persons directly named, could long take offense. The Pullman Strike of 1894, with its attendant sufferings along Archer Avenue, particularly stirred Dunne's efforts. Sometimes, in essays like "When the Trust Is at Work" and "The Idle Apprentice," he went beyond comedy into a new tragic dimension in his compassion for the sufferings of the poor; more often he struck at Chicago's conscience with the equally potent weapon of laughter.

It was not until an incident in the Spanish-American War that Mr. Dooley achieved nation-wide renown. In 1898 Commodore George Dewey was known to have sailed into Manila Harbor to engage the Spanish fleet; because of a cut cable details of Dewey's victory were not known, though rumors of all kinds could be heard. Dunne, to whom the comic-opera aspects of the war had previously supplied ideas, seized upon the national mood and struck just the right note in "On His Cousin George." The essay attained instantaneous approval. A rebellious session of the Texas Bar Association was brought to order by it; Ambassador Choate read it aloud to an English audience. Secretary of the Treasury Lyman J. Gage, seeing one of Mr. Dooley's satires on the President's Cabinet, sent it to Secretary of the Navy John D. Long, who replied that Dooley must be "a fictitious name for somebody near the scene of action." Soon Dooley essays were being read aloud as a regular part of Cabinet meetings. By 1899 the country had gone Dooley-mad: popular songs were being written about Dooley; newspapermen were guessing—correctly—the identity of his creator; college presidents were quoting him;

Henry Adams recommended him to friends. Nor was it Dunne's humor alone that was attractive: Dunne was supplying pertinent answers to some of the troublesome questions that perplexed America as it extended its influence in the wake of the Spanish-American War. Few writers had ever been so powerful in swaying public opinion. It is no wonder that Theodore Roosevelt during his administration sought Dunne's friendship and wrote him long letters of self-defense if he thought Finley Peter Dunne disapproved of any of his actions.

In 1898, at the height of the Dooley craze, Dunne brought together, at the suggestion of his friends, his first authorized collection, *Mr. Dooley in Peace and in War*. It sold at the rate of 10,000 copies a month and was pirated in England. The next year *Mr. Dooley in the Hearts of His Countrymen*—dedicated to the publishers who had, "uninvited, presented Mr. Dooley to a part of the British public" and containing some of Dunne's finest tragic pieces—maintained a similar popularity. Later books, such as *Mr. Dooley's Philosophy* (1900), *Mr. Dooley's Opinions* (1901), *Observations by Mr. Dooley* (1902), and *Dissertations by Mr. Dooley* (1906), were less successful, probably because of the competition they faced from Dunne's own widely syndicated newer essays.

It was, ironically, Dunne's own popularity that first tended to undermine the Dooley articles. As his audience grew wider, Dunne had to select subjects of more and more general appeal; his short satiric pieces about corruption in Chicago tended to become longer examinations of human foibles and weaknesses. His blows, too, became softer as he mellowed, and he apparently found it difficult to recapture the old rowdy feeling of Archey Road. On the other hand, the later work shows greater profundity, and the level of writing, like that of the humor, remains astonishingly high. If anything, it was Dunne's own high artistic standards that slowed down his rate of production—his high standards and the old, half-forgotten urge to be a "serious" writer. This urge he revived when, in 1906, he joined Lincoln Steffens, Ray Stannard Baker, and William Allen White on the editorial staff of *The American Magazine*. Here he produced, in the section "In the Interpreter's House," long, discursive articles, polished and thoughtful, on all the subjects he had never, as Dooley, been able to write about. They were his wisest statements, but the public was uninterested.

The public wanted Dooley, and Dunne refused to revive him even for the First World War. After a bequest in the will of Payne Whitney allowed Dunne to retire in 1927, he wrote very little until his death in 1936. Like Conan Doyle and many another creator, Dunne had been trapped into competing with his own brain child.

It is, nevertheless, the Dooley articles that are the best of Finley Peter Dunne, and those who would turn away from them because the dialect form does not at first sight appear inviting or because a few forgotten names appear in them are depriving themselves of a rare and pleasurable experience. The briefest familiarity with the dialect will reveal that here, in whatever spelling, is some of the richest humor America has ever produced. Whether he is describing Ambassador Choate arriving at Buckingham Palace "as fast as his hands an' knees wud carry him" or misquoting Shakespeare "Be thrue to ye'ersilf an' ye will not thin be false to ivry man," Dunne offers us, in the words of John Kendrick Bangs, "humor boiled down until that which remains is the pure, undiluted essence of humor"—humor, if you like, raised to the third or fourth power. And, far from being dated, what strikes one most about these essays is not their age but their astonishing youthfulness. It is hard to read some of the political essays—on drafting party platforms, on filling Cabinet posts, on electing military men to public office—and believe that they were written, not last week, but sixty years ago. Some views apparently—like ours of the Vice-President or our imagined racial superiority—have not changed at all. Elsewhere Dunne forecasts our own world from his; and automation, superbombs, and the threat of China appear in almost contemporary terms.

It is not that Dunne was interested in predicting the problems of our age, but that he had so remarkable a knowledge of the directions of his own. He is aware, at the moment, of trends historians discover later. And his knowledge is based upon an equally deep insight into human nature. At a time when thought was at its most optimistic in America and modern psychology almost unknown, Dunne saw the human psyche in all its vanity, self-deception, and egoism. "Thrust ivrybody," Dunne says, "but cut the cards." In its total lack of illusion, his view of human history is almost Augustinian, and it is for this reason he grew increasingly wary of reforms: he knew too well the

ambitions of the reformers. " 'Tis only a question," he says,
"iv who does th' robbin'."

It is this hard core of realism that distinguishes Dunne's work
from that of most of his contemporaries. Few other American
humorists could have written the section in "The Pursuit of
Riches" beginning, "Life, Hinnissy, is like a Pullman dinin'-car:
a fine bill of fare but nawthin' to eat." At the same time, few
other American humorists could have risen so gloriously above
their pessimism. "Th' trouble with this house," Dooley's friend
Gallagher tells the forever-cleaning Mrs. Doherty, "is that it is
occpied entirely be human bein's. If 'twas a vacant house, it
cud aisily be kept clean." It is this balance of hard truth and
laughter that keeps Dunne's work so very much alive sixty years
later. In his work, the London *Spectator* wrote, "the whole pot
of civilization boils all the time."

To those of us who encounter it for the first time today, Dunne's
laughter is at once exhilarating, reassuring, and shocking. In our
time it has not been considered good form to joke about the
Supreme Court or the President's age, and in particular our period
is careful to avoid humor that would be offensive to racial and
religious minorities. It must be remembered that Dunne wrote
at a time when such humor was widely accepted. To have
attempted, in the manner of contemporary television, to eliminate
such material from Finley Peter Dunne—the most democratic of
men, who spent a lifetime fighting prejudice of all kinds—would
have seemed to us more shocking than anything in Mr. Dooley's
vocabulary. Those who might be offended by the presence
of certain phrases are invited to look again and at the whole
man.

Certainly no American humorist has ever been more penetrat-
ing in his social criticism or, in his philosophy, more profound.
For a writer of such significance, then, it is all the more surprising
that so little of Dunne's work should have been available in recent
years in book form. Dunne is included in nearly all humor
anthologies; in every campaign Mr. Dooley is widely and fervently
quoted. Yet for many years only a single collection of Dunne's
work has been in print in America.

This Dover edition is an attempt to correct this injustice. It
consists of 102 of the more than 700 dialect essays Dunne wrote
during his lifetime, presented in the order and the form originally
approved by Dunne for book publication. No selection has been

altered or cut; the footnotes are our own.   If the appearance at
this time of the opinions of Mr. Dooley helps to stimulate interest
in one of America's most brilliant humorists, this edition of the
work of Finley Peter Dunne will have fulfilled its purpose.

ROBERT HUTCHINSON

New York, 1962

CONTENTS

MR. DOOLEY IN THE HEARTS OF HIS COUNTRYMEN (*1899*)

MR. DOOLEY'S PHILOSOPHY (*1900*)

MR. DOOLEY'S OPINIONS (*1901*)

OBSERVATIONS BY MR. DOOLEY (*1902*)

DISSERTATIONS BY MR. DOOLEY (*1906*)

MR. DOOLEY IN PEACE AND IN WAR

PREFACE

Archey Road stretches back for many miles from the heart of an ugly city to the cabbage gardens that gave the maker of the seal his opportunity to call the city "urbs in horto." Somewhere between the two—that is to say, forninst th' gas-house and beyant Healey's slough and not far from the polis station—lives Martin Dooley, doctor of philosophy.

There was a time when Archey Road was purely Irish. But the Huns, turned back from the Adriatic and the stock-yards and overrunning Archey Road, have nearly exhausted the original population—not driven them out as they drove out less vigorous races, with thick clubs and short spears, but edged them out with the more biting weapons of modern civilization—overworked and under-eaten them into more languid surroundings remote from the tanks of the gas-house and the blast furnaces of the rolling mill.

But Mr. Dooley remains, and enough remain with him to save the Archey Road. In this community you can hear all the various accents of Ireland, from the awkward brogue of the "far-downer" to the mild and aisy Elizabethan English of the southern Irishman, and all the exquisite variations to be heard between Armagh and Bantry Bay, with the difference that would naturally arise from substituting cinders and sulphuretted hydrogen for soft misty air and peat smoke. Here also you can see the wakes and christenings, the marriages and funerals, and the other fêtes of the ol' counthry somewhat modified and darkened by American usage. The Banshee has been heard many times in Archey Road. On the eve of All Saints' Day it is well known that here alone the pookies play thricks in cabbage gardens. In 1893 it was reported that Malachi Dempsey was called "by the other people," and disappeared west of the tracks, and never came back.

A simple people! "Simple, says ye!" remarked Mr. Dooley. "Simple like th' air or th' deep sea. Not complicated like a watch that stops whin th' shoot iv clothes ye got it with wears out. Whin Father Butler wr-rote a book he niver finished, he said simplicity was not wearin' all ye had on ye'er shirt-front, like a tin-horn gambler with his di'mon' stud. An' 'tis so."

The barbarians around them are moderately but firmly governed, encouraged to passionate votings for the ruling race, but restrained from the immoral pursuit of office.

The most generous, thoughtful, honest, and chaste people in the world are these friends of Mr. Dooley—knowing and innocent; moral, but giving no heed at all to patented political moralities.

Among them lives and prospers the traveller, archæologist, historian, social observer, saloon-keeper, economist, and philosopher, who has not been out of the ward for twenty-five years "but twict." He reads the newspapers with solemn care, heartily hates them, and accepts all they print for the sake of drowning Hennessy's rising protests against his logic. From the cool heights of life in the Archey Road, uninterrupted by the jarring noises of crickets and cows, he observes the passing show, and meditates thereon. His impressions are transferred to the desensitized plate of Mr. Hennessy's mind, where they can do no harm.

"There's no betther place to see what's goin' on thin the Ar-rchey Road," says Mr. Dooley. "Whin th' ilicthric cars is hummin' down th' sthreet an' th' blast goin' sthrong at th' mills, th' noise is that gr-reat ye can't think."

He is opulent in good advice, as becomes a man of his station; for he has mastered most of the obstacles in a business career, and by leading a prudent and temperate life has established himself so well that he owns his own house and furniture, and is only slightly behind on his license. It would be indelicate to give statistics as to his age. Mr. Hennessy says he was a "grown man whin th' pikes was out in forty-eight, an' I was hedge-high, an' I'm near fifty-five." Mr. Dooley says Mr. Hennessy is eighty. He closes discussion on his own age with the remark, "I'm old enough to know betther." He has served his country with distinction. His conduct of the important office of captain of his precinct (1873–75) was highly commended, and there was some talk of nominating him for alderman. At the expiration of his term he was personally thanked by the Hon. M. McGee, at one time a member of the central committee. But the activity of public life was unsuited to a man of Mr. Dooley's tastes; and, while he continues to view the political situation always with interest and sometimes with alarm, he has resolutely declined to leave the bar for the forum. His early experience gave him wisdom in discussing public affairs. "Politics," he says, "ain't bean bag. 'Tis a man's game; an' women, childher, an' pro-hybitionists'd do well to keep out iv it." Again he remarks, "As Shakespeare says, 'Ol' men f'r th' council, young men f'r th' ward.'"

An attempt has been made in this book to give permanent form to a few of the more characteristic and important of Mr. Dooley's utterances. For permission to reprint the articles the thanks of the editor are due to Mr. George G. Booth, of the Chicago *Journal*, and to Mr. Dooley's constant friend, Mr. H. H. Kohlsaat, of the Chicago *Evening Post*.

F. P. D.

ON WAR PREPARATIONS[1]

"Well," Mr. Hennessy asked, "how goes th' war?"

"Splendid, thank ye," said Mr. Dooley. "Fine, fine. It makes me hear-rt throb with pride that I'm a citizen iv th' Sixth Wa-ard."

"Has th' ar-rmy started f'r Cuba yet?"

"Wan ar-rmy, says ye? Twinty! Las' Choosdah an advance ar-rmy iv wan hundherd an' twinty thousand men landed fr'm th' Gussie, with tin thousand cannons hurlin' projick-tyles weighin' eight hundherd pounds sivinteen miles. Winsdah night a second ar-rmy iv injineers, miners, plumbers, an' lawn tinnis experts, numberin' in all four hundherd an' eighty thousand men, ar-rmed with death-dealin' canned goods, was hurried to Havana to storm th' city.

"Thursdah mornin' three thousand full rigimints iv r-rough r-riders swum their hor-rses acrost to Matoonzas, an' afther a spirited battle captured th' Rainy Christiny golf links, two up an' hell to play, an' will hold thim again all comers. Th' same afthernoon th' reg'lar cavalry, con-sistin' iv four hundherd an' eight thousan' well-mounted men, was loaded aboord th' tug Lucy J., and departed on their earned iv death amidst th' cheers iv eight millyon sojers left behind at Chickamaha. These cav'lry'll

---

[1] The disorganized state of the United States army on the eve of the Spanish-American War was a natural subject for Dunne's satire. Here he refers to the arrival of General Nelson A. Miles, his wife, and their two children at the camp at Tampa, Florida.

co-operate with Commodore Schlow; an' whin he desthroys th' Spanish fleet, as he does ivry Sundah an' holy day except in Lent, an' finds out where they ar-re an' desthroys thim, afther batterin' down th' forts where they ar-re con-cealed so that he can't see thim, but thinks they ar-re on their way f'r to fight Cousin George Dooley, th' cav'lry will make a dash back to Tampa, where Gin'ral Miles is preparin' to desthroy th' Spanish at wan blow—an' he's th' boy to blow.

"The gin'ral arrived th' other day, fully prepared f'r th' bloody wurruk iv war. He had his intire fam'ly with him. He r-rode recklessly into camp, mounted on a superb specyal ca-ar. As himsilf an' Uncle Mike Miles, an' Cousin Hennery Miles, an' Master Miles, aged eight years, dismounted fr'm th' specyal train, they were received with wild cheers be eight millyon iv th' bravest sojers that iver give up their lives f'r their counthry. Th' press cinchorship is so pow'rful that no news is allowed to go out; but I have it fr'm th' specyal corryspondint iv Mesilf, Clancy th' Butcher, Mike Casey, an' th' City Direchtry that Gin'ral Miles instantly repaired himsilf to th' hotel, where he made his plans f'r cr-rushin' th' Spanyards at wan blow. He will equip th' ar-rmy with blow-guns at wanst. His uniforms ar-re comin' down in specyal steel protected bullyon trains fr'm th' mint, where they've been kept f'r a year. He has ordhered out th' gold resarve f'r to equip his staff, numberin' eight thousan' men, manny iv whom ar-re clubmen; an', as soon as he can have his pitchers took, he will cr-rush th' Spanish with wan blow. Th' pur-pose iv th' gin'ral is to permit no delay. Decisive action is demanded be th' people. An', whin th' hot air masheens has been sint to th' front, Gin'ral Miles will strike wan blow that'll be th' damdest blow since th' year iv th' big wind in Ireland.

"Iv coorse, they'se dissinsions in th' cabinet; but they don't amount to nawthin'. Th' Sicrety iv War is in favor iv sawin' th' Spanish ar-rmy into two-be-four joists. Th' Sicrety iv th' Threeasury has a scheme f'r roonin' thim be lindin' thim money. Th' Sicrety iv th' Navy wants to sue thim befure th' Mattsachusetts Supreme Coort. I've heerd that th' President is arrangin' a knee dhrill, with th' idee iv prayin' th' villyans to th' divvil. But these diff'rences don't count. We're all wan people, an' we look to Gin'ral Miles to desthroy th' Spanish with wan blow. Whin it comes, trees will be lifted out be th' roots. Morro Castle'll cave in, an' th' air'll be full iv Spanish whiskers. A long blow, a sthrong blow, an' a blow all together."

"We're a gr-reat people," said Mr. Hennessy, earnestly.

"We ar-re," said Mr. Dooley. "We ar-re that. An' th' best iv it is, we know we ar-re."

ON MULES AND OTHERS[1]

"I see," said Mr. Dooley, "th' first gr-reat land battle iv th' war has been fought."

"Where was that?" demanded Mr. Hennessy, in great excitement. "Lord save us, but where was that?"

"Th' Alger gyards," said Mr. Dooley, "bruk fr'm th' corral where they had thim tied up, atin' thistles, an' med a desp'rate charge on th' camp at Tampa. They dayscinded like a whur-rl-wind, dhrivin' th' astonished throops befure thim, an' thin charged back again, completin' their earned iv desthruction. At th' las' account th' brave sojers was climbin' threes an' tillygraft poles, an' a rig'mint iv mules was kickin' th' pink silk linin' out iv th' officers' quarthers. Th' gallant mules was led be a most courage-ous jackass, an' 'tis undhersthud that me frind Mack will appint him a brigadier-gin-ral jus' as soon as he can find out who his father is. 'Tis too bad he'll have no childher to perpituate th' fame iv him. He wint through th' camp at th' head iv his throops iv mules without castin' a shoe. He's th' biggest jackass in Tampa to-day, not exciptin' th' cinsor; an' I doubt if they'se a bigger wan in Wash'n'ton, though I cud name a few that cud thry a race with him. Annyhow, they'll know how to reward him. They know a jackass whin they see wan, an' they see a good manny in that peaceful city.

"Th' charge iv Tampa'll go into histhry as th' first land action iv th' war. An', be th' way, Hinnissy, if this here sociable is f'r to go on at th' prisint rate, I'm sthrong to ar-rm th' wild ar-rmy mules an' the unbridled jackasses iv th' pe-rary an' give thim a chanst to set Cuba free. Up to this time th' on'y hero kilt on th' Spanish side was a jackass that poked an ear above th' batthries at Matoonzas f'r to hear what was goin' on. 'Behold,' says Sampson, 'th' insolince iv th' foe,' he says. 'For-rm in line iv battle, an' hur-rl death an' desthruction at yon Castilyan gin'ral.'

[1] In June, 1898, three thousand army mules stampeded at Tampa, Florida, adding to the comic-opera aspects of the war. Mack: President McKinley. Alger: Russell J. Alger, Secretary of War.

'Wait,' says an officer. 'It may be wan iv our own men. It looks like th' Sicrety iv'— 'Hush!' says th' commander. 'It can't be an American jackass, or he'd speak,' he says. 'Fire on him.' Shot afther shot fell round th' inthrepid ass; but he remained firm till th' dinnymite boat Vesoovyus fired three hundherd an' forty thousand pounds iv gun cotton at him, an' the poor crather was smothered to death. Now, says I, give these Tampa mules a chanst, an' we'll have no need iv wastin' ammun-ni-tion. Properly led, they'd go fr'm wan end iv Cuba to th' other, kickin' th' excelsior out iv ivry stuffed Spanish gin'ral fr'm Bahoohoo Hoondoo to Sandago de Cuba. They'd be no loss iv life. Th' sojers who haven't gone away cud come home an' get cured iv th' measles an' th' whoopin'-cough an' th' cholera infantum befure th' public schools opens in th' fall, an' iverything wud be peaceful an' quiet an' prosp'rous. Th' officers in th' field at prisint is well qualified f'r command iv th' new ar-rmy; an', if they'd put blinders on th' mules, they wudden't be scared back be wan iv thim Spanish fleets that a jackass sees whin he's been up all night, secretly stuffing himsilf with silo. They'd give wan hew-haw, an' follow their leaders through th' hear-rt iv th' inimy's counthry. But give thim th' wurrud to git ap, an' they'd ate their thistles undher th' guns iv some ol' Morro Castle befure night.

"Ye don't see th' diff'rence, says ye. They ain't anny i' th' leaders. As efficient a lot iv mules as iver exposed their ears. Th' throuble is with th' rank an' file. They're men. What's needed to carry on this war as it goes to-day is an ar-rmy iv jacks an' mules. Whin ye say to a man, 'Git ap, whoa, gee, back up, get alang!' he don't know what ye'er dhrivin' at or to. But a mule hears th' ordhers with a melancholy smile, dhroops his ears, an' follows his war-rm, moist breath. Th' ordhers fr'm Washin'ton is perfectly comprehinsible to a jackass, but they don't mane annything to a poor, foolish man. No human bein', Hinnissy, can undherstand what the divvle use it was to sink a ship that cost two hundherd thousan' dollars an' was worth at laste eighty dollars in Sandago Harbor, if we have to keep fourteen ships outside to prevint five Spanish ships fr'm sailin'. Th' poor, tired human mind don't tumble, Hinnissy, to th' raison f'r landin' four hund-herd marines at Guanotommy to clear th' forests, whin Havana is livin' free on hot tamales an' ice-cream. Th' mind iv a Demos-theens or a Tim Hogan would be crippled thryin' to figure out why throops ar-re sint out fr'm Tampa an' thin ordhered back through a speakin' chube, while wan iv th' new brigadeer-gin'rals has his hands manicured an' says good-bye to his nurse. But it ought to be as plain to th' mule that hears it as it is to th' jackasses that gets it up. What we need, Hinnissy, is a perfect undherstandin' between th' ar-rmy an' th' administhration. We need what Hogan calls th' esphrite th' corpse, an' we'll on'y have it whin th' mules begins to move."

"I shud think," said Mr. Hennessy, "now that th' jackasses has begun to be onaisy"—

"We ought to be afraid th' cabinet an' th' Boord iv Sthrateejy 'll be stampeded?" Mr. Dooley interrupted. "Niver fear. They're too near th' fodder."

ON HIS COUSIN GEORGE[1]

"Well," said Mr. Hennessy, in tones of chastened joy: "Dewey didn't do a thing to thim. I hope th' poor la-ad ain't cooped up there in Minneapolis."

"Niver fear," said Mr. Dooley, calmly. "Cousin George is all r-right."

"Cousin George?" Mr. Hennessy exclaimed.

"Sure," said Mr. Dooley. "Dewey or Dooley, 'tis all th' same. We dhrop a letter here an' there, except th' haitches—we niver dhrop thim—but we're th' same breed iv fightin' men. Georgy has th' thraits iv th' fam'ly. Me uncle Mike, that was a handy man, was tol' wanst he'd be sint to hell f'r his manny sins, an' he desarved it; f'r, lavin' out th' wan sin iv runnin' away fr'm annywan, he was booked f'r ivrything from murdher to missin' mass. 'Well,' he says, 'anny place I can get into,' he says, 'I can get out iv,' he says. 'Ye bet on that,' he says.

"So it is with Cousin George. He knew th' way in, an' it's th' same way out. He didn't go in be th' fam'ly inthrance, sneakin' along with th' can undher his coat. He left Ding Dong, or whativer 'tis ye call it, an' says he, 'Thank Gawd,' he says, 'I'm where no man can give me his idees iv how to r-run a quiltin' party, an' call it war,' he says. An' so he sint a man down in a

---

[1] Though Commodore George Dewey was known to have met the Spanish fleet at Manila, news of his victory was delayed by a cut cable. In the nation-wide mood of suspense that followed, Dunne wrote one of his most famous essays.

divin' shute, an' cut th' cables, so's Mack cudden't chat with him.
Thin he prances up to th' Spanish forts, an' hands thim a few
oranges. Tosses thim out like a man throwin' handbills f'r a
circus. 'Take that,' he says, 'an' raymimber th' Maine,' he says.
An' he goes into th' harbor, where Admiral What-th'-'ell is, an',
says he, 'Surrinder,' he says. 'Niver,' says th' Dago. 'Well,'
says Cousin George, 'I'll just have to push ye ar-round,' he says.
An' he tosses a few slugs at th' Spanyards. Th' Spanish admiral
shoots at him with a bow an' arrow, an' goes over an' writes a cable.
'This mornin' we was attackted,' he says. 'An,' he says, 'we
fought the inimy with great courage,' he says. 'Our victhry is
com-plete,' he says. 'We have lost ivrything we had,' he says.
'Th' threachrous foe,' he says, 'afther destroyin' us, sought refuge
behind a mud-scow,' he says; 'but nawthin' daunted us. What
boats we cudden't r-run ashore we surrindered,' he says. 'I
cannot write no more,' he says, 'as me coat-tails are afire,' he says;
'an' I am bravely but rapidly leapin' fr'm wan vessel to another,
followed be me valiant crew with a fire-engine,' he says. 'If I can
save me coat-tails,' he says, 'they'll be no kick comin',' he says.
'Long live Spain, long live mesilf.'

"Well, sir, in twinty-eight minyits be th' clock Dewey he had
all th' Spanish boats sunk, an' that there harbor lookin' like a
Spanish stew. Thin he r-run down th' bay, an' handed a few
war-rm wans into th' town. He set it on fire, an' thin wint
ashore to war-rm his poor hands an' feet. It chills th' blood not
to have annything to do f'r an hour or more."

"Thin why don't he write something?" Mr. Hennessy
demanded.

"Write?" echoed Mr. Dooley. "Write? Why shud he
write? D'ye think Cousin George ain't got nawthin' to do but
to set down with a fountain pen, an' write: 'Dear Mack—At 8
o'clock I begun a peaceful blockade iv this town. Ye can see th'
pieces ivrywhere. I hope ye're injyin' th' same gr-reat blessin'.
So no more at prisint. Fr'm ye'ers thruly, George Dooley.'
He ain't that kind. 'Tis a nice day, an' he's there smokin' a good
tin-cint see-gar, an' throwin' dice f'r th' dhrinks. He don't care
whether we know what he's done or not. I'll bet ye, whin we
come to find out about him, we'll hear he's ilicted himself king
iv th' F'lip-ine Islands. Dooley th' Wanst. He'll be settin' up
there undher a pa'm-three with naygurs fannin' him an' a dhrop
iv licker in th' hollow iv his ar-rm, an' hootchy-kootchy girls

dancin' befure him, an' ivry tin or twinty minyits some wan bringin' a prisoner in. 'Who's this?' says King Dooley. 'A Spanish gin'ral,' says th' copper. 'Give him a typewriter an' set him to wurruk,' says th' king. 'On with th' dance,' he says. An' afther awhile, whin he gits tired iv th' game, he'll write home an' say he's got the islands; an' he'll tur-rn thim over to th' gover'mint an' go back to his ship, an' Mark Hanna'll organize th' F'lip-ine Islands Jute an' Cider Comp'ny, an' th' rivolutchinists'll wish they hadn't. That's what'll happen. Mark me wurrud."

ON SOME ARMY APPOINTMENTS[1]

"Well, sir," said Mr. Dooley, "I didn't vote f'r Mack, but I'm with him now. I had me doubts whether he was th' gr-reatest military janius iv th' cinchry, but they'se no question about it. We go into this war, if we iver do go into it, with th' most fash'n-able ar-rmy that iver creased its pants. 'Twill be a daily hint fr'm Paris to th' crool foe.

"Other gin'rals iv th' r-rough-house kind, like Napoleon Bonypart, th' impror iv th' Frinch, Gin'ral Ulis S. Grant, an' Cousin George Dooley, hired coarse, rude men that wudden't know th' diff'rence between goluf an' crokay, an' had their pants tucked in their boots an' chewed tobacco be th' pound. Thank Hivin, McKinley knows betther thin to sind th' likes iv thim abroad to shock our frinds be dumpin' their coffee into thimsilves fr'm a saucer.

"Th' dure bell rings, an' a futman in liv'ry says: 'I'm Master Willie Dooselbery's man, an' he's come to be examined f'r th' army,' says he. 'Admit him,' says McKinley; an' Master Willie enters, accompanied be his val-lay, his mah an' pah an' th' comity iv th' goluf club. 'Willie,' says th' President, 'ye ar-re enthrin' upon a gloryous car-eer, an' 'tis nic'ssry that ye shud be thurly examined, so that ye can teach th' glories iv civilization to th' tyr-ranies iv Europe that is supported be ye'er pah an' mah,' he says. ''Twud be a turr'ble thing,' he says, 'if some day they shud meet a Spanish gin'ral in Mahdrid, an' have him say to thim, "I seen ye'er son Willie durin' th' war wearin' a stovepipe hat an' tan shoes." Let us begin th' examination,' he says. 'Ar-re ye a good goluf player?' 'I am,' says Willie. 'Thin I appint ye a liftnant. What we need in th' ar-rmy is good goluf players,' he

---

[1] General Miles's fondness for gold braid was one of Dunne's favorite targets.

says. 'In our former war,' he says, 'we had th' misfortune to have men in command that didn't know th' diff'rence between a goluf stick an' a beecycle; an' what was th' raysult? We foozled our approach at Bull R-run,' he says. 'Ar-re ye a mimber iv anny clubs?' he says. 'Four,' says Willie. 'Thin I make ye a major,' he says. 'Where d'ye get ye'er pants?' he says. 'Fr'm England,' says Willie. 'Gloryous,' says McKinley. 'I make ye a colonel,' he says. 'Let me thry ye in tactics,' he says. 'Suppose ye was confronted be a Spanish ar-rmy in th' afthernoon, how wud ye dhress?' he says. 'I'd wear a stovepipe hat, a long coat, a white vest, an' lavender pants,' says Willie. 'An' if th' attack was be night?' he says. 'I'd put on me dhress shoot, an' go out to meet thim,' says Willie. 'A thuro sojer,' says McKinley. 'Suppose th' sociable lasted all night?' he says. 'I'd sound th' rethreat at daybreak, an' have me brave boys change back,' he says, 'to suitable appar'l,' he says. 'Masterly,' says McKinley. 'I will sind ye'er name in as a brigadier-gin'ral,' he says. 'Thank Gawd, th' r-rich,' he says, 'is brave an' pathriotic,' he says. 'Ye will jine th' other boys fr'm th' club at Tampa,' he says. 'Ye shud be careful iv ye'er equipment,' he says. 'I have almost ivrything r-ready,' says Willie. 'Me man attinded to thim details,' he says. 'But I fear I can't go to th' fr-ront immejetly,' he says. 'Me pink silk pijammas hasn't arrived,' he says. 'Well,' says Mack, 'wait f'r thim,' he says. 'I'm anxious f'r to ind this hor'ble war,' he says, 'which has cost me manny a sleepy night,' he says; 'but 'twud be a crime f'r to sind a sojer onprepared to battle,' he says. 'Wait f'r th' pijammas,' he says. 'Thin on to war,' he says; 'an' let ye'er watchword be, "Raymimber ye'er manners,"' he says.

"'They'se a man out here,' says th' privit sicrity, 'that wants to see ye,' he says. 'He's a r-rough-lookin' charackter that was in th' Soo war,' he says. 'His name is Gin'ral Fiteum,' he says. 'Throw th' stiff out,' says Mack. 'I seen him in Pinnsylvania Avnoo yisterdah, r-ridin' in a sthreet ca-ar,' he says. 'Ah, Willie, me boy,' he says, ''tis little ye know what throuble I have fr'm these vulgar sojers with pants that bags at th' knees. Give me a goold-tipped cigareet, an' tell me whether shirt waists is much worn in New York this year.'

"Yis, Hinnissy, we'll put th' tastiest ar-rmy in th' field that iver come out iv a millinery shop. 'Right dhress!' will be an ordher that'll mean somethin'. Th' ar-rmy'll be followed be specyal correspondints fr'm Butthrick's Pattherns an' Harper's Bazar; an', if our brave boys don't gore an' pleat th' inimy, 'twill be because th' inimy'll be r-rude enough to shoot in anny kind iv clothes they find on th' chair whin they wake up."

ON STRATEGY

"A sthrateejan," said Mr. Dooley, in response to Mr. Hennessy's request for information, "is a champeen checker-player. Whin th' war broke out, me frind Mack wint to me frind Hanna, an' says he, 'What,' he says, 'what can we do to cr-rush th' haughty power iv Spain,' he says, 'an' br-ring this hateful war to a early conclusion?" he says. 'Mobilize th' checker-players,' says Hanna. An' fr'm all cor-rners iv th' counthry they've gone to Washin'ton, where they're called th' Sthrateejy Board.

"Day an' night they set in a room with a checker-board on th' end iv a flour bar'l, an' study problems iv th' navy. At night Mack dhrops in. 'Well, boys,' says he, 'how goes th' battle?' he says. 'Gloryous,' says th' Sthrateejy Board. 'Two more moves, an' we'll be in th' king row.' 'Ah,' says Mack, 'this is too good to be thrue,' he says. 'In but a few brief minyits th' dhrinks'll be on Spain,' he says. 'Have ye anny plans f'r Sampson's fleet?' he says. 'Where is it?' says th' Sthrateejy Board. 'I dinnaw,' says Mack. 'Good,' says th' Sthrateejy Board. 'Where's th' Spanish fleet?' says they. 'Bombardin' Boston, at Cadiz, in San June de Matzoon, sighted near th' gashouse be our special correspondint, copyright, 1898, be Mike O'Toole.' 'A sthrong position,' says th' Sthrateejy Board. 'Undoubtedly, th' fleet is headed south to attack and seize Armour's glue facthory. Ordher Sampson to sail north as fast as he can, an' lay in a supply iv ice. Th' summer's comin' on. Insthruct Schley to put on all steam, an' thin put it off again, an' call us up be telephone. R-rush eighty-three millyon throops an' four mules to Tampa, to Mobile, to Chickenmaha, to Coney Island, to Ireland, to th' divvle, an' r-rush thim back again. Don't r-rush thim. Ordher Sampson to pick up th' cable at Lincoln Par-rk, an' run into th' bar-rn. Is th' balloon corpse r-ready? It is? Thin don't sind it up. Sind it up. Have th' Mulligan Gyards co-op'rate with Gomez, an' tell him to cut away his whiskers. They've got tangled in th' riggin'. We need yellow-fever throops. Have ye anny yellow fever in th' house? Give it to twinty thousand three hundherd men, an'

sind thim afther Gov'nor Tanner. Teddy Rosenfelt's r-rough
r-riders ar-re downstairs, havin' their uniforms pressed.   Ordher
thim to th' goluf links at wanst.   They must be no indecision.
Where's Richard Harding Davis ?   On th' bridge iv the New
York ?   Tur-rn th' bridge.   Seize Gin'ral Miles' uniform.   We
must strengthen th' gold resarve.   Where's th' Gussie ?   Runnin'
off to Cuba with wan hundherd men an' ar-rms, iv coorse.   Oh,
war is a dhreadful thing.   It's ye'er move, Claude,' says th'
Sthrateejy Board.

"An' so it goes on ; an' day by day we r-read th' tur-rble story
iv our brave sthrateejans sacrificin' their time on th' altar iv their
counthry, as Hogan says.   Little we thought, whin we wint into
this war, iv th' horrors it wud bring.   Little we thought iv th'
mothers at home weepin' f'r their brave boys down at Washin'ton
hur-rtin their poor eyes over a checker-board.   Little we thought
iv these devoted men, as Hogan says, with achin' heads, plannin'
to sind three hundherd thousand millyon men an' a carload iv
beans to their fate at Tampa, Fla.   But some wan must be
sacrificed, as Hogan says.   An' these poor fellows in Washin'ton
with their r-red eyes an' their tired backs will be an example to
future ginerations, as Hogan says, iv how an American sojer can
face his jooty whin he has to, an' how he can't whin he hasn't to."

" Dewey ain't a sthrateejan ? " inquired Mr. Hennessy.

" No, " said Mr. Dooley.   " Cousin George is a good man, an'
I'm very fond iv him—more be raison iv his doin' that May-o
bosthoon Pat Mountjoy, but he has low tastes.   We niver cud
make a sthrateejan iv him.   They'se a kind iv a vulgar fightin'
sthrain in him that makes him want to go out an' slug some wan
wanst a month.   I'm glad he ain't in Washin'ton.   Th' chances
ar-re he'd go to th' Sthrateejy Board and pull its hair."

ON GENERAL MILES'S MOONLIGHT
EXCURSION[1]

" Dear, oh, dear," said Mr. Dooley, " I'd give five dollars—an'
I'd kill a man f'r three—if I was out iv this Sixth Wa-ard to-night,
an' down with Gin'ral Miles' gran' picnic an' moonlight excursion
in Porther Ricky.   'Tis no comfort in bein' a cow'rd whin ye
think iv thim br-rave la-ads facin' death be suffication in bokays

---

[1] In July, 1898, General Miles invaded Puerto Rico and met surprisingly
little resistance.

an' dyin' iv waltzin' with th' pretty girls iv Porther Ricky.

"I dinnaw whether Gin'ral Miles picked out th' job or whether 'twas picked out f'r him. But, annyhow, whin he got to Sandago de Cubia an' looked ar-round him, he says to his frind Gin'ral Shafter, 'Gin'ral,' says he, 'ye have done well so far,' he says. ''Tis not f'r me to take th' lorls fr'm th' steamin' brow iv a thrue hero,' he says. 'I lave ye here,' he says, 'f'r to complete th' victhry ye have so nobly begun,' he says. 'F'r you,' he says, 'th' wallop in th' eye fr'm th' newspaper rayporther, th' r-round robbing, an' th' sunsthroke,' he says, 'f'r me th' hardship iv th' battlefield, th' late dinner, th' theayter party, an' th' sickenin' polky,' he says. 'Gather,' he says, 'th' fruits iv ye'er bravery,' he says. 'Return,' he says, 'to ye'er native land, an' receive anny gratichood th' Sicrety iv War can spare fr'm his own fam'ly,' he says. 'F'r me,' he says, 'there is no way but f'r to tur-rn me back upon this festive scene,' he says, 'an' go where jooty calls me,' he says. 'Ordherly,' he says, 'put a bottle on th' ice, an' see that me goold pants that I wear with th' pale blue vest with th' di'mon buttons is irned out,' he says. An' with a haggard face he walked aboord th' excursion steamer, an' wint away.

"I'd hate to tell ye iv th' thriles iv th' expedition, Hinnissy. Whin th' picnic got as far as Punch, on th' southern coast iv Porther Ricky, Gin'ral Miles gazes out, an' says he, 'This looks like a good place to hang th' hammicks, an' have lunch,' says he. 'Forward, brave men,' says he, 'where ye see me di'mon's sparkle,' says he. 'Forward, an' plant th' crokay ar-rches iv our beloved counthry,' he says. An' in they wint, like inthrepid warryors that they ar-re. On th' beach they was met be a diligation fr'm th' town of Punch, con-sistin' iv th' mayor, th' common council, th' polis an' fire departments, th' Gr-rand Ar-rmy iv th' Raypublic, an' prominent citizens in carredges. Gin'ral Miles, makin' a hasty tielet, advanced onflinchingly to meet thim. 'Gintlemen,' says he, 'what can I do f'r ye?' he says. 'We come,' says th' chairman iv th' comity, 'f'r to offer ye,' he says, 'th' r-run iv th' town,' he says. 'We have held out,' he says, 'as long as we cud,' he says. 'But,' he says, 'they'se a limit to human endurance,' he says. 'We can withstand ye no longer,' he says. 'We surrinder. Take us prisoners, an' rayceive us into ye'er gloryous an' well-fed raypublic,' he says. 'Br-rave men,' says Gin'ral Miles, 'I congratulate ye,' he says, 'on th' heeroism iv yer definse,' he says. 'Ye stuck manfully to yer colors, whativer they ar-re,' he says. 'I on'y wondher that ye waited f'r me to come befure surrindhrin,' he says. 'I welcome ye into th' Union,' he says. 'I don't know how th' Union'll feel about it, but that's no business iv mine,' he says. 'Ye will get ye'er wur-rkin-cards fr'm th' walkin' diligate,' he says; 'an' ye'll be entitled,' he says, 'to pay ye'er share iv th' taxes an' to live awhile an' die whin ye get r-ready,' he says, 'jus' th' same as if ye was bor-rn at home,' he says. 'I don't know th' names iv ye; but I'll call ye all Casey, f'r short,' he says. 'Put ye'er bokays in th' hammick,' he says, 'an' return to Punch,' he says; 'an' freeze somethin' f'r me,' he says, 'f'r me thrawt is parched with th' labors iv th' day,' he says. Th' r-rest iv th' avenin' was spint in dancin', music, an' boat-r-ridin'; an' an inj'yable time was had.

"Th' nex' day th' army moved on Punch; an' Gin'ral Miles marched into th' ill-fated city, preceded be flower-girls sthrewin' r-roses an' geranyums befure him. In th' afthernoon they was a lawn tinnis party, an' at night the gin'ral attinded a banket at th' Gran' Palace Hotel. At midnight he was serenaded be th' Raymimber th' Maine Banjo an' Mandolin Club. Th' entire popylace attinded, with pork chops in their button-holes to show their pathreetism. Th' nex' day, afther breakfastin' with Mayor Casey, he set out on his weary march over th' r-rough, flower-strewn paths f'r San Joon. He has been in gr-reat purl fr'm a witherin' fire iv bokays, an' he has met an' overpowered some iv th' mos' savage orators in Porther Ricky; but, whin I las' heerd iv him, he had pitched his tents an' ice-cream freezers near the inimy's wall, an' was grajully silencin' thim with proclamations."

"They'll kill him with kindness if he don't look out," said Mr. Hennessy.

"I dinnaw about that," said Mr. Dooley; "but I know this, that there's th' makin' iv gr-reat statesmen in Porther Ricky. A proud people that can switch as quick as thim la-ads have nawthin' to larn in th' way iv what Hogan calls th' signs iv gover'mint, even fr'm th' Supreme Court."

ON THE PHILIPPINES

"I know what I'd do if I was Mack," said Mr. Hennessy. "I'd hist a flag over th' Ph'lippeens, an' I'd take in th' whole lot iv thim."

"An' yet," said Mr. Dooley, "'tis not more thin two months since ye larned whether they were islands or canned goods.

Ye'er back yard is so small that ye'er cow can't turn r-round without buttin' th' wood-shed off th' premises, an' ye wudden't go out to th' stock yards without takin' out a policy on yer life. Suppose ye was standin' at th' corner iv State Sthreet an' Archey R-road, wud ye know what car to take to get to th' Ph'lippeens? If yer son Packy was to ask ye where th' Ph'lippeens is, cud ye give him anny good idea whether they was in Rooshia or jus' west iv th' thracks?"

"Mebbe I cudden't," said Mr. Hennessy, haughtily, "but I'm f'r takin' thim in, annyhow."

"So might I be," said Mr. Dooley, "if I cud on'y get me mind on it. Wan iv the worst things about this here war is th' way it's makin' puzzles f'r our poor, tired heads. Whin I wint into it, I thought all I'd have to do was to set up here behind th' bar with a good tin-cint see-gar in me teeth, an' toss dinnymite bombs into th' hated city iv Havana. But look at me now. Th' war is still goin' on; an' ivry night, whin I'm countin' up the cash, I'm askin' mesilf will I annex Cubia or lave it to the Cubians? Will I take Porther Ricky or put it by? An' what shud I do with the Ph'lippeens? Oh, what shud I do with thim? I can't annex thim because I don't know where they ar-re. I can't let go iv thim because some wan else'll take thim if I do. They are eight thousan' iv thim islands, with a popylation iv wan hundherd millyon naked savages; an' me bedroom's crowded now with me an' th' bed. How can I take thim in, an' how on earth am I goin' to cover th' nakedness iv thim savages with me wan shoot iv clothes? An' yet 'twud break me heart to think iv givin' people I niver see or heerd tell iv back to other people I don't know. An', if I don't take thim, Schwartzmeister down th' sthreet, that has half me thrade already, will grab thim sure.

"It ain't that I'm afraid iv not doin' th' r-right thing in th' end, Hinnissy. Some mornin' I'll wake up an' know jus' what to do, an' that I'll do. But 'tis th' annoyance in th' mane time. I've been r-readin' about th' counthry. 'Tis over beyant ye'er left shoulder whin ye're facin east. Jus' throw ye'er thumb back, an' ye have it as ac'rate as anny man in town. 'Tis farther thin Boohlgahrya an' not so far as Blewchoochoo. It's near Chiny, an' it's not so near; an', if a man was to bore a well through fr'm Goshen, Indianny, he might sthrike it, an' thin again he might not. It's a poverty-sthricken counthry, full iv goold an' precious stones, where th' people can pick dinner off th' threes an' ar-re starvin' because they have no step-ladders. Th' inhabitants is mostly naygurs an' Chinnymen, peaceful, industhrus, an' law-abidin', but savage an' bloodthirsty in their methods. They wear no clothes except what they have on, an' each woman has five husbands an' each man has five wives. Th' r-rest goes into th' discard, th' same as here. Th' islands has been ownded be Spain since befure th' fire; an' she's threated thim so well they're now up in ar-rms again her, except a majority iv thim which is thurly loyal. Th' natives seldom fight, but whin they get mad at wan another they r-run-a-muck. Whin a man r-runs-a-muck, sometimes they hang him an' sometimes they discharge him an' hire a new motorman. Th' women ar-re beautiful, with languishin' black eyes, an' they smoke see-gars, but ar-re hurried an' incomplete in their dhress. I see a pitcher iv wan th' other day with nawthin' on her but a basket of cocoanuts an' a hoop-skirt. They're no prudes. We import juke, hemp, cigar wrappers, sugar, an' fairy tales fr'm th' Ph'lippeens, an' export six-inch shells an' th' like. Iv late th' Ph'lippeens has awaked to th' fact that they're behind th' times, an' has received much American amminition in their midst. They say th' Spanyards is all tore up about it.

"I larned all this fr'm th' papers, an' I know 'tis sthraight. An' yet, Hinnissy, I dinnaw what to do about th' Ph'lippeens. An' I'm all alone in th' wurruld. Ivrybody else has made up his mind. Ye ask anny con-ducthor on Ar-rchy R-road, an' he'll tell ye. Ye can find out fr'm the papers; an', if ye really want to know, all ye have to do is to ask a prom'nent citizen who can mow all th' lawn he owns with a safety razor. But I don't know."

"Hang on to thim," said Mr. Hennessy, stoutly. "What we've got we must hold."

"Well," said Mr. Dooley, "if I was Mack, I'd lave it to George. I'd say: 'George,' I'd say, 'if ye're f'r hangin' on, hang on it is. If ye say, lave go, I dhrop thim.' 'Twas George won thim with th' shells, an' th' question's up to him."

ON PRAYERS FOR VICTORY

"It looks to me," said Mr. Dooley, "as though me frind Mack'd got tired iv th' Sthrateejy Board, an' was goin' to lave th' war to th' men in black."

"How's that?" asked Mr. Hennessy, who has at best but a clouded view of public affairs.

"Well," said Mr. Dooley, "while th' sthrateejans have been wearin' out their jeans on cracker-boxes in Wash'n'ton, they'se been goin' on th' mos' deadly conflict iver heerd tell iv between th' pow'rful preachin' navies iv th' two counthries. Manila is nawthin' at all to th' scenes iv carnage an' slaughter, as Hogan says, that's been brought about be these desthroyers. Th' Spanyards fired th' openin' gun whin th' bishop iv Cades, a powerful tur-reted monitor (ol' style), attackted us with both for'ard guns, an' sint a storm iv brimstone an' hell into us. But th' victhry was not f'r long with th' hated Spanyard. He was answered be our whole fleet iv preachers. Thin he was jined be th' bishop iv Barsaloona an' th' bishop iv Mahdrid an' th' bishop iv Havana, all battle-ships iv th' first class, followed be a fleet iv cruisers r-runnin' all th' way fr'm a full-ar-rmored vicar gin'ral to a protected parish priest. To meet thim, we sint th' bishop iv New York, th' bishop iv Philadelphia, th' bishop iv Baltimore, an' th' bishop iv Chicago, accompanied be a flyin' squadhron iv Methodists, three Presby-teryan monitors, a fleet iv Baptist submarine desthroyers, an' a formidable array iv Universalist an' Unitaryan torpedo boats, with a Jew r-ram. Manetime th' bishop iv Manila had fired a solid prayer, weighin' a ton, at San Francisco; an' a masked batthry iv Congregationalists replied, inflictin' severe damage. Our Atlantic fleet is now sarchin' f'r th' inimy, an' the bishop iv New York is blockadin' th' bishop iv Sandago de Cuba; an' they'se been an exchange iv prayers between th' bishop iv Baltimore an' th' bishop iv Havana without much damage.

"Th' Lord knows how it'll come out. First wan side prays that th' wrath iv Hiven'll descind on th' other, an' thin th' other side returns th' compliment with inthrest. Th' Spanish bishop says we're a lot iv murdherin', irreligious thieves, an' ought to be swept fr'm th' face iv th' earth. We say his people ar-re th' same, an' manny iv thim. He wishes Hivin to sink our ships an' desthroy our men; an' we hope he'll injye th' same gr-reat blessin'. We have a shade th' best iv him, f'r his fleets ar-re all iv th' same class an' ol' style, an' we have some iv th' most modhern prayin' machines in the warruld; but he prays har-rd, an' 'tis no aisy wurruk to silence him."

"What d'ye think about it?" asked Mr. Hennessy.

"Well," said Mr. Dooley. "I dinnaw jus' what to think iv it. Me own idee is that war is not a matther iv prayers so much as a matther iv punchin'; an' th' on'y place a prayer book stops a

bullet is in th' story books. 'Tis like what Father Kelly said.
Three weeks ago las' Sundah he met Hogan; an' Hogan, wantin'
to be smart, ast him if he'd offered up prayers f'r th' success iv th'
cause. 'Faith, I did not,' says th' good man. 'I was in too much
iv a hurry to get away.' 'What was th' matther?' ast Hogan.
'I had me uniform to brush up an' me soord to polish,' says
Father Kelly. 'I am goin' with th' rig'mint to-morrah,' he says;
an' he says, 'If ye hear iv me waitin' to pray,' he says, 'anny time
they'se a call f'r me,' he says, 'to be in a fight,' he says, 'ye may
conclude,' he says, 'that I've lost me mind, an' won't be back to
me parish,' he says. 'Hogan,' he says, 'I'll go into th' battle
with a prayer book in wan hand an' a soord in th' other,' he says;
'an', if th' wurruk calls f'r two hands, 'tis not th' soord I'll dhrop,'
he says. 'Don't ye believe in prayer?' says Hogan. 'I do,' says
th' good man; 'but,' he says, 'a healthy person ought,' he says, 'to
be ashamed,' he says, 'to ask f'r help in a fight,' he says."

"That's th' way I look at it," said Mr. Hennessy. "When
'tis an aven thing in th' prayin', may th' best man win."

"Ye're r-right, Hinnissy," said Mr. Dooley, warmly. "Ye're
r-right. An' th' best man will win."

ON THE ANGLO-SAXON[1]

"Well," said Mr. Dooley, "I see be th' pa-apers that th' snow-
white pigeon iv peace have tied up th' dogs iv war. It's all over
now. All we've got to do is to arrest th' pathrites an' make th'
reconcenthradios pay th' stamp tax, an' be r-ready f'r to take a
punch at Germany or France or Rooshia or anny counthry on th'
face iv th' globe.

"An' I'm glad iv it. This war, Hinnissy, has been a gr-reat
sthrain on me. To think iv th' suffrin' I've endured! F'r weeks
I lay awake at nights fearin' that th' Spanish ar-rmadillo'd lave
the Cape Verde Islands, where it wasn't, an' take th' thrain out
here, an' hur-rl death an' desthruction into me little store. Day
be day th' pitiless exthries come out an' beat down on me. Ye
hear iv Teddy Rosenfelt plungin' into ambus-cades an' Sicrity iv

---

[1] Claims of racial superiority stirred Dunne to anger, and none more so than
the clamor for the spread of Protestantism and Anglo-Saxon allegiance following
the Spanish-American War. When Roosevelt's election in 1904 was hailed
as an "Anglo-Saxon" triumph, Dunne pictured Joseph Choate, American
ambassador to Great Britain, arriving before the king "as fast as his hands an'
knees wud carry him."

Wars; but d'ye hear iv Martin Dooley, th' man behind th' guns, four thousan' miles behind thim, an' willin' to be further? They ar-re no bokays f'r me. I'm what Hogan calls wan iv th' mute, ingloryous heroes iv th' war; an' not so dam mute, ayther. Some day, Hinnissy, justice'll be done me, an' th' likes iv me; an', whin th' story iv a gr-reat battle is written, they'll print th' kilt, th' wounded, th' missin', an' th' seryously disturbed. An' thim that have bore thimsilves well an' bravely an' paid th' taxes an' faced th' deadly newspa-apers without flinchin' 'll be advanced six pints an' given a chanst to tur-rn jack f'r th' game.

"But me wurruk ain't over jus' because Mack has inded th' war an' Teddy Rosenfelt is comin' home to bite th' Sicrety iv War. You an' me, Hinnissy, has got to bring on this here Anglo-Saxon 'lieance. An Anglo-Saxon, Hinnissy, is a German that's forgot who was his parents. They're a lot iv thim in this counthry. There must be as manny as two in Boston: they'se wan up in Maine, an' another lives at Bogg's Ferry in New York State, an' dhrives a milk wagon. Mack is an Anglo-Saxon. His folks come fr'm th' County Armagh, an' their naytional Anglo-Saxon hymn is 'O'Donnell Aboo.' Teddy Rosenfelt is another Anglo-Saxon. An' I'm an Anglo-Saxon. I'm wan iv th' hottest Anglo-Saxons that iver come out iv Anglo-Saxony. Th' name iv Dooley has been th' proudest Anglo-Saxon name in th' County Roscommon f'r many years.

"Schwartzmeister is an Anglo-Saxon, but he doesn't know it, an' won't till some wan tells him. Pether Bowbeen down be th' Frinch church is formin' th' Circle Francaize Anglo-Saxon club, an' me ol' frind Dominigo that used to boss th' Ar-rchey R-road wagon whin Callaghan had th' sthreet conthract will march at th' head iv th' Dago Anglo-Saxons whin th' time comes. There ar-re twinty thousan' Rooshian Jews at a quarther a vote in th' Sivinth Ward; an', ar-rmed with rag hooks, they'd be a tur-rble thing f'r anny inimy iv th' Anglo-Saxon 'lieance to face. Th' Bohemians an' Pole Anglo-Saxons may be a little slow in wakin' up to what th' pa-apers calls our common hurtage, but ye may be sure they'll be all r-right whin they're called on. We've got together an Anglo-Saxon 'lieance in this wa-ard, an' we're goin' to ilict Sarsfield O'Brien prisidint, Hugh O'Neill Darsey vice-prisidint, Robert Immitt Clancy sicrety, an' Wolfe Tone Malone three-as-urer. O'Brien'll be a good wan to have. He was in the Fenian r-raid, an' his father carrid a pike in forty-eight. An' he's in th'

Clan.   Besides, he has a sthrong pull with th' Ancient Ordher iv Anglo-Saxon Hibernyans.

"I tell ye, whin th' Clan an' th' Sons iv Sweden an' th' Banana Club an' th' Circle Francaize an' th' Pollacky Benivolent Society an' th' Rooshian Sons of Dinnymite an' th' Benny Brith an' th' Coffee Clutch that Schwartzmeister r-runs an' th' Tur-rnd'ye-mind an' th' Holland society an' th' Afro-Americans an' th' other Anglo-Saxons begin f'r to raise their Anglo-Saxon battle-cry, it'll be all day with th' eight or nine people in th' wurruld that has th' misfortune iv not bein' brought up Anglo-Saxons."

"They'se goin' to be a debate on th' 'lieance at th' ninety-eight picnic at Ogden's gr-rove," said Mr. Hennessy.

"P'r'aps," said Mr. Dooley, sweetly, "ye might like to borry th' loan iv an ice-pick."

ON OUR CUBAN ALLIES

"Well, sir," said Mr. Dooley, "dam thim Cubians!   If I was Gin'ral Shafter, I'd back up th' wagon in front iv th' dure, an' I'd say to Gin'ral Garshy, I'd say, 'I want you'; an' I'd have thim all down at th' station an' dacently booked be th' desk sergeant befure th' fall iv night.   Th' impydince iv thim!"

"What have they been doin'?" Mr. Hennessy asked.

"Failin' to undherstand our civilization," said Mr. Dooley. "Ye see, it was this way.   This is th' way it was: Gin'ral Garshy with wan hundherd thousan' men's been fightin' bravely f'r two years f'r to liberyate Cubia.   F'r two years he's been marchin' his sivinty-five thousan' men up an' down th' island, desthroyin' th' haughty Spanyard be th' millyons.   Whin war was declared, he offered his own sarvice an' th' sarvices iv his ar-rmy iv fifty thousan' men to th' United States; an', while waitin' f'r ships to arrive, he marched at th' head iv his tin thousan' men down to Sandago de Cuba an' captured a cigar facthry, which they soon rayjooced to smokin' ruins.   They was holdin' this position—Gin'ral Garshy an' his gallant wan thousan' men—whin Gin'ral Shafter arrived. Gin'ral Garshy immedjitly offered th' sarvices iv himsilf an' his two hundherd men f'r th' capture iv Sandago; an', when Gin'ral Shafter arrived, there was Gin'ral Garshy with his gallant band iv fifty Cubians, r-ready to eat at a minyit's notice.

"Gin'ral Shafter is a big, coorse, two-fisted man fr'm Mitchigan, an', whin he see Gin'ral Garshy an' his twenty-five gallant followers, 'Fr-ront,' says he. 'This way,' he says, 'step lively,' he says, 'an' move some iv these things,' he says. 'Sir,' says Gin'ral Garshy, 'd'ye take me f'r a dhray?' he says. 'I'm a sojer,' he says, 'not a baggage car,' he says. 'I'm a Cubian pathrite, an' I'd lay down me life an' the lives iv ivry wan iv th' eighteen brave men iv me devoted ar-rmy,' he says; 'but I'll be dam'd if I carry a thrunk,' he says. 'I'll fight whiniver 'tis cool,' he says, 'an' they ain't wan iv these twelve men here that wudden't follow me to hell if they was awake at th' time,' he says; 'but,' he says, 'if 'twas wurruk we were lookin' f'r, we cud have found it long ago,' he says. 'They'se a lot iv it in this counthry that nobody's usin',' he says. 'What we want,' he says, 'is freedom,' he says; 'an', if ye think we have been in th' woods dodgin' th' savage corryspondint f'r two year,' he says, 'f'r th' sake iv r-rushin' yer laundhry home,' he says, ''tis no wondher,' he says, 'that th' r-roads fr'm Marinette to Kalamazoo is paved with goold bricks bought be th' people iv ye'er native State,' he says.

"So Shafter had to carry his own thrunk; an' well it was f'r him that it wasn't Gin'ral Miles', the weather bein' hot. An' Shafter was mad clear through; an', whin he took hold iv Sandago, an' was sendin' out invitations, he scratched Garshy. Garshy took his gallant band iv six back to th' woods; an' there th' three iv thim ar-re now, ar-rmed with forty r-rounds iv canned lobster, an' ready to raysist to th' death. Him an' th' other man has written to Gin'ral Shafter to tell him what they think iv him, an' it don't take long."

"Well," said Mr. Hennessy, "I think Shafter done wrong. He might've asked Garshy in f'r to see th' show, seein' that he's been hangin' ar-round f'r a long time, doin' th' best he cud."

"It isn't that," explained Mr. Dooley. "Th' throuble is th' Cubians don't undherstand our civilization. Over here freedom means hard wurruk. What is th' ambition iv all iv us, Hinnissy? 'Tis ayether to hold our job or to get wan. We want wurruk. We must have it. D'ye raymimber th' sign th' mob carrid in th' procession las' year? 'Give us wurruk, or we perish,' it said. They had their heads bate in be polismen because no philan-thropist'd come along an' make thim shovel coal. Now, in Cubia, whin th' mobs turns out, they carry a banner with the wurruds, 'Give us nawthin' to do, or we perish.' Whin a Cubian comes home at night with a happy smile on his face, he don't say to his wife an' childher, 'Thank Gawd, I've got wurruk at last!' He

says, 'Thank Gawd, I've been fired.' An' th' childher go out,
and they say, 'Pah-pah has lost his job.' And Mrs. Cubian buys
hersilf a new bonnet; and where wanst they was sorrow an'
despair all is happiness an' a cottage organ.

"Ye can't make people here undherstand that, an' ye can't
make a Cubian undherstand that freedom means th' same thing as
a pinitinchry sintince. Whin we thry to get him to wurruk, he'll
say: 'Why shud I? I haven't committed anny crime.' That's
goin' to be th' throuble. Th' first thing we know we'll have
another war in Cubia whin we begin disthributin' good jobs,
twelve hours a day, wan sivinty-five. Th' Cubians ain't civilized
in our way. I sometimes think I've got a touch iv Cubian blood
in me own veins."

ON THE DESTRUCTION OF CERVERA'S FLEET[1]

[These comments were made by Mr. Dooley during a strike of the stereo-
typers, which caused the English newspapers of Chicago temporarily to
suspend publication.]

"I hear," said Mr. Hennessy, "that th' stereopticons on th'
newspapers have sthruck."

"I sh'd think they wud," said Mr. Dooley. "Th' las' time I
was down town was iliction night, whin Charter Haitch's big la-ad
was ilicted, an' they was wurrukin' th' stereopticons till they was
black in th' face. What's th' news?"

"Th' What Cheer, Ioway, Lamp iv Freedom is on th' sthreets
with a tillygram that Shafter has captured Sandago de Cuba, an'
is now settin' on Gin'ral Pando's chest with his hands in his hair.
But this is denied be th' Palo Gazoot, the Macoupin County
Raygisther, an' th' Meridyan Sthreet Afro-American. I also see
be th' Daily Scoor Card, th' Wine List, th' Deef Mute's Spokes-
man, th' Morgue Life, the Bill iv Fare, th' Stock Yards Sthraight
Steer, an' Jack's Tips on th' Races, the on'y daily paper printed in
Chicago, that Sampson's fleet is in th' Suez Canal bombarding
Cades. Th' Northwestern Christyan Advycate says this is not
thrue, but that George Dixon was outpointed be an English boxer
in a twinty-r-round go in New York."

"Ye've got things mixed up," said Mr. Dooley. "I get th'

[1] After the destruction of the Spanish fleet under Cervera in July, 1898,
controversy raged at home about whether Admiral W. T. Sampson or Admiral
W. S. Schley should be credited with the victory.

news sthraight. 'Twas this way. Th' Spanish fleet was bottled up in Sandago Harbor, an' they dhrew th' cork. That's a joke. I see it in th' pa-apers. Th' gallant boys iv th' navy was settin' out on th' deck, defindin' their counthry an' dhrawin' three ca-ards apiece, whin th' Spanish admiral con-cluded 'twud be better f'r him to be desthroyed on th' ragin' sea, him bein' a sailor, thin to have his fleet captured be cav'lry. Annyhow, he was willin' to take a chance; an' he says to his sailors: 'Spanyards,' he says, 'Castiles,' he says, 'we have et th' las' bed-tick,' he says; 'an', if we stay here much longer,' he says, 'I'll have to have a steak off th' armor plate fried f'r ye,' he says. 'Lave us go out where we can have a r-run f'r our money,' he says. An' away they wint. I'll say this much f'r him, he's a brave man, a dam brave man. I don't like a Spanyard no more than ye do, Hinnissy. I niver see wan. But, if this here man was a—was a Zulu, I'd say he was a brave man. If I was aboord wan iv thim yachts that was converted, I'd go to this here Cervera, an' I'd say: 'Manuel,' I'd say, 'ye're all right, me boy. Ye ought to go to a doctor an' have ye'er eyes re-set, but ye're a good fellow. Go downstairs,' I'd say, 'into th' basemint iv the ship,' I'd say, 'an' open th' cupboard jus'· nex' to th' head iv th' bed, an' find th' bottle marked "Floridy Wather," an' threat ye'ersilf kindly.' That's what I'd say to Cervera. He's all right.

"Well, whin our boys see th' Spanish fleet comin' out iv th' harbor, they gathered on th' deck an' sang th' naytional anthem, 'They'll be a hot time in th' ol' town to-night.' A lift-nant come up to where Admiral Sampson was settin' playin' sivin up with Admiral Schley. 'Bill,' he says, 'th' Spanish fleet is comin' out,' he says. 'What talk have ye?' says Sampson. 'Sind out some row-boats an' a yacht, an' desthroy thim. Clubs is thrumps,' he says, and he wint on playin'. Th' Spanish fleet was attackted on all sides be our br-rave la-ads, nobly assisted be th' dispatch boats iv the newspapers. Wan by wan they was desthroyed. Three battleships attackted th' converted yacht Gloucester. Th' Gloucester used to be owned be Pierpont Morgan; but 'twas converted, an' is now leadin' a dacint life. Th' Gloucester sunk thim all, th' Christobell Comma, the Viscera, an' th' Admiral O'Quinn. It thin wint up to two Spanish torpedo boats an' giv thim wan punch, an' away they wint. Be this time th' sojers had heerd of the victhry, an' they gathered on th' shore, singin' th' naytional anthem, 'They'll be a hot time in th' ol' town to-night,

me babby.' Th' gloryous ol' chune, to which Washington an'
Grant an' Lincoln marched, was took up be th' sailors on th'
ships, an' Admiral Cervera r-run wan iv his boats ashore, an'
jumped into th' sea.　At last accounts th' follyin' dispatches had
been received: 'To Willum McKinley: Congratulations on ye'er
noble victhry.　(Signed) Willum McKinley.'　'To Russell A.
Alger: Ye done splendid.　(Signed) Russell A. Alger.'　'To
James Wilson, Sicrety iv Agriculture: This is a gr-reat day f'r
Ioway.　Ar-re ye much hur-rted?　(Signed) James Wilson.'"

"Where did ye hear all this?" asked Mr. Hennessy, in great
amazement.

"I r-read it," said Mr. Dooley, impressively, "in the Staats
Zeitung."

ON A SPEECH BY PRESIDENT McKINLEY

"I hear-r that Mack's in town," said Mr. Dooley.

"Didn't ye see him?" asked Mr. Hennessy.

"Faith, I did not!" said Mr. Dooley.　"If 'tis meetin' me
he's afther, all he has to do is to get on a ca-ar an' r-ride out to
number nine-double-naught-nine Archey R-road, an' stop whin
he sees th' sign iv th' Tipp'rary Boodweiser Brewin' Company.
I'm here fr'm eight in the mornin' till midnight, an' th' r-rest iv
th' time I'm in the back room in th' ar-rms iv Or-rpheus, as
Hogan says.　Th' Presidint is as welcome as anny rayspictable
marrid man.　I will give him a chat an' a dhrink f'r fifteen cints;
an', as we're not, as a frind iv mine in th' grocery an' pothry
business says, intirely a commercial an' industhreel nation, if he
has th' Sicrety iv th' Threasury with him, I'll give thim two f'r
twinty-five cints, which is th' standard iv value among civilized
nations th' wurruld over.　Prisidint iv th' United States, says
ye?　Well, I'm prisidint iv this liquor store, fr'm th' pitcher iv th'
Chicago fire above th' wash-stand in th' back room to th' dure-
step.　Beyond that belongs to th' polisman on th' bate. An
Amurrican's home, as wan iv th' potes says, is his castle till th'
morgedge falls due.　An' divvle a fut will I put out iv this dure
to see e'er a prisidint, prince, or potentate, fr'm th' czar iv Rooshia
to th' king iv Chiny.　There's Prisidint Mack at th' Audjiotoroom,
an' here's Prisidint Dooley at nine-double-naught-nine, an' th'
len'th iv th' sthreet between thim.　Says he, 'Come over to th'

hotel an' see me.' Says I, 'If ye find ye'ersilf thrun fr'm a ca-ar in me neighborhood, dhrop in.' An' there ye ar-re.

"I may niver see him. I may go to me grave without gettin' an' eye on th' wan man besides mesilf that don't know what th' furrin' policy iv th' United States is goin' to be. An he, poor man, whin some wan asts him, 'Did ye iver meet Dooley ?' 'll have to say, 'No, I had th' chanst wanst, but me accursed pride kept me from visitin' him.'

"I r-read his speeches, though, an' know what he's doin'. Some iv thim ar-re gr-reat. He attinded th' banket given be th' Prospurity Brigade at th' hotel where he's stoppin'. 'Twas a magnificent assimblage iv th' laborin' classes, costin' fifteen dollars a plate, an' on'y disturbed whin a well-to-do gintleman in th' dhry-goods business had to be thrun out f'r takin' a kick at a waiter. I r-read be th' papers that whin Mack come in he was rayceived be th' gatherin' with shouts iv approval. Th' pro-ceedin's was opened with a prayer that Providence might r-remain undher th' protection iv th' administhration. Th' Sicrety iv th' Treasury followed with a gran' speech, highly commindin' th' action iv th' threasury department durin' th' late war; 'but,' says he, 'I cannot,' he says, 'so far forget mesilf,' he says, 'as not to mintion,' he says, 'that,' he says, 'if it hadn't been f'r the sublime pathreetism an' courage,' he says, 'iv th' gintleman whom we honor,' he says, 'in puttin' me on th' foorce,' he says, 'I might not be here to-night,' he says.

"Th' Sicrety iv th' Threasury was followed be th' Gin'ral Shafter. 'Gintlemen,' says he, 'it gives me,' he says, 'gr-reat pleasure,' he says, 'to be prisint in th' mist iv so manny an' so various vittles,' he says. 'Iv coorse,' he says, 'I re-elize me own gr-reat worth,' he says; 'but,' he says, 'I wud have to be more thin human,' he says, 'to overlook th' debt iv gratichood,' he says, 'th' counthry owes,' he says, 'to th' man whose foresight, wisdom, an' prudence brought me for-ard at such an opparchune time,' he says. 'Gintlemen,' he says, 'onless ye have lived in th' buck-board f'r months on th' parched deserts iv Cubia,' he says, 'ye little know what a pleasure it is,' he says, 'to dhrink,' he says, 'to th' author iv our bein' here,' he says. An' Gin'ral Miles wint out an' punched th' bell-boy. Mack r-rose up in a perfect hur-cane iv applause, an' says he, 'Gintlemen,' he says, 'an' fellow-heroes,' he says, 'ye do me too much honor,' he says. 'I alone shud not have th' credit iv this gloryous victhry. They ar-re others.' [A voice:

'Shafter.' Another voice: 'Gage.' Another voice: 'Dooley.'] 'But I pass to a more conganial line iv thought,' he says. 'We have just emerged fr'm a turrible war,' he says. 'Again,' he says, 'we ar-re a united union,' he says. 'No north,' he says, 'no south, no east,' he says, 'no west. No north east a point east,' he says. 'Th' inimies iv our counthry has been cr-rushed,' he says, 'or is stuck down in Floridy with his rig'mint talkin',' he says, 'his hellish docthrines to th' allygatars,' he says. 'Th' nation is wanst more at peace undher th' gran' goold standard,' he says. 'Now,' he says, 'th' question is what shall we do with th' fruits iv victhry?' he says. [A voice, 'Can thim.'] 'Our duty to civilization commands us to be up an' doin',' he says. 'We ar-re bound,' he says, 'to—to re-elize our destiny, whativer it may be,' he says. 'We can not tur-rn back,' he says, 'th' hands iv th' clock that, even as I speak,' he says, 'is r-rushin' through th' hear-rts iv men,' he says, 'dashin' its spray against th' star iv liberty an' hope, an' no north, no south, no east, no west, but a steady purpose to do th' best we can, considerin' all th' circumstances iv the case,' he says. 'I hope I have made th' matther clear to ye,' he says, 'an', with these few remarks,' he says, 'I will tur-rn th' job over to destiny,' he says, 'which is sure to lead us iver on an' on, an' back an' forth, a united an' happy people, livin',' he says, 'undher an administhration that, thanks to our worthy Prisidint an' his cap-ble an' earnest advisers is second to none,' he says."

"What do you think ought to be done with th' fruits iv victhry?" Mr. Hennessy asked.

"Well," said Mr. Dooley, "if 'twas up to me, I'd eat what was r-ripe an' give what wasn't r-ripe to me inimy. An' I guess that's what Mack means."

ON NEW YEAR'S RESOLUTIONS

Mr. Hennessy looked out at the rain dripping down in Archey Road, and sighed, "A-ha, 'tis a bad spell iv weather we're havin'."

"Faith, it is," said Mr. Dooley, "or else we mind it more thin we did. I can't remimber wan day fr'm another. Whin I was young, I niver thought iv rain or snow, cold or heat. But now th' heat stings an' th' cold wrenches me bones; an', if I go out in th' rain with less on me thin a ton iv rubber, I'll pay dear f'r it in achin' j'ints, so I will. That's what old age means; an' now

another year has been put on to what we had befure, an' we're
expected to be gay. 'Ring out th' old,' says a guy at th' Brothers'
School. 'Ring out th' old, ring in th' new,' he says. 'Ring out
th' false, ring in th' thrue,' says he. It's a pretty sintimint,
Hinnissy; but how ar-re we goin' to do it? Nawthin'd please me
betther thin to turn me back on th' wicked an' ingloryous past,
rayform me life, an' live at peace with th' wurruld to th' end iv me
days. But how th' divvle can I do it? As th' fellow says,
'Can th' leopard change his spots,' or can't he?

"You know Dorsey, iv coorse, th' cross-eyed May-o man that
come to this counthry about wan day in advance iv a warrant f'r
sheep-stealin'? Ye know what he done to me, tellin' people I was
caught in me cellar poorin' wather into a bar'l? Well, last night
says I to mesilf, thinkin' iv Dorsey, I says: 'I swear that henceforth
I'll keep me temper with me fellow-men. I'll not let anger or
jealousy get th' betther iv me,' I says. 'I'll lave off all me old
feuds; an' if I meet me inimy goin' down th' sthreet, I'll go up an'
shake him be th' hand, if I'm sure he hasn't a brick in th' other
hand.' Oh, I was mighty compliminthry to mesilf. I set be th'
stove dhrinkin' hot wans, an' ivry wan I dhrunk made me more iv a
pote. 'Tis th' way with th' stuff. Whin I'm in dhrink, I have
manny a fine thought; an', if I wasn't too comfortable to go an'
look f'r th' ink-bottle, I cud write pomes that'd make Shakespeare
an' Mike Scanlan think they were wur-rkin' on a dredge. 'Why,'
says I, 'carry into th' new year th' hathreds iv th' old?' I says.
'Let th' dead past bury its dead,' says I. 'Tur-rn ye'er lamps up
to th' blue sky,' I says. (It was rainin' like th' divvle, an' th' hour
was midnight; but I give no heed to that, bein' comfortable with
th' hot wans.) An' I wint to th' dure, an', whin Mike Duffy come
by on number wan hundherd an' five, ringin' th' gong iv th' ca-ar,
I hollered to him: 'Ring out th' old, ring in th' new.' 'Go back
into ye'er stall,' he says, 'an' wring ye-ersilf out,' he says. 'Ye'er
wet through,' he says.

"Whin I woke up this mornin', th' pothry had all disappeared,
an' I begun to think th' las' hot wan I took had somethin' wrong
with it. Besides, th' lumbago was grippin' me till I cud hardly
put wan foot befure th' other. But I remimbered me promises to
mesilf, an' I wint out on th' sthreet, intindin' to wish ivry wan a
'Happy New Year,' an' hopin' in me hear-rt that th' first wan I
wished it to'd tell me to go to th' divvle, so I cud hit him in th' eye.
I hadn't gone half a block befure I spied Dorsey acrost th' shtreet.

I picked up a half a brick an' put it in me pocket, an' Dorsey done th' same. Thin we wint up to each other. 'A Happy New Year,' says I. 'Th' same to you,' says he, 'an' manny iv thim,' he says. 'Ye have a brick in ye'er hand,' says I. 'I was thinkin' iv givin' ye a New Year's gift,' says he. 'Th' same to you, an' manny iv thim,' says I, fondlin' me own ammunition. ''Tis even all around,' says he. 'It is,' says I. 'I was thinkin' las' night I'd give up me gredge again ye,' says he. 'I had th' same thought mesilf,' says I. 'But, since I seen ye'er face,' he says, 'I've con- cluded that I'd be more comfortable hatin' ye thin havin' ye f'r a frind,' says he. 'Ye're a man iv taste,' says I. An' we backed away fr'm each other. He's a Tip, an' can throw a stone like a rifleman; an', Hinnissy, I'm somethin' iv an amachoor shot with a half-brick mesilf.

"Well, I've been thinkin' it over, an' I've argied it out that life'd not be worth livin' if we didn't keep our inimies. I can have all th' frinds I need. Anny man can that keeps a liquor sthore. But a rale sthrong inimy, specially a May-o inimy—wan that hates ye ha-ard, an' that ye'd take th' coat off yer back to do a bad tur-rn to—is a luxury that I can't go without in me ol' days. Dorsey is th' right sort. I can't go by his house without bein' in fear he'll spill th' chimbly down on me head; an', whin he passes my place, he walks in th' middle iv th' sthreet, an' crosses himsilf. I'll swear off on annything but Dorsey. He's a good man, an' I despise him. Here's long life to him."

ON GOLD-SEEKING

"Well, sir," said Mr. Hennessy, "that Alaska's th' gr-reat place. I thought 'twas nawthin' but an iceberg with a few seals roostin' on it, an' wan or two hundherd Ohio politicians that can't be killed on account iv th' threaty iv Pawrs. But here they tell me 'tis fairly smothered in goold. A man stubs his toe on th' ground, an lifts th' top off iv a goold mine. Ye go to bed at night, an' wake up with goold fillin' in ye'er teeth."

"Yes," said Mr. Dooley, "Clancy's son was in here this mornin', an' he says a frind iv his wint to sleep out in th' open wan night, an' whin he got up his pants assayed four ounces iv goold to th' pound, an' his whiskers panned out as much as thirty dollars net."

"If I was a young man an' not tied down here," said Mr. Hennessy, "I'd go there: I wud so."

"I wud not," said Mr. Dooley. "Whin I was a young man in th' ol' counthry, we heerd th' same story about all America. We used to set be th' tur-rf fire o' nights, kickin' our bare legs on th' flure an' wishin' we was in New York, where all ye had to do was to hold ye'er hat an' th' goold guineas'd dhrop into it. An' whin I got to be a man, I come over here with a ham and a bag iv oatmeal, as sure that I'd return in a year with money enough to dhrive me own ca-ar as I was that me name was Martin Dooley. An' that was a cinch.

"But, faith, whin I'd been here a week, I seen that there was nawthin' but mud undher th' pavement—I larned that be means iv a pick-axe at tin shillin's th' day—an' that, though there was plenty iv goold, thim that had it were froze to it; an' I come west, still lookin' f'r mines. Th' on'y mine I sthruck at Pittsburgh was a hole f'r sewer pipe. I made it. Siven shillin's th' day. Smaller thin New York, but th' livin' was cheaper, with Mon'gahela rye at five a throw, put ye'er hand around th' glass.

"I was still dreamin' goold, an' I wint down to Saint Looey. Th' nearest I come to a fortune there was findin' a quarther on th' sthreet as I leaned over th' dashboord iv a car to whack th' off mule. Whin I got to Chicago, I looked around f'r the goold mine. They was Injuns here thin. But they wasn't anny mines I cud see. They was mud to be shovelled an' dhrays to be dhruv an' beats to be walked. I choose th' dhray; f'r I was niver cut out f'r a copper, an' I'd had me fill iv excavatin'. An' I dhruv th' dhray till I wint into business.

"Me experyence with goold minin' is it's always in th' nex' county. If I was to go to Alaska, they'd tell me iv th' finds in Seeberya. So I think I'll stay here. I'm a silver man, annyhow; an' I'm contint if I can see goold wanst a year, whin some prominent citizen smiles over his newspaper. I'm thinkin' that ivry man has a goold mine undher his own durestep or in his neighbor's pocket at th' farthest."

"Well, annyhow," said Mr. Hennessy, "I'd like to kick up th' sod, an' find a ton iv goold undher me fut."

"What wud ye do if ye found it?" demanded Mr. Dooley.

"I—I dinnaw," said Mr. Hennessy, whose dreaming had not gone this far. Then, recovering himself, he exclaimed with great enthusiasm, "I'd throw up me job an'—an' live like a prince."

"I tell ye what ye'd do," said Mr. Dooley. "Ye'd come back here an' sthrut up an' down th' sthreet with ye'er thumbs in ye'er armpits; an' ye'd dhrink too much, an' ride in sthreet ca-ars. Thin ye'd buy foldin' beds an' piannies, an' start a reel estate office. Ye'd be fooled a good deal an' lose a lot iv ye'er money, an' thin ye'd tighten up. Ye'd be in a cold fear night an' day that ye'd lose ye'er fortune. Ye'd wake up in th' middle iv th' night, dhreamin' that ye was back at th' gas-house with ye'er money gone. Ye'd be prisidint iv a charitable society. Ye'd have to wear ye'er shoes in th' house, an' ye'er wife'd have ye around to rayciptions an' dances. Ye'd move to Mitchigan Avnoo, an' ye'd hire a coachman that'd laugh at ye. Ye'er boys'd be joods an' ashamed iv ye, an' ye'd support ye'er daughters' husbands. Ye'd rackrint ye'er tinants an' lie about ye'er taxes. Ye'd go back to Ireland on a visit, an' put on airs with ye'er cousin Mike. Ye'd be a mane, close-fisted, onscrupulous ol' curmudgeon; an', whin ye'd die, it'd take half ye'er fortune f'r rayqueems to put ye r-right. I don't want ye iver to speak to me whin ye get rich, Hinnissy."

"I won't," said Mr. Hennessy.

ON BOOKS

"Ivry time I pick up me mornin' paper to see how th' scrap come out at Batthry D," said Mr. Dooley, "th' first thing I r-run acrost is somethin' like this: 'A hot an' handsome gift f'r Christmas is Lucy Ann Patzooni's "Jims iv Englewood Thought"'; or 'If ye wud delight th' hear-rt iv yer child, ye'll give him Dr. Harper's monymental histhry iv th' Jewish thribes fr'm Moses to Dhryfuss' or 'Ivrybody is r-readin' Roodyard Kiplin's "Busy Pomes f'r Busy People."' Th' idee iv givin' books f'r Christmas prisints whin th' stores are full iv tin hor-rns an' dhrums an' boxin' gloves an choo-choo ca-ars! People must be crazy."

"They ar-re," said Mr. Hennessy. "My house is so full iv books ye cudden't tur-rn around without stumblin' over thim. I found th' life iv an ex-convict, the 'Prisoner iv Zinders,' in me high hat th' other day, where Mary Ann was hidin' it fr'm her sister. Instead iv th' childher fightin' an' skylarkin' in th' evenin', they're settin' around th' table with their noses glued into books. Th' ol' woman doesn't read, but she picks up what's goin' on. 'Tis 'Honoria, did Lor-rd What's-his-name marry th' fair Aminta?' or 'But that Lady Jane was a case.' An' so it goes.

There's no injymint in th' house, an' they're usin' me cravats f'r bookmarks."

" 'Tis all wrong," said Mr. Dooley. "They're on'y three books in th' wurruld worth readin'—Shakespeare, th' Bible, an' Mike Ahearn's histhry iv Chicago. I have Shakespeare on thrust, Father Kelly r-reads th' Bible f'r me, an' I didn't buy Mike Ahearn's histhry because I seen more thin he cud put into it. Books is th' roon iv people, specially novels. Whin I was a young man, th' parish priest used to preach again thim; but nobody knowed what he meant. At that time Willum Joyce had th' on'y library in th' Sixth Wa-ard. Th' mayor give him th' bound volumes iv th' council proceedings, an' they was a very handsome set. Th' on'y books I seen was th' kind that has th' life iv th' pope on th' outside an' a set iv dominos on th' inside. They're good readin'. Nawthin' cud be better f'r a man whin he's tired out afther a day's wurruk thin to go to his library an' take down wan iv the gr-reat wurruks iv lithratchoor an' play a game iv dominos f'r th' dhrinks out iv it. Anny other kind iv r-readin', barrin' th' newspapers, which will niver hurt anny onedycated man, is desthructive iv morals.

"I had it out with Father Kelly th' other day in this very matther. He was comin' up fr'm down town with an ar-rmful iv books f'r prizes at th' school. 'Have ye th' Key to Heaven there?' says I. 'No,' says he, 'th' childher that'll get these books don't need no key. They go in under th' turnstile,' he says, laughin'. 'Have ye th' Lives iv th' Saints, or the Christyan Dooty, or th' Story iv Saint Rose iv Lima?' I says. 'I have not,' says he. 'I have some good story books. I'd rather th' kids'd r-read Char-les Dickens than anny iv th' tales iv thim holy men that was burned in ile or et up be lines,' he says. 'It does no good in these degin'rate days to prove that th' best that can come to a man f'r behavin' himsilf is to be cooked in a pot or di-gisted be a line,' he says. 'Ye're wrong,' says I. 'Beggin' ye'er riv'rince's pardon, ye're wrong,' I says. 'What ar-re ye goin' to do with thim young wans? Ye're goin' to make thim near-sighted an' round-shouldered,' I says. 'Ye're goin' to have thim believe that, if they behave thimsilves an' lead a virchous life, they'll marry rich an' go to Congress. They'll wake up some day, an' find out that gettin' money an behavin' ye'ersilf don't always go together,' I says. 'Some iv th' wickedest men in th' wur-ruld have marrid rich,' I says. 'Ye're goin' to teach thim that a man doesn't have

to use an ax to get along in th' wur-ruld.   Ye're goin' to teach thim
that a la-ad with a curlin' black mustache an' smokin' a cigareet is
always a villyan, whin he's more often a barber with a lar-rge
family.   Life, says ye!   There's no life in a book.   If ye want to
show thim what life is, tell thim to look around thim.   There's
more life on a Saturdah night in th' Ar-rchy Road thin in all th'
books fr'm Shakespeare to th' rayport iv th' drainage thrustees.
No man,' I says, 'iver wrote a book if he had annything to write
about, except Shakespeare an' Mike Ahearn.   Shakespeare was
all r-right.   I niver read anny of his pieces, but they sound good;
an' I know Mike Ahearn is all r-right.'"

"What did he say?" asked Mr. Hennessy.

"He took it all r-right," said Mr. Dooley.   "He kind o'
grinned, an' says he: 'What ye say is thrue, an' it's not thrue,' he
says.   'Books is f'r thim that can't injye thimsilves in anny other
way,' he says.   'If ye're in good health, an' ar-re atin' three squares
a day, an' not ayether sad or very much in love with ye'er lot, but
just lookin' on an' not carin' a'—he said rush—'not carin' a rush,
ye don't need books,' he says.   'But if ye're a down-spirited
thing an' want to get away an' can't, ye need books.   'Tis betther
to be comfortable at home thin to go to th' circus, an' 'tis betther
to go to th' circus thin to r-read anny book.   But 'tis betther to
r-read a book thin to want to go to th' circus an' not be able to,'
he says.   'Well,' says I, 'whin I was growin' up, half th' congregation heard mass with their prayer books tur-rned upside down,
an' they were as pious as anny.   Th' Apostles' Creed niver was as
con-vincin' to me afther I larned to r-read it as it was whin I
cudden't read it, but believed it.'"

ON CRIMINALS

"Lord bless my sowl," said Mr. Dooley, "childher is a gr-reat
responsibility—a gr-reat risponsibility.   Whin I think iv it, I
praise th' saints I niver was married, though I had opporchunities
enough whin I was a young man; an' even now I have to wear me
hat low whin I go down be Cologne Sthreet on account iv th'
Widow Grogan.   Jawn, that woman'll take me dead or alive.
I wake up in a col' chill in th' middle iv th' night, dhreamin' iv
her havin' me in her clutches.

"But that's not here or there, avick.   I was r-readin' in th'
pa-apers iv a lad be th' name iv Scanlan bein' sint down th' short

r-road f'r near a lifetime; an' I minded th' first time I iver see him—
a bit iv a curly-haired boy that played tag around me place, an'
'd sing 'Blest Saint Joseph' with a smile on his face like an angel's.
Who'll tell what makes wan man a thief an' another man a saint?
I dinnaw. This here boy's father wurrked fr'm morn till night in
th' mills, was at early mass Sundah mornin' befure th' alkalis lit
th' candles, an' niver knowed a month whin he failed his jooty.
An' his mother was a sweet-faced little woman, though fr'm th'
County Kerry, that nursed th' sick an' waked th' dead, an' niver
had a hard thought in her simple mind f'r anny iv Gawd's creatures.
Poor sowl, she's dead now. May she rest in peace!

"He didn't git th' shtreak fr'm his father or fr'm his mother.
His brothers an' sisters was as fine a lot as iver lived. But this
la-ad Petey Scanlan growed up fr'm bein' a curly-haired angel f'r
to be th' toughest villyun in th' r-road. What was it at all, at all?
Sometimes I think they'se poison in th' life iv a big city. Th'
flowers won't grow here no more thin they wud in a tannery, an'
th' bur-rds have no song; an' th' childher iv dacint men an' women
come up hard in th' mouth an' with their hands raised again their
kind.

"Th' la-ad was th' scoorge iv th' polis. He was as quick as a
cat an' as fierce as a tiger, an' I well raymimber him havin' laid
out big Kelly that used to thravel this post—'Whistlin'' Kelly
that kep' us awake with imitations iv a mockin' bur-rd—I well
raymimber him scuttlin' up th' alley with a score iv polismin
laborin' afther him, thryin' f'r a shot at him as he wint around th'
bar-rns or undher th' thrucks. He slep' in th' coal-sheds afther
that until th' poor ol' man cud square it with th' loot. But, whin
he come out, ye cud see how his face had hardened an' his ways
changed. He was as silent as an animal, with a sideways manner
that watched ivrything. Right here in this place I seen him stand
f'r a quarther iv an' hour, not seemin' to hear a dhrunk man
abusin' him, an' thin lep out like a snake. We had to pry him
loose.

"Th' ol' folks done th' best they cud with him. They hauled
him out iv station an' jail an' bridewell. Wanst in a long while
they'd dhrag him off to church with his head down: that was
always afther he'd been sloughed up f'r wan thing or another.
Between times th' polis give him his own side iv th' sthreet, an'
on'y took him whin his back was tur-rned. Thin he'd go in the
wagon with a mountain iv thim on top iv him, swayin' an' swearin'

an' sthrikin' each other in their hurry to put him to sleep with their clubs.

"I mind well th' time he was first took to be settled f'r good. I heerd a noise in th' ya-ard, an' thin he come through th' place with his face dead gray an' his lips just a turn grayer. 'Where ar-re ye goin', Petey?' says I. 'I was jus' takin' a short cut home,' he says. In three minyits th' r-road was full iv polismin. They'd been a robbery down in Halsted Sthreet. A man that had a grocery sthore was stuck up, an' whin he fought was clubbed near to death; an' they'd r-run Scanlan through th' alleys to his father's house. That was as far as they'd go. They was enough iv thim to've kicked down th' little cottage with their heavy boots, but they knew he was standin' behind th' dure with th' big gun in his hand; an', though they was manny a good lad there, they was none that cared f'r that short odds.

"They talked an' palavered outside, an' telephoned th' chief iv polis, an' more pathrol wagons come up. Some was f'r settin' fire to th' buildin', but no wan moved ahead. Thin th' fr-ront dure opened, an' who shud come out but th' little mother. She was thin an' pale, an' she had her apron in her hands, pluckin' at it. 'Gintlemin,' she says, 'what is it ye want iv me?' she says. 'Liftinant Cassidy,' she says, ''tis sthrange f'r ye that I've knowed so long to make scandal iv me befure me neighbors,' she says. 'Mrs. Scanlan,' says he, 'we want th' boy. I'm sorry, ma'am, but he's mixed up in a bad scrape, an' we must have him,' he says. She made a curtsy to thim, an' wint indures. 'Twas less than a minyit befure she come out, clingin' to th' la-ad's ar-rm. 'He'll go,' she says. 'Thanks be, though he's wild, they'se no crime on his head. Is there, dear?' 'No,' says he, like th' game kid he is. Wan iv th' polismin stharted to take hold iv him, but th' la-ad pushed him back; an' he wint to th' wagon on his mother's ar-rm."

"And was he really innocent?" Mr. McKenna asked.

"No," said Mr. Dooley. "But she niver knowed it. Th' ol' man come home an' found her: she was settin' in a big chair with her apron in her hands an th' picture iv th' la-ad in her lap."

ON THE NEW WOMAN

"Molly Donahue have up an' become a new woman!

"It's been a good thing f'r ol' man Donahue, though, Jawn. He shtud ivrything that mortal man cud stand. He seen her appearin' in th' road wearin' clothes that no lady shud wear an' ridin' a bicycle; he was humiliated whin she demanded to vote; he put his pride under his ar-rm an' ma-arched out iv th' house whin she committed assault-an'-batthry on th' piannah. But he's got to th' end iv th' rope now. He was in here las' night, how-come-ye-so, with his hat cocked over his eye an' a look iv risolution on his face; an' whin he left me, he says, says he, 'Dooley,' he says, 'I'll conquir, or I'll die,' he says.

"It's been comin' f'r months, but it on'y bust on Donahue las' week. He'd come home at night tired out, an' afther supper he was pullin' off his boots, whin Mollie an' th' mother begun talkin' about th' rights iv females. ''Tis th' era iv th' new woman,' says Mollie. 'Ye're right,' says th' mother. 'What d'ye mean be the new woman?' says Donahue, holdin' his boot in his hand. 'Th' new woman,' says Mollie, ''ll be free fr'm th' opprission iv man,' she says. 'She'll wurruk out her own way, without help or hinderance,' she says. 'She'll wear what clothes she wants,' she says, 'an' she'll be no man's slave,' she says. 'They'll be no such thing as givin' a girl in marredge to a clown an' makin' her dipindant on his whims,' she says. 'Th' women'll earn their own livin',' she says; 'an' mebbe,' she says, 'th' men'll stay at home an' dredge in th' house wurruk,' she says. 'A-ho,' says Donahue. 'An' that's th' new woman, is it?' he says. An' he said no more that night.

"But th' nex' mornin' Mrs. Donahue an' Mollie come to his dure. 'Get up,' says Mrs. Donahue, 'an' bring in some coal,' she says. 'Ye drowsy man, ye'll be late f'r ye'er wurruk.' 'Divvle th' bit iv coal I'll fetch,' says Donahue. 'Go away an' lave me alone,' he says. 'Ye're inthruptin' me dreams.' 'What ails ye, man alive?' says Mrs. Donahue. 'Get up.' 'Go away,' says Donahue, 'an' lave me slumber,' he says. 'Th' idee iv a couple iv big strong women like you makin' me wurruk f'r ye,' he says. 'Mollie 'll bring in th' coal,' he says. 'An' as f'r you, Honoria, ye'd best see what there is in th' cupboord an' put it in ye'er dinner-pail,' he says. 'I heerd th' first whistle blow a minyit ago,' he says; 'an' there's a pile iv slag at th' mills that has to be wheeled off befure th' sup'rintindint comes around,' he says. 'Ye know ye can't afford to lose ye'er job with me in this dilicate condition,' he says. 'I'm going to sleep now,' he says. 'An', Mollie, do ye bring me in a cup iv cocoa an' a pooched igg at tin,' he says. 'I ixpect me music-teacher about that time. We have to take a wallop out iv Wagner an' Bootoven befure noon.' 'Th' Lord save us fr'm harm," says Mrs. Donahue. 'Th' man's clean crazy.' 'Divvle's th' bit,' says Donahue, wavin' his red flannel undhershirt in th' air. 'I'm the new man,' he says.

"Well, sir, Donahue said it flured thim complete. They didn't know what to say. Mollie was game, an' she fetched in th' coal; but Mrs. Donahue got nervous as eight o'clock come around. 'Ye're not goin' to stay in bed all day an' lose ye'er job,' she says. 'Th' 'ell with me job,' says Donahue. 'I'm not th' man to take wurruk whin they'se industhrees women with nawthin' to do,' he says. 'Show me th' pa-apers,' he says. 'I want to see where I can get an eighty-cint bonnet f'r two and a half.' He's that stubborn he'd've stayed in bed all day, but th' good woman weakened. 'Come,' she says, 'don't be foolish,' she says. 'Ye wudden't have th' ol' woman wurrukin' in th' mills,' she says. ''Twas all a joke,' she says. 'Oh-ho, th' ol' woman!' he says. 'Th' ol' woman! Well, that's a horse iv another color,' he says. 'An' I don't mind tellin' ye th' mills is closed down to-day, Honoria.' So he dhressed himsilf an' wint out; an' says he to Mollie, he says: 'Miss Newwoman,' says he, 'ye may find wurruk enough around th' house,' he says. 'An', if ye have time, ye might paint th' stoop,' he says. 'Th' ol' man is goin' to take th' ol' woman down be Halsted Sthreet an' blow himsilf f'r a new shawl f'r her.'

"An' he's been that proud iv th' victhry that he's been a reg'lar customer f'r a week."

ON THE POPULARITY OF FIREMEN

"I knowed a man be th' name iv Clancy wanst, Jawn. He was fr'm th' County May-o, but a good man f'r all that; an', whin he'd growed to be a big, sthrappin' fellow, he wint on to th' fire departmint. They'se an Irishman 'r two on th' fire departmint an' in th' army, too, Jawn, though ye'd think be hearin' some talk they was all runnin' prim'ries an' thryin' to be cinthral comitymen. So ye wud. Ye niver hear iv thim on'y whin they die; an' thin, murther, what funerals they have!

"Well, this Clancy wint on th' fire departmint, an' they give him a place in thruck twenty-three. All th' r-road was proud iv him, an' faith he was proud iv himsilf. He r-rode free on th' sthreet ca-ars, an' was th' champeen hand-ball player f'r miles

around. Ye shud see him goin' down th' sthreet, with his blue
shirt an' his blue coat with th' buttons on it, an' his cap on his ear.
But ne'er a cap or coat'd he wear whin they was a fire. He might
be shiv'rin' be th' stove in th' ingine house with a buffalo robe over
his head; but, whin th' gong sthruck, 'twas off with coat an' cap an'
buffalo robe, an' out come me brave Clancy, bare-headed an' bare
hand, dhrivin' with wan line an' spillin' th' hose cart on wan
wheel at ivry jump iv th' horse. Did anny wan iver see a fireman
with his coat on or a polisman with his off? Why, wanst, whin
Clancy was standin' up f'r Grogan's eighth, his son come runnin'
in to tell him they was a fire in Vogel's packin' house. He
dhropped th' kid at Father Kelly's feet, an' whipped off his long
coat an' wint tearin' f'r th' dure, kickin' over th' poorbox an'
buttin' ol' Mis' O'Neill that'd come in to say th' stations. 'Twas
lucky 'twas wan iv th' Grogans. They're a fine family f'r falls.
Jawn Grogan was wurrukin' on th' top iv Metzri an' O'Connell's
brewery wanst, with a man be th' name iv Dorsey. He slipped an'
fell wan hundherd feet. Whin they come to see if he was dead, he
got up, an' says he: 'Lave me at him.' 'At who?' says they.
'He's deliryous,' they says. 'At Dorsey,' says Grogan. 'He
thripped me.' So it didn't hurt Grogan's eighth to fall four 'r
five feet.

"Well, Clancy wint to fires an' fires. Whin th' big organ
facthry burnt, he carrid th' hose up to th' fourth story an' was
squirtin' whin th' walls fell. They dug him out with pick an'
shovel, an' he come up fr'm th' brick an' boards an' saluted th'
chief. 'Clancy,' says th' chief, 'ye betther go over an' get a
dhrink.' He did so, Jawn. I heerd it. An' Clancy was that
proud!

"Whin th' Hogan flats on Halsted Sthreet took fire, they got
all th' people out but wan; an' she was a woman asleep on th'
fourth flure. 'Who'll go up?' says Bill Musham. 'Sure, sir,'
says Clancy, 'I'll go'; an' up he wint. His captain was a man be
th' name iv O'Connell, fr'm th' County Kerry; an' he had his fut
on th' ladder whin Clancy started. Well, th' good man wint into
th' smoke, with his wife faintin' down below. 'He'll be kilt,' says
his brother. 'Ye don't know him,' says Bill Musham. An' sure
enough, whin ivry wan'd give him up, out comes me brave
Clancy, as black as a Turk, with th' girl in his arms. Th' others
wint up like monkeys, but he shtud wavin' thim off, an' come down
th' ladder face forward. 'Where'd ye larn that?' says Bill

Musham. 'I seen a man do it at th' Lyceem whin I was a kid,' says Clancy. 'Was it all right?' 'I'll have ye up before th' ol' man,' says Bill Musham. 'I'll teach ye to come down a laddher as if ye was in a quadhrille, ye horse-stealin', ham-sthringin' May-o man,' he says. But he didn't. Clancy wint over to see his wife. 'O Mike,' says she, ''twas fine,' she says. 'But why d'ye take th' risk?' she says. 'Did ye see th' captain?' he says with a scowl. 'He wanted to go. Did ye think I'd follow a Kerry man with all th' ward lukkin' on?' he says.

"Well, so he wint dhrivin' th' hose-cart on wan wheel, an' jumpin' whin he heerd a man so much as hit a glass to make it ring. All th' people looked up to him, an' th' kids followed him down th' sthreet; an' 'twas th' gr-reatest priv'lige f'r anny wan f'r to play dominos with him near th' joker. But about a year ago he come in to see me, an' says he, 'Well, I'm goin' to quit.' 'Why,' says I, 'ye'er a young man yet,' I says. 'Faith,' he says, 'look at me hair,' he says—'young heart, ol' head. I've been at it these twinty year, an' th' good woman's wantin' to see more iv me thin blowin' into a saucer iv coffee,' he says. 'I'm goin' to quit,' he says, 'on'y I want to see wan more good fire,' he says. 'A rale good ol' hot wan,' he says, 'with th' win' blowin' f'r it an' a good dhraft in th' ilivator-shaft, an' about two stories, with pitcher-frames an' gasoline an' excelsior, an' to hear th' chief yellin': "Play 'way, sivinteen. What th' hell an' damnation are ye standin' aroun' with that pipe f'r? Is this a fire 'r a dam livin' pitcher? I'll break ivry man iv eighteen, four, six, an' chem'cal five to-morrah mornin' befure breakfast." Oh,' he says, bringin' his fist down, 'wan more, an' I'll quit.'

"An' he did, Jawn. Th' day th' Carpenter Brothers' box factory burnt. 'Twas wan iv thim big, fine-lookin' buildings that pious men built out iv celluloid an' plasther iv Paris. An' Clancy was wan iv th' men undher whin th' wall fell. I seen thim bringin' him home; an' th' little woman met him at th' dure, rumplin' her apron in her hands."

ON THE GAME OF FOOTBALL

"Whin I was a young man," said Mr. Dooley, "an' that was a long time ago—but not so long ago as manny iv me inimies'd like to believe, if I had anny inimies—I played fut-ball, but 'twas not th' fut-ball I see whin th' Brothers' school an' th' Saint Aloysius Tigers played las' week on th' pee-raries.

"Whin I was a la-ad, iv a Sundah afthernoon we'd get out in th' field where th' oats'd been cut away, an' we'd choose up sides. Wan cap'n'd pick one man, an' th' other another. 'I choose Dooley,' 'I choose O'Connor,' 'I choose Dimpsey,' 'I choose Riordan,' an' so on till there was twinty-five or thirty on a side. Thin wan cap'n'd kick th' ball, an' all our side'd r-run at it an' kick it back; an' thin wan iv th' other side'd kick it to us, an' afther awhile th' game'd get so timpischous that all th' la-ads iv both sides'd be in wan pile, kickin' away at wan or th' other or at th' ball or at th' impire, who was mos'ly a la-ad that cudden't play an' that come out less able to play thin he was whin he wint in. An', if anny wan laid hands on th' ball, he was kicked be ivry wan else an' be th' impire. We played fr'm noon till dark, an' kicked th' ball all th' way home in the moonlight.

"That was futball, an' I was a great wan to play it. I'd think nawthin' iv histin' th' ball two hundherd feet in th' air, an' wanst I give it such a boost that I stove in th' ribs iv th' Prowtestant minister—bad luck to him, he was a kind man—that was lookin' on fr'm a hedge. I was th' finest player in th' whole county, I was so.

"But this here game that I've been seein' ivry time th' pagan fistival iv Thanksgivin' comes ar-round, sure it ain't th' game I played. I seen th' Dorgan la-ad comin' up th' sthreet yesterdah in his futball clothes—a pair iv matthresses on his legs, a pillow behind, a mask over his nose, an' a bushel measure iv hair on his head. He was followed be three men with bottles, Dr. Ryan, an' th' Dorgan fam'ly. I jined thim. They was a big crowd on th' peerary —a bigger crowd than ye cud get to go f'r to see a prize fight. Both sides had their frinds that give th' colledge cries. Says wan crowd: 'Take an ax, an ax, an ax to thim. Hooroo, hooroo, hellabaloo. Christyan Bro-others!' an' th' other says, 'Hit thim, saw thim, gnaw thim, chaw thim, Saint Alo-ysius!' Well, afther awhile they got down to wur-ruk. 'Sivin, eighteen, two, four,' says a la-ad. I've seen people go mad over figures durin' th' free silver campaign, but I niver see figures make a man want f'r to go out an' kill his fellow-men befure. But these here figures had th' same effect on th' la-ads that a mintion iv Lord Castlereagh'd have on their fathers. Wan la-ad hauled off, an' give a la-ad acrost fr'm him a punch in th' stomach. His frind acrost th' way caught him in th' ear. Th'

cinter rush iv th' Saint Aloysiuses took a runnin' jump at th' left
lung iv wan iv th' Christyan Brothers, an' wint to th' grass with
him.   Four Christyan Brothers leaped most crooly at four Saint
Aloysiuses, an' rolled thim.   Th' cap'n iv th' Saint Aloysiuses he
took th' cap'n iv th' Christyan Brothers be th' leg, an' he pounded
th' pile with him as I've seen a section hand tamp th' thrack.   All
this time young Dorgan was standin' back, takin' no hand in th'
affray.   All iv a suddent he give a cry iv rage, an' jumped feet
foremost into th' pile.   'Down!' says th' impire.   'Faith, they
are all iv that,' says I, 'Will iver they get up ?'   'They will,' says
ol' man Dorgan.   'Ye can't stop thim,' says he.

   "It took some time f'r to pry thim off.   Near ivry man iv th'
Saint Aloysiuses was tied in a knot around wan iv th' Christyan
Brothers.   On'y wan iv them remained on th' field.   He was
lyin' face down, with his nose in th' mud.   'He's kilt,' says I.
'I think he is,' says Dorgan, with a merry smile.   ''Twas my boy
Jimmy done it, too,' says he.   'He'll be arrested f'r murdher,' says
I.   'He will not,' says he.   'There's on'y wan polisman in town
cud take him, an' he's down town doin' th' same f'r somebody,' he
says.   Well, they carried th' corpse to th' side, an' took th' ball
out iv his stomach with a monkey wrinch, an' th' game was ray-
shumed.   'Sivin, sixteen, eight, eleven,' says Saint Aloysius ; an'
young Dorgan started to run down th' field.   They was another
young la-ad r-runnin' in fr-front iv Dorgan ; an', as fast as wan iv
th' Christyan Brothers come up an' got in th' way, this here young
Saint Aloysius grabbed him be th' hair iv th' head an' th' sole iv
th' fut, an' thrun him over his shoulder.   'What's that la-ad
doin' ?' says I.   'Interferin',' says he.   'I shud think he was,'
says I, 'an' most impudent,' I says.   ''Tis such interference as
this,' I says, 'that breaks up fam'lies' ; an' I come away.

   "'Tis a noble sport, an' I'm glad to see us Irish ar-re gettin'
into it.   Whin we larn it thruly, we'll teach thim colledge joods
fr'm th' pie belt a thrick or two."

   "We have already," said Mr. Hennessy.   "They'se a team
up in Wisconsin with a la-ad be th' name iv Jeremiah Riordan f'r
cap'n, an' wan named Patsy O'Dea behind him.   They come
down here, an' bate th' la-ads fr'm th' Chicawgo Colledge down be
th' Midway."

   "Iv coorse, they did,' said Mr. Dooley.   "Iv coorse, they did.
An' they cud bate anny collection iv Baptists that iver come out
iv a tank."

ON THE POWER OF LOVE[1]

" 'Twas this way," said Mr. Hennessy, sparring at Mr. Dooley. "Fitz led his right light on head, thin he stuck his thumb in Corbett's hear-rt, an' that was th' end iv th' fight an' iv Pompydour Jim. I tol' ye how it wud come out. Th' punch over th' hear-rt done th' business."

"Not at all," said Mr. Dooley. "Not at all. 'Twas Mrs. Fitzsimmons done th' business. Did ye see the pitcher iv that lady ? Did ye ? Well, 'twud've gone har-rd with th' lad if he'd lost th' fight in th' ring. He'd have to lose another at home. I'll bet five dollars that th' first lady iv th' land licks th' champeen without th' aid iv a stove lid. I know it.

"As me good frind, Jawn Sullivan, says, 'tis a great comfort to have little reminders iv home near by whin ye're fightin'. Jawn had none, poor lad; an' that accounts f'r th' way he wint down at last. Th' home infloo-ence is felt in ivry walk iv life. Whin Corbett was poundin' th' first jintleman iv th' land like a man shinglin' a roof, th' first lady iv th' land stood in th' corner, cheerin' on th' bruised an' bleedin' hero. 'Darlin',' she says, 'think iv ye'er home, me love. Think,' she says, 'iv our little child larnin' his caddychism in Rahway, New Jersey,' she says. 'Think iv th' love I bear ye,' she says, 'an' paste him,' she says, 'in th' slats. Don't hit him on th' jaw,' she says. 'He's well thrained there. But tuck ye'er lovin' hooks into his diseased an' achin' ribs,' she says. 'Ah, love!' she says, 'recall thim happy goolden days iv our coortship, whin we walked th' counthry lane in th' light iv th' moon,' she says, 'an' hurl yer maulies into his hoops,' she says. 'Hit him on th' slats!' An' Fitz looked over his shoulder an' seen her face, an' strange feelin's iv tendherness come over him; an' thinks he to himself: 'What is so good as th' love iv a pure woman ? If I don't nail this large man, she'll prob'ly kick in me head.' An' with this sacred sintimint in his heart he wint over an' jolted Corbett wan over th' lathes that retired him to th' home f'r decayed actors.

" 'Twas woman's love that done it, Hinnissy. I'll make a bet with ye that, if th' first lady iv th' land had been in th' ring instead iv th' first jintleman, Corbett wudden't have lasted wan r-round. I'd like to have such a wife as that. I'd do th' cookin',

---

[1] Written on the occasion of the Fitzsimmons-Corbett fight of March, 1897. Fitzsimmons won by a knockout in the fourteenth round.

an' lave th' fightin' to her. There ought to be more like her.
Th' throuble with th' race we're bringin' up is that th' fair sect, as
Shakespeare calls thim, lacks inthrest in their jooty to their
husbands. It's th' business iv men to fight, an' th' business iv
their wives f'r to make thim fight. Ye may talk iv th' immyrality
iv nailin' a man on th' jaw, but 'tis in this way on'y that th' wurruld
increases in happiness an' th' race in strenth. Did ye see annywan
th' other day that wasn't askin' to know how th' fight come out?
They might say that they re-garded th' exhibition as brutal an'
disgustin', but divvle a wan iv thim but was waitin' around th'
corner f'r th' rayturns, an' prayin' f'r wan or th' other iv th' big
lads. Father Kelly mentioned th' scrap in his sermon last
Sundah. He said it was a disgraceful an' corruptin' affair, an'
he was ashamed to see th' young men iv th' parish takin' such an
inthrest in it in Lent. But late Winsdah afthernoon he came
bustlin' down th' sthreet. 'Nice day,' he says. It was poorin'
rain. 'Fine,' says I. 'They was no parade to-day,' he says.
'No,' says I. 'Too bad,' says he; an' he started to go. Thin he
turned, an' says he: 'Be th' way, how did that there foul an'
outhrajous affray in Carson City come out?' 'Fitz,' says I, 'in th'
fourteenth.' 'Ye don't say,' he says, dancin' around. 'Good,'
he says. 'I told Father Doyle this mornin' at breakfuss that if
that red-headed man iver got wan punch at th' other lad, I'd bet a
new cassock—Oh, dear!' he says, 'what am I sayin'?' 'Ye're
sayin',' says I, 'what nine-tenths iv th' people, laymen an' clargy,
are sayin',' I says. 'Well,' he says, 'I guess ye're right,' he says.
'Afther all,' he says, 'an' undher all, we're mere brutes; an' it on'y
takes two lads more brutal than th' rest f'r to expose th' sthreak in
th' best iv us. Foorce rules th' wurruld, an' th' churches is
empty whin th' blood begins to flow,' he says. 'It's too bad, too
bad,' he says. 'Tell me, was Corbett much hurted?' he says."

ON THE VICTORIAN ERA

"Ar-re ye goin' to cillybrate th' queen's jubilee?" asked Mr.
Dooley.

"What's that?" demanded Mr. Hennessy, with a violent
start.

"To-day," said Mr. Dooley, "her gracious Majesty Victorya,
Queen iv Great Britain an' that part iv Ireland north iv Sligo, has
reigned f'r sixty long and tiresome years."

"I don't care if she has snowed f'r sixty years," said Mr. Hennessy. "I'll not cillybrate it. She may be a good woman f'r all I know, but dam her pollytics."

"Ye needn't be pro-fane about it," said Mr. Dooley. "I on'y ast ye a civil question. F'r mesilf, I have no feelin' on th' subject. I am not with th' queen an' I'm not again her. At th' same time I corjally agree with me frind Captain Finerty, who's put his newspaper in mournin' f'r th' ivint. I won't march in th' parade, an' I won't put anny dinnymite undher thim that does. I don't say th' marchers an' dinnymiters ar-re not both r-right. 'Tis purely a question iv taste, an', as the ixicutive says whin both candydates are mimbers iv th' camp, 'Pathrites will use their own discreetion.'

"Th' good woman niver done me no har-rm; an', beyond throwin' a rock or two into an orangey's procission an' subscribin' to tin dollars' worth iv Fenian bonds, I've threated her like a lady. Anny gredge I iver had again her I burrid long ago. We're both well on in years, an' 'tis no use carrying har-rd feelin's to th' grave. About th' time th' lord chamberlain wint over to tell her she was queen, an' she came out in her nitey to hear th' good news, I was announced into this wurruld iv sin an' sorrow. So ye see we've reigned about th' same lenth iv time, an' I ought to be cillybratin' me di'mon' jubilee. I wud, too, if I had anny di'mon's. Do ye r-run down to Aldherman O'Brien's an' borrow twinty or thirty f'r me.

"Great happenin's have me an' Queen Victorya seen in these sixty years. Durin' our binificent prisince on earth th' nations have grown r-rich an' prosperous. Great Britain has ixtinded her domain until th' sun niver sets on it. No more do th' original owners iv th' sile, they bein' kept movin' be th' polis. While she was lookin' on in England, I was lookin' on in this counthry. I have seen America spread out fr'm th' Atlantic to th' Pacific, with a branch office iv the Standard Ile Comp'ny in ivry hamlet. I've seen th' shackles dropped fr'm th' slave, so's he cud be lynched in Ohio. I've seen this gr-reat city desthroyed be fire fr'm De Koven Sthreet to th' Lake View pumpin' station, and thin rise felix-like fr'm its ashes, all but th' West Side, which was not burned. I've seen Jim Mace beat Mike McCool, an' Tom Allen beat Jim Mace, an' somebody beat Tom Allen, an' Jawn Sullivan beat him, an' Corbett beat Sullivan, an' Fitz beat Corbett; an', if I live to cillybrate me goold-watch-an'-chain jubilee, I may see some wan put it all over Fitz.

"Oh, what things I've seen in me day an' Victorya's! Think
iv that gran' procission iv lithry men—Tinnyson an' Longfellow
an' Bill Nye an' Ella Wheeler Wilcox an' Tim Scanlan an'—an' I
can't name thim all: they're too manny. An' th' brave gin'rals—
Von Molkey an' Bismarck an' U. S. Grant an' gallant Phil
Shurdan an' Coxey. Think iv thim durin' me reign. An' th'
invintions—th' steam-injine an' th' printin'-press an' th' cotton-
gin an' the gin sour an' th' bicycle an' th' flyin'-machine an' th'
nickel-in-th'-slot machine an' th' Croker machine an' th' sody
fountain an'—crownin' wur-ruk iv our civilization—th' cash raygisther. What gr-reat advances has science made in my time an'
Victorya's! f'r, whin we entered public life, it took three men to
watch th' bar-keep, while to-day ye can tell within eight dollars an
hour what he's took in.

"Glory be, whin I look back fr'm this day iv gin'ral rejoicin' in
me rhinestone jubilee, an' see what changes has taken place an'
how manny people have died an' how much betther off th' wurruld
is, I'm proud iv mesilf. War an' pest'lence an' famine have
occurred in me time, but I count thim light compared with th'
binifits that have fallen to th' race since I come on th' earth."

"What ar-re ye talkin' about?" cried Mr. Hennessy, in deep
disgust. "All this time ye've been standin' behind this bar ladlin'
out disturbance to th' Sixth Wa-ard, an' ye haven't been as far
east as Mitchigan Avnoo in twinty years. What have ye had to do
with all these things?"

"Well," said Mr. Dooley, "I had as much to do with thim as
th' queen."

ON POLITICAL PARADES

Mr. Hennessy, wearing a silver-painted stove-pipe hat and a
silver cape and carrying a torch, came in, looking much the worse
for wear. The hat was dented, the cape was torn, and there were
marks on Mr. Hennessy's face.

"Where ye been?" asked Mr. Dooley.

"Ma-archin'," said Mr. Hennessy.

"Be th' looks iv ye, ye might have been th' line iv ma-arch f'r
th' p'rade. Who's been doin' things to ye?"

"I had a currency debate with a man be th' name iv Joyce, a
towny iv mine, in th' Audjiotoroom Hotel," said Mr. Hennessy.
"Whin we got as far as th' price iv wheat in th' year iv th' big wind,

we pushed each other. Give me a high glass iv beer. I'm as dhry as a gravel roof."

"Well," said Mr. Dooley, handing over the glass, "ye're an ol' man; an', as th' good book says, an ol' fool is th' worst yet. So I'll not thry to con-vince ye iv th' error iv ye'er ways. But why anny citizen that has things in his head shud dhress himself up like a sandwich-man, put a torch on his shoulder, an' toddle over this blessid town with his poor round feet, is more than I can come at with all me intelligence.

"I agree with ye perfectly, Hinnissy, that this here is a crisis in our histhry. On wan hand is arrayed th' Shylocks an' th' pathrites, an' on th' other side th' pathrites an' th' arnychists. Th' Constitution must be upheld, th' gover'mint must be maintained, th' down-throdden farmer an' workin'man must get their rights. But do ye think, man alive, that ye're goin' to do this be pourin' lard ile frim ye'er torch down ye'er spine or thrippin' over sthreet-car tracks like a dhray-horse thryin' to play circus? Is th' Constitution anny safer to-night because ye have to have ye'er leg amputated to get ye'er boot off, or because Joyce has made ye'er face look like th' back dure-step iv a German resthrant?

"Jawnny Mack took me down in th' afthernoon f'r to see th' monsthrous p'rade iv th' goold men. It was a gloryous spectacle. Th' sthreets were crowded with goold bugs an' women an' polismin an' ambulances. Th' procission was miles an' miles long. Labor an' capital marched side be side, or annyhow labor was in its usual place, afther th' capitalists. It was a noble sight f'r to see th' employer iv workin'men marchin' ahead iv his band iv sturdy toilers that to rest thimsilves afther th' layboryous occupations iv th' week was reelin' undher banners that dhrilled a hole in their stomachs or carryin' two-be-four joists to show their allegance to th' naytional honor. A man that has to shovel coke into a dhray or shove lumber out iv th' hole iv a barge or elevate his profession be carryin' a hod iv mort to th' top iv a laddher doesn't march with th' grace iv an antelope, be a blamed sight. To march well, a man's feet have to be mates; an', if he has two left feet both runnin' sideways, he ought to have interference boots to keep him fr'm settin' fire to his knees. Whin a man walks as if he expected to lave a leg stuck in th' sthreet behind him, he has th' gait proper f'r half-past six o'clock th' avenin' befure pay-day. But 'tis not th' prance iv an American citizen makin' a gloryous spectacle iv himsilf."

"They were coerced," said Mr. Hennessy, gloomily.

"Don't ye believe it," replied the philosopher. "It niver requires coercion to get a man to make a monkey iv himsilf in a prisidintial campaign. He does it as aisily as ye dhrink ye'er liquor, an' that's too aisy. Don't ye believe thim lads with lumber ya-ards on their necks an' bar'ls on their feet was co-erced. There wasn't wan iv thim that wudden't give his week's wages f'r a chanst to show how many times he cud thrip over a manhole in a mile. No more co-erced than ye are whin ye r-run down town an' make an ape iv ye-ersilf. I see ye marchin' away fr'm Finucane's with th' Willum J. O'Briens. Th' man nex' to ye had a banner declarin' that he was no slave. 'Twas th' la-ad Johnson. He was r-right. He is no slave, an' he won't be wan as long as people have washin' to give to his wife. Th' man I see ye takin' a dhrink with had a banner that said if th' mines was opened th' mills would be opened, too. He meant be that, that if money was plenty enough f'r him to get some without wur-rukin', he'd open a gin mill. An' ye ma-arched afther Willum J. O'Brien, didn't ye? Well, he's a good la-ad. If I didn't think so, I wudden't say it until I got me strenth back or cud buy a gun. But did Willum J. O'Brien march? Not Willie. He was on horseback; an', Hinnissy, if dollars was made out iv Babbit metal, an' horses was worth sixty-sivin cints a dhrove, ye cudden't buy a crupper."

"Well," said Mr. Hennessy, "annyhow, I proved me hathred iv capital."

"So ye did," said Mr. Dooley. "So ye did. An' capital this afthernoon showed its hatred iv ye. Ye ought to match blisters to see which hates th' worst. Capital is at home now with his gams in a tub iv hot wather; an', whin he comes down to-morrah to oppriss labor an' square his protisted notes, he'll have to go on all fours. As f'r you, Hinnissy, if 'twill aise ye anny, ye can hang f'r a few minyits fr'm th' gas fixtures. Did th' goold Dimmycrats have a p'rade?"

"No," said Mr. Hennessy. "But they rayviewed th' day procission fr'm th' Pammer House. Both iv thim was on th' stand."

ON A FAMILY REUNION

"Why aren't you out attending the reunion of the Dooley family?" Mr. McKenna asked the philosopher.

"Thim's no rel-ations to me," Mr. Dooley answered.

"Thim's farmer Dooleys. No wan iv our fam'ly iver lived in th' counthry. We live in th' city, where they burn gas an' have a polis foorce to get on to. We're no farmers, divvle th' bit. We belong to th' industhreel classes. Thim must be th' Fermanagh Dooleys, a poor lot, Jawn, an' always on good terms with th' landlord, bad ciss to thim, says I. We're from Roscommon. They'se a Dooley family in Wixford an' wan near Ballybone that belonged to th' constabulary. I met him but wanst. 'Twas at an iviction; an', though he didn't know me, I inthrajooced mesilf be landin' him back iv th' ear with a bouldher th' size iv ye'er two fists together. He didn't know me afterwards, ayether.

"We niver had but wan reunion iv th' Dooley fam'ly, an' that was tin years ago. Me cousin Felix's boy Aloysius—him that afterwards wint to New York an' got a good job dhrivin' a carredge f'r th' captain iv a polis station—he was full iv pothry an' things; an' he come around wan night, an' says he, 'D'ye know,' he says, ''twud be th' hite iv a good thing f'r th' Dooleys to have a reunion,' he says. 'We ought to come together,' he says, 'an' show the people iv this ward,' he says, 'how sthrong we are,' he says. 'Ye might do it betther, me buck,' says I, 'shovellin' slag at th' mills,' I says. 'But annyhow, if ye'er mind's set on it, go ahead,' I says, 'an' I'll attind to havin' th' polis there,' I says, 'f'r I have a dhrag at th' station.'

"Well, he sint out letthers to all th' Roscommon Dooleys; an' on a Saturdah night we come together in a rinted hall an' held th' reunion. 'Twas great sport f'r a while. Some iv us hadn't spoke frindly to each other f'r twinty years, an' we set around an' tol' stories iv Roscommon an' its green fields, an' th' stirabout pot that was niver filled, an' th' blue sky overhead an' th' boggy ground undherfoot. 'Which Dooley was it that hamsthrung th' cows?' 'Mike Dooley's Pat.' 'Naw such thing: 'twas Pat Dooley's Mike. I mane Pat Dooley's Mike's Pat.' F'r 'tis with us as with th' rest iv our people. Ye take th' Dutchman: he has as manny names to give to his childher as they'se nails in his boots, but an Irishman has th' pick iv on'y a few. I knowed a man be th' name iv Clancy —a man fr'm Kildare. He had fifteen childher; an', whin th' las' come, he says, 'Dooley, d'ye happen to know anny saints?' 'None iv thim thrades here,' says I. 'Why?' says I. 'They'se a new kid at th' house,' he says; 'an', be me troth, I've run out iv all th' saints I knew, an', if somewan don't come to me assistance,

I'll have to turn th' child out on th' wurruld without th' rag iv a name to his back,' he says.

"But I was tellin' ye about th' reunion. They was lashins iv dhrink an' story-tellin', an' Felix's boy Aloysius histed a banner he had made with 'Dooley aboo' painted on it. But, afther th' night got along, some iv us begun to raymimber that most iv us hadn't been frinds f'r long. Mrs. Morgan Dooley, she that was Molly Dooley befure she married Morgan, she turns to me, an' says she, ' 'Tis sthrange they let in that Hogan woman,' she says—that Hogan woman, Jawn, bein' th' wife iv her husband's brother. She heerd her say it, an' she says, ' I'd have ye to undherstand that no wan iver come out iv Roscommon that cud hold up their heads with th' Hogans,' she says. ' 'Tis not f'r th' likes iv ye to slandher a fam'ly that's iv th' landed gintry iv Ireland, an' f'r two pins I'd hit ye a poke in th' eye,' she says. If it hadn't been f'r me bein' between thim, they'd have been trouble; f'r they was good frinds wanst. What is it th' good book says about a woman scorned? Faith, I've forgotten.

"Thin me uncle Mike come in, as rough a man as iver laid hands on a polisman. Felix Dooley was makin' a speech on th' vartues iv th' fam'ly. 'Th' Dooleys,' says he, 'can stand befure all th' wurruld, an' no man can say ought agin ayether their honor or their integrity,' says he. 'Th' man that's throwin' that at ye,' says me uncle Mike, 'stole a saw fr'm me in th' year sivinty-five.' Felix paid no attintion to me uncle Mike, but wint on, 'We point proudly to th' motto, "Dooley aboo—Dooley f'river."' 'Th' saw aboo,' says me uncle Mike. 'Th' Dooleys,' says Felix, 'stood beside Red Hugh O'Neill; an', whin he cut aff his hand—' 'He didn't cut it off with anny wan else's saw,' says me uncle Mike. 'They'se an old sayin',' wint on Felix. 'An' ol' saw,' says me uncle Mike. 'But 'twas new whin ye stole it.'

" 'Now look here,' says Aloysius, 'this thing has gone far enough. 'Tis an outrage that this here man shud come here f'r to insult th' head iv th' fam'ly.' 'Th' head iv what fam'ly?' says Morgan Dooley, jumpin' up as hot as fire. 'I'm th' head iv th' fam'ly,' he says, 'be right iv histhry.' 'Ye're an ol' cow,' says me uncle Mike. 'Th' back iv me hand an' th' sowl iv me fut to all iv ye,' he says. 'I quit ye,' he says. 'Ye're all livin' here undher assumed names'; an' he wint out, followed be Morgan Dooley with a chair in each hand.

"Well, they wasn't two Dooleys in th' hall'd speak whin th'

meetin' broke up; an' th' Lord knows, but I don't to this day, who's th' head iv th' Dooley fam'ly. All I know is that I had wan th' nex' mornin'."

ON ORATORY IN POLITICS

"I mind th' first time Willum J. O'Brien r-run f'r office, th' Raypublicans an' th' Indypindants an' th' Socialists an' th' Prohybitionist (he's dead now, his name was Larkin) nommynated a young man be th' name iv Dorgan that was in th' law business in Halsted Sthreet, near Cologne, to r-run again' him. Smith O'Brien Dorgan was his name, an' he was wan iv th' most iloquint young la-ads that iver made a speakin' thrumpet iv his face. He cud holler like th' impire iv a base-ball game; an', whin he delivered th' sintimints iv his hear-rt, ye'd think he was thryin' to confide thim to a man on top iv a high buildin'. He was prisidint iv th' lithry club at th' church; an' Father Kelly tol' me that, th' day afther he won th' debate on th' pen an' th' soord in favor iv th' pen, they had to hire a carpenter to mend th' windows, they'd sagged so. They called him th' boy or-rator iv Healey's slough.

"He planned th' campaign himsilf. 'I'll not re-sort,' says he, 'to th' ordin'ry methods,' he says. 'Th' thing to do,' he says, 'is to prisint th' issues iv th' day to th' voters,' he says. 'I'll burn up ivry precin't in th' ward with me iloquince,' he says. An' he bought a long black coat, an' wint out to spread th' light.

"He talked ivrywhere. Th' people jammed Finucane's Hall, an' he tol' thim th' time had come f'r th' masses to r-rise. 'Raymimber,' says he, 'th' idees iv Novimb'r,' he says. 'Raymimber Demosthens an' Cicero an' Oak Park,' he says. 'Raymimber th' thraditions iv ye'er fathers, iv Washin'ton an' Jefferson an' Andhrew Jackson an' John L. Sullivan,' he says. 'Ye shall not, Billy O'Brien,' he says, 'crucify th' voters iv th' Sixth Ward on th' double cross,' he says. He spoke to a meetin' in Deerin' Sthreet in th' same wuruds. He had th' sthreet-car stopped while he coughed up reemarks about th' Constitution until th' bar-rn boss sint down an' threatened to discharge Mike Dwyer that was dhrivin' wan hundherd an' eight in thim days, though thransferred to Wintworth Avnoo later on. He made speeches to polismin in th' squadroom an' to good la-ads hoistin' mud out iv th' dhraw at th' red bridge. People'd be settin' quite in th' back room playin' forty-fives whin Smith O'Brien Dorgan'd burst in, an' addhress thim on th' issues iv th' day.

"Now all this time Bill O'Brien was campaignin' in his own way. He niver med wan speech. No wan knew whether he was f'r a tariff or again wan, or whether he sthud be Jefferson or was knockin' him, or whether he had th' inthrests iv th' toilin' masses at hear-rt or whether he wint to mass at all, at all. But he got th' superintindint iv th' rollin'-mills with him; an' he put three or four good fam'lies to wurruk in th' gas-house, where he knew th' main guy, an' he made reg'lar calls on th' bar-rn boss iv th' sthreet-ca-ars. He wint to th' picnics, an' hired th' or-chesthry f'r th' dances, an' voted himsilf th' most pop'lar man at th' church fair at an expinse iv at laste five hundherd dollars. No wan that come near him wanted f'r money. He had headquarthers in ivry saloon fr'm wan end iv th' ward to th' other. All th' pa-apers printed his pitcher, an' sthud by him as th' frind iv th' poor.

"Well, people liked to hear Dorgan at first, but afther a few months they got onaisy. He had a way iv breakin' into festive gatherin's that was enough to thry a saint. He delayed wan prize fight two hours, encouragin' th' voters prisint to stand be their principles, while th' principles sat shiverin' in their cor-rners until th' polis r-run him out. It got so that men'd bound into alleys whin he come up th' sthreet. People in th' liquor business rayfused to let him come into their places. His fam'ly et in th' coal-shed f'r fear iv his speeches at supper. He wint on talkin', and Willum J. O'Brien wint on handin' out th' dough that he got fr'm th' gas company an' con-ciliatin' th' masses; an', whin iliction day come, th' judges an' clerks was all f'r O'Brien, an' Dorgan didn't get votes enough to wad a gun. He sat up near all night in his long coat, makin' speeches to himsilf; but tord mornin' he come over to my place where O'Brien sat with his la-ads. 'Well,' says O'Brien, 'how does it suit ye?' he says. 'It's sthrange,' says Dorgan. 'Not sthrange at all,' says Willum J. O'Brien. 'Whin ye've been in politics as long as I have, ye'll know,' he says, 'that th' rolyboly is th' gr-reatest or-rator on earth,' he says. 'Th' American nation in th' Sixth Ward is a fine people,' he says. 'They love th' eagle,' he says, 'on th' back iv a dollar,' he says. 'Well,' says Dorgan, 'I can't undherstand it,' he says. 'I med as manny as three thousan' speeches,' he says. 'Well,' says Willum J. O'Brien, 'that was my majority,' he says. 'Have a dhrink,' he says."

ON ANARCHISTS

" 'Tis ha-ard bein' a king these days," said Mr. Dooley. " Manny's th' man on a throne wishes his father'd brought him up a cooper, what with wages bein' docked be parlymints an' ragin' arnychists r-runnin' wild with dinnymite bombs undher their ar-rms an' carvin'-knives in their pockets.

"Onaisy, as Hogan says, is th' head that wears a crown. They'se other heads that're onaisy, too; but ye don't hear iv thim. But a man gr-rows up in wan iv thim furrin counthries, an' he's thrained f'r to be a king. Hivin may've intinded him f'r a dooce or a jack, at th' most; but he has to follow th' same line as his father. 'Tis like pawnbrokin' that way. Ye niver heerd iv a pawnbroker's son doin' annything else. Wanst a king, always a king. Other men's sons may pack away a shirt in a thrunk, an' go out into th' wurruld, brakin' on a freight or ladin' Indyanny bankers up to a shell game. But a man that's headed f'r a throne can't r-run away. He's got to take th' job. If he kicks, they blindfold him an' back him in. He can't ask f'r his time at th' end iv th' week, an' lave. He pays himsilf. He can't sthrike, because he'd have to ordher out th' polis to subjoo himsilf. He can't go to th' boss, an' say: 'Me hours is too long an' th' wurruk is tajious. Give me me pay-check.' He has no boss. A man can't be indipindint onless he has a boss. 'Tis thrue. So he takes th' place, an' th' chances ar-re he's th' biggest omadhon in th' wurruld, an' knows no more about r-runnin' a counthry thin I know about ladin' an orchesthry. An', if he don't do annything, he's a dummy, an', if he does do annything, he's crazy; an', whin he dies, his foreman says: 'Sure, 'tis th' divvle's own time I had savin' that bosthoon fr'm desthroyin' himsilf. If it wasn't f'r me, th' poor thing'd have closed down the wurruks, an' gone to th' far-rm long ago.' An' wan day, whin he's takin' th' air, p'raps, along comes an Eyetalyan, an' says he, 'Ar-re ye a king?' 'That's my name,' says his majesty. 'Betther dead,' says th' Eyetalyan; an' they'se a scramble, an' another king goes over th' long r-road.

"I don't know much about arnychists. We had thim here— wanst. They wint again polismen, mostly. Mebbe that's because polismen's th' nearest things to kings they cud find. But, annyhow, I sometimes think I know why they're arnychists some-where, an' why they ain't in other places. It minds me iv what happened wanst in me cousin Terence's fam'ly. They was livin'

down near Healey's slough in wan iv thim ol' Doherty's houses—
not Doherty that ye know, th' j'iner, a good man whin he don't
dhrink.   No, 'twas an ol' grouch iv a man be th' name iv Malachi
Doherty that used to keep five-day notices in his thrunk, an'
ownded his own privit justice iv th' peace.   Me cousin Terence
was as dacint a man as iver shoed a hor-rse; an' his wife was a good
woman, too, though I niver took much to th' Dolans.   Fr'm
Tipperary, they was, an' too handy throwin' things at ye.   An' he
had a nice fam'ly growin' up, an' I niver knowed people that lived
together more quite an' amyable.   'Twas good f'r to see thim
settin' ar-roun' th' parlor—Terence spellin' out th' newspaper, an'
his good woman mendin' socks, an' Honoria playin' th' 'Vale iv
Avoca' on th' pianny, an' th' kids r-rowlin' on th' flure.

"But wan day it happened that that whole fam'ly begun to rasp
on wan another.   Honoria'd set down at th' pianny, an' th' ol'
man'd growl: 'F'r th' love iv th' saints, close down that hurdy-
gurdy, an' lave a man injye his headache!'   An' th' good woman
scolded Terence, an' th' kids pulled th' leg fr'm undher th' stove;
an', whin th' big boy Mike come home fr'm Omaha, he found none
iv thim speakin' to th' others.   He cud do nawthin', an' he wint
f'r Father Kelly.   Father Kelly sniffed th' air whin he come in; an'
says he, 'Terence, what's th' matther with ye'er catch basin?'
'I dinnaw,' growled Terence.   "Well,' says Father Kelly, 'ye
put on ye'er hat this minyit, an' go out f'r a plumber,' he says.
'I'm not needed here,' he says.   'Ye'er sowls ar-re all r-right,'
he says; 'but ye'er systems ar-re out iv ordher,' he says.   'Fetch
in a plumber,' he says, 'whilst I goes down to Doherty, an' make
him think his lease on th' hereafther is defective,' he says."

"Ye're right," said Mr. Hennessy, who had followed the
argument dimly.

"Iv coorse I'm right," said Mr. Dooley.   "What they need
over there in furrin' counthries is not a priest, but a plumber.
'Tis no good prayin' again arnychists, Hinnissy.   Arnychists is
sewer gas."

ON THE DREYFUS CASE

"I see be th' pa-apers," said Mr. Dooley, "that Col. Hinnery,
th' man that sint me frind Cap. Dhry-fuss to th' cage, has moved
on.   I sup-pose they'll give th' Cap a new thrile now."

"I hope they won't," said Mr. Hennessy.   "I don't know
annything about it, but I think he's guilty.   He's a Jew."

"Well," said Mr. Dooley, "ye're thoughts on this subject is inthrestin', but not conclusive, as Dorsey said to th' Pollack that thought he cud lick him. Ye have a r-right to ye'er opinyon, an' ye'll hold it annyhow, whether ye have a r-right to it or not. Like most iv ye'er fellow-citizens, ye start impartial. Ye don't know annything about th' case. If ye knew annything, ye'd not have an opinyon wan way or th' other. They'se niver been a matther come up in my time that th' American people was so sure about as they ar-re about th' Dhry-fuss case. Th' Frinch ar-re not so sure, but they'se not a polisman in this counthry that can't tell ye jus' where Dhry-fuss was whin th' remains iv th' poor girl was found. That's because th' thrile was secret. If 'twas an open thrile, an' ye heerd th' tisti-mony, an' knew th' language, an' saw th' safe afther 'twas blown open, ye'd be puzzled, an' not care a rush whether Dhry-fuss was naked in a cage or takin' tay with his uncle at th' Benny Brith Club.

"I haven't made up me mind whether th' Cap done th' shootin' or not. He was certainly in th' neighborhood whin th' fire started, an' th' polis dug up quite a lot iv lead pipe in his back yard. But it's wan thing to sus-pect a man iv doin' a job an' another thing to prove that he didn't. Me frind Zola thinks he's innocint, an' he raised th' divvle at th' thrile. Whin th' judge come up on th' bench an' opined th' coort, Zola was settin' down below with th' lawyers. 'Let us pro-ceed,' says th' impartial an' fair-minded judge, 'to th' thrile iv th' haynious monsther Cap Dhry-fuss,' he says. Up jumps Zola, an' says he in Frinch: 'Jackuse,' he says, which is a hell of a mane thing to say to anny man. An' they thrun him out. 'Judge,' says th' attorney f'r th' difinse, 'an' gintlemen iv th' jury,' he says. 'Ye're a liar,' says th' judge. 'Cap, ye're guilty, an' ye know it,' he says. 'Th' decision iv th' coort is that ye be put in a cage, an' sint to th' Divvle's own island f'r th' r-rest iv ye'er life,' he says. 'Let us pro-ceed to hearin' th' tisti-mony,' he says. 'Call all th' witnesses at wanst,' he says, 'an' lave thim have it out on th' flure,' he says. Be this time Zola has come back; an' he jumps up, an', says he, 'Jackuse,' he says. An' they thrun him out.

"'Befure we go anny farther,' says th' lawyer f'r th' difinse, 'I wish to sarve notice that, whin this thrile is over, I intind,' he says, 'to wait outside,' he says, 'an' hammer th' hon'rable coort into an omelet,' he says. 'With these few remarks I will close,' he says. 'Th' coort,' says th' judge, 'is always r-ready to defind

th' honor iv France,' he says; 'an', if th' larned counsel will consint,' he says, 'to step up here f'r a minyit,' he says, 'th' coort'll put
a sthrangle hold on him that'll not do him a bit iv good,' he says.
'Ah!' he says. 'Here's me ol' frind Pat th' Clam,' he says. 'Pat,
what d'ye know about this case?' he says. 'None iv ye'er business,' says Pat. 'Answered like a man an' a sojer,' says th' coort.
'Jackuse,' says Zola fr'm th' dureway. An' they thrun him out.
'Call Col. Hinnery,' says th' coort. 'He ray-fuses to answer.'
'Good. Th' case is clear. Cap forged th' will. Th' coort will
now adjourn f'r dools, an' all ladin' officers iv th' ar-rmy not in
disgrace already will assimble in jail, an' com-mit suicide,' he says.
'Jackuse,' says Zola, an' started f'r th' woods, pursued be his
fellow-editors. He's off somewhere in a three now hollerin'
'Jackuse' at ivry wan that passes, sufferin' martyrdom f'r his
counthry an' writin' now an' thin about it all.

"That's all I know about Cap Dhry-fuss' case, an' that's all
anny man knows. Ye didn't know as much, Hinnissy, till I told
ye. I don't know whether Cap stole th' dog or not."

"What's he charged with?" Mr. Hennessy asked, in bewilder-
ment.

"I'll niver tell ye," said Mr. Dooley. "It's too much to ask."

"Well, annyhow," said Mr. Hennessy, "he's guilty, ye can
bet on that."

MR. DOOLEY IN THE HEARTS
OF HIS COUNTRYMEN

EXPANSION[1]

"Whin we plant what Hogan calls th' starry banner iv Freedom in th' Ph'lippeens," said Mr. Dooley, "an' give th' sacred blessin' iv liberty to the poor, down-trodden people iv thim unfortunate isles—dam thim!—we'll larn thim a lesson."

"Sure," said Mr. Hennessy, sadly, "we have a thing or two to larn oursilves."

"But it isn't f'r thim to larn us," said Mr. Dooley. " 'Tis not f'r thim wretched an' degraded crathers, without a mind or a shirt iv their own, f'r to give lessons in politeness an' liberty to a nation that mannyfacthers more dhressed beef than anny other imperyal nation in th' wurruld. We say to thim: 'Naygurs,' we say, 'poor, dissolute, uncovered wretches,' says we, 'whin th' crool hand iv Spain forged man'cles f'r ye'er limbs, as Hogan says, who was it crossed th' say an' sthruck off th' comealongs? We did —by dad, we did. An' now, ye mis'rable, childish-minded apes, we propose f'r to larn ye th' uses iv liberty. In ivry city in this unfair land we will erect school-houses an' packin' houses an' houses iv correction; an' we'll larn ye our language, because 'tis aisier to larn ye ours than to larn oursilves yours. An' we'll give ye clothes, if ye pay f'r thim; an', if ye don't, ye can go without. An', whin ye're hungry, ye can go to th' morgue—we mane th' resth'rant—an' ate a good square meal iv ar-rmy beef. An' we'll sind th' gr-reat Gin'ral Eagan over f'r to larn ye etiquette, an' Andhrew Carnegie to larn ye pathriteism with blow-holes into it, an' Gin'ral Alger to larn ye to hould onto a job; an', whin ye've become edycated an' have all th' blessin's iv civilization that we don't want, that'll count ye one. We can't give ye anny votes,

---

[1] Andrew Carnegie's steel company had been accused of supplying the navy with armor plate with blow-holes in it.

55

because we haven't more thin enough to go round now; but we'll threat ye th' way a father shud threat his childher if we have to break ivry bone in ye'er bodies. So come to our ar-rms,' says we.

"But, glory be, 'tis more like a rasslin' match than a father's embrace. Up gets this little monkey iv an Aggynaldoo, an' says he, 'Not for us,' he says. 'We thank ye kindly; but we believe,' he says, 'in pathronizin' home industhries,' he says. 'An',' he says, 'I have on hand,' he says, 'an' f'r sale,' he says, 'a very superyor brand iv home-made liberty, like ye'er mother used to make,' he says. ' 'Tis a long way fr'm ye'er plant to here,' he says, 'an' be th' time a cargo iv liberty,' he says, 'got out here an' was handled be th' middlemen,' he says, 'it might spoil,' he says. 'We don't want anny col' storage or embalmed liberty,' he says. 'What we want an' what th' ol' reliable house iv Aggynaldoo,' he says, 'supplies to th' thrade,' he says, 'is fr-resh liberty r-right off th' far-rm,' he says. 'I can't do annything with ye'er proposition,' he says. 'I can't give up,' he says, 'th' rights f'r which f'r five years I've fought an' bled ivry wan I cud reach,' he says. 'Onless,' he says, 'ye'd feel like buyin' out th' whole business,' he says. 'I'm a pathrite,' he says; 'but I'm no bigot,' he says.

"An' there it stands, Hinnissy, with th' indulgent parent kneelin' on th' stomach iv his adopted child, while a dillygation fr'm Boston bastes him with an umbrella. There it stands, an' how will it come out I dinnaw. I'm not much iv an expansionist mesilf. F'r th' las' tin years I've been thryin' to decide whether 'twud be good policy an' thrue to me thraditions to make this here bar two or three feet longer, an manny's th' night I've laid awake tryin' to puzzle it out. But I don't know what to do with th' Ph'lippeens anny more thin I did las' summer, befure I heerd tell iv thim. We can't give thim to anny wan without makin' th' wan that gets thim feel th' way Doherty felt to Clancy whin Clancy med a frindly call an' give Doherty's childher th' measles. We can't sell thim, we can't ate thim, an' we can't throw thim into th' alley whin no wan is lookin'. An' 'twud be a disgrace f'r to lave befure we've pounded these frindless an' ongrateful people into insinsibility. So I suppose, Hinnissy, we'll have to stay an' do th' best we can, an' lave Andhrew Carnegie secede fr'm th' Union. They'se wan consolation; an' that is, if th' American people can govern thimsilves, they can govern annything that walks."

"An' what 'd ye do with Aggy—what-d'ye-call-him?" asked Mr. Hennessy.

"Well," Mr. Dooley replied, with brightening eyes, "I know what they'd do with him in this ward. They'd give that pathrite what he asks, an' thin they'd throw him down an' take it away fr'm him."

RUDYARD KIPLING[1]

"I think," said Mr. Dooley, "th' finest pothry in th' wurruld is wrote be that frind iv young Hogan's, a man be th' name iv Roodyard Kipling. I see his pomes in th' pa-aper, Hinnissy; an' they're all right. They're all right, thim pomes. They was wan about scraggin' Danny Deever that done me a wurruld iv good. They was a la-ad I wanst knew be th' name iv Deever, an' like as not he was th' same man. He owed me money. Thin there was wan that I see mintioned in th' war news wanst in a while—th' less we f'rget, th' more we raymimber. That was a hot pome an' a good wan. What I like about Kipling is that his pomes is right off th' bat, like me con-versations with you, me boy. He's a minyit-man, a r-ready pote that sleeps like th' dhriver iv thruck 9, with his poetic pants in his boots beside his bed, an' him r-ready to jump out an' slide down th' pole th' minyit th' alarm sounds.

"He's not such a pote as Tim Scanlan, that hasn't done annything since th' siege iv Lim'rick; an' that was two hundherd year befure he was bor-rn. He's prisident iv th' Pome Supply Company—fr-resh pothry delivered ivry day at ye'er dure. Is there an accident in a grain illyvator? Ye pick up ye'er mornin' pa-aper, an' they'se a pome about it be Roodyard Kipling. Do ye hear iv a manhole cover bein' blown up? Roodyard is there with his r-ready pen. ' 'Tis written iv Cashum-Cadi an' th' book iv th' gr-reat Gazelle that a manhole cover in anger is tin degrees worse thin hell.' He writes in all dialects an' anny language, plain an' fancy pothry, pothry f'r young an' old, pothry be weight or linyar measuremint, pothry f'r small parties iv eight or tin a specialty. What's the raysult, Hinnissy? Most potes I despise. But Roodyard Kipling's pothry is aisy. Ye can skip through it while ye're atin' breakfuss an' get a c'rrect idee iv th' current news iv th' day—who won th' futball game, how Sharkey is thrainin' f'r th' fight, an' how manny votes th' pro-hybitionist got f'r gov'nor iv th' State iv Texas. No col' storage pothry f'r Kipling. Ivrything fr-resh an' up to date. All lays laid this mornin'.

---

[1] Though Dunne had admired Kipling in his youth, he felt sufficiently detached to satirize Kipling's poem, "The Truce of the Bear."

"Hogan was in to-day readin' Kipling's Fridah afthernoon pome, an' 'tis a good pome. He calls it 'Th' Thruce iv th' Bear.' This is th' way it happened: Roodyard Kipling had just finished his mornin' batch iv pothry f'r th' home-thrade, an' had et his dinner, an' was thinkin' iv r-runnin' out in th' counthry f'r a breath iv fr-resh air, whin in come a tillygram sayin' that th' Czar iv Rooshia had sint out a circluar letther sayin' ivrybody in th' wurrld ought to get together an' stop makin' war an' live a quite an' dull life. Now Kipling don't like the czar. Him an' th' czar fell out about something, an' they don't speak. So says Roodyard Kipling to himsilf, he says: 'I'll take a crack at that fellow,' he says. 'I'll do him up,' he says. An' so he writes a pome to show that th' czar's letter's not on th' square. Kipling's like me, Hinnissy. When I want to say annything lib-lous, I stick it on to me Uncle Mike. So be Roodyard Kipling. He doesn't come r-right out, an' say, 'Nick, ye're a liar!' but he tells about what th' czar done to a man he knowed be th' name iv Muttons. Muttons, it seems, Hinnissy, was wanst a hunter; an' he wint out to take a shot at th' czar, who was dhressed up as a bear. Well, Muttons r-run him down, an' was about to plug him, whin th' czar says, 'Hol' on,' he says—'hol' on there,' he says. 'Don't shoot,' he says. 'Let's talk this over,' he says. An' Muttons, bein' a foolish man, waited till th' czar come near him; an' thin th' czar feinted with his left, an' put in a right hook an' pulled off Muttons's face. I tell ye 'tis so. He jus' hauled it off th' way ye'd haul off a porous plascher—raked off th' whole iv Muttons's fr-ront ilivation. 'I like ye'er face,' he says, an' took it. An' all this time, an' 'twas fifty years ago, Muttons hasn't had a face to shave. Ne'er a one. So he goes ar-round exhibitin' th' recent site, an' warnin' people that, whin they ar-re shootin' bears, they must see that their gun is kept loaded an' their face is nailed on securely. If ye iver see a bear that looks like a man, shoot him on th' spot, or, betther still, r-run up an alley. Ye must niver lose that face, Hinnissy.

"I showed th' pome to Father Kelly," continued Mr. Dooley.

"What did he say?" asked Mr. Hennessy.

"He said," Mr. Dooley replied, "that I cud write as good a wan mesilf; an' he took th' stub iv a pencil, an' wrote this. Lemme see—Ah! here it is:—

Whin he shows as seekin' frindship with paws that're thrust in thine,
That is th' time iv pearl, that is th' thruce iv th' line.

Collarless, coatless, hatless, askin' a dhrink at th' bar,
Me Uncle Mike, the Fenyan, he tells it near and far,

Over an' over th' story: 'Beware iv th' gran' flimflam,
There is no thruce with Gazabo, th' line that looks like a lamb.''

"That's a good pome, too," said Mr. Dooley; "an' I'm goin'
to sind it to th' nex' meetin' iv th' Anglo-Saxon 'liance."

HANGING ALDERMEN

Chicago is always on the point of hanging some one and
quartering him and boiling him in hot pitch, and assuring him that
he has lost the respect of all honorable men. Rumors of a
characteristic agitation had come faintly up Archey Road, and
Mr. Hennessy had heard of it.

"I hear they're goin' to hang th' aldhermen," he said. "If
they thry it on Willum J. O'Brien, they'd betther bombard him
first. I'd hate to be th' man that 'd be called to roll with him to
his doom. He cud lick th' whole Civic Featheration."

"I believe ye," said Mr. Dooley. "He's a powerful man.
But I hear there is, as ye say, what th' pa-apers 'd call a movement
on fut f'r to dec'rate Chris'mas threes with aldhermen, an' 'tis
wan that ought to be encouraged. Nawthin' cud be happyer, as
Hogan says, thin th' thought iv cillybratin' th' season be sthringin'
up some iv th' fathers iv th' city where th' childher cud see thim.
But I'm afraid, Hinnissy, that you an' me won't see it. 'Twill all
be over soon, an' Willum J. O'Brien 'll go by with his head just
as near his shoulders as iver. 'Tis har-rd to hang an aldherman,
annyhow. Ye'd have to suspind most iv thim be th' waist.

"Man an' boy, I've been in this town forty year an' more; an'
divvle th' aldherman have I see hanged yet, though I've sthrained
th' eyes out iv me head watchin' f'r wan iv thim to be histed anny
pleasant mornin'. They've been goin' to hang thim wan week an'
presintin' thim with a dimon' star th' next iver since th' year iv th'
big wind, an' there's jus' as manny iv thim an' jus' as big robbers
as iver there was.

"An' why shud they hang thim, Hinnissy? Why shud they?
I'm an honest man mesilf, as men go. Ye might have ye'er watch,
if ye had wan, on that bar f'r a year, an' I'd niver touch it. It

wudden't be worth me while. I'm an honest man. I pay me
taxes, whin Tim Ryan isn't assessor with Grogan's boy on th'
books. I do me jooty; an' I believe in th' polis foorce, though not
in polismen. That's diff'rent. But honest as I am, between you
an' me, if I was an aldherman, I wudden't say, be hivins, I think
I'd stand firm; but—well, if some wan come to me an' said,
'Dooley, here's fifty thousan' dollars f'r ye'er vote to betray th'
sacred inthrests iv Chicago,' I'd go to Father Kelly an' ask th'
prayers iv th' congregation.

"'Tis not, Hinnissy, that this man Yerkuss goes up to an
aldherman an' says out sthraight, 'Here, Bill, take this bundle, an'
be an infamyous scoundhrel.' That's th' way th' man in Mitchigan
Avnoo sees it, but 'tis not sthraight. D'ye mind Dochney that
was wanst aldherman here? Ye don't. Well, I do. He ran a
little conthractin' business down be Halsted Sthreet. 'Twas him
built th' big shed f'r th' ice comp'ny. He was a fine man an' a
sthrong wan. He begun his political career be lickin' a plasthrer
be th' name iv Egan, a man that had th' County Clare thrip an'
was thought to be th' akel iv anny man in town. Fr'm that he
growed till he bate near ivry man he knew, an' become very
pop'lar, so that he was sint to th' council. Now Dochney was an
honest an' sober man whin he wint in; but wan day a man come
up to him, an' says he, 'Ye know that ordhnance Schwartz
inthrajooced?' 'I do,' says Dochney, 'an' I'm again it. 'Tis a
swindle,' he says. 'Well,' says th' la-ad, 'they'se five thousan' in
it f'r ye,' he says. They had to pry Dochney off iv him. Th'
nex' day a man he knowed well come to Dochney, an' says he,
'That's a fine ordhnance iv Schwartz.' 'It is, like hell,' says
Dochney. '"Tis a plain swindle,' he says. '"Tis a good thing f'r
th' comp'nies,' says this man; 'but look what they've done f'r th'
city,' he says, 'an' think,' he says, 'iv th' widdies an' orphans,' he
says, 'that has their har-rd-earned coin invisted,' he says. An' a
tear rolled down his cheek. 'I'm an orphan mesilf,' says Dochney;
'an' as f'r th' widdies, anny healthy widdy with sthreet-car stock
ought to be ashamed iv hersilf if she's a widdy long,' he says. An'
th' man wint away.

"Now Dochney thought he'd put th' five thousan' out iv his
mind, but he hadn't. He'd on'y laid it by, an' ivry time he closed
his eyes he thought iv it. 'Twas a shame to give th' comp'nies
what they wanted, but th' five thousan' was a lot iv money. 'Twud
lift th' morgedge. 'Twud clane up th' notes on th' new conthract.

'Twud buy a new dhress f'r Mrs. Dochney. He begun to feel sorrowful f'r th' widdies an' orphans. 'Poor things!' says he to himsilf, says he. 'Poor things, how they must suffer!' he says; 'an' I need th' money. Th' sthreet-car comp'nies is robbers,' he says; 'but 'tis thrue they've built up th' city,' he says, 'an' th' money'd come in handy,' he says. 'No wan 'd be hurted, annyhow,' he says; 'an', sure, it ain't a bribe f'r to take money f'r doin' something ye want to do, annyhow,' he says. 'Five thousan' widdies an' orphans,' he says; an' he wint to sleep.

"That was th' way he felt whin he wint down to see ol' Simpson to renew his notes, an' Simpson settled it. 'Dochney,' he says, 'I wisht ye'd pay up,' he says. 'I need th' money,' he says. 'I'm afraid th' council won't pass th' Schwartz ordhnance,' he says; 'an' it manes much to me,' he says. 'Be th' way,' he says, 'how're ye goin' to vote on that ordhnance?' he says. 'I dinnaw,' says Dochney. 'Well,' says Simpson (Dochney tol' me this himsilf), 'whin ye find out, come an' see me about th' notes,' he says. An' Dochney wint to th' meetin'; an', whin his name was called, he hollered 'Aye,' so loud a chunk iv plaster fell out iv th' ceilin' an' stove in th' head iv a rayform aldherman."

"Did they hang him?" asked Mr. Hennessey.

"Faith, they did not," said Mr. Dooley. "He begun missin' his jooty at wanst. Aldhermen always do that after th' first few weeks. 'Ye got ye'er money,' says Father Kelly; 'an' much good may it do ye,' he says. 'Well,' says Dochney, 'I'd be a long time prayin' mesilf into five thousan',' he says. An' he become leader in th' council. Th' las' ordhnance he inthrojooced was wan establishin' a license f'r churches, an' compellin' thim to keep their fr-ront dure closed an' th' blinds drawn on Sundah. He was expelled fr'm th' St. Vincent de Pauls, an' ilicted a director iv a bank th' same day.

"Now, Hinnissy, that there man niver knowed he was bribed —th' first time. Th' second time he knew. He ast f'r it. An' I wudden't hang Dochney. I wudden't if I was sthrong enough. But some day I'm goin' to let me temper r-run away with me, an' get a comity together, an' go out an' hang ivry dam widdy an' orphan between th' rollin' mills an' th' foundlin's' home. If it wasn't f'r thim raypechious crathers, they'd be no boodle annywhere."

"Well, don't forget Simpson," said Mr. Hennessy.

"I won't," said Mr. Dooley. "I won't."

THE GRIP

Mr. Dooley was discovered making a seasonable beverage, consisting of one part syrup, two parts quinine, and fifteen parts strong waters.

"What's the matter?" asked Mr. McKenna.

"I have th' lah gr-rip," said Mr. Dooley, blowing his nose and wiping his eyes. "Bad cess to it! Oh, me poor back! I feels as if a dhray had run over it. Did ye iver have it? Ye did not? Well, ye're lucky. Ye're a lucky man.

"I wint to McGuire's wake las' week. They gave him a dacint sind-off. No porther. An' himsilf looked natural, as fine a corpse as iver Gavin layed out. Gavin tould me so himsilf. He was as proud iv McGuire as if he owned him. Fetched half th' town in to look at him, an' give ivry wan iv thim cards. He near frightened ol' man Dugan into a faint. 'Misther Dugan, howold a-are ye?' 'Sivinty-five, thanks be,' says Dugan. 'Thin,' says Gavin, 'take wan iv me cards,' he says. 'I hope ye'll not forget me,' he says.

"'Twas there I got th' lah grip. Lastewise, it is me opinion iv it, though th' docthor said I swallowed a bug. It don't seem right, Jawn, f'r th' McGuires is a clane fam'ly; but th' docthor said a bug got into me system. 'What sort iv bug?' says I. 'A lah grip bug,' he says. 'Ye have Mickrobes in ye'er lungs,' he says. 'What's thim?' says I. 'Thim's th' lah grip bugs,' says he. 'Ye took wan in, an' warmed it,' he says; 'an' it has growed an' multiplied till ye'er system does be full iv' thim,' he says, 'millions iv thim,' he says, 'marchin' an' counthermarchin' through ye.' 'Glory be to the saints!' says I. 'Had I better swallow some insect powdher?' I says. 'Some iv thim in me head has a fallin' out, an' is throwin' bricks.' 'Foolish man,' says he. 'Go to bed,' he says, 'an' lave thim alone,' he says. 'Whin they find who they're in,' he says, 'they'll quit ye.'

"So I wint to bed, an' waited while th' Mickrobes had fun with me. Mondah all iv thim was quite but thim in me stummick. They stayed up late dhrinkin' an' carousin' an' dancin' jigs till wurruds come up between th' Kerry Mickrobes an' thim fr'm Wexford; an' th' whole party wint over to me left lung, where they cud get th' air, an' had it out. Th' nex' day th' little Mickrobes made a toboggan slide iv me spine; an' manetime some Mickrobes that was wurkin' f'r th' tilliphone comp'ny got it in their heads that me legs was poles, an' put on their spikes an' climbed all night long.

"They was tired out th' nex' day till about five o'clock, whin thim that was in me head begin flushin' out th' rooms; an' I knew there was goin' to be doin's in th' top flat. What did thim Mickrobes do but invite all th' other Mickrobes in f'r th' ev'nin'. They all come. Oh, by gar, they was not wan iv them stayed away. At six o'clock they begin to move fr'm me shins to me throat. They come in platoons an' squads an' dhroves. Some iv thim brought along brass bands, an' more thin wan hundhred thousand iv thim dhruv through me pipes on dhrays. A throlley line was started up me back, an' ivry car run into a wagonload iv scrap iron at th' base iv me skull.

"Th' Mickrobes in me head must 've done thimsilves proud. Ivry few minyits th' kids 'd be sint out with th' can, an' I'd say to mesilf: 'There they go, carryin' th' thrade to Schwartzmeister's because I'm sick an' can't wait on thim.' I was daffy, Jawn, d'ye mind. Th' likes iv me fillin' a pitcher f'r a little boy-bug! Such dhreams! An' they had a game iv forty-fives; an' there was wan Mickrobe that larned to play th' game in th' County Tipp'rary, where 'tis played on stone, an' ivry time he led thrumps he'd like to knock me head off. 'Whose thrick is that?' says th' Tipp'rary Mickrobe. ''Tis mine,' says th' red-headed Mickrobe fr'm th' County Roscommon. They tipped over th' chairs an' tables: an', in less time thin it takes to tell, th' whole party was at it. They'd been a hurlin' game in th' back iv me skull, an' th' young folks was dancin' breakdowns an' havin' leppin' matches in me forehead; but they all stopped to mix in. Oh, 'twas a grand shindig—tin millions iv men, women, an' childher rowlin' on th' flure, hands an' feet goin', ice-picks an' hurlin' sticks, clubs, brickbats, an' beer kags flyin' in th' air! How manny iv thim was kilt I niver knew; f'r I wint as daft as a hen, an' dhreamt iv organizin' a Mickrobe Campaign Club that 'd sweep th' prim'ries, an' maybe go acrost an' free Ireland. Whin I woke up, me legs was as weak as a day old baby's, an' me poor head empty as a cobbler's purse. I want no more iv thim. Give me anny bug fr'm a cockroach to an aygle save an' excipt thim West iv Ireland Fenians, th' Mickrobes."

SHAUGHNESSY

"Jawn," said Mr. Dooley in the course of the conversation, "whin ye come to think iv it, th' heroes iv th' wurruld—an' be thim I mean th' lads that've buckled on th' gloves, an' gone out to do th' best they cud—they ain't in it with th' quite people nayether you nor me hears tell iv fr'm wan end iv th' year to another.''

"I believe it," said Mr. McKenna; "for my mother told me so."

"Sure," said Mr. Dooley, "I know it is an old story. Th' wurruld's been full iv it fr'm th' beginnin'; an' 'll be full iv it till, as Father Kelly says, th' pay-roll's closed. But I was thinkin' more iv it th' other night thin iver befure, whin I wint to see Shaughnessy marry off his on'y daughter. You know Shaughnessy—a quite man that come into th' road befure th' fire. He wurruked f'r Larkin, th' conthractor, f'r near twinty years without skip or break, an' seen th' fam'ly grow up be candle-light. Th' oldest boy was intinded f'r a priest. 'Tis a poor fam'ly that hasn't some wan that's bein' iddycated f'r the priesthood while all th' rest wear thimsilves to skeletons f'r him, an' call him Father Jawn 'r Father Mike whin he comes home wanst a year, light-hearted an' free, to eat with thim.

"Shaughnessy's lad wint wrong in his lungs, an' they fought death f'r him f'r five years, sindin' him out to th' Wist an' havin' masses said f'r him; an', poor divvle, he kept comin' back cross an' crool, with th' fire in his cheeks, till wan day he laid down, an' says he: 'Pah,' he says, 'I'm goin' to give up,' he says. 'An' I on'y ask that ye'll have th' mass sung over me be some man besides Father Kelly,' he says. An' he wint, an' Shaughnessy come clumpin' down th' aisle like a man in a thrance.

"Well, th' nex' wan was a girl, an' she didn't die; but, th' less said, th' sooner mended. Thin they was Terrence, a big, bould, curly-headed lad that cocked his hat at anny man—or woman f'r th' matter iv that—an' that bruk th' back iv a polisman an' swum to th' crib, an' was champeen iv th' South Side at hand ball. An' he wint. Thin th' good woman passed away. An' th' twins they growed to be th' prettiest pair that wint to first communion; an' wan night they was a light in th' window of Shaughnessy's house till three in th' mornin'. I raymimber it; f'r I had quite a crowd iv Willum Joyce's men in, an' we wondhered at it, an' wint home whin th' lamp in Shaughnessy's window was blown out.

"They was th' wan girl left—Theresa, a big, clean-lookin' child that I see grow up fr'm hello to good avnin'. She thought on'y iv th' ol' man, an' he leaned on her as if she was a crutch. She was out to meet him in th' evnin'; an' in th' mornin' he, th' simple ol' man, 'd stop to blow a kiss at her an' wave his dinner-pail, lookin' up an' down th' r-road to see that no wan was watchin' him.

"I dinnaw what possessed th' young Donahue, fr'm th' Nineteenth. I niver thought much iv him, a stuck-up, aisy-come la-ad that niver had annything but a civil wurrud, an' is prisident iv th' sodality. But he came in, an' married Theresa Shaughnessy las' Thursdah night. Th' ol' man took on twinty years, but he was as brave as a gin'ral iv th' army. He cracked jokes an' he made speeches; an' he took th' pipes fr'm under th' elbow iv Hogan, th' blindman, an' played 'Th' Wind that shakes th' Barley' till ye'd have wore ye'er leg to a smoke f'r wantin' to dance. Thin he wint to th' dure with th' two iv thim; an' says he, 'Well,' he says, 'Jim, be good to her,' he says, an' shook hands with her through th' carredge window.

"Him an' me sat a long time smokin' across th' stove. Fin'lly, says I, 'Well,' I says, 'I must be movin'.' 'What's th' hurry?' says he. 'I've got to go,' says I. 'Wait a moment,' says he. 'Theresa 'll'— He stopped right there f'r a minyit, holdin' to th' back iv th' chair. 'Well,' says he, 'if ye've got to go, ye must,' he says. 'I'll show ye out,' he says. An' he come with me to th' dure, holdin' th' lamp over his head. I looked back at him as I wint by; an' he was settin' be th' stove, with his elbows on his knees an' th' empty pipe between his teeth."

TIMES PAST

Mr. McKenna, looking very warm and tired, came into Mr. Dooley's tavern one night last week, and smote the bar with his fist.

"What's the matter with Hogan?" he said.

"What Hogan?" asked Mr. Dooley. "Malachy or Matt? Dinnis or Mike? Sarsfield or William Hogan? There's a Hogan f'r ivry block in th' Ar-rchey Road, an' wan to spare. There's nawthin' th' matter with anny iv thim; but, if ye mean Hogan, th' liquor dealer, that r-run f'r aldherman, I'll say to ye he's all right. Mind ye, Jawn, I'm doin' this because ye're me frind; but, by gar, if anny wan else comes in an' asks me that question, I'll kill him, if I have to go to th' bridewell f'r it. I'm no health officer."

Having delivered himself of this tirade, Mr. Dooley scrutinized Mr. McKenna sharply, and continued: "Ye've been out ilictin'

some man, Jawn, an' ye needn't deny it.   I seen it th' minyit ye
come in.   Ye'er hat's dinted, an' ye have ye'er necktie over ye'er
ear; an' I see be ye'er hand ye've hit a Dutchman.   Jawn, ye
know no more about politics thin a mimber iv this here Civic
Featheration.   Didn't ye have a beer bottle or an ice-pick?
Ayether iv thim is good, though, whin I was a young man an'
precinct captain an' intherested in th' welfare iv th' counthry, I
found a couplin' pin in a stockin' about as handy as annything.

"Thim days is over, though, Jawn, an' between us politics
don't intherest me no more.   They ain't no liveliness in thim.
Whin Andy Duggan r-run f'r aldherman against Schwartzmeister,
th' big Dutchman—I was precinct captain then, Jawn—there was
an iliction f'r ye.   'Twas on our precinct they relied to ilict
Duggan; f'r the Dutch was sthrong down be th' thrack, an'
Schwartzmeister had a band out playin' 'Th' Watch on th'
Rhine.'   Well, sir, we opened th' polls at six o'clock, an' there
was tin Schwartzmeister men there to protect his intherests.
At sivin o'clock there was only three, an' wan iv thim was goin' up
th' sthreet with Hinnissy kickin' at him.   At eight o'clock, be
dad, there was on'y wan; an' he was sittin' on th' roof iv Gavin's
blacksmith shop, an' th' la-ads was thryin' to borrow a laddher
fr'm th' injine-house f'r to get at him.   'Twas thruck eighteen;
an' Hogan, that was captain, wudden't let thim have it.   Not ye'er
Hogan, Jawn, but th' meanest fireman in Bridgeport.   He got
kilt afthwards.   He wudden't let th' la-ads have a laddher, an'
th' Dutchman stayed up there; an', whin there was nawthin' to do,
we wint over an' thrun bricks at him.   'Twas gr-reat sport.

"About four in th' afthernoon Schwartzmeister's band come
up Ar-rchey Road, playin' 'Th' Watch on th' Rhine.'   Whin it
got near Gavin's, big Peter Nolan tuk a runnin' jump, an' landed
feet first in th' big bass dhrum.   Th' man with th' dhrum walloped
him over th' head with th' dhrumstick, an' Dorsey Quinn wint
over an' tuk a slide trombone away fr'm the musician an' clubbed
th' bass dhrum man with it.   Thin we all wint over, an' ye niver
see th' like in ye'er born days.   Th' las' I see iv th' band it was
goin' down th' road towards th' slough with a mob behind it,
an' all th' polis foorce fr'm Deerin' Sthreet afther th' mob.   Th'
la-ads collected th' horns an th' dhrums, an' that started th'
Ar-rchey Road brass band.   Little Mike Doyle larned to play
'Th' Rambler fr'm Clare' beautifully on what they call a pickle-e-o
befure they sarved a rayplivin writ on him.

"We cast twinty-wan hundherd votes f'r Duggan, an' they was on'y five hundherd votes in th' precinct. We'd cast more, but th' tickets give out. They was tin votes in th' box f'r Schwartz-meister whin we counted up; an' I felt that mortified I near died, me bein' precinct captain, an' res-sponsible. 'What'll we do with thim? Out th' window,' says I. Just thin Dorsey's nanny-goat that died next year put her head through th' dure. 'Monica,' says Dorsey (he had pretty names for all his goats), 'Monica, are ye hungry,' he says, 'ye poor dear?' Th' goat give him a pleadin' look out iv her big brown eyes. 'Can't I make ye up a nice supper?' says Dorsey. 'Do ye like paper?' he says. 'Would ye like to help desthroy a Dutchman,' he says, 'an' perform a sarvice f'r ye'er counthry?' he says. Thin he wint out in th' next room, an' come back with a bottle iv catsup; an' he poured it on th' Schwartzmeister ballots, an' Monica et thim without winkin'.

"Well, sir, we ilicted Duggan; an' what come iv it? Th' week befure iliction he was in me house ivry night, an' 'twas 'Misther Dooley, this,' an' 'Mr. Dooley, that,' an' 'What 'll ye have, boys?' an' 'Niver mind about th' change.' I niver see hide nor hair iv him f'r a week afther iliction. Thin he come with a plug hat on, an' says he: 'Dooley,' he says, 'give me a shell iv beer,' he says: 'give me a shell iv beer,' he says, layin' down a nickel. 'I suppose ye're on th' sub-scription,' he says. 'What for?' says I. 'F'r to buy me a goold star,' says he. With that I eyes him, an' says I: 'Duggan,' I says, 'I knowed ye whin ye didn't have a coat to ye'er back,' I says, 'an' I'll buy no star f'r ye,' I says. 'But I'll tell ye what I'll buy f'r ye,' I says. 'I'll buy rayqueem masses f'r th' raypose iv ye'er sowl, if ye don't duck out iv this in a minyit.' Whin I seen him last, he was back dhrivin' a dhray an' atin' his dinner out iv a tin can."

THE SKIRTS OF CHANCE

The people of Bridgeport are not solicitous of modern improve-ments, and Mr. Dooley views with distaste the new and garish. But he consented to install a nickel-in-the-slot machine in his tavern last week, and it was standing on a table when Mr. McKenna came in. It was a machine that looked like a house; and, when you put a nickel in at the top of it, either the door opened and released three other nickels or it did not.   Mostly it did not.

Mr. Dooley saluted Mr. McKenna with unusual cordiality, and Mr. McKenna inspected the nickel-in-the-slot machine with affectation of much curiosity.

"What's this you have here, at all ?" said Mr. McKenna.

"'Tis an aisy way iv gettin' rich," said Mr. Dooley.   "All ye have to do is to dhrop a nickel in th' slot, an' three other nickels come out at th' dure.   Ye can play it all afthernoon, an' take a fortune fr'm it if y'er nickels hould out."

"And where do th' nickels come fr'm ?" asked Mr. McKenna.

"I put thim in," said Mr. Dooley.   "Ivry twinty minutes I feed th' masheen a hatful iv nickels, so that whin me frinds dhrop in they won't be dissypinted, d'ye mind.   'Tis a fine invistment for a young man.   Little work an' large profits.   It rayminds me iv Hogan's big kid an' what he done with his coin.   He made a lot iv it in dhrivin' a ca-ar, he did, but he blew it all in again good liquor an' bad women; an', bedad, he was broke half th' time an' borrowin' th' other half.   So Hogan gets in Father Kelly fr'm up west iv th' bridge, an' they set in with Dinnis to talk him out iv his spindthrift ways.   'I have plenty to keep mesilf,' says Hogan, he says.   'But,' he says, 'I want ye to save ye'er money,' he says, 'f'r a rainy day.'   'He's right, Dinnis,' says th' soggarth—'he's right,' he says.   'Ye should save a little in case ye need it,' he says.   'Why don't ye take two dollars,' says th' priest, 'an' invist it ivry month,' says he, 'in somethin',' says he, 'that'll give ye profits,' says he. 'I'll do it,' says Dinnis—'I'll do it,' he says.   Well, sir, Hogan was that tickled he give th' good man five bones out iv th' taypot; but, faith, Dinnis was back at his reg'lar game before th' week was out, an', afther a month or two, whin Hogan had to get th' tayspoons out iv soak, he says to th' kid, he says, 'I thought ye was goin' to brace up,' he says, 'an' here ye're burnin' up ye'er money,' he says.   'Didn't ye promise to invist two dollars ivry month ?' he says.   'I'm doin' it,' says Dinnis.   'I've kept me wurrud.' 'An' what are ye invistin' it in ?' says Hogan.   'In lotthry tickets,' says th' imp'dent kid."

While delivering these remarks, Mr. Dooley was peeping over his glasses at Mr. McKenna, who was engaged in a struggle with the machine.   He dropped a nickel and it rattled down the slot, but it did not open the door.

"Doesn't it open ?" said Mr. Dooley.

"It does not."

"Shake it thin," said Mr. Dooley. "Something must be wrong."

Mr. McKenna shook the machine when he inserted the next nickel, but there was no compensatory flow of coins from the door.

"Perhaps the money is bad," suggested Mr. Dooley. "It won't open f'r bad money."

Thereupon he returned to his newspaper, observing which Mr. McKenna drew from his pocket a nickel attached to a piece of string and dropped it into the slot repeatedly. After a while the door popped open, and Mr. McKenna thrust in his hand expectantly. There was no response, and he turned in great anger to Mr. Dooley.

"There ain't any money there," he said.

"Ye're right, Jawn," responded Mr. Dooley. "If ye expect to dhraw anny coin fr'm that there masheen, ye may call on some iv ye'er rough frinds down town f'r a brace an' bit an' a jimmy. Jawn, me la-ad, I see th' nickel with th' string befure; an' to provide again it, I improved th' masheen. Thim nickels ye dhropped in are all in th' dhrawer iv that there table, an' to-morrow mornin' ye may see me havin' me hair cut be means iv thim. An' I'll tell ye wan thing, Jawn McKenna, an' that's not two things, that if ye think ye can come up here to Ar-rchey Road an' rob an honest man, by gar, ye've made th' mistake iv ye'er life. Goowan, now, befure I call a polisman."

Mr. McKenna stopped at the door only long enough to shake his fist at the proprietor, who responded with a grin of pure contentment.

WHEN THE TRUST IS AT WORK

"Which d'ye think makes th' best fun'ral turnout, th' A-ho-aitches or th' Saint Vincent de Pauls, Jawn?" asked Mr. Dooley.

"I don't know," said Mr. McKenna. "Are you thinking of leaving us?"

"Faith, I am not," said Mr. Dooley. "Since th' warm weather's come an' th' wind's in th' south, so that I can tell at night that A-armoor an' me ol' frind, Jawn Brinnock, are attindin' to business, I have a grip on life like th' wan ye have on th' shank iv that shell iv malt. Whether 'tis these soft days, with th'

childher beginnin' to play barefutted in th' sthreet an' th' good
women out to palaver over th' fence without their shawls, or
whether 'tis th' wan wurrud Easter Sundah that comes on me, an'
jolts me up with th' thoughts iv th' la-ads goin' to mass an' th'
blackthorn turnin' green beyant, I dinnaw. But annyhow I'm as
gay as a babby an' as fresh as a lark. I am so.

"I was on'y thinkin'. Ol' Gran'pah Grogan died las' Mondah
—as good a man as e'er counted his beads or passed th' plate.
A thrue man. Choosdah a Connock man up back iv th' dumps
laid down th' shovel. Misther Grogan had a grand notice in th'
pa-apers: 'Grogan, at his late risidence, 279 A-archoor Avnoo,
Timothy Alexander, beloved husband iv th' late Mary Grogan,
father iv Maurice, Michael, Timothy, Edward, James, Peter,
Paul, an' Officer Andrew Grogan, iv Cologne Sthreet station, an'
iv Mrs. Willum Sarsfield Cassidy, nee Grogan' (which manes that
was her name befure she marrid Cassidy, who wurruks down be
Haley's packin'-house). 'Fun'ral be carriages fr'm his late
risidence to Calv'ry cimithry. Virginia City, Nivada; St.
Joseph, Mitchigan; an' Clonmel Tipp'rary pa-apers please copy.'

"I didn't see e'er a nee about th' fam'ly iv th' little man back
iv th' dumps, though maybe he had wan to set aroun' th' fire in
th' dark an' start at th' tap iv a heel on th' dure-step. Mebbe he
had a fam'ly, poor things. A fun'ral is great la-arks f'r th'
neighbors, an' 'tis not so bad f'r th' corpse. But in these times,
Jawn dear, a-ho th' gray hearts left behind an' th' hungry mouths
to feed. They done th' best they cud f'r th' Connock man back
iv th' dumps—give him all th' honors, th' A-ho-aitches ma-archin'
behind th' hearse an' th' band playin' th' Dead March. 'Twas
almost as good a turnout as Grogan had, though th' Saint
Vincents had betther hats an' looked more like their fam'lies kept
a cow.

"But they was two hacks back iv th' pall-bearers. I wondhered
what was passin' behind th' faces I seen again their windys.
'Twas well f'r himself, too. Little odds to him, afther th' last
screw was twisted be Gavin's ol' yellow hands, whether beef was
wan cint or a hundherd dollars th' pound. But there's comin'
home as well as goin' out. There's more to a fun'ral thin th' lucks
parpitua, an' th' clod iv sullen earth on th' top iv th' crate. Sare a
pax vobiscum is there f'r thim that's huddled in th' ol' hack,
sthragglin' home in th' dust to th' empty panthry an' th' fireless
grate.

"Mind ye, Jawn, I've no wurrud to say again thim that sets back in their own house an' lot an' makes th' food iv th' people dear. They're good men, good men. Whin they tilt th' price iv beef to where wan pound iv it costs as much as manny th' man in this Ar-rchey Road 'd wurruk fr'm th' risin' to th' settin' iv th' sun to get, they have no thought iv th' likes iv you an' me. 'Tis aisy come, aisy go with thim; an' ivry cint a pound manes a new art musoom or a new church, to take th' edge off hunger. They're all right, thim la-ads, with their own pork-chops delivered free at th' door. 'Tis ,'Will ye have a new spring dhress, me dear? Willum, ring thim up, an' tell thim to hist th' price iv beef. If we had a few more pitchers an' statoos in th' musoom, 'twud ilivate th' people a sthory or two. Willum, afther this steak 'll be twinty cints a pound.' Oh, they're all right, on'y I was thinkin' iv th' Connock man's fam'ly back iv th' dumps."

"For a man that was gay a little while ago, it looks to me as if you'd grown mighty solemn-like," said Mr. McKenna.

"Mebbe so," said Mr. Dooley. "Mebbe so. What th' 'ell, annyhow. Mebbe 'tis as bad to take champagne out iv wan man's mouth as round steak out iv another's. Lent is near over. I seen Doherty out shinin' up his pipe that's been behind th' clock since Ash Winsdah. Th' girls 'll be layin' lilies on th' altar in a day or two. Th' spring's come on. Th' grass is growin' good; an', if th' Connock man's children back iv th' dumps can't get meat, they can eat hay."

A BRAND FROM THE BURNING

"I see be th' pa-apers," said Mr. Dooley, "that Boss have flew th' coop. 'Tis too bad, too bad. He wa-as a gr-reat man."

"Is he dead?" asked Mr. McKenna.

"No, faith, worse thin that; he's resigned. He calls th' la-ads about him, an' says he: 'Boys,' he says, 'I'm tired iv politics,' he says. 'I'm goin' to quit it f'r me health,' he says. 'Do ye stay in, an' get ar-rested f'r th' good iv th' party.' Ye see thim mug-wumps is afther th' Boss, an' he's gettin' out th' way Hogan got out iv Connock. Wan day he comes over to me fa-ather's house, an' says he, 'Dooley,' he says, 'I'm goin' to lave this hole iv a place,' he says. 'F'r why?' says th' ol' man; 'I thought ye liked it.' 'Faith,' says Hogan, 'I niver liked a blade iv grass in it,' he says. 'I'm sick iv it,' he says. 'I don't want niver to see it no more.' And he wint away. Th' next mornin' th' polis was lookin' f'r him to lock him up f'r stealin' joo'lry in the fair town. Yes, by dad.

"'Tis th' way iv th' boss, Jawn. I seen it manny's th' time. There was wanst a boss in th' Sixth Wa-ard, an' his name was Flannagan; an' he came fr'm th' County Clare, but so near th' bordher line that no wan challenged his vote, an' he was let walk down Ar-rchey Road just 's though he come fr'm Connock. Well, sir, whin I see him first, he'd th' smell iv Castle Garden on him, an' th' same is no mignonette, d'ye mind; an' he was goin' out with pick an' shovel f'r to dig in th' canal—a big, shtrappin', black-haired lad, with a neck like a bull's an' covered with a hide as thick as wan's, fr'm thryin' to get a crop iv oats out iv a Clare farm that growed divvle th' thing but nice, big boldhers.

"He was de-termined, though, an' th' first man that made a face at him he walloped in th' jaw; an' he'd been on th' canal no more thin a month befure he licked ivry man in th' gang but th' section boss, who'd been a Dublin jackeen, an' weighed sixteen stone an' was great with a thrip an' a punch. Wan day they had some wurruds, whin me bold Dublin man sails into Flannagan. Well, sir, they fought fr'm wan o'clock till tin in th' night, an' nayther give up; though Flannagan had th' best iv it, bein' young. 'Why don't ye put him out?' says wan iv th' la-ads. 'Whisht,' says Flannagan. 'I'm waitin' f'r th' moon to come up,' he says, 'so's I can hit him right,' he says, 'an' scientific.' Well, sir, his tone was that fierce th' section boss he dhropped right there iv sheer fright; an' Flannagan was cock iv th' walk.

"Afther a while he begun f'r to go out among th' other gangs, lookin' f'r fight; an', whin th' year was over, he was knowed fr'm wan end iv th' canal to th' other as th' man that no wan cud stand befure. He got so pop'lar fr'm lickin' all his frinds that he opened up a liquor store beyant th' bridge, an' wan night he shot some la-ads fr'm th' ya-ards that come over f'r to r-run him. That made him sthronger still. When they got up a prize f'r th' most pop'lar man in th' parish, he loaded th' ballot box an' got th' goold-headed stick, though he was r-runnin' against th' aldherman, an' th' little soggarth thried his best to down him. Thin he give a cock fight in th' liquor shop, an' that atthracted a gang iv bad men; an' he licked thim wan afther another, an' made thim his frinds. An' wan day lo an' behold, whin th' aldherman thried f'r to carry th' prim'ries that'd niver failed him befure, Flannagan wint down with his gang an' illicted his own dilligate ticket, an' thrun th' aldherman up in th' air!

"Thin he was a boss, an' f'r five years he r-run th' ward. He niver wint to th' council, d'ye mind; but, whin he was gin'rous, he give th' aldhermen tin per cint iv what they made. In a convintion, whin anny iv th' candydates passed roun' th' money, 'twas wan thousand dollars f'r Flannagan an' have a nice see-gar with me f'r th' rest iv thim. Wan year fr'm th' day he done th' aldherman he sold th' liquor shop. Thin he built a brick house in th' place iv th' little frame wan he had befure, an' moved in a pianny f'r his daughter. 'Twas about this time he got a dimon as big as ye'er fist, an' begun to dhrive down town behind a fast horse. No wan knowed what he done, but his wife said he was in th' r-rale estate business. D'ye mind, Jawn, that th' r-rale estate business includes near ivrything fr'm vagrancy to manslaughter?

"Whativer it was he done, he had money to bur-rn; an' th' little soggarth that wanst despised him, but had a hard time payin' th' debt iv th' church, was glad enough to sit at his table. Wan day without th' wink iv th' eye he moved up in th' avnoo, an' no wan seen him in Bridgeport afther that. 'Twas a month or two later whin a lot iv th' la-ads was thrun into jail f'r a little diviltry they'd done f'r him. A comity iv th' fathers iv th' la-ads wint to see him. He raceived thim in a room as big as wan iv their whole houses, with pitchers on th' walls an' a carpet as deep an' soft as a bog. Th' comity asked him to get th' la-ads out on bail.

"'Gintlemen,' he says, 'ye must excuse me,' he says, 'in such matthers.' 'D'ye mane to say,' says Cassidy, th' plumber, 'that ye won't do annything f'r my son?' 'Do annything,' says Flannagan. (I'll say this f'r him: a more darin' man niver drew breath; an', whin his time come to go sthandin' off th' mob an' defindin' his sthone quarry in th' rites iv sivinty-siven, he faced death without a wink.) 'Do?' he says, risin' an' sthandin' within a fut iv Cassidy's big cane. 'Do?' he says. 'Why,' he says, 'yes,' he says; 'I've subscribed wan thousand dollars,' he says, 'to th' citizen's comity,' he says, 'f'r to prosecute him; an',' he says, 'gintlemen,' he says, 'there's th' dure.'

"I seen Cassidy that night, an' he was as white as a ghost. 'What ails ye?' says I. 'Have ye seen th' divvle?' 'Yes,' he says, bendin' his head over th' bar, an' lookin' sivinty years instead iv forty-five."

A WINTER NIGHT

Any of the Archey Road cars that got out of the barns at all were pulled by teams of four horses, and the snow hung over the shoulders of the drivers' big bearskin coats like the eaves of an old-fashioned house on the blizzard night. There was hardly a soul in the road from the red bridge, west, when Mr. McKenna got laboriously off the platform of his car and made for the sign of somebody's celebrated Milwaukee beer over Mr. Dooley's tavern. Mr. Dooley, being a man of sentiment, arranges his drinks to conform with the weather. Now anybody who knows anything at all knows that a drop of "J.J." and a whisper (subdued) of hot water and a lump of sugar and lemon peel (if you care for lemon peel) and nutmeg (if you are a "jood") is a drink calculated to tune a man's heart to the song of the wind slapping a beer-sign upside down and the snow drifting in under the door. Mr. Dooley was drinking this mixture behind his big stove when Mr. McKenna came in.

"Bad night, Jawn," said Mr. Dooley.

"It is that," said Mr. McKenna.

"Blowin' an' stormin', yes," said Mr. Dooley. "There hasn' been a can in to-night but wan, an' that was a pop bottle. Is the snow-ploughs out, I dinnaw?"

"They are," said Mr. McKenna.

"I suppose Doherty is dhrivin'," said Mr. Dooley. "He's a good dhriver. They do say he do be wan iv the best dhrivers on th' road. I've heerd that th' prisident is dead gawn on him. He's me cousin. Ye can't tell much about what a man 'll be fr'm what th' kid is. That there Doherty was th' worst omadhon iv a boy that iver I knowed. He niver cud larn his a-ah-bee, abs. But see what he made iv himsilf! Th' best dhriver on th' road; an', by dad, 'tis not twinty to wan he won't be stharter befure he dies. 'Tis in th' fam'ly to make their names. There niver was anny fam'ly in th' ol' counthry that turned out more priests than th' Dooleys. By gar, I believe we hol' th' champeenship iv th' wurruld. At M'nooth th' profissor that called th' roll got so fr'm namin' th' Dooley la-ads that he came near bein' tur-rned down on th' cha-arge that he was whistlin' at vespers. His mouth, d'ye mind, took that there shape fr'm sayin' 'Dooley,' 'Dooley,' that he'd looked as if he was whistlin'. D'ye mind? Dear, oh dear, 'tis th' divvle's own fam'ly f'r religion."

Mr. McKenna was about to make a jeering remark to the effect that the alleged piety of the Dooley family had not penetrated to the Archey Road representative, when a person, evidently of wayfaring habits, entered and asked for alms. Mr. Dooley arose, and, picking a half-dollar from the till, handed it to the visitor with great unconcern. The departure of the wayfarer with profuse thanks was followed by a space of silence.

"Well, Jawn," said Mr. Dooley.

"What did you give the hobo?" asked Mr. McKenna.

"Half a dollar," said Mr. Dooley.

"And what for?"

"Binivolence," said Mr. Dooley, with a seraphic smile.

"Well," said Mr. McKenna, "I should say that was benevolence."

"Well," said Mr. Dooley, "'tis a bad night out, an' th' poor divvle looked that mis'rable it brought th' tears to me eyes, an'"—

"But," said Mr. McKenna, "that ain't any reason why you should give half a dollar to every tramp who comes in."

"Jawn," said Mr. Dooley, "I know th' ma-an. He spinds all his money at Schneider's, down th' block."

"What of that?" asked Mr. McKenna.

"Oh, nawthin'," said Mr. Dooley, "on'y I hope Herman won't thry to bite that there coin. If he does"—

THE BLUE AND THE GRAY

"A-ho," said Mr. Dooley, "th' blue an' th' gray, th' blue an' th' gray. Well, sir, Jawn, d'ye know that I see Mulligan marchin' ahead with his soord on his side, an' his horse dancin' an' backin' into th' crowd; an' th' la-ads chowlder arms an' march, march away. Ye shud've been there. Th' women come down fr'm th' peeraries with th' childher in their arms, an' 'twas like a sind-off to a picnic. 'Good-by, Mike.' 'Timothy, darlin', don't forget your prayers.' 'Cornalius, if ye do but look out f'r th' little wans, th' big wans'll not harm ye.' 'Teddy, lad, always wear ye'er Agnus Day.' An', whin th' time come f'r th' thrain to lave, th' girls was up to th' lines; an' 'twas, 'Mike, love, ye'll come back alive, won't ye?' an' 'Pat, there does be a pair iv yarn socks in th' hoomp on ye'er back. Wear thim, lad. They'll be good f'r ye'er poor, dear feet.' An' off they wint.

"Well, some come back, an' some did not come back. An' some come back with no rale feet f'r to put yarn socks on thim. Mulligan quit down somewhere in Kentucky; an' th' las' wurruds he was heard to utter was, 'Lay me down, boys, an' save th' flag.' An' there was manny th' other that had nawthin' to say but to call f'r a docthor; f'r 'tis on'y, d'ye mind, th' heroes that has somethin' writ down on typewriter f'r to sind to th' newspapers whin they move up. Th' other lads that dies because they cudden't r-run away—not because they wudden't—they dies on their backs, an' calls f'r th' docthor or th' priest. It depinds where they're shot.

" But, annyhow, no wan iv thim lads come back to holler because he was in th' war or to war again th' men that shot him. They wint to wurruk, carryin' th' hod 'r shovellin' cindhers at th' rollin' mills. Some iv thim took pinsions because they needed thim; but divvle th' wan iv thim ye'll see paradin' up an' down Ar-rchey Road with a blue coat on, wantin' to fight th' war over with Schwartzmeister's bar-tinder that niver heerd iv but wan war, an' that th' rites iv sivinty-sivin. Sare a wan. No, faith. They'd as lave decorate a confeatherate's grave as a thrue pathrite's. All they want is a chanst to go out to th' cimitry; an', faith, who doesn't enjoy that? No wan that's annything iv a spoort.

"I know hundherds iv thim. Ye know Pat Doherty, th' little man that lives over be Grove Sthreet. He inlisted three times, by dad, an' had to stand on his toes three times to pass. He was that ager. Well, he looks to weigh about wan hundherd an' twinty pounds; an' he weighs wan fifty be raison iv him havin' enough lead to stock a plumber in his stomach an' his legs. He showed himsilf wanst whin he was feelin' gay. He looks like a sponge. But he ain't. He come in here Thursdah night to take his dhrink in quite; an' says I, 'Did ye march to-day?' 'Faith, no,' he says, 'I can get hot enough runnin' a wheelbarrow without makin' a monkey iv mesilf dancin' around th' sthreets behind a band.' 'But didn't ye go out to decorate th' graves?' says I. 'I hadn't th' price,' says he. 'Th' women wint out with a gyranium to put over Sarsfield, the first born,' he says.

"Just thin Morgan O'Toole come in, an' laned over th' ba-ar. He's been a dillygate to ivry town convention iv th' Raypublicans since I dinnaw whin. 'Well,' says he, 'I see they're pilin' it on,'

he says. 'On th' dead?' says I, be way iv a joke.   No,' he says;
'but did ye see they're puttin' up a monnymint over th' rebils out
here be Oakwoods?' he says.   'By gar,' he says, ''tis a disgrace to
th' mim'ries iv thim devoted dead who died f'r their counthry,' he
says.   'If,' he says, 'I cud get ninety-nine men to go out an' blow
it up, I'd be th' hundherth,' he says.   'Yes,' says I, 'ye wud,' I
says.   'Ye'd be th' last,' I says.

"Doherty was movin' up to him.   'What rig'ment?' says he.
'What's that?' says O'Toole.   'Did ye inlist in th' army, brave
man?' says Pat.   'I swore him over age,' says I.   'Was ye
dhrafted in?' says th' little man.   'No,' says O'Toole.   'Him an'
me was in th' same cellar,' says I.   'Did ye iver hear iv Ree-saca,
'r Vicksburg, 'r Lookout Mountain?' th' little man wint on.
'Did anny man iver shoot at ye with annything but a siltzer
bottle?   Did ye iver have to lay on ye'er stummick with ye'er nose
burrid in th' Lord knows what while things was whistlin' over ye
that, if they iver stopped whistlin', 'd make ye'er backbone look
like a broom?   Did ye iver see a man that ye'd slept with th' night
befure cough, an' go out with his hands ahead iv his face?   Did
ye iver have to wipe ye'er most intimate frinds off ye'er clothes,
whin ye wint home at night?   Where was he durin' th' war?' he
says.   'He was dhrivin' a grocery wagon f'r Philip Reidy,' says I.
'An' what's he makin' th' roar about?' says th' little man.   'He
don't want anny man to get onto him,' says I.

"O'Toole was gone be this time, an' th' little man laned over
th' bar.   'Now,' says he, 'what d'ye think iv a gazabo that don't
want a monniment put over some wan?   Where is this here pole?
I think I'll go out an' take a look at it.   Where'd ye say th' la-ad
come fr'm?   Donaldson?   I was there.   There was a man in our
mess—a Wicklow man be th' name iv Dwyer—that had th' best
come-all-ye I iver heerd.   It wint like this,' an' he give it to me."

THE IDLE APPRENTICE

"They hanged a man to-day," said Mr. Dooley.
"They did so," said Mr. McKenna.
"Did he die game?"
"They say he did."
"Well, he did," said Mr. Dooley.   "I read it all in th' pa-apers.
He died as game as if he was wan iv th' Christyan martyrs instead

iv a thief that'd hit his man wan crack too much. Saint or murdherer, 'tis little difference whin death comes up face front.

"I read th' story iv this man through, Jawn; an', barrin' th' hangin', 'tis th' story iv tin thousan' like him. D'ye raymimber th' Carey kid? Ye do. Well, I knowed his grandfather; an' a dacinter ol' man niver wint to his jooty wanst a month. Whin he come over to live down be th' slip, 'twas as good a place as iver ye see. Th' honest men an' honest women wint as they pleased, an' laid hands on no wan. His boy Jim was as straight as th' r-roads in Kildare, but he took to dhrink; an', whin Jack Carey was born, he was a thramp on th' sthreets an' th' good woman was wurrukin' down-town, scrubbin' away at th' flures in th' city hall, where Dennehy got her.

"Be that time around th' slip was rough-an'-tumble. It was dhrink an' fight ivry night an' all day Sundah. Th' little la-ads come together under sidewalks, an' rushed th' can over to Burke's on th' corner an' listened to what th' big lads tol' thim. Th' first instruction that Jack Carey had was how to take a man's pocket handkerchief without his feelin' it, an' th' nex' he had was larnin' how to get over th' fence iv th' Reform School at Halsted Sthreet in his stockin' feet.

"He was a thief at tin year, an' th' polis 'd run f'r him if he'd showed his head. At twelve they sint him to th' bridewell f'r breakin' into a freight car. He come out, up to anny game. I see him whin he was a lad hardly to me waist stand on th' roof iv Finucane's Hall an' throw bricks at th' polisman.

"He hated th' polis, an' good reason he had f'r it. They pulled him out iv bed be night to search him. If he turned a corner, they ran him f'r blocks down th' sthreet. Whin he got older, they begun shootin' at him; an' it wasn't manny years befure he begun to shoot back. He was right enough whin he was in here. I cud conthrol him. But manny th' night whin he had his full iv liquor I've see him go out with his gun in his outside pocket; an' thin I'd hear shot after shot down th' sthreet, an' I'd know him an' his ol' inimy Clancy 'd met an' was exchangin' compliments. He put wan man on th' polis pension fund with a bullet through his thigh.

"They got him afther a while. He'd kept undher cover f'r months, livin' in freight cars an' hidin' undher viadocks with th' pistol in his hand. Wan night he come out, an' broke into Schwartzmeister's place. He sneaked through th' alley with th'

German man's damper in his arms, an' Clancy leaped on him fr'm th' fence. Th' kid was tough, but Clancy played fut-ball with th' Finerty's on Sundah, an' was tougher; an', whin th' men on th' other beats come up, Carey was hammered so they had to carry him to th' station an' nurse him f'r trile.

"He wint over th' road, an come back gray an' stooped. I was afraid iv th' boy with his black eyes; an' wan night he see me watchin' him, an' he says: 'Ye needn't be afraid,' he says. 'I won't hurt ye. Ye're not Clancy,' he says.

"I tol' Clancy about it, but he was a brave man; an' says he: ''Tis wan an' wan, an' a thief again an' honest man. If he gets me, he must get me quick.' Th' nex' night about dusk he come saunterin' up th' sthreet, swingin' his club an' jokin' with his frind, whin some wan shouted, 'Look out, Clancy.' He was not quick enough. He died face forward, with his hands on his belt; an' befure all th' wurruld Jack Carey come across th' sthreet, an' put another ball in his head.

"They got him within twinty yards iv me store. He was down in th' shadow iv th' house, an' they was shootin' at him fr'm roofs an' behind barns. Whin he see it was all up, he come out with his eyes closed, firin' straight ahead; an' they filled him so full iv lead he broke th' hub iv th' pathrol wagon takin' him to th' morgue."

"It served him right," said Mr. McKenna.

"Who?" said Mr. Dooley. "Carey or Clancy?"

SLAVIN CONTRA WAGNER

"Ol' man Donahue bought Molly a pianny las' week," Mr. Dooley said in the course of his conversation with Mr. McKenna. "She'd been takin' lessons fr'm a Dutchman down th' sthreet, an' they say she can play as aisy with her hands crossed as she can with wan finger. She's been whalin' away iver since, an' Donahue is dhrinkin' again.

"Ye see th' other night some iv th' la-ads wint over f'r to see whether they cud smash his table in a frindly game iv forty-fives. I don't know what possessed Donahue. He niver asked his frinds into the parlor befure. They used to set in th' dining-room; an', whin Mrs. Donahue coughed at iliven o'clock, they'd toddle out th' side dure with their hats in their hands. But this here night, whether 'twas that Donahue had taken on a dhrink or two too much or not, he asked thim all in th' front room, where Mrs. Donahue was settin' with Molly. 'I've brought me frinds,' he says, 'f'r to hear Molly take a fall out iv th' music-box,' he says. 'Let me have ye'er hat, Mike,' he says. 'Ye'll not feel it whin ye get out,' he says.

"At anny other time Mrs. Donahue'd give him th' marble heart. But they wasn't a man in th' party that had a pianny to his name, an' she knew they'd be throuble whin they wint home an' tould about it. ' 'Tis a mel-odjious insthrument,' says she. 'I cud sit here be the hour an' listen to Bootoven and Choochooski,' she says.

" 'What did thim write?' says Cassidy. 'Chunes,' says Donahue, 'chunes. Molly,' he says, 'fetch 'er th' wallop to make th' gintlemen feel good,' he says. 'What'll it be, la-ads?' 'D'ye know "Down be th' Tan-yard Side"?' says Slavin. 'No,' says Molly. 'It goes like this,' says Slavin. 'A-ah, din yadden, yooden a-yadden, arrah yadden ay-a.' 'I dinnaw it,' says th' girl. ' 'Tis a low chune, annyhow,' says Mrs. Donahue. 'Misther Slavin ividintly thinks he's at a polis picnic,' she says. 'I'll have no come-all-ye's in this house,' she says. 'Molly, give us a few ba-ars fr'm Wagner.' 'What Wagner's that?' says Flanagan. 'No wan ye know,' says Donahue; 'he's a German musician.' 'Thim Germans is hot people f'r music,' says Cassidy. 'I knowed wan that cud play th' "Wacht am Rhine" on a pair iv cymbals,' he says. 'Whisht!' says Donahue. 'Give th' girl a chanst.'

"Slavin tol' me about it. He says he niver heerd th' like in his born days. He says she fetched th' pianny two or three wallops that made Cassidy jump out iv his chair, an' Cassidy has charge iv th' steam whistle at th' quarry at that. She wint at it as though she had a gredge at it. First 'twas wan hand an' thin th' other, thin both hands, knuckles down; an' it looked, says Slavin, as if she was goin' to leap into th' middle iv it with both feet, whin Donahue jumps up. 'Hol' on!' he says. 'That's not a rented pianny, ye daft girl,' he says. 'Why, pap-pah,' says Molly, 'what d'ye mean?' she says. 'That's Wagner,' she says. ' 'Tis th' music iv th' future,' she says. 'Yes,' says Donahue, 'but I don't want me hell on earth. I can wait f'r it,' he says, 'with th' kind permission iv Mrs. Donahue,' he says. 'Play us th' "Wicklow Mountaineer,"' he says, 'an' threat th' masheen kindly,' he says.

'She'll play no "Wicklow Mountaineer,"' says Mrs. Donahue.
'If ye want to hear that kind iv chune, ye can go down to
Finucane's Hall,' she says, 'an' call in Crowley, th' blind piper,'
she says. 'Molly,' she says, 'give us wan iv thim Choochooski
things,' she said. 'They're so ginteel.'

"With that Donahue rose up. 'Come on,' says he. 'This is
no place f'r us,' he says. Slavin, with th' politeness iv a man
who's gettin' even, turns at th' dure. 'I'm sorry I can't remain,'
he says. 'I think th' wurruld an' all iv Choochooski,' he says.
'Me brother used to play his chunes,' he says—'me brother Mike,
that run th' grip ca-ar,' he says. 'But there's wan thing missin'
fr'm Molly's playin',' he says. 'And what may that be?' says Mrs.
Donahue. 'An ax,' says Slavin, backin' out.

"So Donahue has took to dhrink."

THE WANDERERS

"Poor la-ads, poor la-ads," said Mr. Dooley, putting aside his
newspaper and rubbing his glasses. "'Tis a hard lot theirs, thim
that go down into th' sea in ships, as Shakespeare says. Ye niver
see a storm on th' ocean? Iv coorse ye didn't. How cud ye, ye
that was born away fr'm home? But I have, Jawn. May th'
saints save me fr'm another! I come over in th' bowels iv a big
crazy balloon iv a propeller, like wan iv thim ye see hooked up to
Dempsey's dock, loaded with lumber an' slabs an' Swedes. We
watched th' little ol' island fadin' away behind us, with th' sun
sthrikin' th' white house-tops iv Queenstown an' lightin' up th'
chimbleys iv Martin Hogan's liquor store. Not wan iv us but had
left near all we loved behind, an' sare a chance that we'd iver
spoon th' stirabout out iv th' pot above th' ol' peat fire again. Yes,
by dad, there was wan—a lad fr'm th' County Roscommon.
Divvle th' tear he shed. But, whin we had parted fr'm land, he
turns to me, an' says, 'Well, we're on our way,' he says. 'We are
that,' says I. 'No chanst f'r thim to turn around an' go back,' he
says. 'Divvle th' fut,' says I. 'Thin,' he says, raisin' his voice, 'to
'ell with th' Prince iv Wales,' he says. 'To 'ell with him,' he says.

"An' that was th' last we see of sky or sun f'r six days. That
night come up th' divvle's own storm. Th' waves tore an'
walloped th' ol' boat, an' th' wind howled, an' ye cud hear th'
machinery snortin' beyant. Murther, but I was sick. Wan
time th' ship 'd be settin' on its tail, another it'd be standin' on its

head, thin rollin' over cow-like on th' side; an' ivry time it lurched me stummick lurched with it, an' I was tore an' rint an' racked till, if death come, it 'd found me willin'.   An' th' Roscommon man—glory be, but he was disthressed.   He set on th' flure, with his hands on his belt an' his face as white as stone, an' rocked to an' fro.   'Ahoo,' he says, 'ahoo, but me insides has torn loose,' he says, 'an' are tumblin' around,' he says.   'Say a pather an' avy,' says I, I was that mad f'r th' big bosthoon f'r his blatherin'. 'Say a pather an' avy,' I says; 'f'r ye're near to death's dure, avick.' 'Am I?' says he, raising up.   'Thin,' he says, 'to 'ell with the whole rile fam'ly,' he says.   Oh, he was a rebel!

"Through th' storm there was a babby cryin'.   'Twas a little wan, no more thin a year ol'; an' 'twas owned be a Tipp'rary man who come fr'm near Clonmel, a poor, weak, scarey-lookin' little divvle that lost his wife, an' see th' bailiff walk off with th' cow, an' thin see him come back again with th' process servers.   An' so he was comin' over with th' babby, an' bein' mother an' father to it.   He'd rock it be th' hour on his knees, an' talk nonsense to it, an' sing it songs, 'Aha, 'twas there I met a maiden,' an' 'Th' Wicklow Mountaineer,' an' 'Th' Rambler fr'm Clare,' an' 'O'Donnel Aboo,' croonin' thim in th' little babby's ears, an' payin' no attintion to th' poorin' thunder above his head, day an' night, day an' night, poor soul.   An' th' babby cryin' out his heart, an' him settin' there with his eyes as red as his hair, an' makin' no kick, poor soul.

"But wan day th' ship settled down steady, an' ragin' stummicks with it; an' th' Roscommon man shakes himself, an' says, 'To 'ell with th' Prince iv Wales an' th' Dook iv Edinboroo,' an' goes out.   An' near all th' steerage followed; f'r th' storm had done its worst, an' gone on to throuble those that come afther, an' may th' divvle go with it.   'Twill be rest f'r that little Tipp'rary man; f'r th' waves was r-runnin' low an' peaceful, an' th' babby have sthopped cryin'.

"He had been settin' on a stool, but he come over to me. 'Th' storm,' says I, 'is over.   'Twas wild while it lasted,' says I. 'Ye may say so,' says he.   'Well, please Gawd,' says I, 'that it left none worse off thin us.'   'It blew ill f'r some an' aise f'r others,' says he.   'Th' babby is gone.'

"An' so it was, Jawn, f'r all his rockin' an' singin'.   An' in th' avnin' they burried it over th' side into th' sea.   An' th' little man see thim do it."

MAKING A CABINET

"I suppose, Jawn," said Mr. Dooley, "ye do be afther a governmint job. Is it council to Athlone or what, I dinnaw?"

"I haven't picked out the place yet," said Mr. McKenna. "Bill wrote me the day after election about it. He says: 'John,' he says, 'take anything you want that's not nailed to the wall,' he says. He heard of my good work in the Twenty-ninth. We rolled up eight votes in Carey's precinct, and had five of them counted; and that's more of a miracle than carrying New York by three hundred thousand."

"It is so," said Mr. Dooley. "It is f'r a fact. Ye must've give the clerks an' judges morphine, an' ye desarve great credit. Ye ought to have a place; an' I think ye'll get wan, if there's enough to go round among th' Irish Raypublicans. 'Tis curious what an effect an iliction has on th' Irish Raypublican vote. In October an Irish Raypublican's so rare people point him out on th' sthreet, an' women carry their babies to see him. But th' day afther iliction, glory be, ye run into thim ivrywhere—on th' sthreet-car, in the sthreet, in saloons principally, an' at th' meetin's iv th' Raypublican Comity. I've seen as manny iv them as twinty in here to-day, an' ivry wan iv thim fit to run anny job in th' governmint, fr'm directin' th' Departmint iv State to carryin' ashes out an' dumpin' thim in th' white lot.

"They can't all have jobs, but they've got to be attinded to first; an', whin Mack's got through with thim, he can turn in an' make up that cabinet iv his. Thin he'll have throuble iv his own, th' poor man, on'y comin' into fifty thousand a year and rint free. If 'twas wan iv th' customs iv th' great raypublic iv ours, Jawn, f'r to appoint th' most competent men f'r th' places, he'd have a mighty small lot f'r to pick fr'm. But, seein' that on'y thim is iligible that are unfit, he has th' divvle's own time selectin'. F'r Sicrety iv State, if he follows all iv what Casey calls recent precidints, he's limited to ayether a jack-leg counthry lawyer, that has set around Washington f'r twinty years, pickin' up a dollar or two be runnin' errands f'r a foreign imbassy, or a judge that doesn't know whether th' city of Booloogne-sure-Mere, where Tynan was pinched, is in Boolgahria or th' County Cavan. F'r Sicrety iv th' Threasury he has a choice iv three kinds iv proud and incompetent fi-nanceers. He can ayether take a bank prisident, that'll see that his little bank an' its frinds doesn't get th' worst iv

it, or a man that cudden't maintain th' par'ty iv a counthry dhry-
good store long enough to stand off th' sheriff, or a broken-down
Congressman, that is full iv red liquor half the year, an' has
remorse settin' on his chest th' other half.

"On'y wan class is iligible f'r Attorney-gin'ral. To fill that
job, a man's got to be a first-class thrust lawyer. If he ain't, th'
Lord knows what'll happen. Be mistake he might prosecute a
thrust some day, an' th' whole counthry'll be rooned. He must be
a man competint f'r to avoid such pitfalls an' snares, so 'tis th' rule
f'r to have him hang on to his job with th' thrust afther he gets to
Washington. This keeps him in touch with th' business intherests.

"F'r Sicrety iv War, th' most like wan is some good prisident
iv a sthreet-car company. 'Tis exthraordinney how a man learns
to manage military affairs be auditin' thrip sheets an' rentin' signs
in a sthreet-car to chewin' gum imporyums. If Gin'ral Washington iv sacred mimory 'd been under a good sthreet-car Sicrety
iv War, he'd 've wore a bell punch to ring up ivry time he killed a
Hessian. He wud so, an' they'd 've kep' tab on him, an', if he
thried to wurruk a brother-in-law on thim, they'd give him his
time.

"F'r th' Navy Departmint ye want a Southern Congressman
fr'm th' cotton belt. A man that iver see salt wather outside iv
a pork bar'l 'd be disqualified f'r th' place. He must live so far
fr'm th' sea that he don't know a capstan bar fr'm a sheet anchor.
That puts him in th' proper position to inspect armor plate f'r th'
imminent Carnegie, an' insthruct admirals that's been cruisin'
an' fightin' an' dhrinkin' mint juleps f'r thirty years. He must
know th' difference bechune silo an' insilage, how to wean a bull
calf, an' th' best way to cure a spavin. If he has that information, he is fixed f'r th' job.

"Whin he wants a good Postmaster-gin'ral, take ye'er ol' law
partner f'r awhile, an', be th' time he's larned to stick stamps, hist
him out, an' put in a school-teacher fr'm a part iv th' counthry
where people communicate with each other through a conch.
Th' Sicrety iv th' Interior is an important man. If possible, he
ought to come fr'm Maine or Florida. At anny rate, he must be a
resident iv an Atlantic seacoast town, an' niver been west iv Cohoes.
If he gets th' idee there are anny white people in Ann Arbor or
Columbus, he loses his job.

"Th' last place on th' list is Sicrety iv Agriculture. A good,
lively business man that was born in th' First Ward an' moved to

th' Twinty-foorth after th' fire is best suited to this office. Thin he'll have no prejudices against sindin' a farmer cactus seeds whin he's on'y lookin' f'r wheat, an' he will have a proper understandin' iv th' importance iv an' early Agricultural Bureau rayport to th' bucket-shops.

"No President can go far away that follows Cleveland's cabinet appintmints, although it may be hard f'r Mack, bein' new at th' business, to select th' right man f'r th' wrong place. But I'm sure he'll be advised be his frinds, an' fr'm th' lists iv candy-dates I've seen he'll have no throuble in findin' timber."

THE DIVIDED SKIRT

"Jawn," said Mr. Dooley, "did ye iver hear th' puzzle whin a woman's not a woman?"

"Faith, I have," said Mr. McKenna. "When I was a kid, I knew the answer."

"Ye didn't know this answer," said Mr. Dooley. "Whin is a woman not a woman? 'Twas give to me las' Satthurdah night be young Callaghan, th' sthreet-car man that have all th' latest jokes that does be out. Whin is a woman not a woman? mind ye. Whin's she's on a bicycle, by dad. Yes, yes. Whin she's on a bicycie, Jawn. D'ye know Molly Donahue?"

"I know her father," said Mr. McKenna.

"Well, well, the dacint man sint his daughter Molly to have a convint schoolin'; an' she larned to pass th' butther in Frinch an' to paint all th' chiny dishes in th' cubb'rd, so that, whin Donahue come home wan night an' et his supper, he ate a green paint ha-arp along with his cabbage, an' they had to sind f'r Docthor Hinnissy f'r to pump th' a-art work out iv him. So they did. But Donahue, bein' a quite man, niver minded that, but let her go on with her do-se-does an' bought her a bicycle. All th' bicycles th' poor man had himsilf whin he was her age was th' dhray he used to dhrive f'r Comiskey; but he says, '"Tis all th' thing,' he says. 'Let th' poor child go her way,' he says to his wife, he says. 'Honoria,' he says, 'she'll get over it.'

"No wan knowed she had th' bicycle, because she wint out afther dark an' practised on it down be th' dump. But las' Friday evnin', lo an' behold, whin th' r-road was crowded with people fr'm th' brick-yards an' th' gas-house an' th' mills, who shud come ridin' along be th' thracks, bumpin' an' holdin' on, but Molly Donahue ? An' dhressed ! How d'ye suppose she was dhressed ? In pa-ants, Jawn avick. In pa-ants. Oh, th' shame iv it ! Ivry wan on th' sthreet stopped f'r to yell. Little Julia Dorgan called out, 'Who stole Molly's dhress ?' Ol' man Murphy was settin' asleep on his stoop. He heerd th' noise, an' woke up an' set his bull tarrier Lydia Pinkham on her. Malachi Dorsey, vice-prisident iv th' St. Aloysius Society, was comin' out iv th' German's, an' see her. He put his hands to his face, an' wint back to th' house.

"But she wint bumpin' on, Jawn, till she come up be th' house. Father Kelly was standin' out in front, an' ol' man Donahue was layin' down th' law to him about th' tariff, whin along come th' poor foolish girl with all th' kids in Bridgeport afther her. Donahue turned white. 'Say a pather an' avy quick,' he says to the priest. Thin he called out to his wife. 'Honoria,' he says, 'bring a bar'l,' he says. 'Molly has come away without annything on,' he says, 'but Sarsfield's pa-ants.' Thin he turned on his daughter. 'May th' Lord forgive ye, Molly Donahue,' he says, 'this night !' he says. 'Child, where is ye'er dhress ?' 'Tut, tut !' says th' good man. 'Molly,' he says, 'ye look well on that there bicycle,' he says. 'But 'tis th' first time I ever knowed ye was bow-legged,' he says, says th' soggarth aroon.

"Well, sir, she wint into th' house as if she'd been shot fr'm a gun, an' th' nex' mornin' I see Doheny's express wagon haulin' th' bicycle away."

"Didn't Father Kelly do anything about it ?" asked Mr. McKenna.

"No," replied Mr. Dooley. "There was some expicted she'd be read fr'm th' altar at high mass, but she wasn't."

THE OPTIMIST

"Aho," said Mr. Dooley, drawing a long, deep breath. "Ah-ho, glory be to th' saints ! "

He was sitting out in front of his liquor shop with Mr. Mc-Kenna, their chairs tilted against the door-posts. If it had been hot elsewhere, what had it been in Archey Road ? The street-car horses reeled in the dust from the tracks. The drivers, leaning over the dash-boards, flogged the brutes with the viciousness of weakness. The piles of coke in the gas-house yards sent up waves of heat like smoke. Even the little girls playing on the sidewalks were flaming pink in color. But the night saw Archey Road out in all gayety, its flannel shirt open at the breast to the cooling blast and the cries of its children filling the air. It also saw Mr. Dooley luxuriating like a polar bear, and bowing cordially to all who passed.

"Glory be to th' saints," he said, "but it's been a thryin' five days. I've been mean enough to commit murdher without th' strength even to kill a fly. I expect to have a fight on me hands; f'r I've insulted half th' road, an' th' on'y thing that saved me was that no wan was sthrong enough to come over th' bar. 'I cud lick ye f'r that, if it was not so hot,' said Dorsey, whin I told him I'd change no bill f'r him. 'Ye cud not,' says I, 'if 'twas cooler,' I says. It's cool enough f'r him now. Look, Jawn dear, an' see if there's an ice-pick undher me chair.

"It 'd be more thin th' patience iv Job 'd stand to go through such weather, an' be fit f'r society. They's on'y wan man in all th' wurruld cud do it, an' that man's little Tim Clancy. He wurruks out in th' mills, tin hours a day, runnin' a wheelbarrow loaded with cindhers. He lives down beyant. Wan side iv his house is up again a brewery, an' th' other touches elbows with Twinty-Percint Murphy's flats. A few years back they found out that he didn't own on'y th' front half iv th' lot, an' he can set on his back stoop an' put his feet over th' fince now. He can, faith. Whin he's indures, he breathes up th' chimbley; an' he has a wife an' eight kids. He dhraws wan twinty-five a day—whin he wurruks.

"He come in here th' other night to talk over matthers; an' I was stewin' in me shirt, an' sayin' cross things to all th' wurruld fr'm th' tail iv me eye. ''Tis hot,' says I. ''Tis war-rum,' he says. ''Tis dam hot,' says I. 'Well,' he says, ''tis good weather f'r th' crops,' he says. 'Things grows in this weather. I mind wanst,' he says, 'we had days just like these, an' we raised forty bushels iv oats to an acre,' he says. 'Whin Neville, th' landlord, come with wagons to take it off, he was that surprised ye cud iv knocked him down with a sthraw. 'Tis great growin' weather,' he says. An', Jawn, by dad, barrin' where th' brewery horse spilt oats on th' durestep an' th' patches iv grass on th' dump, sare a growin' thing but childher has that little man seen in twinty years.

"''Twas hotter whin I seen him nex', an' I said so. ''Tis

war-rum,' he says, laughin'. 'By dad, I think th' ice 'll break up in th' river befure mornin',' he says. 'But look how cold it was last winter,' he says. 'Th' crops need weather like this,' he says. I'd like to have hit him with a chair. Sundah night I wint over to see him. He was sittin' out in front, with a babby on each knee. 'Good avnin',' says I. 'Good avnin',' he says. 'This is th' divvle's own weather,' I says. 'I'm suffocatin'.' ''Tis quite a thaw,' he says. 'How's all th' folks?' says I. 'All well, thank ye kindly,' he says, 'save an' except th' wife an' little Eleen,' he says. 'They're not so well,' he says. 'But what can ye expect? They've had th' best iv health all th' year.' 'It must be har-rd wurrukin' at th' mills this weather,' I says. ''Tis war-rum,' he says; 'but ye can't look f'r snow-storms this time iv th' year,' he says. 'Thin,' says he, 'me mind's taken aff th' heat be me wurruk,' he says. 'Dorsey that had th' big cinder-pile—the wan near th' fence—was sun-struck Fridah, an' I've been promoted to his job. 'Tis a most re-sponsible place,' he says; 'an' a man, to fill it rightly an' properly, has no time to think f'r th' crops,' he says. An' I wint away, lavin' him singin' 'On th' Three-tops' to th' kids on his knees.

"Well, he comes down th' road tonight afther th' wind had turned, with his old hat on th' back iv his head, whistlin' 'Th' Rambler fr'm Clare' and I stopped to talk with him. 'Glory be,' says I, ''tis pleasant to breathe th' cool air,' says I. 'Ah,' he says, ''tis a rale good avnin',' he says. 'D'ye know,' he says, 'I haven't slept much these nights, f'r wan reason 'r another. But,' he says, 'I'm afraid this here change won't be good f'r th' crops,' he says. 'If we'd had wan or two more war-rum days an' thin a sprinkle iv rain,' he says, 'how they would grow, how they would grow!'"

Mr. Dooley sat up in his chair, and looked over at Mr. McKenna.

"Jawn," he said, "d'ye know that, whin I think iv th' thoughts that's been in my head f'r a week, I don't dare to look Tim Clancy in th' face."

PROSPERITY[1]

"Th' defeat iv Humanity be Prosperity was wan iv th' raysults iv th' iliction," said Mr. Dooley.

"What are you talking about?" asked Mr. McKenna, gruffly.

[1] Written on the occasion of McKinley's election over Bryan in November, 1896.

"Well," said Mr. Dooley, "I thought it was McKinley an' Hobart that won out, but I see now that it's McKinley an' Prosperity. If Bryan had been elected, Humanity would have had a front seat an' a tab. Th' sufferin's iv all th' wurruld would have ended; an' Jawn H. Humanity would be in th' White House, throwin' his feet over th' furniture an' receivin' th' attintions iv diplomats an' pleeniapotentiaries. It was decided otherwise be th' fates, as th' Good Book says. Prosperity is th' bucko now. Barrin' a sthrike at th' stock-yards an' a hold-up here an' there, Prosperity has come leapin' in as if it had jumped fr'm a spring-board. Th' mills are opened, th' factories are goin' to go, th' railroads are watherin' stocks, long processions iv workin'men are marchin' fr'm th' pay-car to their peaceful saloons, their wives are takin' in washin' again, th' price iv wheat is goin' up an' down, creditors are beginnin' to sue debtors; an' thus all th' wurruld is merry with th' on'y rational enjoyments iv life.

"An' th' stock exchange has opened. That's wan iv th' strongest signs iv prosperity. I min' wanst whin me frind Mike McDonald was controllin' th' city, an' conductin' an exchange down be Clark Sthreet. Th' game had been goin' hard again th' house. They hadn't been a split f'r five deals. Whin ivrybody was on th' queen to win, with th' sivin spot coppered, th' queen won, th' sivin spot lost. Wan lad amused himsilf be callin' th' turn twenty-wan times in succession, an' th' check rack was down to a margin iv eleven whites an' fifty-three cints in change. Mike looked around th' crowd, an' turned down th' box. 'Gintlemen,' says he, 'th' game is closed. Business conditions are such,' he says, 'that I will not be able to cash in ye'er checks,' he says. 'Please go out softly, so's not to disturb th' gintlemen at th' roulette wheel,' he says, 'an' come back afther th' iliction, whin confidence is restored an' prosperity returns to th' channels iv thrade an' industhry,' he says. 'Th' exchange 'll be opened promptly; an' th' usual rule iv chips f'r money an' money f'r chips, fifty on cases an' sivinty-five f'r doubles, a hard-boiled egg an' a dhrink f'r losers, will prevail,' he says. 'Return with th' glad tidings iv renewed commerce, an' thank th' Lord I haven't took ye'er clothes.' His was th' first stock exchange we had.

"Yes, Prosperity has come hollerin' an screamin'. To read th' papers, it seems to be a kind iv a vagrancy law. No wan can loaf anny more. Th' end iv vacation has gone f'r manny a happy lad that has spint six months ridin' through th' counthry, dodgin'

wurruk, or loafin' under his own vine or hat-three.   Prosperity
grabs ivry man be th' neck, an' sets him shovellin' slag or coke or
runnin' up an' down a ladder with a hod iv mortar.   It won't let
th' wurruld rest.   If Humanity 'd been victoryous, no wan 'd
iver have to do a lick again to th' end iv his days.   But Prosperity's
a horse iv another color.   It goes round like a polisman givin' th'
hot fut to happy people that are snoozin' in th' sun.   'Get up,'
says Prosperity.   'Get up, an' hustle over to th' rollin' mills:
there's a man over there wants ye to carry a ton iv coal on ye'er
back.'   'But I don't want to wurruk,' says th' lad.   'I'm very
comfortable th' way I am.'   'It makes no difference,' says
Prosperity.   'Ye've got to do ye'er lick.   Wurruk, f'r th' night is
comin'.   Get out, an' hustle.   Wurruk, or ye can't be unhappy;
an', if th' wurruld isn't unhappy, they'se no such a thing as
Prosperity.'

"That's wan thing I can't understand," Mr. Dooley went on.
"Th' newspapers is run be a lot iv gazabos that thinks wurruk is
th' ambition iv mankind.   Most iv th' people I know 'd be
happiest layin' on a lounge with a can near by, or stretchin'
thimsilves f'r another nap at eight in th' mornin'.   But th' papers
make it out that there'd be no sunshine in th' land without you an'
me, Hinnissy, was up befure daybreak pullin' a sthreet-car or
poundin' sand with a shovel.   I seen a line, 'Prosperity effects on
th' Pinnsylvania Railroad'; an' I read on to find that th' road
intinded to make th' men in their shops wurruk tin hours instead
iv eight, an' it says 'there's no reasons why they should not
wurruk Sundahs if they choose.'   If they choose!   An' what
chance has a man got that wants to make th' wurruld brighter an'
happier be rollin' car-wheels but to miss mass an' be at th' shops ?"

"We must all work," said Mr. McKenna, sententiously.

"Yes," said Mr. Dooley, "or be wurruked."

KEEPING LENT

Mr. McKenna had observed Mr. Dooley in the act of spinning
a long, thin spoon in a compound which reeked pleasantly and
smelt of the humming water of commerce; and he laughed and
mocked at the philosopher.

"Ah-ha," he said, "that's th' way you keep Lent, is it ?   Two
weeks from Ash Wednesday, and you tanking up."

Mr. Dooley went on deliberately to finish the experiment,

leisurely dusting the surface with nutmeg and tasting the product before setting down the glass daintily. Then he folded his apron, and lay back in ample luxury while he began: "Jawn, th' holy season iv Lent was sent to us f'r to teach us th' weakness iv th' human flesh. Man proposes, an' th' Lord disposes, as Hinnissy says.

"I mind as well as though it was yesterday th' struggle iv me father f'r to keep Lent. He began to talk it a month befure th' time. 'On Ash Winsdah,' he'd say, 'I'll go in f'r a rale season iv fast an' abstinince,' he'd say. An' sure enough, whin Ash Winsdah come round at midnight, he'd take a long dhraw at his pipe an' knock th' ashes out slowly again his heel, an' thin put th' dhudeen up behind th' clock. 'There,' says he, 'there ye stay till Easter morn,' he says. Ash Winsdah he talked iv nawthin but th' pipe. ''Tis exthrordinney how easy it is f'r to lave off,' he says. 'All ye need is will power,' he says. 'I dinnaw that I'll iver put a pipe in me mouth again. 'Tis a bad habit, smokin' is,' he says; 'an' it costs money. A man's betther off without it. I find I dig twict as well,' he says; 'an', as f'r cuttin' turf, they'se not me like in th' parish since I left off th' pipe,' he says.

"Well, th' nex' day an' th' nex' day he talked th' same way; but Fridah he was sour, an' looked up at th' clock where th' pipe was. Saturdah me mother, thinkin' to be plazin' to him, says: 'Terrence,' she says, 'ye're iver so much betther without th' tobacco,' she says. 'I'm glad to find you don't need it. Ye'll save money,' she says. 'Be quite, woman,' says he. 'Dear, oh dear,' he says, 'I'd like a pull at th' clay,' he says. 'Whin Easter comes, plaze Gawd, I'll smoke mesilf black an' blue in th' face,' he says.

"That was th' beginin' iv th' downfall. Choosdah he was settin' in front iv th' fire with a pipe in his mouth. 'Why, Terrence,' says me mother, 'ye're smokin' again.' 'I'm not,' says he: ''tis a dhry smoke,' he says; ''tisn't lighted,' he says. Wan week afther th' swear-off he came fr'm th' field with th' pipe in his face, an' him puffin' away like a chimney. 'Terrence,' says me mother, 'it isn't Easter morn.' 'Ah-ho,' says he, 'I know it,' he says; 'but,' he says, 'what th' divvle do I care?' he says. 'I wanted f'r to find out whether it had th' masthery over me; an',' he says, 'I've proved that it hasn't,' he says. 'But what's th' good iv swearin' off, if ye don't break it?' he says. 'An' annyhow,' he says, 'I glory in me shame.'

"Now, Jawn," Mr. Dooley went on, "I've got what Hogan calls

a theery, an' it's this: that what's thrue iv wan man's thrue iv all
men. I'm me father's son a'most to th' hour an' day. Put me in
th' County Roscommon forty year ago, an' I'd done what he'd
done. Put him on th' Ar-rchey Road, an' he'd be deliverin' ye a
lecture on th' sin iv thinkin' ye're able to overcome th' pride iv
th' flesh, as Father Kelly says. Two weeks ago I looked with
contimpt on Hinnissy f'r an' because he'd not even promise to
fast an' obstain fr'm croquet durin' Lent. To-night you see me
mixin' me toddy without th' shadow iv remorse about me. I'm
proud iv it. An' why not? I was histin' in me first wan whin th'
soggarth come down fr'm a sick call, an' looked in at me. 'In
Lent?' he says, half-laughin' out iv thim quare eyes iv his.
'Yes,' said I. 'Well,' he says, 'I'm not authorized to say this be
th' propaganda,' he says, 'an' 'tis no part iv th' directions f'r
Lent,' he says; 'but,' he says, 'I'll tell ye this, Martin,' he says,
'that they'se more ways than wan iv keepin' th' season,' he says.
'I've knowed thim that starved th' stomach to feast th' evil
temper,' he says. 'They'se a little priest down be th' Ninth Ward
that niver was known to keep a fast day; but Lent or Christmas
tide, day in an' day out, he goes to th' hospital where they put th'
people that has th' small-pox. Starvation don't always mean
salvation. If it did,' he says, 'they'd have to insure th' pavemint
in wan place, an' they'd be money to burn in another. Not,' he
says, 'that I want ye to undherstand that I look kindly on th' sin
iv'—

   "''Tis a cold night out,' says I.
   "'Well,' he says, th' dear man, 'ye may. On'y,' he says,
''tis Lent.'
   "'Yes,' says I.
   "'Well, thin,' he says, 'by ye'er lave I'll take but half a lump
iv sugar in mine,' he says."

THE QUICK AND THE DEAD

   Mr. Dooley and Mr. McKenna sat outside the ample door of
the little liquor store, the evening being hot, and wrapped their
legs around the chair, and their lips around two especially long
and soothing drinks. They talked politics and religion, the
people up and down the street, the chances of Murphy, the
tinsmith, getting on the force, and a great deal about the weather.
A woman in white started Mr. McKenna's nerves.
   "Glory be, I thought it was a ghost!" said Mr. McKenna,

whereupon the conversation drifted to those interesting phenomena. Mr. Dooley asked Mr. McKenna if he had ever seen one. Mr. McKenna replied that he hadn't, and didn't want to. Had Mr. Dooley? "No," said the philosopher, "I niver did; an' it's always been more thin sthrange to me that annywan shud come back afther he'd been stuck in a crate five feet deep, with a ton iv mud upon him. 'Tis onplisint iv thim, annyhow, not to say ongrateful. F'r mesilf, if I was wanst pushed off, an' they'd waked me kindly, an' had a solemn rayqueem high mass f'r me, an' a funeral with Roddey's Hi-beryan band, an' th' A-ho-aitches, I have too much pride to come back f'r an encore. I wud so, Jawn. Whin a man's dead, he ought to make th' best iv a bad job, an' not be thrapsin' around, lookin' f'r throuble among his own kind.

"No, I niver see wan, but I know there are such things; f'r twinty years ago all th' road was talkin' about how Flaherty, th' tailor, laid out th' ghost iv Tim O'Grady. O'Grady was a big sthrappin' Connock man, as wide across th' shoulders as a freight car. He was a plastherer be thrade whin wages was high, an' O'Grady was rowlin' in wealth. Ivry Sundah ye'd see him, with his horse an' buggy an' his goold watch an' chain, in front iv th' Sullivans' house, waitin' f'r Mary Ann Sullivan to go f'r a buggy ride with him over to McAllister Place; an' he fin'lly married her, again th' wishes iv Flaherty, who took to histin' in dhrinks, an' missed his jooty, an' was a scandal in th' parish f'r six months.

"O'Grady didn't improve with mathrimony, but got to lanin' again th' ol' stuff, an' walkin' up an' down th' sidewalk in his shirt-sleeves, with his thumbs stuck in his vest, an' his little pipe turned upside down; an', whin he see Flaherty, 'twas his custom to run him up an alley, so that th' little tailor man niver had a minyit iv peace. Ivry wan supposed he lived in a three most iv th' time, to be out iv th' way iv O'Grady.

"Well, wan day O'Grady he seen Flaherty walkin' down th' sthreet with a pair iv lavender pants f'r Willum Joyce to wear to th' Ogden Grove picnic, an' thried to heave a brick at him. He lost his balance, an' fell fr'm th' scaffoldin' he was wurrukin' on; an' th' last wurruds he said was, 'Did I get him or didn't I?' Mrs. O'Grady said it was th' will iv Gawd; an' he was burrid at Calvary with a funeral iv eighty hacks, an' a great manny people in their own buggies. Dorsey, th' conthractor, was there with his wife. He thought th' wurruld an' all iv O'Grady.

"Wan year afterward Flaherty begun makin' up to Mrs.

O'Grady; an' ivry wan in th' parish seen it, an' was glad iv it, an' said it was scandalous. How it iver got out to O'Grady's pew in th' burryin' ground, I'll niver tell ye, an' th' Lord knows; but wan evenin' th' ghost iv O'Grady come back. Flaherty was settin' in th' parlor, smokin' a seegar, with O'Grady's slippers on his feet, whin th' spook come in in th' mos' natural way in the wurruld, kickin' th' dog. 'What ar-re ye doin' here, ye little farryer iv pants?' he says. Mrs. O'Grady was f'r faintin'; but O'Flaherty he says, says he: 'Be quite,' he says. 'I'll dale with him.' Thin to th' ghost: 'Have ye paid th' rint here, ye big ape?' he says. 'What d'ye mane be comin' back, whin th' landlord ain't heerd fr'm ye f'r a year?' he says. Well, O'Grady's ghost was that surprised he cud hardly speak. 'Ye ought to have betther manners thin insultin' th' dead,' he says. 'Ye ought to have betther manners thin to be lavin' ye'er coffin at this hour iv th' night, an' breakin' in on dacint people,' says Flaherty. 'What good does it do to have rayqueem masses f'r th' raypose iv th' like iv you,' he says, 'that doesn't know his place?' he says. 'I'm masther iv this house,' says th' ghost. 'Not on ye'er life,' says Flaherty. 'Get out iv here, or I'll make th' ghost iv a ghost out iv ye. I can lick anny dead man that iver lived,' he said.

"With that th' ghost iv O'Grady made a pass at him, an' they clinched an' rowled on th' flure. Now a ghost is no aisy mark f'r anny man, an' O'Grady's ghost was as sthrong as a cow. It had Flaherty down on th' flure an' was feedin' him with a book they call th' 'Christyan Martyrs,' whin Mrs. O'Grady put a bottle in Flaherty's hands. 'What's this?' says Flaherty. 'Howly wather,' says Mrs. O'Grady. 'Sprinkle it on him,' says Mrs. O'Grady. 'Woman,' says th' tailor between th' chapters iv th' book, 'this is no time f'r miracles,' he says. An' he give O'Grady's ghost a treminjous wallop on th' head. Now, whether it was th' wather or th' wallop, I'll not tell ye; but, annyhow, th' ghost give wan yell an' disappeared. An' th' very next Sundah, whin Father Kelly wint into th' pulpit at th' gospel, he read th' names iv Roger Kickham Flaherty an' Mary Ann O'Grady."

"Did the ghost ever come back?" asked Mr. McKenna.

"Niver," said Mr. Dooley. "Wanst was enough. But, mind ye, I'd hate to have been wan iv th' other ghosts th' night O'Grady got home fr'm th' visit to O'Flaherty's. There might be ghosts that cud stand him off with th' gloves, but in a round an' tumble fight he cud lick a St. Patrick's Day procession iv thim."

THE HAY FLEET[1]

Mr. Dooley had been reading about General Shafter's unfortunately abandoned enterprise for capturing Santiago by means of a load of hay, and it filled him with great enthusiasm. Laying down his paper, he said: "By dad, I always said they give me frind Shafter th' worst iv it. If they'd left him do th' job th' way he wanted to do it, he'd 've taken Sandago without losin' an ounce."

"How was it he wanted to do it?" Mr. Hennessy asked.

"Well," said Mr. Dooley, "'twas this way. This is th' way it was. Ol' Cervera's fleet was in th' harbor an' bottled up, as th' man says. Shafter he says to Sampson: 'Look here, me bucko, what th' divvle ar-re ye loafin' ar-round out there f'r,' he says, 'like a dep'ty sheriff at a prize fight?' he says. 'Why don't ye go in, an' smash th' Castiles?' he says. 'I'm doin' well where I am,' says Sampson. 'Th' navy iv th' United States,' he says, 'which is wan iv th' best, if not th' best, in th' wurruld,' he says, 'was not,' he says, 'intinded f'r sthreet fightin',' he says. 'We'll stay here,' he says, 'where we ar-re,' he says, 'until,' he says, 'we can equip th' ships with noomatic tire wheels,' he says, 'an' ball bearin's,' he says.

"'Well,' says Shafter, 'if ye won't go in,' he says, 'we'll show ye th' way,' he says. An' he calls on Cap Brice, that was wan iv th' youngest an' tastiest dhressers in th' whole crool an' devastatin' war. 'Cap,' he says, 'is they anny hay in th' camp?' he says. 'Slathers iv it,' says th' cap. 'Onless,' he says, 'th' sojers et it,' he says. 'Th' las' load iv beef that come down fr'm th' undhertakers,' he says, 'was not good,' he says. 'Ayether,' he says, ''twas improperly waked,' he says, 'or,' he says, 'th' pall-bearers was careless,' he says. 'Annyhow,' he says, 'th' sojers won't eat it; an', whin I left, they was lookin' greedily at th' hay,' he says. 'Cap,' says Gin'ral Shafter, 'if anny man ates a wisp, shoot him on th' spot,' he says. 'Those hungry sojers may desthroy me hopes iv victhry,' he says. 'What d'ye mane?' says Cap Brice. 'I mane this,' says Gin'ral Shafter. 'I mane to take yon fortress,' he says. 'I'll sind ye in, Cap,' he says, 'in a ship protected be hay,' he says. 'Her turrets 'll be alfalfa, she'll have three inches iv solid timithy to th' water line, an' wan inch iv th' best clover below

[1] General W. R. Shafter, commander of the expeditionary force to Santiago de Cuba, was subjected to considerable press criticism for alleged deficiencies in subsistence and equipment.

th' wather line,' he says. 'Did ye iver see an eight-inch shell pinithrate a bale iv hay?' he says. 'I niver did,' says Cap Brice. 'Maybe that was because I niver see it thried,' he says. 'Be that as it may,' says Gin'ral Shafter, 'ye niver see it done. No more did I,' he says. 'Onless,' he says, 'they shoot pitchforks,' he says, 'they'll niver hur-rt ye,' he says. 'Ye'll be onvincible,' he says. 'Ye'll pro-ceed into th' harbor,' he says, 'behind th' sturdy armor iv projuce,' he says. 'Let ye'er watchword be "Stay on th' far-rm,"' an' go on to victhry,' he says. 'Gin'ral,' says Cap Brice, 'how can I thank ye f'r th' honor?' he says. ''Tis no wondher th' men call ye their fodder,' he says. 'Twas a joke Cap Brice med at th' time. 'I'll do th' best I can,' he says; 'an', if I die in th' attempt,' he says, 'bury me where the bran-mash 'll wave over me grave,' he says.

"An' Gin'ral Shafter he got together his fleet, an' put th' armor on it. 'Twas a formidable sight. They was th' cruiser 'Box Stall,' full armored with sixty-eight bales iv th' finest grade iv chopped feed; th' 'R-red Barn,' a modhern hay battleship, protected be a whole mow iv timothy; an' th' gallant little 'Haycock,' a torpedo boat shootin' deadly missiles iv explosive oats. Th' expedition was delayed be wan iv th' mules sthrollin' down to th' shore an' atin' up th' affther batthry an' par-rt iv th' ram iv th' 'R-red Barn' an', befure repairs was made, Admiral Cervera heerd iv what was goin' on. 'Glory be to the saints,' he says, 'what an injaynious thribe these Yankees is!' says he. 'On'y a few weeks ago they thried to desthroy me be dumpin' a load iv coal on me,' he says; 'an' now,' he says, 'they're goin' to smother me in feed,' he says. 'They'll be rollin' bar'ls iv flour on me fr'm th' heights next,' he says. 'I'd betther get out,' he says. ''Tis far nobler,' he says, 'to purrish on th' ragin' main,' he says, 'thin to die with ye'er lungs full iv hayseed an' ye'er eyes full iv dust,' he says. 'I was born in a large city,' he says; 'an' I don't know th' rules iv th' barn,' he says. An' he wint out, an' took his lickin'.

"'Twas too bad Shafter didn't get a chanst at him, but he's give th' tip to th' la-ads that makes th' boats. No more ixpinsive steel an' ir'n, but good ol' grass fr'm th' twinty-acre meadow. Th' ship-yards 'll be moved fr'm th' say, an' laid down in th' neighborhood iv Polo, Illinye, an' all th' Mississippi Valley'll ring with th' sound iv th' scythe an' th' pitchfork buildin' th' definse iv our counthry's honor. Thank th' Lord, we've winrows an' winrows iv Shafter's armor plate between here an' Dubuque."

Mr. Hennessy said good-night. "As me cousin used to say," he remarked, "we're through with wan hell iv a bad year, an' here goes f'r another like it."

"Well," said Mr. Dooley, "may th' Lord niver sind us a foolisher wan than this!"

THE DECLINE OF NATIONAL FEELING

"What ar-re ye goin' to do Patrick's Day?" asked Mr. Hennessy.

"Patrick's Day?" said Mr. Dooley. "Patrick's Day? It seems to me I've heard th' name befure. Oh, ye mane th' day th' low Irish that hasn't anny votes cillybrates th' birth iv their naytional saint, who was a Fr-rinchman."

"Ye know what I mane," said Mr. Hennessy, with rising wrath. "Don't ye get gay with me now."

"Well," said Mr. Dooley, "I may cillybrate it an' I may not. I'm thinkin' iv savin' me enthusyasm f'r th' queen's birthday, whiniver it is that that blessid holiday comes ar-round. Ye see, Hinnissy, Patrick's Day is out iv fashion now. A few years ago ye'd see the Prisident iv th' United States marchin' down Pinnsyl-vanya Avnoo, with the green scarf iv th' Ancient Ordher on his shoulders an' a shamrock in his hat. Now what is Mack doin'? He's settin' in his parlor, writin' letthers to th' queen, be hivins, askin' afther her health. He was fr'm th' north iv Ireland two years ago, an' not so far north ayether—just far enough north f'r to be on good terms with Derry an' not far enough to be bad frinds with Limerick. He was raised on butthermilk an' haggis, an' he dhrank his Irish nate with a dash iv orange bitthers in it. He's been movin' steadily north since; an', if he keeps on movin', he'll go r-round th' globe, an' bring up somewhere in th' south iv England.

"An' Hinnery Cabin Lodge! I used to think that Hinnery would niver die contint till he'd took th' Prince iv Wales be th' hair iv th' head—an' 'tis little th' poor man's got—an' dhrag him fr'm th' tower iv London to Kilmainham Jail, an' hand him over to th' tindher mercies, as Hogan says, iv Michael Davitt. Thim was th' days whin ye'd hear Hinnery in th' Sinit, spreadin' fear to th' hear-rts iv th' British aristocracy. 'Gintlemen,' he says, 'an' fellow-sinitors, th' time has come,' he says, 'whin th' eagle burrud iv freedom,' he says, 'lavin',' he says, 'its home in th' mountains,' he says, 'an' circlin',' he says; 'undher th' jool'd hivin,' he says, 'fr'm where,' he says, 'th' Passamaquoddy rushes into Lake Erastus K. Ropes,' he says, 'to where rowls th' Oregon,' he says, 'fr'm th' lakes to th' gulf,' he says, 'fr'm th' Atlantic to th' Passific where rowls th' Oregon,' he says, 'an' fr'm ivry American who has th' blood iv his ancesthors' hathred iv tyranny in his veins—your ancesthors an' mine, Mr. McAdoo,' he says—'there goes up a mute prayer that th' nation as wan man, fr'm Bangor, Maine, to where rowls th' Oregon, that,' he says, 'is full iv salmon, which is later put up in cans, but has th' same inthrest as all others in this question,' he says, 'that,' he says, 'th' descindants iv Wash'nton an',' he says, 'iv Immitt,' he says, 'will jine hands f'r to protect,' he says, 'th' codfisheries again th' Vandal hand iv th' British line,' he says. 'I therefore move ye, Mr. Prisident, that it is th' sinse iv this house, if anny such there be, that Tay Pay O'Connor is a greater man thin Lord Salisberry,' he says.

"Now where's Hinnery? Where's th' bould Fenian? Where's th' moonlighter? Where's th' pikeman? Faith, he's changed his chune, an' 'tis 'Sthrangers wanst, but brothers now,' with him, an' 'Hands acrost th' sea an' into some wan's pocket,' an' 'Take up th' white man's burden an' hand it to th' coons,' an' 'An open back dure an' a closed fr-ront dure.' 'Tis th' same with all iv thim. They'se me frind Joe Choate. Where'd Joe spind th' night? Whisper, in Windsor Castle, no less, in a night-shirt iv th' Prince iv Wales; an' the nex' mornin', whin he come down-stairs, they tol' him th' rile fam'ly was late risers, but, if he wanted a good time, he cud go down an' look at th' cimit'ry! An' he done it. He went out an' wept over th' grave iv th' Father iv his Counthry. Ye'er man, George Washington, Hinnissy, was on'y th' stepfather.

"Well, glory be, th' times has changed since me frind Jawn Finerty come out iv th' House iv Riprisintatives; an', whin some wan ast him what was goin' on, he says, 'Oh, nawthin' at all but some damned American business.' Thim was th' days! An' what's changed thim? Well, I might be sayin' 'twas like wanst whin me cousin Mike an' a Kerry man be th' name iv Sullivan had a gredge again a man named Doherty, that was half a Kerry man himsilf. They kept Doherty indures f'r a day, but by an' by me cousin Mike lost intherest in th' gredge, havin' others that was newer, an' he wint over to th' ya-ards; an' Doherty an' Sullivan begin to bow to each other, an' afther a while they found that they were blood relations, an', what's closer thin that whin ye're away fr'm home, townies. An' they hooked arms, an' sthrutted up an' down th' road, as proud as imprors. An' says they, 'We can lick annything in th' ward,' says they. But, befure they injyed th' 'lieance f'r long, around th' corner comes me cousin Mike, with a half-brick in each hand; an' me brave Sullivan gives Doherty th' Kerry man's thrip, an' says he, 'Mike,' he says, 'I was on'y pullin' him on to give ye a crack at him,' he says. An' they desthroyed Doherty, so that he was in bed f'r a week."

"Well, I wondher will Mike come back?" said Mr. Hennessy.

"Me cousin Mike," said Mr. Dooley, "niver missed an iliction. An' whin th' campaign opened, there wasn't a man on th' ticket, fr'm mayor to constable, that didn't claim him f'r a first cousin. There are different kinds iv hands from acrost th' sea. There are pothry hands an' rollin'-mill hands; but on'y wan kind has votes."

"CYRANO DE BERGERAC"

"Ivry winter Hogan's la-ad gives a show with what he calls th' Sixth Wa-ard Shakspere an' Willum J. Bryan Club, an' I was sayjooced into goin' to wan las' night at Finucane's hall," said Mr. Dooley.

"Th' girls was goin'," said Mr. Hennessy; "but th' sthovepipe come down on th' pianny, an' we had a minsthrel show iv our own. What was it about, I dinnaw?"

"Well, sir," said Mr. Dooley, "I ain't much on th' theayter. I niver wint to wan that I didn't have to stand where I cud see a man in blue overalls scratchin' his leg just beyant where the heeroyne was prayin' on th' palace stairs, an' I don't know much about it; but it seemed to me, an' it seemed to Hartigan, th' plumber, that was with me, that 'twas a good play if they'd been a fire in th' first act. They was a lot iv people there; an', if it cud've been arranged f'r to have injine company fifteen with Cap'n Duffy at th' head iv thim come in through a window an' carry off th' crowd, 'twud've med a hit with me.

"'Tis not like anny play I iver see befure or since. In 'Tur-rble Tom; or, th' Boys iv Ninety-eight,' that I see wanst, th' man that's th' main guy iv th' thing he waits till ivry wan has said what he has to say, an' he has a clean field; an' thin he jumps in as th' man that plays th' big dhrum gives it an upper cut.   But with this here play iv 'Cyrus O'Bergerac' 'tis far diff'rent.   Th' curtain goes up an' shows Bill Delaney an' little Tim Scanlan an' Mark Toolan an' Packy Dugan, that wurruks in the shoe store, an' Molly Donahue an' th' Casey sisters, thim that scandalized th' parish be doin' a skirt dance at th' fair, all walkin' up an' down talkin'.   'Tin to wan on Sharkey,' says Toolan.   'I go ye, an' make it a hundherd,' says Tim Scanlan.   'Was ye at th' cake walk?'   'Who stole me hat?'   'Cudden't ye die waltzin'?' 'They say Murphy has gone on th' foorce.'   'Hivins, there goes th' las' car!'   'Pass th' butther, please: I'm far fr'm home.'   All iv thim talkin' away at once, niver carin' f'r no wan, whin all at wanst up stheps me bold Hogan with a nose on him—glory be, such a nose!   I niver see th' like on a man or an illyphant.

"Well, sir, Hogan is Cy in th' play; an' th' beak is pa-art iv him. What does he do?   He goes up to Toolan, an' says he: 'Ye don't like me nose.   It's an ilicthric light globe.   Blow it out.   It's a Swiss cheese.   Cut it off, if ye want to.   It's a brick in a hat. Kick it.   It's a balloon.   Hang a basket on it, an' we'll have an' ascinsion.   It's a dure-bell knob.   Ring it.   It's a punchin' bag. Hit it, if ye dahr.   F'r two pins I'd push in th' face iv ye.'   An', mind ye, Hinnissy, Toolan had said not wan wurrud about th' beak—not wan wurrud.   An' ivry wan in th' house was talkin' about it, an' wondhrin' whin it'd come off an' smash somewan's fut.   I looked f'r a fight there an' thin.   But Toolan's a poor-spirited thing, an' he wint away.   At that up comes Scanlan; an' says he: 'Look here, young fellow,' he says, 'don't get gay,' he says, 'don't get gay,' he says.   'What's that?' says Hogan.   Whin a man says, 'What's that?' in a bar-room, it manes a fight, if he says it wanst.   If he says it twict, it manes a fut race.   'I say,' says Scanlan, 'that, if ye make anny more funny cracks, I'll hitch a horse to that basket fender,' he says, 'an' dhrag it fr'm ye,' he says. At that Hogan dhrew his soord, an' says he: 'Come on,' he says, 'come on, an' take a lickin',' he says.   An' Scanlan dhrew his soord, too.   'Wait,' says Hogan.   'Wait a minyit,' he says.   'I must think,' he says.   'I must think a pome,' he says.   'Whiniver I fight,' he says, 'I always have a pome,' he says.   'Glory be,' says I, 'there's Scanlan's chanst to give it to him,' I says.   But Scanlan was as slow as a dhray; an', befure he cud get action, Hogan was at him, l'adin' with th' pome an' counthrin' with the soord. 'I'll call this pome,' he says, 'a pome about a gazabo I wanst had a dool with in Finucane's hall,' he says. 'I'll threat ye r-right,' he says, 'an' at the last line I'll hand ye wan,' he says. An' he done it. 'Go in,' he says in th' pome, 'go in an do ye'er worst,' he says. 'I make a pass at ye'er stomach,' he says, 'I cross ye with me right,' he says; 'an',' he says, at th' last line he says, 'I soak ye,' he says. An' he done it. Th' minyit 'twas over with th' pome 'twas off with Scanlan. Th' soord wint into him, an' he sunk down to th' flure; an' they had to carry him off. Well, sir, Hogan was that proud ye cudden't hold him f'r th' rest iv th' night. He wint around ivrywhere stickin' people an' soakin' thim with pothry. He's a gr-reat pote is this here Hogan, an' a gr-reat fighter. He done thim all at both; but, like me ol' frind Jawn L., he come to th' end. A man dhropped a two-be-four on his head wan day, an' he died. Honoria Casey was with him as he passed away, an' she says, 'How d'ye feel?' 'All right,' says Hogan. 'But wan thing I'll tell ye has made life worth livin',' he says. 'What's that?' says Miss Casey. 'I know,' says I. 'Annywan cud guess it. He manes his nose,' I says. But ivry-wan on th' stage give it up. 'Ye don't know,' says Hogan. ''Tis me hat,' he says; an', makin a low bow to th' audjence, he fell to th' flure so hard that his nose fell off an' rowled down on Mike Finnegan. 'I don't like th' play,' says Finnegan, 'an' I'll break ye'er nose,' he says; an' he done it. He's a wild divvle. Hogan thried to rayturn th' compliment on th' sidewalk afterward; but he cudden't think iv a pome, an' Finnegan done him."

"Well," said Mr. Hennessy, "I'd like to've been there to see th' fightin'."

"In th' play?" asked Mr. Dooley.

"No," said Mr. Hennessy. "On th' sidewalk."

THE UNION OF TWO GREAT FORTUNES

"They'se wan thing that always makes me feel sure iv what Hogan calls th' safety iv our dimmycratic institutions," said Mr. Dooley, "an' that's th' intherest th' good people iv New York takes in a weddin' iv th' millyionaires. Anny time a millyionaire condiscinds to enther th' martial state, as Hogan says, an', as Hogan says, make vows to Hyman, which is the Jew god iv mar-redge, he can fill th' house an' turn people away fr'm th' dure.

An' he does. Th' sthreets is crowded. Th' cars can har'ly get
through. Th' polis foorce is out, an' hammerin' th' heads iv th'
delighted throng. Riprisintatives iv th' free an' inlightened press,
th' pollutyem iv our liberties, as Hogan says, bright, intilligent
young journalists, iver ready to probe fraud an' sham, disgeesed
as waithers, is dashin' madly about, makin' notes on their cuffs.
Business is suspinded. They'se no money in Wall Sthreet. It's
all at th' sacred scene. Hour be hour, as th' prisints ar-re
delivered, th' bank rates go up. Th' Threeasury Departmint
has to go on a silver basis, there bein' no goold to mannyfacther
into plunks.

"Inside th' house th' prisints cast a goolden gleam on th'
beauchious scene. Th' happy father is seen seated at a table,
dictattin' millyion-dollar checks to a stinographer. Th' goold
chandeliers is draped with r-ropes iv dimon's an' pearls. Th'
hired girl is passin' dhrinks in goolden goblets. Twinty firemen
fr'm th' New York Cinthral Railroad is shovellin' di'mon'-
studded pickle crutes into th' back yard, among th' yachts an'
horses. Chansy Depoo enthers an' thrips over a box iv bonds.
'Ar-re these th' holy bonds iv mathrimony?' he says; f'r he is a
wild divvle, an' ye can't stop his jokin', avin on solemn occasions.

"Th' soggarth comes in afther a while, carryin' a goold prayer-
book, th' gift iv th' Rothscheelds, an' stands behind a small but
valyable pree Doo. To th' soft, meelojous chune iv th' Wagner
Palace Weddin' March fr'm 'Long Green,' th' groom enthers,
simply but ixpinsively attired in governmint fours, an' fannin'
himsilf with a bunch iv first morgedge bonds.

"Th' prayers f'r th' occasion, printed on negotyable paper, is
disthributed among th' guests. Th' bride was delayed be th'
crowd outside. Women screamed an' waved their handkerchefs,
sthrong men cheered an' wept; an' 'twas not until th' polis had
clubbed tin hardy pathrites to death that th' lady cud enther th'
house where her fate was to be sealed. But fin'lly she med it;
an' th' two happy, happy childher, whose sunshiny youth riprisinted five thousan' miles iv thrack, eight goold mines, wan hundherd millyion dollars' worth iv rollin' stock, an' a majority
intherest in th' Chicago stock yards, was r-ready f'r th' nicissary
thransfers that wud establish th' com-bination.

"Th' ceremony was brief, but intherestin'. Th' happy father
foorced his way through dimon' stomachers; an' they was tears in
his eyes as he handed th' clargyman, whose name was Murphy—

but he carried himsilf as well as if he was used to it—handed him
a check f'r tin millyion dollars. I don't blame him. Divvle th'
bit! Me own hear-rt is har-rd an' me eyes ar-re dhry, but I'd
break down if I had to hand anny wan that much. 'I suppose th'
check is good,' says th' clargyman. ''Tis certified,' says th'
weepin' father. 'Do ye take this check,' says th' clargyman, 'to
have an' to hold, until some wan parts ye fr'm it?' he says. 'I do,'
says th' young man. 'Thin,' says th' clargyman, 'I see no reason
why ye shudden't be marrid an' live comfortable,' he says. An'
marrid they were, in th' same ol' foolish way that people's been
marrid in f'r cinchries. 'Tis a wondher to me th' ceremony ain't
changed. Th' time is comin', Hinnissy, whin millyionaires 'll
not be marrid be Father Murphy, but be th gov'nors iv th' stock
exchange. They'll be put through th' clearin' house, me faith, an'
securities 'll be issued be th' combination. Twinty-year, goold-
secured, four per cint bonds iv mathrimony! Aha, 'tis a joke that
Chansy Depoo might 've med!

"Th' crowd outside waited, cheerin' an' fightin' th' polis. In
this here land iv liberty an' akequality, Hinnissy, ivry man is as
good as ivry other man, except a polisman. An' it showed how
thrue th' people in New York is to th' thraditions iv Jefferson that
divvle a wan iv thim 'd move away till th' check 'd been passed
fr'm father to son, an' th' important part iv th' sacred ceremony
was over. Thin a few iv thim wint home to cook dinner f'r their
husbands, who was previnted be their jooties at th' gas-house
fr'm attindin' th' function. Th' rest raymained an' see th' two
gr-reat fortunes get into their carredge, pursued be th' guests to
th' amount iv five hundhred millyions, peltin' thim with seed
pearls."

"Sure," said Mr. Hennessy, "mebbe 'twasn't as bad as th'
pa-apers let on. Ye can't always thrust thim."

"P'rhaps not," said Mr. Dooley. "Th' pa-apers say, 'Two
gr-reat fortunes united'; an', if that's it, they didn't need th'
sarvices iv a priest, but a lawyer an' a thrust comp'ny. P'rhaps,
with all th' certyfied checks, 'twas two rale people that was marrid;
an', if that's so, it explains th' prisince iv Father Murphy."

MR. DOOLEY'S PHILOSOPHY

A BOOK REVIEW[1]

"Well sir," said Mr. Dooley, "I jus' got hold iv a book, Hinnissy, that suits me up to th' handle, a gran' book, th' grandest iver seen. Ye know I'm not much throubled be lithrachoor, havin' manny worries iv me own, but I'm not prejudiced again' books. I am not. Whin a rale good book comes along I'm as quick as anny wan to say it isn't so bad, an' this here book is fine. I tell ye 'tis fine."

"What is it?" Mr. Hennessy asked languidly.

"'Tis 'Th' Biography iv a Hero be Wan who Knows.' 'Tis 'Th' Darin' Exploits iv a Brave Man be an Actual Eye Witness.' 'Tis 'Th' Account iv th' Desthruction iv Spanish Power in th' Ant Hills,' as it fell fr'm th' lips iv Tiddy Rosenfelt an' was took down be his own hands. Ye see 'twas this way, Hinnissy, as I r-read th' book. Whin Tiddy was blowed up in th' harbor iv Havana he instantly con-cluded they must be war. He debated th' question long an' earnestly an' fin'lly passed a jint resolution declarin' war. So far so good. But there was no wan to carry it on. What shud he do? I will lave th' janial author tell th' story in his own wurruds.

"'Th' sicrety iv war had offered me,' he says, 'th' command of a rig'mint,' he says, 'but I cud not consint to remain in Tampa while perhaps less audacious heroes was at th' front,' he says. 'Besides,' he says, 'I felt I was incompetent f'r to command a

[1] This review of Theodore Roosevelt's *The Rough Riders*—published when Roosevelt was Governor of New York—was one of Dunne's most famous essays. Roosevelt, perhaps to ward off a second attack, wrote to Dunne saying, "I regret to state that my family and intimate friends are delighted with your review of my book." After they met and became friends, Roosevelt—according to Elmer Ellis in *Mr. Dooley's America* (Knopf, 1941)—reportedly told Dunne of meeting a young woman who disclosed that her favorite of T.R.'s books was the one called *Alone in Cuba*.

rig'mint raised be another,' he says. 'I detarmined to raise wan iv me own,' he says. 'I selected fr'm me acquaintances in th' West,' he says, 'men that had thravelled with me acrost th' desert an' th' storm-wreathed mountain,' he says, 'sharin' me burdens an' at times confrontin' perils almost as gr-reat as anny that beset me path,' he says. 'Together we had faced th' turrors iv th' large but vilent West,' he says, 'an' these brave men had seen me with me trusty rifle shootin' down th' buffalo, th' elk, th' moose, th' grizzly bear, th' mountain goat,' he says, 'th' silver man, an' other ferocious beasts iv thim parts,' he says. 'An' they niver flinched,' he says. 'In a few days I had thim perfectly tamed,' he says, 'an' ready to go annywhere I led,' he says. 'On th' thransport goin' to Cubia,' he says, 'I wud stand beside wan iv these r-rough men threatin' him as a akel, which he was in ivrything but birth, education, rank an' courage, an' together we wud look up at th' admirable stars iv that tolerable southern sky an' quote th' bible fr'm Walt Whitman,' he says. 'Honest, loyal, thrue-hearted la-ads, how kind I was to thim,' he says.

"'We had no sooner landed in Cubia than it become nicessry f'r me to take command iv th' ar-rmy which I did at wanst. A number of days was spint be me in reconnoitring, attinded on'y be me brave an' fluent body guard, Richard Harding Davis. I discovered that th' inimy was heavily inthrenched on th' top iv San Joon hill immejiately in front iv me. At this time it become apparent that I was handicapped be th' prisence iv th' ar-rmy,' he says. 'Wan day whin I was about to charge a block house sturdily definded be an ar-rmy corps undher Gin'ral Tamale, th' brave Castile that I aftherwards killed with a small ink-eraser that I always carry, I r-ran into th' entire military force iv th' United States lying on its stomach. 'If ye won't fight,' says I, 'let me go through,' I says. 'Who ar-re ye?' says they. 'Colonel Rosenfelt,' says I. 'Oh, excuse me,' says the gin'ral in command (if me mimry serves me thrue it was Miles) r-risin' to his knees an' salutin'. This showed me 'twud be impossible f'r to carry th' war to a successful con-clusion unless I was free, so I sint th' ar-rmy home an' attackted San Joon hill. Ar-rmed on'y with a small thirty-two which I used in th' West to shoot th' fleet prairie dog, I climbed that precipitous ascent in th' face iv th' most gallin' fire I iver knew or heerd iv. But I had a few r-rounds iv gall mesilf an' what cared I? I dashed madly on cheerin' as I wint. Th' Spanish throops was dhrawn up in a long line in th' formation known among military men as a long line. I fired at th' man nearest to me an' I knew be th' expression iv his face that th' trusty bullet wint home. It passed through his frame, he fell, an' wan little home in far-off Catalonia was made happy be th' thought that their riprisintative had been kilt be th' future governor iv New York. Th' bullet sped on its mad flight an' passed through th' intire line fin'lly imbeddin' itself in th' abdomen iv th' Ar-rch-bishop iv Santiago eight miles away. This ended th' war.

"'They has been some discussion as to who was th' first man to r-reach th' summit iv San Juon hill. I will not attempt to dispute th' merits iv th' manny gallant sojers, statesmen, corryspondints an' kinetoscope men who claim th' distinction. They ar-re all brave men an' if they wish to wear my laurels they may. I have so manny annyhow that it keeps me broke havin' thim blocked an' irned. But I will say f'r th' binifit iv Posterity that I was th' on'y man I see. An' I had a tillyscope.'

"I have thried, Hinnissy," Mr. Dooley continued, "to give you a fair idee iv th' contints iv this remarkable book, but what I've tol' ye is on'y what Hogan calls an outline iv th' principal pints. Ye'll have to r-read th' book ye'ersilf to get a thrue conciption. I haven't time f'r to tell ye th' wurruk Tiddy did in ar-rmin' an' equippin' himself, how he fed himsilf, how he steadied himsilf in battle an' encouraged himsilf with a few well-chosen wurruds whin th' sky was darkest. Ye'll have to take a squint into th' book ye'ersilf to l'arn thim things."

"I won't do it," said Mr. Hennessy. "I think Tiddy Rosenfelt is all r-right an' if he wants to blow his hor-rn lave him do it."

"Thrue f'r ye," said Mr. Dooley, "an' if his valliant deeds didn't get into this book 'twud be a long time befure they appeared in Shafter's histhry iv th' war. No man that bears a gredge again' himself 'll iver be governor iv a state. An' if Tiddy done it all he ought to say so an' relieve th' suspinse. But if I was him I'd call th' book 'Alone in Cubia.'"

AMERICANS ABROAD[1]

"I wondher," said Mr. Dooley, "what me Dutch frind Oom Paul'll think whin he hears that Willum Waldorf Asthor has given four thousan' pounds or twinty thousan' iv our money as a conthribution to th' British governmint?"

[1] Dunne wrote this essay soon after returning from his first trip to Europe.

"Who's Willum Waldorf Asthor?" Mr. Hennessy asked. "I niver heerd iv him."

"Ye wudden't," said Mr. Dooley. "He don't thravel in ye'er set. Willum Waldorf Asthor is a gintleman that wanst committed th' sin iv bein' bor-rn in this counthry. Ye know what orig-inal sin is, Hinnissy. Ye was bor-rn with wan an' I was bor-rn with wan an' ivrybody was bor-rn with wan. 'Twas took out iv me be Father Tuomy with holy wather first an' be me father aftherward with a sthrap. But I niver cud find out what it was. Th' sins I've committed since, I'm sure iv. They're painted red an' carry a bell an' whin I'm awake in bed they stan' out on th' wall like th' ilicthric signs they have down be State sthreet in front iv th' clothin' stores. But I'll go to th' grave without knowin' exactly what th' black orig-inal sin was I committed. All I know is I done wrong. But with Willum Waldorf Asthor 'tis diff'rent. I say 'tis diff'rent with Willum Waldorf Asthor. His orig-inal sin was bein' bor-rn in New York. He cudden't do anything about it. Nawthin' in this counthry wud wipe it out. He built a hotel intinded f'r jooks who had no sins but thim iv their own makin', but even th' sight iv their haughty bills cud not efface th' stain. He thried to live down his crime without success an' he thried to live down to it be runnin' f'r congress, but it was no go. No matther where he wint among his counthrymen in England some wan wud find out he was bor-rn in New York an' th' man that ownded th' house where he was spindin' th' night wud ast him if he was a cannibal an' had he anny Indyan blood in his veins. 'Twas like seein' a fine lookin' man with an intellecjal forehead an' handsome, dar-rk brown eyes an' admirin' him, an' thin larnin' his name is Mudd J. Higgins. His accint was proper an' his clothes didn't fit him right, but he was not bor-rn in th' home iv his dayscindants, an' whin he walked th' sthreets iv London he knew ivry polisman was sayin': 'There goes a man that pretinds to be happy, but a dark sorrow is gnawin' at his bosom. He looks as if he was at home, but he was bor-rn in New York, Gawd help him.'

"So this poor way-worn sowl, afther thryin' ivry other rimidy fr'm dhrivin' a coach to failin' to vote, at las' sought out th' rile high clark iv th' coort an' says he: 'Behold,' he says, 'an onhappy man,' he says. 'With millyons in me pocket, two hotels an' onlimited credit,' he says, 'me hear-rt is gray,' he says. 'Poor sowl,' says th' clark iv th' coort, 'What's ailin' ye?' he says. 'Have ye committed some gr-reat crime?' he says. 'Partly,' says

Willum Waldorf Asthor. 'It was partly me an' partly me folks,'
he says. 'I was,' he says, in a voice broken be tears, 'I was,' he
says, 'bor-rn in New York,' he says. Th' clark made th' sign iv
th' cross an' says he: 'Ye shudden't have come here,' he says.
'Poor afflicted wretch,' he says, 'ye need a clargyman,' he says.
'Why did ye seek me out?' he says. 'Because,' says Willum
Waldorf Asthor, 'I wish,' he says, 'f'r to renounce me sinful life,'
he says. 'I wish to be bor-rn anew,' he says. An' th' clark bein'
a kind man helps him out. An' Willum Waldorf Asthor renounced fealty to all foreign sovereigns, princes an' potentates an'
especially Mack th' Wanst, or Twict, iv th' United States an'
Sulu an' all his wur-ruks an' he come out iv th' coort with his hat
cocked over his eye, with a step jaunty and high, afther years iv
servile freedom a bondman at last!

"So he's a citizen iv Gr-reat Britain now an' a lile subject iv
th' Queen like you was Hinnissy befure ye was r-run out."

"I niver was," said Mr. Hennessy. "Sure th' Queen iv
England was renounced f'r me long befure I did it f'r mesilf—to
vote."

"Well, niver mind," Mr. Dooley continued, "he's a citizen iv
England an' he has a castle that's as big as a hotel, on'y nobody goes
there excipt thim that's ast, an' not all of those, an' he owns a
newspaper an' th' editor iv it's the Prince iv Wales an' th' ray-
porthers is all jooks an' th' Archbishop iv Canterbury r-runs th'
ilivator, an' slug wan in th' printin' office is th' Impror iv Germany
in disgeese. 'Tis a pa-per I'd like to see. I'd like to know how
th' Jook iv Marlbro'd do th' McGovern fight. An' some day
Willum Waldorf Asthor'll be able to wurruk f'r his own pa-aper,
f'r he's goin' to be a earl or a markess or a jook or somethin' gran'.
Ye can't be anny iv these things without money, Hinnissy, an'
he has slathers iv it."

"Where does he get it?" demanded Mr. Hennessy.

"F'rm this counthry," said Mr. Dooley.

"I shud think," Mr. Hennessey protested stoutly, "if he's
ashamed iv this counthry he wudden't want to take money f'rm
it."

"That's where ye're wrong," Mr. Dooley replied. "Take
money annywhere ye find it. I'd take money f'rm England, much
as I despise that formerly haughty but now dejected land, if I cud
get anny from there. An' whin ye come down to it, I dinnaw as I
blame Willum Waldorf Asthor f'r shiftin' his allegiance. Ivry

wan to his taste as th' man said whin he dhrank out iv th' fire extinguisher. It depinds on how ye feel. If ye ar-re a tired la-ad an' wan without much fight in ye, livin' in this counthry is like thryin' to read th' Lives iv the Saints at a meetin' iv th' Clan-na-Gael. They'se no quiet f'r annybody. They's a fight on ivry minyit iv th' time. Ye may say to ye'ersilf: 'I'll lave these la-ads roll each other as much as they plaze, but I'll set here in th' shade an' dhrink me milk punch,' but ye can't do it. Some wan 'll say, 'Look at that gazabo settin' out there alone. He's too proud f'r to jine in our simple dimmycratic festivities. Lave us go over an' bate him on th' eye.' An' they do it. Now if ye have fightin' blood in ye'er veins ye hastily gulp down ye'er dhrink an' hand ye'er assailant wan that does him no kind iv good, an' th' first thing ye know ye're in th' thick iv it an' it's scrap, scrap, scrap till th' undhertaker calls f'r to measure ye. An' 'tis tin to wan they'se somethin' doin' at th' fun'ral that ye're sorry ye missed. That's life in America. 'Tis a gloryous big fight, a rough an' tumble fight, a Donnybrook fair three thousan' miles wide an' a ruction in ivry block. Head an' han's an' feet an' th' pitchers on th' wall. No holds barred. Fight fair but don't f'rget th' other la-ad may not know where th' belt line is. No polisman in sight. A man's down with twinty on top iv him wan minyit. Th' next he's settin' on th' pile usin' a base-ball bat on th' neighbor next below him. 'Come on, boys, f'r 'tis growin' late, an' no wan's been kilt yet. Glory be, but this is th' life!'

"Now, if I'm tired I don't want to fight. A man bats me in th' eye an' I call f'r th' polis. They isn't a polisman in sight. I say to th' man that poked me: 'Sir, I fain wud sleep.' 'Get up,' he says, 'an' be doin',' he says. 'Life is rale, life is earnest,' he says, 'an' man was made to fight,' he says, fetchin' me a kick. An' if I'm tired I say, 'What's th' use? I've got plenty iv money in me inside pocket. I'll go to a place where they don't know how to fight. I'll go where I can get something but an argymint f'r me money an' where I won't have to rassle with th' man that bates me carpets, ayether,' I says, 'f'r fifty cints overcharge or good govermint,' I says. An' I pike off to what Hogan calls th' effete monarchies iv Europe an' no wan walks on me toes, an' ivry man I give a dollar to becomes an acrobat an' I live comfortably an' die a markess! Th' divvle I do!"

"That's what I was goin' to say," Mr. Hennessy remarked. "Ye wudden't live annywhere but here."

"No," said Mr. Dooley, "I wudden't. I'd rather be Dooley iv Chicago than th' Earl iv Peltville. It must be that I'm iv th' fightin' kind."

SERVANT GIRL PROBLEM

"Whin Congress gets through expellin' mimbers that believes so much in mathrimony that they carry it into ivry relation iv life an' opens th' dure iv Chiny so that an American can go in there as free as a Chinnyman can come into this refuge iv th' opprissed iv th' wurruld, I hope 'twill turn its attintion to th' gr-reat question now confrontin' th' nation—th' question iv what we shall do with our hired help. What shall we do with thim?"

"We haven't anny," said Mr. Hennessy.

"No," said Mr. Dooley. "Ar-rchey r-road has no servant girl problem. Th' rule is ivry woman her own cook an' ivry man his own futman, an' be th' same token we have no poly-gamy problem an' no open dure problem an' no Ph'lippeen problem. Th' on'y problem in Ar-rchey r-road is how manny times does round steak go into twelve at wan dollar-an-a-half a day. But east iv th' r-red bridge, Hinnissy, wan iv th' most cryin' issues iv th' hour is: What shall we do with our hired help? An' if Congress don't take hold iv it we ar-re a rooned people.

"'Tis an ol' problem an' I've seen it arise an' shake its gory head ivry few years whiniver th' Swede popylation got wurruk an' begun bein' marrid, thus rayjoocin' th' visible supply iv help. But it seems 'tis deeper thin that. I see be letters in th' pa-apers that servants is insolent, an' that they won't go to wurruk onless they like th' looks iv their employers, an' that they rayfuse to live in th' counthry. Why anny servant shud rayfuse to live in th' counthry is more thin I can see. Ye'd think that this disreputable class'd give annything to lave th' crowded tinimints iv a large city where they have frinds be th' hundherds an' know th' polisman on th' bate an' can go out to hateful dances an' moonlight picnics— ye'd think these unforchnate slaves'd be delighted to live in Mulligan's subdivision, amid th' threes an' flowers an' bur-rds. Gettin' up at four o'clock in th' mornin' th' singin' iv th' full-throated alarm clock is answered be an invisible choir iv songsters, as Shakespere says, an' ye see th' sun rise over th' hills as ye go out to carry in a ton iv coal. All day long ye meet no wan as ye thrip over th' coal-scuttle, happy in ye'er tile an' ye'er heart is

enlivened be th' thought that th' childher in th' front iv th' house
ar-re growin' sthrong on th' fr-resh counthry air.   Besides they'se
always cookin' to do.   At night ye can set be th' fire an' improve
ye'er mind be r-readin' half th' love story in th' part iv th' pa-aper
that th' cheese come home in, an' whin ye're through with that,
all ye have to do is to climb a ladder to th' roof an' fall through th'
skylight an' ye're in bed.

   " But wud ye believe it, Hinnissy, manny iv these misguided
women rayfuse f'r to take a job that ain't in a city.   They prefer
th' bustle an' roar iv th' busy marts iv thrade, th' sthreet car, th'
saloon on three corners an' th' church on wan, th' pa-apers ivry
mornin' with pitchers iv th' s'ciety fav'rite that's just thrown up a
good job at Armours to elope with th' well-known club man who
used to be yard-masther iv th' three B's, G, L, & N., th' shy peek
into th' dhry-goods store, an' other base luxuries, to a free an'
healthy life in th' counthry between iliven P.M. an' four A.M.
Wensdahs an' Sundahs.   'Tis worse thin that, Hinnissy, f'r whin
they ar-re in th' city they seem to dislike their wurruk an' manny
iv thim ar-re givin' up splindid jobs with good large families where
they have no chanst to spind their salaries, if they dhraw thim, an'
takin' places in shops, an' gettin' marrid an' adoptin' other
devices that will give thim th' chanst f'r to wear out their good
clothes.   'Tis a horrible situation.   Riley th' conthractor dhropped in here th' other day in his horse an' buggy on his way to
the dhrainage canal an' he was all wurruked up over th' question.
'Why,' he says, ''tis scand'lous th' way servants act,' he says.
'Mrs. Riley has hystrics,' he says.   'An' ivry two or three nights
whin I come home,' he says, 'I have to win a fight again' a cook
with a stove lid befure I can move me family off th' fr-ront stoop,'
he says.   'We threat thim well too,' he says.   'I gave th' las' wan
we had fifty cints an' a cook book at Chris'mas an' th' next day she
left befure breakfast,' he says.   'What naytionalties do ye hire ?'
says I.   'I've thried thim all,' he says, 'an',' he says, 'I'll say this
in shame,' he says, 'that th' Irish ar-re th' worst,' he says.   'Well,'
says I, 'ye need have no shame,' I says, 'f'r 'tis on'y th' people
that ar-re good servants that'll niver be masthers,' I says.   'Th'
Irish ar-re no good as servants because they ar-re too good,' I says.
'Th' Dutch ar-re no good because they ain't good enough.   No
matther how they start they get th' noodle habit.   I had wan,
wanst, an' she got so she put noodles in me tay,' I says.   'Th'
Swedes ar-re all right but they always get marrid th' sicond day.

Ye'll have a polisman at th' dure with a warrant f'r th' arrist iv ye'er cook if ye hire a Boheemyan,' I says. 'Coons'd be all right but they're liable f'r to hand ye ye'er food in ragtime, an' if ye ordher pork-chops f'r dinner an' th' hall is long, 'tis little ye'll have to eat whin th' platter's set down,' I says. 'No,' says I, 'they'se no naytionality now livin' in this counthry that're nathral bor-rn servants,' I says. 'If ye want to save throuble,' I says, 'ye'll import ye'er help. They'se a race iv people livin' in Cinthral Africa that'd be jus' r-right. They niver sleep, they can carry twice their weight on their backs, they have no frinds, they wear no clothes, they can't read, they can't dance an' they don't dhrink. Th' fact is they're thoroughly oneddycated. If ye cud tache thim to cook an' take care iv childher they'd be th' best servants,' says I. 'An' what d'ye call thim ?' says he. 'I f'rget,' says I. An' he wint away mad."

"Sure an' he's a nice man to be talkin' iv servants," said Mr. Hennessy. "He was a gintleman's man in th' ol' counthry an' I used to know his wife whin she wurruked f'r—"

"S-sh," said Mr. Dooley. "They're beyond that now. Besides they speak fr'm experyence. An' mebbe that's th' throuble. We're always harder with our own kind thin with others. 'Tis I that'd be th' fine cinsor iv a bartinder's wurruk. Th' more ye ought to be a servant ye'ersilf th' more difficult 'tis f'r ye to get along with servants. I can holler to anny man fr'm th' top iv a buildin' an' make him tur-rn r-round, but if I come down to th' sthreet where he can see I ain't anny bigger thin he is, an' holler at him, 'tis twinty to wan if he tur-rns r-round he'll hit me in th' eye. We have a servant girl problem because, Hinnissy, it isn't manny years since we first begun to have servant girls. But I hope Congress'll take it up. A smart Congress like th' wan we have now ought to be able to spare a little time fr'm its prepara-tion iv new jims iv speech f'r th' third reader an' rig up a bill that'd make keepin' house a recreation while so softenin' th' spirit iv th' haughty sign iv a noble race in th' kitchen that cookin' buckwheat cakes on a hot day with th' aid iv a bottle iv smokeless powdher'd not cause her f'r to sind a worthy man to his office in slippers an' without a hat."

"Ah," said Mr. Hennessy, the simple democrat. "It wud be all r-right if women'd do their own cookin'."

"Well," said Mr. Dooley. "'Twud be a return to Jacksonyan simplicity, an' 'twud be a gr-reat thing f'r th' resthrant business."

UNDERESTIMATING THE ENEMY

"What d'ye think iv th' war?" Mr. Hennessy asked.

"I think I want to go out an' apologize to Shafter," said Mr. Dooley. "I'm like ivrybody else, be hivins, I thought war was like shootin' glass balls. I niver thought iv th' glass balls thrainin' a dinnymite gun on me. 'Tis a thrait iv us Anglo-Saxons that we look on an inimy as a target. If ye hit him ye get three good seegars. We're like people that dhreams iv fights. In me dhreams I niver lost wan fight. A man I niver saw befure comes up an' says something mane to me, that I can't raymimber, an' I climb into him an' 'tis all over in a minyit. He niver hits me, or if he does I don't feel it. I put him on his back an' bate him to death. An' thin I help mesilf to his watch an' chain an' me frinds come down an' say, 'Martin, ye haven't a scratch,' an' congrathlate me, an' I wandher ar-roun' th' sthreets with a chip on me shoulder till I look down an' see that I haven't a stitch on me but a short shirt. An' thin I wake up. Th' list iv knock-outs to me credit in dhreams wud make Fitzsimmons feel poor. But ne'er a wan iv thim was printed in th' pa-apers.

"'Tis so with me frinds, th' hands acrost th' sea. They wint to sleep an' had a dhream. An' says they: 'We will sind down to South Africa thim gallant throops that have won so manny hard-fought reviews,' they says, 'captained,' they says, 'be th' flower iv our aristocracy,' they says. 'An' whin th' Boers come out ar-rmed with rollin' pins an' bibles,' they says, 'we'll just go at thim,' they says, 'an' walk through thim an' that night we'll have a cotillyon at Pretoria to which all frinds is invited,' they says. An' so they deposit their intellects in th' bank at home, an' th' absent-minded beggars goes out in thransports iv pathreetism an' pothry. An' they'se a meetin' iv th' cabinet an' 'tis decided that as th' war will on'y las' wan week 'twill be well f'r to begin renamin' th' cities iv th' Thransvaal afther pop'lar English statesmen—Joechamberlainville an' Rhodesdorp an' Beitfontein. F'r they have put their hands to th' plough an' th' sponge is squeezed dhry, an' th' sands iv th' glass have r-run out an' th' account is wiped clean.

"An' what's th' Boer doin' all this time? What's me frind th' Boer doin'? Not sleepin', Hinnissy, mind ye. He hasn't anny dhreams iv conquest. But whin a man with long whiskers comes r-ridin' up th' r-road an' says: 'Jan Schmidt or Pat O'Toole or

whativer his name is, ye're wanted at th' front,' he goes home an'
takes a rifle fr'm th' wall an' kisses his wife an' childher good-bye
an' puts a bible in th' tails iv his coat an' a stovepipe hat on his
head an' thramps away. An' his wife says: 'Good-bye, Jan.
Don't be long gone an' don't get shooted.' An' he says: 'Not
while I've got a leg undher me an' a rock in front iv me,' he says.
I tell ye, Hinnissy, ye can't beat a man that fights f'r his home an'
counthry in a stovepipe hat. He might be timpted f'r to come
out fr'm cover f'r his native land, but he knows if he goes home to
his wife with his hat mussed she won't like it, an' so he sets behind
a rock an' plugs away. If th' lid is knocked off he's fatally
wounded.

"What's th' raysult, Hinnissy? Th' British marches up with
their bands playin' an' their flags flyin'. An' th' Boers squat
behind a bouldher or a three or set comfortable in th' bed iv a
river an' bang away. Their on'y thradition is that it's betther to be
a live Boer thin a dead hero, which comes, perhaps, to th' same
thing. They haven't been taught f'r hundherds iv years that 'tis a
miracle f'r to be an officer an' a disgrace to be a private sojer.
They know that if they're kilt they'll have their names printed in
th' pa-apers as well as th' Markess iv Doozleberry that's had his
eyeglass shot out. But they ain't lookin' f'r notoriety. All they
want is to get home safe, with their counthry free, their honor
protected an' their hats in good ordher. An' so they hammer
away an' th' inimy keeps comin', an' th' varyous editions iv th'
London pa-apers printed in this counthry have standin' a line iv
type beginnin', 'I regret to state.'

"All this, Hinnissy, comes fr'm dhreamin' dhreams. If th'
British had said, 'This unclean an' raypeecious people that we're
against is also very tough. Dirty though they be, they'll fight.
Foul though their nature is, they have ca'tridges in their belts.
This not bein' England an' th' inimy we have again us not bein'
our frinds, we will f'rget th' gloryous thraditions iv th' English an'
Soudan ar-rmies an' instead iv r-rushin' on thim sneak along yon
kindly fence an' hit thim on th' back iv th' neck'—they'd be less,
'I r-regret-to-states' and more 'I'm plazed-to-reports.' They
wud so, an' I'm a man that's been through columns an' columns iv
war. Ye'll find, Hinnissy, that 'tis on'y ar-rmies fights in th' open.
Nations fights behind threes an' rocks. Ye can put that in ye're
little book. 'Tis a sayin' I made as I wint along."

"We done th' same way oursilves," said Mr. Hennessy.

"We did that," said Mr. Dooley. "We were in a dhream, too. Th' on'y thing is th' other fellow was in a thrance. We woke up first. An' annyhow I'm goin' to apologize to Shafter. He may not have anny medals f'r standin' up in range iv th' guns but, be hivins, he niver dhrove his buckboard into a river occypied be th' formerly loathed Castile."

MODERN EXPLOSIVES

"If iver I wanted to go to war," said Mr. Dooley, "an' I niver did, th' desire has passed fr'm me iv late. Ivry time I read iv th' desthructive power iv modhern explosives col' chills chase each other up an' down me spine."

"What's this here stuff they calls lyddite?" Mr. Hennessy asked.

"Well, 'tis th' divvle's own med'cine," said Mr. Dooley. "Compared with lyddite joynt powdher is Mrs. Winslow's soothin' surup, an' ye cud lave th' childher play base-ball with a can iv dinnymite. 'Tis as sthrong as Gin'ral Crownjoy's camp th' day iv th' surrinder an' almost as sthrong as th' pollytics iv Montana. Th' men that handles it is cased in six inch armor an' played on be a hose iv ice wather. Th' gun that shoots it is always blown up be th' discharge. Whin this deadly missile flies through th' air, th' threes ar-re withered an' th' little bur-rds falls dead fr'm th' sky, fishes is kilt in th' rivers, an' th' tillyphone wires won't wurruk. Th' keen eyed British gunners an' corry-spondints watches it in its hellish course an' tur-rn their faces as it falls into th' Boer trench. An' oh! th' sickly green fumes it gives off, jus' like pizen f'r potato bugs! There is a thremenjous explosion. Th' earth is thrown up f'r miles. Horses, men an' gun carredges ar-re landed in th' British camp whole. Th' sun is obscured be Boer whiskers turned green. Th' heart iv th' corryspondint is made sick be th' sight, an' be th' thought iv th' fearful carnage wrought be this dhread desthroyer in th' ranks iv th' brave but misguided Dutchmen. Th' nex' day deserters fr'm th' Boer ranks reports that they have fled fr'm th' camp, needin' a dhrink an' onable to stand th' scenes iv horror. They announce that th' whole Boer ar-rmy is as green as wall paper, an' th' Irish brigade has sthruck because ye can't tell their flag fr'm th' flag iv th' r-rest iv th' Dutch. Th' Fr-rinch gin'ral in command iv th'

Swedish corps lost his complexion an' has been sint to th' hospital, an' Mrs. Gin'ral Crownjoy's washin' that was hangin' on th' line whin th' bombardmint comminced is a total wreck which no amount iv bluin' will save. Th' deserters also report that manny iv th' Boers ar-re outspannin', trekkin', loogerin', kopjein' an' veldtin' home to be dyed, f'r 'tis not known whether lyddite is a fast color or will come out in th' wash.

"In spite iv their heavy losses th' Boers kept up a fierce fire. They had no lyddite, but with their other divvlish modhern explosives they wrought thremenjous damage. F'r some hours shells burst with turr'ble precision in th' British camp. Wan man who was good at figures counted as manny as forty-two thousan' eight hundherd an' sivin burstin' within a radyus iv wan fut. Ye can imagine th' hor-rible carnage. Colonel C. G. F. K. L. M. N. O. P. Hetherington-Casey-Higgins lost his eye-glass tin times, th' las' time almost swallowin' it, while ye'er faithful corryspondint was rindered deaf be th' explosions. Another Irish rig'mint has disappeared, th' Twelve Thousandth an' Eighth, Dublin Fusiliers. Brave fellows, 'tis suspected they mistook th' explosion of lyddite f'r a Pathrick's Day procession an' wint acrost to take a look at it.

"Murdher, but 'tis dhreadful to r-read about. We have to change all our conciptions iv warfare. · Wanst th' field was r-red, now 'tis a br-right lyddite green. Wanst a man wint out an' died f'r his counthry, now they sind him out an' lyddite dyes him. What do I mane? 'Tis a joke I made. I'll not explane it to ye. Ye wudden't undherstand it. 'Tis f'r th' eddycated classes.

"How they're iver goin' to get men to fight afther this I cudden't tell ye. 'Twas bad enough in th' ol' days whin all that happened to a sojer was bein' pinithrated be a large r-round gob iv solder or stuck up on th' end iv a baynit be a careless inimy. But now-a-days, they have th' bullet that whin it enthers ye tur-rns ar-round like th' screw iv a propeller, an' another wan that ye might say goes in be a key-hole an' comes out through a window, an' another that has a time fuse in it an' it doesn't come out at all but stays in ye, an' mebbe twinty years afther, whin ye've f'rgot all about it an' ar-re settin' at home with ye'er fam'ly, bang! away it goes an' ye with it, carryin' off half iv th' roof. Thin they have guns as long as fr'm here to th' rollin' mills that fires shells as big as a thrunk. Th' shells are loaded like a docthor's bag an' have all kinds iv things in thim that won't do a bit iv good to man or beast. If a sojer has a weak back there's something in th' shell that removes a weak back; if his head throubles him, he can lose it; if th' odher iv vilets is distasteful to him th' shell smothers him in vilet powdher. They have guns that anny boy or girl who knows th' typewriter can wurruk, an' they have other guns on th' music box plan, that ye wind up an' go away an' lave, an' they annoy anny wan that comes along. They have guns that bounces up out iv a hole in th' groun', fires a millyon shells a minyit an' dhrops back f'r another load. They have guns that fire dinnymite an' guns that fire th' hateful, sickly green lyddite that makes th' inimy look like fiat money, an' guns that fire canned beef f'r th' inimy an' distimper powdher for th' inimy's horses. An' they have some guns that shoot straight."

"Well, thin," Mr. Hennessy grumbled, "it's a wondher to me that with all thim things they ain't more people kilt. Sure, Gin'ral Grant lost more men in wan day thin th' British have lost in four months, an' all he had to keep tab on was ol' fashioned bullets an' big, bouncin' iron balls."

"Thrue," said Mr. Dooley. "I don't know th' reason, but it mus' be that th' betther gun a man has th' more he thrusts th' gun an' th' less he thrusts himsilf. He stays away an' shoots. He says to himsilf, he says: 'They'se nawthin' f'r me to do,' he says, 'but load up me little lyddite cannon with th' green goods,' he says, 'an' set here at the organ,' he says, 'pull out th' stops an' paint th' town iv Pretoria green,' he says. 'But,' he says, 'on sicond thought, suppose th' inimy shud hand it back to me,' he says. ''Twud be oncomfortable,' he says. 'So,' he says, 'I'll jus' move me music back a mile,' he says, 'an' peg away, an' th' longest gun takes th' persimmons,' he says. 'Tis this way: If ye an' I fall out an' take rifles to each other, 'tis tin to wan nayether iv us gets clost enough to hit. If we take pistols th' odds is rayjooced. If we take swords I may get a hack at ye, but if we take a half-nelson lock 'tis even money I have ye'er back broke befure th' polis comes.

"I can see in me mind th' day whin explosives'll be so explosive an' guns'll shoot so far that on'y th' folks that stay at home'll be kilt, an' life insurance agents'll be advisin' people to go into th' ar-rmy. I can so. 'Tis thrue what Hogan says about it."

"What's that?" Mr. Hennessy asked.

"Th' nation," said Mr. Dooley, "that fights with a couplin' pin extinds its bordhers at th' cost iv th' nation that fights with a clothes pole."

THE BOER MISSION

"Well, sir," said Mr. Dooley, "'tis a fine rayciption th' Boer dillygates is havin' in this counthry."

"They'll be out here nex' week," said Mr. Hennessy.

"They will that," Mr. Dooley replied, "an' we'll show thim that our inthrest in small raypublics fightin' f'r their liberty ain't disappeared since we become an impeeryal nation. No, sir. We have as much inthrest as iver, but we have more inthrests elsewhere.

"Oom Paul, he says to th' la-ads: 'Go,' he says, 'to me good an' great frind, Mack th' Wanst, an' lay th' case befure him,' he says. 'Tell him,' he says, 'that th' situation is just th' same as it was durin' Wash'nton's time,' he says, 'on'y Wash'nton won, an' we're rapidly losin' kopjes till we soon won't have wan to sthrike a match on,' he says. An' off goes th' good men. Whin they started the Boers was doin' pretty well, Hinnissy. They were fightin' Englishmen, an' that's a lawn tinnis to a rale fightin' man. But afther awhile the murdherin' English gover'mint put in a few recreent but gallant la-ads fr'm th' ol' dart—we ought to be proud iv thim, curse thim—Pat O'Roberts, an' Mike McKitchener, an' Terrence O'Fr-rinch—an' they give th' view-halloo an' wint through th' Dutch like a party comin' home fr'm a fifteenth iv August picnic might go through a singerbund. So be th' time th' dillygates got to Europe it was: 'James, if thim br-rave but misguided Dutch appears, squirt th' garden hose on thim. I'll see th' British embassadure this afthernoon.' Ye see, Hinnissy, 'twas ol' Kruger's play to keep on winnin' battles till th' dillygates had their say. Th' amount iv sympathy that goes out f'r a sthrugglin' people is reg'lated, Hinnissy, be th' amount iv sthrugglin' th' people can do. Th' wurruld, me la-ad, is with th' undher dog on'y as long as he has a good hold an' a chanst to tur-rn over.

"Well, sir, whin th' dillygates see they cudden't do business in Europe, says they to thimsilves: 'We'll pike acrost th' ragin' sea,' they says, 'an' in th' home iv Wash'nton, Lincoln, an' Willum J. Bryan, ye bet we'll have a hearin',' an' they got wan. Ivrybody's listenin' to thim. But no wan replies. If they'd come here three months ago, befure Crownjoy was suffocated out iv his hole in th' groun', they'd be smokin' their pipes in rockin' chairs on th' veranda iv th' white house an' passin' th' bucket between thim an' Mack. But 'tis diff'rent now. 'Tis diff'rent now. Says

Willum J. Bryan: 'I can't see thim mesilf, f'r it may not be long befure I'll have to dale with these inthricate problems, I hope an' pray, but Congressman Squirtwather, do ye disguise ye'ersilf as a private citizen an' go down to th' hotel an' tell these la-ads that I'm with thim quietly if public opinyon justifies it an' Mack takes th' other side. Tell thim I frequently say to mesilf that they're all r-right, but I wudden't want it to go further. Perhaps they cud be injooced to speak at a dimmycratic meetin' unbeknown to me,' he says.

"Sicrety Hay meets thim in a coal cellar, wearin' a mask. 'Gintlemen,' says he, 'I can assure ye th' prisidint an' mesilf feels mos' deeply f'r ye. I needn't tell ye about mesilf,' he says. 'Haven't I sint me own son into ye'er accursed but liberty-lovin' counthry,' he says. 'As f'r Mack, I assure ye he's hear-rtbroken over th' tur-rn affairs have taken,' he says. 'Early in th' war he wrote to Lord Salisberry, sayin' he hoped 'twud not be continyued to iliction day, an' Salisberry give him a gruff response. Tur-rned him down, though both ar-re Anglo-Saxons,' he says. 'Las' night his sobs fairly shook th' white house as he thought iv ye an' ye'er sthruggle. He wants to tell ye how much he thinks iv ye, an' he'll meet ye in th' carredge house if ye'll shave off ye'er whiskers an' go as clam-peddlers. Ye'll reco'nize him in a green livery. He'll wear a pink carnation in his buttonhole. Give th' names iv Dorsey an' Flannagan, an' if th' English ambassadure goes by get down on ye'er han's an' knees an' don't make a sign till he's out iv sight,' he says. 'Th' stout party in blue near by 'll be Mark Hanna. He may be able to arrange a raypublican meetin' f'r ye to addhress,' he says. 'The gr-reat hear-rt iv th' raypublican party throbs f'r ye. So does Mack's,' he says. 'So does mine,' he says.

"Well, th' dillygates met Mack an' they had a pleasant chat. 'Will ye,' says they, 'inthervene an' whistle off th' dogs iv war?' they says. 'Whisper,' says Mack, th' tears flowin' down his cheeks. 'Iver since this war started me eyes have been fixed on th' gallant or otherwise, nation or depindancy, fightin' its brave battle f'r freedom or rebellin' again' th' sov'reign power, as the case may be,' he says. 'Unofficially, my sympathy has gone out to ye, an' bur-rnin' wurruds iv unofficial cheer has been communicated unofficially be me to me official fam'ly, not, mind ye, as an official iv this magnificent an' liberty-lovin' raypublic, but as a private citizen,' he says. 'I feel, as a private citizen, that so long,' he says, as the br-right star iv liberty shines resplindent over our common counthries, with th' example iv Washin'ton in ye'er eyes, an' th' iliction comin' on, that ye must go forward an' conker or die,' he says. 'An',' he says, 'Willum McKinley is not th' man to put annything in ye'er way,' he says. 'Go back to me gr-reat an' good frind an' tell him that th' hear-rt iv th' ray-publican party throbs f'r him,' he says. 'An' Sicrety Hay's,' he says, 'an' mine,' he says, 'unofficially,' he says. 'Me official hear-rt,' he says, 'is not permitted be th' constitootion to throb durin' wurrukin' hours,' he says.

"An' so it goes. Ivrywhere th' dillygates tur-rns they see th' sign: 'This is me busy day.' An' whin they get back home they can tell th' people they found th' United States exudin' sympathy at ivry pore—'marked private.'"

"Don't ye think th' United States is enthusyastic f'r th' Boers?" asked the innocent Hennessy.

"It was," said Mr. Dooley. "But in th' las' few weeks it's had so manny things to think iv. Th' enthusyasm iv this counthry, Hinnissy, always makes me think iv a bonfire on an ice-floe. It burns bright so long as ye feed it, an' it looks good, but it don't take hold, somehow, on th' ice."

THE CHINESE SITUATION

"Well, sir," said Mr. Hennessy, "to think iv th' audacity iv thim Chinymen! It do bate all."

"It do that," said Mr. Dooley. "It bates th' wurruld. An' what's it comin' to? You an' me looks at a Chinyman as though he wasn't good f'r annything but washin' shirts, an' not very good at that. 'Tis wan iv th' spoorts iv th' youth iv our gr-reat cities to rowl an impty beer keg down th' steps iv a Chinee laundhry, an' if e'er a Chinyman come out to resint it they'd take him be th' pigtail an' do th' joynt swing with him. But th' Chinyman at home's a diff'rent la-ad. He's with his frinds an' they're manny iv thim an' he's rowlin' th' beer kegs himsilf an' Westhren Civiliza-tion is down in th' laundhry wondhrin' whin th' police'll come along.

"Th' Lord f'rgive f'r sayin' it, Hinnissy, but if I was a Chiny-man, which I will fight anny man f'r sayin', an' was livin' at home,

I'd tuck me shirt into me pants, put me braid up in a net, an' go out an' take a fall out iv th' in-vader if it cost me me life. Here am I, Hop Lung Dooley, r-runnin' me little liquor store an' p'rhaps raisin' a family in th' town iv Koochoo. I don't like foreigners there anny more thin I do here. Along comes a bald-headed man with chin whiskers from Baraboo, Wisconsin, an' says he: 'Benighted an' haythen Dooley,' says he, 'ye have no God,' he says. 'I have,' says I. 'I have a lot iv thim,' says I. 'Ye ar-re an oncultivated an' foul crather,' he says. 'I have come six thousan' miles f'r to hist ye fr'm th' mire iv ignorance an' irrellijon in which ye live to th' lofty plane iv Baraboo,' he says. An' he sets down on an aisy chair, an' his wife an' her friends come in an' they inthrojooce Mrs. Dooley to th' modhren improvements iv th' corset an' th' hat with th' blue bur-rd onto it, an' put shame into her because she hasn't let her feet grow, while th' head mission'ry reads me a pome out iv th' *Northwesthren Christyan Advocate*. 'Well,' says I, 'look here, me good fellow,' I says. 'Me an' me people has occupied these here primises f'r manny years,' I says, 'an' here we mean to stay,' I says. 'We're doin' th' best we can in th' matther iv gods,' says I. 'We have thim cast at a first-rate foundhry,' I says, 'an' we sandpa-aper thim ivry week,' says I. 'As f'r knowin' things,' I says, 'me people wrote pomes with a markin' brush whin th' likes iv ye was r-runnin' ar-round wearin' a short pelisse iv sheep-skins an' batin' each other to death with stone hammers,' says I. An' I'm f'r firin' him out, but bein' a quite man I lave him stay.

"Th' nex' day in comes a man with a suit iv clothes that looks like a tablecloth in a section house, an' says he: 'Poor ignorant haythen,' he says, 'what manner iv food d'ye ate?' he says. 'Rice,' says I, 'an' rats is me fav'rite dish,' I says. 'Deluded wretch,' says he. 'I riprisint Armour an' Company, an' I'm here to make ye change ye'er dite,' he says. 'Hinceforth ye'll ate th' canned roast beef iv merry ol' stock yards or I'll have a file iv sojers in to fill ye full iv ondygistible lead,' he says. An' afther him comes th' man with Aunt Miranda's Pan Cakes an' Flaked Bran an' Ye'll-perish-if-ye-don't-eat-a-biscuit an' other riprisinta-tives iv Westhern Civilization, an' I'm to be shot if I don't take thim all.

"Thin a la-ad runs down with a chain an' a small glass on three sticks an' a gang iv section men that answers to th' name iv Casey, an' pro-ceeds f'r to put down a railroad. 'What's this

f'r ?' says I. 'We ar-re th' advance guard iv Westhren Civilization,' he says, 'an' we're goin' to give ye a railroad so ye can go
swiftly to places that ye don't want to see,' he says. 'A counthry
that has no railroads is beneath contimpt,' he says. 'Casey,' he
says, 'sthretch th' chain acrost yon graveyard,' he says. 'I aim
f'r to put th' thrack just befure that large tombstone marked
Riquiescat in Pace, James H. Chung-a-lung,' he says. 'But,'
says I, 'ye will disturb pah's bones,' says I, 'if ye go to layin' ties,'
I says. 'Ye'll be mixin' up me ol' man with th' Cassidy's in th'
nex' lot that,' I says, 'he niver spoke to save in anger in his life,'
I says. 'Ye're an ancestor worshiper, heathen,' says the la-ad,
an' he goes on to tamp th' mounds in th' cimitry an' ballast th'
thrack with th' remains iv th' deceased. An' afther he's got
through along comes a Fr-rinchman, an' an Englishman, an' a
Rooshan, an' a Dutchman, an' says wan iv them: 'This is a
comfortable lookin' saloon,' he says. 'I'll take th' bar, ye take
th' ice-box an' th' r-rest iv th' fixtures.' 'What f'r ?' says I.
'I've paid th' rent an' th' license,' says I. 'Niver mind,' says he.
'We're th' riprisintatives iv Westhren Civilization,' he says, 'an'
'tis th' business iv Westhren Civilization to cut up th' belongings
iv Easthren Civilization,' he says. 'Be off,' he says, 'or I'll pull
ye'er hair,' he says. 'Well,' says I, 'this thing has gone far
enough,' I says. 'I've heerd me good ol' cast-iron gods or josses
abused,' I says, 'an' I've been packed full iv canned goods, an' th'
Peking Lightnin' Express is r-runnin' sthraight through th' lot
where th' bones iv me ancesthors lies,' I says. 'I've shtud it all,'
I says, 'but whin ye come here to bounce me off iv me own
primises,' I says, 'I'll have to take th' leg iv th' chair to ye,' I says.
An' we're to th' flure.

"That's th' way it stands in Chiny, Hinnissy, an' it looks to
me as though Westhren Civilization was in f'r a bump. I mind
wanst whin a dhrunk prize fighter come up th' r-road and wint to
sleep on Slavin's steps. Some iv th' good sthrong la-ads happened
along an' they were near bein' at blows over who shud have his
watch an' who shud take his hat. While they were debatin' he
woke up an' begin cuttin' loose with hands an' feet, an' whin he
got through he made a collection iv th' things they dhropped in
escapin' an' marched ca'mly down th' sthreet. Mebbe 'twill
tur-rn out so in Chiny, Hinnissy. I see be th' pa-apers that they'se
four hundherd millyons iv thim boys an' be hivins! 'twudden't
surprise me if whin they got through batin' us at home, they

might say to thimsilves: 'Well, here goes f'r a jaunt ar-roun' the wurruld.' Th' time may come, Hinnissy, whin ye'll be squirtin' wather over Hop Lee's shirt while a man named Chow Fung kicks down ye'er sign an' heaves rocks through ye'er windy. The time may come, Hinnissy. Who knows?"

"End ye'er blather," said Mr. Hennessy. "They won't be anny Chinymen left whin Imp'ror Willum gets through."

"Mebbe not," says Mr. Dooley. "He's a sthrong man. But th' Chinymen have been on earth a long time, an' I don't see how we can push so manny iv thim off iv it. Annyhow, 'tis a good thing f'r us they ain't Christyans an' haven't larned properly to sight a gun."

MINISTER WU[1]

"Well, sir, me little Chinee frind Woo must be havin' th' time iv his life in Wash'nton these warm days," said Mr. Dooley.

"Who's he?" asked Mr. Hennessy.

"He's th' Chinee ministher," said Mr. Dooley, "an' his business is f'r to supply fresh hand-laundhried misinformation to the sicrety iv state. Th' sicrety iv state is settin' in his office feelin' blue because he's just heerd be a specyal corryspondint iv th' London Daily Pail at Sydney, Austhreelya, who had it fr'm a slatewriter in Duluth that an ar-rmy iv four hundherd an' eight thousan' millyon an' sivinty-five bloodthirsty Chinee, ar-rmed with flatirnes an' cryin', 'Bung Loo!' which means, Hinnissy, 'Kill th' foreign divvles, dhrive out th' missionries, an' set up in Chiny a gover'mint f'r the Chinee,' is marchin' on Vladivostook in Siberyia, not far fr'm Tinsin. A knock comes at th' dure an' Woo enthers. 'Well,' says he, with a happy smile, ''tis all right." 'What's all right?' says the sicrety iv state. 'Ivrything,' says Woo. 'I have just found a letter sewed in a shirt fr'm me frind Lie Much, th' viceroy iv Bumbang. It is dated th' fourth hour iv th' third day iv th' eighth or green-cheese moon,' he says. 'What day is that?' says the sicrety iv state. 'It's Choosdah, th' fourth iv July; Windsah, th' eighth iv October, an' Thursdah, the sivinteenth iv March,' he says. 'Pathrick's day,' says th' sicrety

---

[1] Minister Wu: Wu T'ing-fang (1842–1922), Chinese minister to the United States, 1897–1902, 1908–1909.

iv state. 'Thrue f'r ye,' says Woo. 'What year?' says Jawn Hay. 'The year iv th' big wind,' says Woo. 'Good,' says John Hay, 'proceed with ye'er story.' 'Here's th' letther,' says Woo. 'I know 'tis genooyine because it is an ol' dhress patthern used be th' impress. It says: 'Oscar Woo, care iv himsilf, annywhere: Dear Woo, brother iv th' moon, uncle iv th' sun, an' roommate iv th' stars, dear sir: Yours iv th' eighth day iv th' property moon rayceived out iv th' air yesterdah afthernoon or to-morrow, an' was glad to note ye ar-re feelin' well. Ivrything over here is th' same ol' pair iv boots. Nawthin' doin'. Peking is as quiet as th' gr-rave. Her majesty, th' impress, is sufferin' slightly fr'm death be poison, but is still able to do th' cookin' f'r the Rooshan ambassadure. Th' impror was beheaded las' week an' feels so much betther f'r the op'ration that he expicts to be quarthered nex' Sundah. He's always wanted to rayjooce his weight. Some iv th' Boxers called on th' foreigners at Tinsin las' week an' met a warrum rayciption. Th' foreigners afthervard paid a visit to thim through a hole in th' wall, an' a jolly day concluded with a foot race, at which our people are becomin' expert. Some iv th' boys expicts to come up to Peking nex' week, an' th' people along th' line iv th' railroad are gettin' ready f'r thim. This is really all the news I have, excipt that cherries ar-re ripe. Me pin is poor, me ink is dhry, me love f'r you can niver die. Give me regards to Sicrety Hay whin he wakes up. I remain, illusthrus cousin iv th' risin' dawn, thruly ye'ers, Li. P.S.—If ye need anny more information take a longer dhraw.'

"'That,' says Woo, 'is wan way iv r-readin' it. Read upside down it says that the impress has become a Swedenboorjan. I will r-read it standin' on me head whin I get home where I can pin down me overskirt; thin I'll r-read it in a lookin' glass; thin I'll saw it into sthrips an' r-run it through a wringer an' lave it stand in a tub iv bluein', an' whin it's properly starched I'll find out what it says. Fin'lly I'll cut it into small pieces an' cook with rice an' lave it to rest in a cool place, an' thin 'twill r-read even betther. I hope ye're satisfied,' he says. 'I am,' says Jawn Hay. 'I'll tillygraft to Mark that ivrything is all r-right,' he says, 'an' that our relations with his majesty or her majesty or their Boxerships or th' Down-with-th'-foreign-divvlers or whoiver's runnin' th' shop over beyant are as they ought to be or worse or betther, as th' case may be,' he says. 'Good,' says Woo, 'ye're a man afther me own heart,' he says. 'I'll sind ye a little book wrote be a frind iv mine in Peking,' he says. ' 'Tis called "Heart to Heart Lies I Have Had," he says. 'Ye'll like it,' he says. 'In the manetime,' he says, ' I must write a secret message to go out be to-night's hot-air express to me corryspondint in Meriden, Connecticut, urgin' him to sind more impeeryal edicks iv a fav'rable nature,' he says. 'I've on'y had twinty so far, an' I'm gettin' scrivener's palsy,' he says. 'But befure I go,' he says, ' I bet ye eight millyon yens, or three dollars an' eighty-four cints iv ye'er money, that ye can't pick out th' shell this here pea is undher,' he says. An' they set down to a game iv what is known at Peking as diplomacy, Hinnissy, but on Randolph sthreet viadock is called the double dirty."

"I don't believe wan wurrud iv what's in th' pa-apers about Chiny," said Mr. Hennessy.

"Well," said Mr. Dooley, "if ye believe annything ye'll believe ivrything. 'Tis a grand contist that's goin' on between Westhren an' Easthren civilliezation. 'Tis a joke iv me own, Hinnissy, an' ye'd undherstand it if ye knew spellin'. Th' Westhren civilization, Hinnissy—that's us—is a pretty good liar, but he's a kind iv rough-an'-tumble at it. He goes in head down, an' ivry lie he tells looks like all th' others. Ye niver see an Englishman that had anny judgment in lyin'. Th' corryspondint iv th' Daily Pail is out iv his class. He's carryin' lies to Lieville. How in th' wurruld can we compete with a counthry where ivry lab'rer's cottage projooces lies so delicate that th' workmen iv th' West can't undherstand thim ? We make our lies be machinery; they tur-rn out theirs be hand. They imitate th' best iv our canned lies to deceive people that likes that kind, but f'r artists they have lies that appeals to a more refined taste. Sure I'd like to live among thim an' find out th' kind iv bouncers they tell each other. They must be gr-rand. I on'y know their export lies now—th' surplus lies they can't use at home. An' th' kind they sind out ar-re betther thin our best. Our lies is no more thin a conthradiction iv th' thruth; their lies appeals to th' since iv honesty iv anny civilized man."

"They can't hurt us with their lies," said Mr. Hennessy of our Western civilization. "We have th' guns an' we'll bate thim yet."

"Yes," said Mr. Dooley, "an' 'twill be like a man who's had his house desthroyed be a cyclone gettin' up an' kickin' at th' air."

THE FUTURE OF CHINA

"Be th' time th' Chinese gets through with this here job o' theirs," said Mr. Dooley, "they'll know a thing or two about good manners an' Christyan idees."

"They need thim," said Mr. Hennessy.

"They do so," said Mr. Dooley. "An' they'll get thim. By an' by th' allied foorces will proceed to Peking. It may not be in ye'er life time or in mine, or in th' life time iv th' ministhers, Hinnissy. They ar-re in no hurry. Th' ministhers ar-re as comfortable as they can be on a dite iv polo ponies an' bamboo, an' they have exercise enough dodgin' cannon balls to have no fear iv indygisthion. They'se no need of haste. Th' allied foorces must take no step forward while wan ar-rmed foe survives. It was rayported last week that th' advance had begun, but on sindin' out scouts 'twas discovered that th' asphalt road to th' capital was not r-ready an' th' gallant sojer boys was afraid to risk their beecycles on a defictive pavement. Thin th' parlor cars ordhered be th' Rooshan admiral has not arrived an' wan iv th' Frinch gin'rals lost an omelette, or whativer 'tis they wear on their shouldhers, an' he won't budge till it can be replaced fr'm Pahrs. A sthrong corps iv miners an' sappers has gone ahead f'r to lo-cate good resthrants on th' line iv march, but th' weather is cloudy an' th' silk umbrellys haven't arrived, an' they'se supposed to be four hundhred millyon Chinymen with pinwheels an' Roman candles blockin' th' way, so th' advance has been postponed indifinitely. Th' American foorces is r-ready f'r to start im-mejately, but they ar-re not there yet. Th' British gin'ral is waitin' f'r th' Victorya cross befure he does annything, an' th' Japanese an' th' Rooshan is dancin' up an' down sayin' 'Afther you, me boy.'

"But afther awhile, whin th' frost is on th' pumpkin an' th' corn is in th' shock, whin th' roads has been repaired, an' ivry gin'ral's lookin' his best, an' in no danger iv a cold on th' chist, they'll prance away. An' whin they get to th' city iv Peking a fine cillybration is planned be th' mission'ries. I see th' pro-gramme in th' pa-aper: First day, 10 A.M., prayers be th' allied mission'ries; 1 P.M., massacree iv the impress an' rile fam'ly; sicond day, 10 A.M., scatthrin' iv remains iv former kings; 11 A.M., disecration iv graves gin'rally; 2. P.M., massacree iv all gin'rals an' coort officials; third day, 12 noon, burnin' iv Peking; foorth day, gran' pop'lar massacree an' division iv territ'ry, th' cillybration to close with a rough-an'-tumble fight among th' allies.

"'Twill be a gr-reat occasion, Hinnissy, an' bedad I'd like to be there to see it. Ye can't go too sthrong again' th' Chinee. Me frind th' impror iv Germany put it right. 'Brave boys,' says he, 'ye ar-re goin' out now,' he says, 'f'r to carry th' light iv Christyanity,' he says, 'an' th' teachin's iv th' German Michael,' he says, 'to th' benighted haythen beyant,' he says. 'Me an' Mike is watchin' ye,' he says, 'an' we ixpict ye to do ye'er duty,' he says. 'Through you,' he says, 'I propose to smash th' vile Chinee with me mailed fist,' he says. 'This is no six-ounce glove fight, but demands a lunch-hook done up in eight-inch armor plate,' he says. 'Whin ye get among th' Chinee,' he says, 'ray-mimber that ye ar-re the van guard iv Christyanity,' he says, 'an' stick ye'er baynet through ivry hated infidel ye see,' he says. 'Lave thim undherstand what our westhren civilization means,' he says, 'an' prod thim good an' hard,' he says. 'Open their heads with ye'er good German swords to Eu-ropyan culture an' refinement,' he says. 'Spare no man that wears a pigtail,' he says. 'An',' he says, 'me an' th' German Michael will smile on ye as ye kick th' linin' out iv th' dhragon an' plant on th' walls iv Peking th' banner,' he says, 'iv th' cross, an',' he says, 'th' double cross,' he says. 'An' if be chance ye shud pick up a little land be th' way, don't lave e'er a Frinchman or Rooshan take it fr'm ye, or ye'll feel me specyal delivery hand on th' back iv ye'er neck in a way that'll do ye no kind iv good. Hock German Michael,' he says, 'hock me gran'father, hoch th' penny postage fist,' he says, 'hock mesilf,' he says. An th' German impror wint back to his bedroom f'r to wurruk on th' book he's goin' to br-ring out nex' year to take th' place iv th' bible.

"He's th' boy f'r me money. Whin th' German throops takes their part in th' desthruction iv Peking they'll be none iv th' allied foorces 'll stick deeper or throw th' backbone iv th' impress' ol' father higher thin th' la-ads fr'm th' home iv th' sausage. I hope th' cillybration 'll occur on Chris'mas day. I'd like to hear th' sojers singin' 'Gawd r-rest ye, merry Chinnymen' as they punchered thim with a baynit."

"'Twill be a good thing," said Mr. Hennessy.

"It will that," said Mr. Dooley.

"'Twill civilize th' Chinnymen," said Mr. Hennessy.

"'Twill civilize thim stiff," said Mr. Dooley. "An' it may

not be a bad thing f'r th' r-rest iv th' wurruld.   Perhaps contack with th' Chinee may civilize th' Germans."

PLATFORM MAKING

"That sthrikes me as a gran' platform," said Mr. Hennessy. "I'm with it fr'm start to finish."

"Sure ye are," said Mr. Dooley, "an' so ye'd be if it begun: 'We denounce Terence Hinnissy iv th' Sixth Ward iv Chicago as a thraitor to his country, an' inimy iv civilization, an' a poor thing.' Ye'd say: 'While there are wan or two things that might be omitted, th' platform as a whole is a statesmanlike docymint, an' wan that appeals to th' intelligince iv American manhood.' That's what ye'd say, an' that's what all th' likes iv ye'd say.   An' whin iliction day comes 'round th' on'y question ye'll ast ye'ersilf is: 'Am I with Mack or am I with Billy Bryan?'   An' accordin'ly ye'll vote.

"'Tis always th' same way, an' all platforms is alike.   I mind wanst whin I was an alter-nate to th' county con-vintion—'twas whin I was a power in pollytics an' th' on'y man that cud do anny-thing with th' Bohemian vote—I was settin' here wan night with a pen an' a pot iv ink befure me, thryin' to compose th' platform f'r th' nex' day, f'r I was a lithry man in a way, d'ye mind, an' I knew th' la-ads'd want a few crimps put in th' raypublicans in a ginteel style, an' 'd be sure to call on me f'r to do it.   Well, I'd got as far down as th' tariff an' was thryin' f'r to express me opinyon without swearin', whin who shud come in but Lafferty, that was sicrety iv McMahon, that was th' Main Guy in thim days, but aftherward thrun down on account iv him mixin' up between th' Rorkes an' th' Dorseys.   Th' Main Guy Down Town said he wudden't have no throuble in th' ward, an' he declared Mc-Mahon out.   McMahon had too much money annyhow.   If he'd kept on, dollar bills'd have been extinct outside iv his house.   But he was a sthrong man in thim days an' much liked.

"Anyhow, Lafferty, that was his sicrety, come in, an' says he: 'What are ye doin' there?' says he.   'Step soft,' says I; 'I am at wurruk,' I says.   'Ye shudden't do lithry wurruk on an empty stomach,' says he.   'I do nawthin' on an empty stomach but eat,' says I.   'I've had me supper,' I says.   'Go 'way,' says I, 'till I finish th' platform,' I says.   'What's th' platform?' says he.

'F'r th' county con-vintion,' says I.

"Well, sir, he set down on a chair, an' I thought th' man was goin' to die right there on the premises with laughter. 'Whin ye get through with ye'er barkin',' says I, 'I'll throuble ye to tell me what ye may be doin' it f'r,' I says. 'I see nawthin' amusin' here but ye'er prisince,' I says, 'an' that's not a divvle iv a lot funnier than a wooden leg,' I says, f'r I was mad. Afther awhile he come to, an' says he: 'Ye don't really think,' says he, 'that ye'll get a chanct to spring that platform,' he says. 'I do,' says I. 'Why,' he says, 'the platform has been adopted,' he says. 'Whin?' says I. 'Befure ye were born,' says he. 'In th' reign iv Bildad th' first,' says he—he was a larned man, was Lafferty, though a dhrinkin' man. All sicreties iv pollyticians not in office is dhrinkin' men, Hinnissy. 'I've got th' copy iv it here in me pocket,' he says. 'Th' boss give it to me to bring it up to date,' he says. 'They was no sthrike last year an' we've got to put a sthrike plank in th' platform or put th' president iv th' Lumber Shovers' union on th' county board, an',' he says, 'they ain't room,' he says.

"'Why,' says Lafferty, 'ye ought to know th' histhry iv platforms,' he says. An' he give it to me, an' I'll give it to ye. Years ago, Hinnissy, manny years ago, they was a race between th' dimmycrats an' th' raypublicans f'r to see which shud have a choice iv principles. Th' dimmycrats lost. I dinnaw why. Mebbe they stopped to take a dhrink. Annyhow, they lost. Th' raypublicans come up an' they choose th' 'we commind' principles, an' they was nawthin' left f'r the dimmycrats but th' 'we denounce an' deplores.' I dinnaw how it come about, but th' dimmycrats didn't like th' way th' thing shtud, an' so they fixed it up between thim that whichiver won at th' iliction shud commind an' congratulate, an' thim that lost shud denounce an' deplore. An' so it's been, on'y the dimmycrats has had so little chanct f'r to do annything but denounce an' deplore that they've almost lost th' use iv th' other wurruds.

"Mack sets back in Wash'nton an' writes a platform f'r th' comity on risolutions to compose th' week afther. He's got a good job—forty-nine ninety-two, sixty-six a month—an' 'tis up to him to feel good. 'I—I mean we,' he says, 'congratulate th' counthry on th' matchless statesmanship, onshrinkin' courage, steady devotion to duty an' principle iv that gallant an' hon'rable leader, mesilf,' he says to his sicrety. 'Take that,' he says, 'an' elaborate it,' he says. 'Ye'll find a ditchnry on th' shelf near the dure,' he says, 'if ye don't think I've put what I give ye sthrong enough,' he says. 'I always was,' he says, 'too retirin' f'r me own good,' he says. 'Spin out th' r-rest,' he says, 'to make about six thousan' wurruds,' he says, 'but be sure don't write annything too hot about th' Boer war or th' Ph'lippeens or Chiny, or th' tariff, or th' goold question, or our relations with England, or th' civil sarvice,' he says. ''Tis a foolish man,' he says, 'that throws a hunk iv coal fr'm his own window at th' dhriver iv a brick wagon,' he says.

"But with Billy Bryan 'tis diff'rent. He's out in Lincoln, Neebrasky, far fr'm home, an' he says to himsilf: 'Me throat is hoarse, an' I'll exercise me other fac'lties,' he says. 'I'll write a platform,' he says. An' he sets down to a typewriter, an' denounces an' deplores till th' hired man blows th' dinner horn. Whin he can denounce an' deplore no longer he views with alarm an' declares with indignation. An' he sinds it down to Kansas City, where th' cot beds come fr'm."

"Oh, ye're always pitchin' into some wan," said Mr. Hennessy. "I bet ye Willum Jennings Bryan niver see th' platform befure it wint in. He's too good a man."

"He is all iv that," said Mr. Dooley. "But ye bet he knows th' rale platform f'r him is: 'Look at th' bad breaks Mack's made,' an' Mack's platform is: 'Ye'd get worse if ye had Billy Bryan.' An' it depinds on whether most iv th' voters ar-re tired out or on'y a little tired who's ilicted. All excipt you, Hinnissy. Ye'll vote f'r Bryan?"

"I will," said Mr. Hennessy.

"Well," said Mr. Dooley, "d'ye know, I suspicted ye might."

PUBLIC FICKLENESS

Mr. Dooley put his paper aside and pushed his spectacles up on his forehead. "Well," he said, "I suppose, afther all, we're th' mos' lively nation in th' wurruld. It doesn't seem many months ago since ye, Hinnissy, was down at th' depot cheerin' th' departin' heroes—"

"I niver was," said Mr. Hennessy. "I stayed at home."

"Since ye was down cheerin' th' departin' heroes," Mr. Dooley continued, "an' thryin' to collect what they owed ye. Th' papers was full iv news iv th' war. Private Jawn Thomas

Bozoom iv Woonsocket, a mimber iv th' gallant an' devoted Wan Hundhred an' Eighth Rhode Island, accidentally slipped on a orange peel while attimptin' to lave th' recruitin' office an' sustained manny con-tu-sions. He rayfused to be taken home an' insisted on jinin' his rig'mint at th' rayciption in th' fair groun's. Gallant Private Bozoom! That's th' stuff that American heroes ar-re made iv. Ye find thim at th' forge an' at th' plough, an' dhrivin' sthreet cars, an' ridin' in th' same. The favoured few has th' chanst to face th' bullets iv th' inimy. 'Tis f'r these unknown pathrites to prove that a man can sarve his counthry at home as well as abroad. Private Bozoom will not be f'rgot be his fellow-counthrymen. A rayciption has been arranged f'r him at th' Woonsocket op'ry-house, an' 'tis said if he will accipt it, th' vote iv th' State iv Rhode Island'll be cast f'r him f'r prisidint. 'Tis at such times as this that we reflict that th' wurruld has wurruk f'r men to do, an' mere politicians mus' retire to th' rear.

"That was a few months ago. Where's Bozoom now? If iver ye go to Woonsocket, Hinnissy, which Gawd f'rbid, ye'll find him behind th' counther iv th' grocery store ladlin' out rutabaga turnips into a brown paper cornucopy an' glad to be alive. An' 'tis tin to wan, an' more thin that, that th' town humorist has named him th' orange-peel hero, an' he'll go to his grave with that name. Th' war is over an' th' state iv war exists. If ye saw a man fall fr'm th' top iv a tin-story buildin' 'twud startle ye, wanst. If it happened again, 'twud surprise ye. But if ye saw a man fall ivry fifteen minyits ye'd go home afther awhile f'r supper an' ye wudden't even mintion it to ye'er wife.

"I don't know how manny heroes they ar-re in th' Philippeens. Down there a man is ayether a sojer or a casualty. Bein' a casualty is no good. I cud say about a man: 'He was a hero in th' war with Spain,' but how can I say: 'Shake hands with Bill Grady, wan iv th' ladin' casualties iv our late war?' 'Twud be no more thin to say he was wan iv th' gallant men that voted f'r prisidint in 1896.

"No, Hinnissy, people wants novelties in war. Th' war fashions iv 1898 is out iv style. They ar-re too full in th' waist an' too long in th' skirt. Th' style has changed. There ar-re fifty thousand backward men in th' fair isles iv th' Passyfic fightin' to free th' Philippeen fr'm himsilf an' becomin' a casualty in th' operation, but no one is charterin' ar-rmy hospital ships f'r thim.

"No one is convartin' anny steam yachts f'r thim.   No wan is sindin' eighty tons iv plum puddin' to complete th' wurruk iv destruction.   They ar-re in a war that'd make th' British throops in Africa think they were drillin' f'r a prize banner.   But 'tis an onfashionable war.   'Tis an ol' war made over fr'm garments formerly worn be heroes.   Whin a man is out in th' counthry with wan newspaper an' has read th' authentic dispatches fr'm Lady-smith an' Harrismith an' Willumaldensmith an' Mysterious-billysmith an' the meetin' iv th' czar iv Rooshia with th' Impror Willum an' th' fire in th' packin' house an' th' report iv th' canal thrustees an' th' fightin' news an' th' want ads, an' afther he has r-read thim over twinty times he looks at his watch an' says he, 'Holy smoke, 'tis two hours to thrain time an' I suppose I'll have to r-read th' news fr'm th' Philippeens.'   War, be hivins, is so common that I believe if we was to take on a fight with all th' wurruld not more thin half th' popylation iv New England'd die iv hear-rt disease befure they got into th' cellars.

"Th' new style iv war is made in London an' all our set is simply stuck on it.   Th' casualties in th' Philippeens can walk home, but is it possible that any thrue an' well-dhressed American can stand to see th' signs iv th' ancient British aristocracy taken care iv be their own gover'mint ?   'What,' says Lady what's-her-name (her that was th' daughter iv wan iv our bravest an' best racontoors).   'What,' she says, 'will anny American woman residin' in London see men shot down,' she says, 'that has but recently played polo in our very sight,' she says, 'an' be brought home in mere thransports ?' she says.   'Ladies,' she says, 'lave us equip a hospital ship,' she says.   'I thrust,' she says, 'that all iv us has been long enough fr'm home to f'rget our despicable domestic struggles,' she says, 'an' think on'y iv human-ity,' she says.   An' whin she opens up th' shop f'r subscriptions ye'd think fr'm th' crowd that 'twas th' first night iv th' horse show.   I don't know what Lem Stiggins iv Kansas, marked down in th' roll, Private in th' Twintieth Kansas, Severely, I don't know what Private Severely thinks iv it.   An' I wudden't like to know till afther Thanksgivin'."

"Don't be blatherin'," said Mr. Hennessy.   "Sure ye can't ixpict people to be inthrested f'river in a first performance."

"No," said Mr. Dooley, "but whin th' audjeence gives th' comp'ny an encore it ought at laste to pretind that it's not lavin' f'r th' other show."

ALCOHOL AS FOOD

"If a man come into this saloon——" Mr. Hennessy was saying.
"This ain't no saloon," Mr. Dooley interrupted. "This is a resthrant."

"A what?" Mr. Hennessy exclaimed.

"A resthrant," said Mr. Dooley. "Ye don't know, Hinnissy, that liquor is food. It is though. Food—an' dhrink. That's what a doctor says in the pa-apers, an' another doctor wants th' gover'mint to sind tubs iv th' stuff down to th' Ph'lipeens. He says 'tis almost issintial that people shud dhrink in thim hot climates. Th' prespiration don't dhry on thim afther a hard pursoot iv Aggynaldoo an' th' capture iv Gin'ral Pantaloons de Garshy; they begin to think iv home an' mother sindin' down th' lawn-sprinkler to be filled with bock, an' they go off somewhere, an' not bein' able to dhry thimsilves with dhrink, they want to die. Th' disease is called nostalgia or home-sickness, or thirst.

"'What we want to do f'r our sojer boys in th' Ph'lipeens besides killin' thim,' says th' ar-rmy surgeon, 'is make th' place more homelike,' he says. 'Manny iv our heroes hasn't had th' deleeryum thremens since we first planted th' stars an' sthripes,' he says, 'an' th' bay'nits among th' people,' he says. 'I wud be in favor iv havin' th' rigimints get their feet round wanst a week, at laste,' he says. 'Lave us,' he says, 'reform th' reg'lations,' he says, 'an' insthruct our sojers to keep their powdher dhry an' their whistles wet,' he says.

"Th' idee ought to take, Hinnissy, f'r th' other doctor la-ad has discovered that liquor is food. 'A man,' says he, 'can live f'r months on a little booze taken fr'm time to time,' he says. 'They'se a gr-reat dale iv nourishment in it,' he says. An' I believe him, f'r manny's th' man I know that don't think iv eatin' whin he can get a dhrink. I wondher if the time will iver come whin ye'll see a man sneakin' out iv th' fam'ly enthrance iv a lunch-room hurridly bitin' a clove! People may get so they'll carry a light dinner iv a pint iv rye down to their wurruk, an' a man'll tell ye he niver takes more thin a bottle iv beer f'r breakfast. Th' cook'll give way to th' bartinder an' th' doctor 'll ordher people f'r to ate on'y at meals. Ye'll r-read in th' pa-apers that 'Anton Boozinski, while crazed with ham an' eggs, thried to kill his wife an' childher.' On Pathrick's day ye'll see th' Dr. Tanner Anti-Food Fife an' Drum corpse out at th' head iv th' procession instead iv th' Father Macchews, an' they'll be places where a man can be took whin he gets th' monkeys fr'm immodhrate eatin'. Th' sojers 'll complain that th' liquor was unfit to dhrink an' they'll be inquiries to find out who sold embammin' flood to th' ar-rmy. Poor people 'll have simple meals—p'raps a bucket iv beer an' a little crame de mint, an' ye'll r-read in th' pa-apers about a family found starvin' on th' North side, with nawthin' to sustain life but wan small bottle iv gin, while th' head iv th' family, a man well known to the polis, spinds his wages in a low doggery or bakeshop fuddlin' his brains with custard pie. Th' r-rich 'll inthrajoose novelties. P'raps they'll top off a fine dinner with a little hasheesh or proosic acid. Th' time'll come whin ye'll see me in a white cap fryin' a cocktail over a cooksthove, while a nigger hollers to me: 'Dhraw a stack iv Scotch,' an' I holler back: 'On th' fire.' Ye will not."

"That's what I thought," said Mr. Hennessy.

"No," said Mr. Dooley. "Whisky wudden't be so much iv a luxury if 'twas more iv a necissity. I don't believe 'tis a food, though whin me frind Schwartzmeister makes a cocktail all it needs is a few noodles to look like a biled dinner. No, whisky ain't food. I think betther iv it thin that. I wudden't insult it be placin' it on th' same low plane as a lobster salad. Father Kelly puts it r-right, and years go by without him lookin' on it even at Hallowe'en. 'Whisky,' says he, 'is called the divvle, because,' he says, ''tis wan iv the fallen angels,' he says. 'It has its place,' he says, 'but its place is not in a man's head,' says he. 'It ought to be th' reward iv action, not th' cause iv it,' he says. 'It's f'r th' end iv th' day, not th' beginnin',' he says. 'Hot whisky is good f'r a cold heart, an' no whisky's good f'r a hot head,' he says. 'Th' minyit a man relies on it f'r a crutch he loses th' use iv his legs. 'Tis a bad thing to stand on, a good thing to sleep on, a good thing to talk on, a bad thing to think on. If it's in th' head in th' mornin' it ought not to be in th' mouth at night. If it laughs in ye, dhrink; if it weeps, swear off. It makes some men talk like good women, an' some women talk like bad men. It is a livin' f'r orators an' th' death iv bookkeepers. It doesn't sustain life, but, whin taken hot with wather, a lump iv sugar, a piece iv lemon peel, and just th' dustin' iv a nutmeg-grater, it makes life sustainable."

"D'ye think ye-ersilf it sustains life?" asked Mr. Hennessy.

"It has sustained mine f'r many years," said Mr. Dooley.

CHRISTIAN JOURNALISM

"I see," said Mr. Dooley, "that th' la-ad out in Kansas that thried to r-run a paper like what th' Lord wud r-run if he had lived in Topeka, has thrun up th' job."

"Sure, I niver heerd iv him," said Mr. Hennessy.

"Well, 'twus this way with him," Mr. Dooley explained. "Ye see, he didn't like th' looks iv th' newspapers. He got tired iv r-readin' how many rows iv plaits Mrs. Potther Pammer had on th' las' dhress she bought, an' whether McGovern oughtn't to go into th' heavy-weight class an' fight Jeffries, an' he says, says th' la-ad, 'This is no right readin' f'r th' pure an' passionless youth iv Kansas,' he says. 'Give me,' he says, 'a chanst an' I'll projooce th' kind iv organ that'd be got out in hiven,' he says, 'price five cints a copy,' he says, 'f'r sale be all newsdealers; f'r advertisin' rates consult th' cashier,' he says. So a man in Topeka that had a newspaper, he says: 'I will not be behindhand,' he says, 'in histin' Kansas up fr'm its prisint low an' irrellijous position,' he says. 'I don't know how th' inhabitants iv th' place ye refer to is fixed,' he says, 'f'r newspapers,' he says, 'an' I niver heerd iv annybody fr'm Kansas home-stakin' there,' he says, 'but if ye'll attind to th' circulation iv thim parts,' he says, 'I'll see that th' paper is properly placed in th' hands iv th' vile an' wicked iv this earth, where,' he says, 'th' returns ar-re more quick,' he says.

"Well, th' la-ad wint at it, an' 'twas a fine paper he made. Hogan was in here th' other day with a copy iv it an' I r-read it. I haven't had such a lithry threat since I was a watchman on th' canal f'r a week with nawthin' to r-read but th' delinquent tax list an' the upper half iv a weather map. 'Twas gran'. Th' editor, it seems, Hinnissy, wint into th' editoryal rooms iv th' pa-aper an' he gathered th' force around him fr'm their reg'lar jobs in th' dhrug stores, an' says he, 'Gintlemen,' he says, 'tell me ye'er plans f'r to enoble this here Christyan publication f'r to-day!' he says. 'Well,' says th' horse rayporther, 'they's a couple iv rabbits goin' to sprint around th' thrack at th' fair groun's,' he says. 'I think 'twud be a good thing f'r rellijon if ye'd lind me tin that I might br-reak th' sin-thralled bookys that come down here fr'm Kansas City f'r to skin th' righteous,' he says. 'No,' says th' editor, he says, 'no horse racin' in this paper,' he says. ''Tis th' roonation iv th' young, an' ye can't beat it,' he says. 'An' you, fair-haired youth,' he says, 'what d'ye do that

makes ye'er color so good an' ye'er eye so bright?' 'I,' says th'
la-ad, 'am th' boy that writes th' fightin' dope,' he says. 'They'se
a couple iv good wans on at th' op'ra house to-night, an' if his
Spiklets don't tin-can 'tis like findin' money in an ol' coat that—'
'Fightin',' says th' editor, 'is a crool an' onchristyan spoort,' he
says. 'Instead iv chroniclin' th' ruffyanism iv these misguided
wretches that weigh in at th' ringside at 125 poun's, an' I see in a
pa-aper I r-read in a barber shop th' other day that Spike's gone
away back—what's that I'm sayin'? Niver mind. D'ye go
down to th' home iv th' Rivrind Aloysius Augustus Morninbinch
an' interview him on th' question iv man's co-operation with
grace in conversion. Make a nice chatty article about it an' I'll
give ye a copy iv wan iv me books.' 'I will,' says th' la-ad, 'if he
don't swing on me,' he says. The editor thin addhressed th'
staff. 'Gintlemen,' he says, 'I find that th' wurruk ye've been
accustomed to doin',' he says, 'is calc'lated f'r to disthroy th'
morality an' debase th' home life iv Topeka, not to mintion th'
surroundin' methrolopuses iv Valencia, Wanamaker, Sugar
Works, Paxico an' Snokomo,' he says. 'Th' newspaper, instead
iv bein' a pow'rful agent f'r th' salvation iv mankind, has become
something that they want to r-read,' he says. 'Ye can all go home,'
he says. 'I'll stay here an' write th' paper mesilf,' he says.
'I'm th' best writer ar-round here, annyhow, an' I'll give thim
something that'll prepare thim f'r death,' he says.

"An' he did, Hinnissy, he did. 'Twas a gran' paper. They
was an article on sewerage an' wan on prayin' f'r rain, an' another
on muni-cipal ownership iv gas tanks, an' wan to show that they
niver was a good milker ownded be a pro-fane man. They was
pomes, too, manny iv thim, an' fine wans: 'Th' Man with th'
Shovel,' 'Th' Man with th' Pick,' 'Th' Man with th' Cash-
Raygisther,' 'Th' Man with th' Snow Plow,' 'Th' Man with th'
Bell Punch,' 'Th' Man with th' Skate,' 'Th' Man with No Kick
Comin'.' Fine pothry, th' editor askin' who pushed this here
man's forehead back an' planed down his chin, who made him
wear clothes that didn't fit him and got him a job raisin' egg-plant
f'r th' monno-polists in Topeka at a dollar a day. A man in th'
editor's position ought to know, but he didn't, so he ast in th'
pomes. An' th' advertisin', Hinnissy! I'd be scandalized f'r
to go back readin' th' common advertisin' in th' vile daily press
about men's pantings, an' DoesannyoneknowwhereIcangeta
biscuit, an' In th' spring a young man's fancy lightly turns to

Pocohontas plug, not made be th' thrusts. Th' editor left thim sacrilegious advertisements f'r his venal contimp'raries. His was pious an' nice: 'Do ye'er smokin' in this wurruld. Th' Christyan Unity Five-Cint See-gar is made out iv th' finest grades iv excelsior iver projooced in Kansas!' 'Nebuchednezzar grass seed, f'r man an' beast.' 'A handful iv meal in a barrel an' a little ile in a cruse. Swedenborgian bran fried in kerosene makes th' best breakfast dish in th' wurruld.' 'Twus nice to r-read. It made a man feel as if he was in church—asleep.

"How did th' pa-aper sthrike th' people?" says ye. "Oh, it sthruck thim good. Says th' Topeka man, skinnin' over th' gossip about Christyan citizenship an' th' toolchest iv pothry: 'Eliza, here's a good paper, a fine wan, f'r ye an' th' childher. Sind Tommy down to th' corner an' get me a copy iv th' Polis Gazette.'

"Ye see, Hinnissy, th' editor wint to th' wrong shop f'r what Hogan calls his inspiration. Father Kelly was talkin' it over with me, an' says he: 'They ain't anny news in bein' good. Ye might write th' doin's iv all th' convents iv th' wurruld on th' back iv a postage stamp, an' have room to spare. Supposin' ye took out iv a newspaper all th' murdhers, an' suicides, an' divorces, an' elopements, an' fires, an' disease, an' war, an' famine,' he says, 'ye wudden't have enough left to keep a man busy r-readin' while he rode ar-roun' th' block on th' lightnin' express. No,' he says, 'news is sin an' sin is news, an' I'm worth on'y a line beginnin': "Kelly, at the parish-house, April twenty-sicond, in th' fiftieth year iv his age," an' pay f'r that, while Scanlan's bad boy is good f'r a column anny time he goes dhrunk an' thries to kill a polisman. A rellijious newspaper? None iv thim f'r me. I want to know what's goin' on among th' murdher an' burglary set. Did ye r-read it?' he says. 'I did,' says I. 'What did ye think iv it?' says he. 'I know,' says I, 'why more people don't go to church,' says I."

THE ADMIRAL'S CANDIDACY

"I see," said Mr. Hennessy, "that Dewey is a candydate f'r prisidint."

"Well, sir," said Mr. Dooley, "I hope to hiven he won't get it. No rilitive iv mine iver held a pollytical job barrin' mesilf. I was precint captain, an' wan iv th' best they was in thim days, if I do say so that shudden't. I was called Cap f'r manny years afther-

ward, an' I'd've joined th' Gr-rand Army iv th' Raypublic if it
hadn't been f'r me poor feet. Manny iv me rilitives has been
candydates, but they niver cud win out again th' r-rest iv th'
fam'ly. 'Tis so with Cousin George. I'm again him. I've been
a rayspictable saloon-keeper f'r forty years in this ward, an' I'll
not have th' name dhragged into pollytics.

"Iv coorse, I don't blame Cousin George. I'm with him f'r
annything else in th' gift iv th' people, fr'm a lovin'-cup to a
house an' lot. He don't mean annything be it. Did ye iver see a
sailor thryin' to ride a horse ? 'Tis a comical sight. Th' reason a
sailor thrics to ride a horse is because he niver r-rode wan befure.
If he knew annything about it he wouldn't do it. So be Cousin
George. Afther he'd been over here awhile an' got so 'twas safe
f'r him to go out without bein' torn to pieces f'r soovenirs or
lynched be a mob, he took a look ar-round him an' says he to a
polisman: 'What's th' governmint iv this counthry ?' ' 'Tis a
raypublic,' says th' polisman. 'What's th' main guy called ?' says
George. 'He's called prisidint,' says th' polisman. 'Is it a good
job ?' says Cousin George. ' 'Tis betther thin thravelin' beat,'
says th' bull. 'What's th' la-ad's name that's holdin' it now ?'
says Cousin George. 'Mack,' says th' cop. 'Irish ?' says George.
'Cross,' says th' elbow. 'Where fr'm ?' says George. 'Ohio,'
says the peeler. 'Where's that ?' says George. 'I dinnaw,' says
th' bull. An' they parted th' best iv frinds.

" 'Well,' says George to himsilf, 'I guess I'll have to go up
an' have a look at this la-ad's place,' he says, 'an' if it looks good,'
he says, 'p'raps I cud nail it,' he says. An' he goes up an' sees
Mack dictatin' his Porther Rickyan policy to a kinetoscope, an' it
looks like a nice employmint f'r a spry man, an' he goes back home
an' sinds f'r a rayporther, an' says he: 'I always believe since I got
home in dealin' frankly with th' press. I haven't seen manny
papers since I've been at sea, but whin I was a boy me father used
to take the Montpelier Paleejum. 'Twas r-run be a man be th'
name iv Horse Clamback. He was quite a man whin sober.
Ye've heerd iv him, no doubt. But what I ast ye up here f'r was
to give ye a item that ye can write up in ye'er own way an' hand
to th' r-rest iv th' boys. I'm goin' to be prisidint. I like th'
looks iv the job an' nobody seems to care f'r it, an' I've got so
blame tired since I left th' ship that if I don't have somethin' to do
I'll go crazy,' he says. 'I wisht ye'd make a note iv it an' give
it to th' other papers,' he says. 'Ar-re ye a raypublican or a

dimmycrat?' says the rayporter. 'What's that?' says Cousin
George. 'D'ye belong to th' raypublican or th' dimmycrat
party?' 'What ar-re they like?' says Cousin George. 'Th'
raypublicans ar-re in favor iv expansion.' 'Thin I'm a raypublican.' 'Th' dimmycrats ar-re in favor iv free thrade.'
'Thin I'm a dimmycrat.' 'Th' raypublicans ar-re f'r upholdin'
th' goold standard.' 'So'm I. I'm a raypublican there.'
'An' they're opposed to an income tax.' 'On that,' says Cousin
George, 'I'm a dimmycrat. I tell ye, put me down as a dimmycrat. Divvle th' bit I care. Just say I'm a dimmycrat with
sthrong raypublican leanings. Put it this way: I'm a dimmycrat,
be a point raypublican, dimmycrat. Anny sailor man'll undherstand that.' 'What'll I say ye'er platform is?' 'Platform?'
'Ye have to stand on a platform.' 'I do, do I? Well, I don't.
I'll stand on no platform, an' I'll hang on no sthrap. What d'ye
think th' prisidincy is—a throlley car? No, sir, whin ye peek in
th' dure to sell ye'er paper ye'll see ye'er Uncle George settin'
down comfortable with his legs crossed, thrippin' up annywan that
thries to pass him. Go out now an' write ye'er little item, f'r 'tis
late an' all hands ar-re piped to bed,' he says.

"An' there ye ar-re. Well, sir, 'tis a hard year Cousin George
has in store f'r him. Th' first thing he knows he'll have to pay f'r
havin' his pitchers in th' pa-aper. Thin he'll larn iv siv'ral
prevyous convictions in Vermont. Thin he'll discover that they
was no union label on th' goods he delivered at Manila. 'Twill be
pointed out be careful observers that he was ilicted prisidint iv th'
A.P.A. be th' Jesuits. Thin somewan'll dig up that story about
his not feelin' anny too well th' mornin' iv th' fight, an' ye can
imajine th' pitchers they'll print, an' th' jokes that'll be made,
an' th' songs: 'Dewey Lost His Appetite at th' Battle iv Manila.
Did McKinley Iver Lose His?' An' George'll wake up th'
mornin' afther iliction an' he'll have a sore head an' a sorer heart,
an' he'll find that th' on'y support he got was fr'm th' goold
dimmycratic party, an' th' chances ar-re he caught cold fr'm goin'
out without his shawl an' cudden't vote. He'll find that a man
can be r-right an' be prisidint, but he can't be both at th' same
time. An' he'll go down to breakfast an' issue Gin'ral Ordher
Number Wan, 'To All Superyor Officers Commandin' Admirals
iv th' United States navy at home or on foreign service: If anny
man mintions an admiral f'r prisidint, hit him in th' eye an'
charge same to me.' An' thin he'll go to his office an' prepare a

plan f'r to capture Dublin, th' capital iv England, whin th' nex' war begins. An' he'll spind th' r-rest iv his life thryin' to live down th' time he was a candydate."

"Well, be hivins, I think if Dewey says he's a dimmycrat an' Joyce is with him, I'll give him a vote," said Mr. Hennessy. "It's no sin to be a candydate f'r prisidint."

"No," said Mr. Dooley. "'Tis sometimes a misfortune an' sometimes a joke. But I hope ye won't vote f'r him. He might be ilicted if ye did. I'd like to raymimber him, an' it might be I cudden't if he got th' job. Who was the prisidint befure Mack? Oh, tubby sure!"

THE NEGRO PROBLEM

"What's goin' to happen to th' naygur?" asked Mr. Hennessy.

"Well," said Mr. Dooley, "he'll ayther have to go to th' north an' be a subjick race, or stay in th' south an' be an objick lesson. 'Tis a har-rd time he'll have, annyhow. I'm not sure that I'd not as lave be gently lynched in Mississippi as baten to death in New York. If I was a black man, I'd choose th' cotton belt in prifrince to th' belt on th' neck fr'm th' polisman's club. I wud so.

"I'm not so much throubled about th' naygur whin he lives among his opprissors as I am whin he falls into th' hands iv his liberators. Whin he's in th' south he can make up his mind to be lynched soon or late an' give his attintion to his other pleasures iv composin' rag-time music on a banjo, an' wurrukin' f'r th' man that used to own him an' now on'y owes him his wages. But 'tis th' divvle's own hardship f'r a coon to step out iv th' rooms iv th' S'ciety f'r th' Brotherhood iv Ma-an where he's been r-readin' a pome on th' 'Future of th' Moke' an' be pursooed be a mob iv abolitionists till he's dhriven to seek polis protection, which, Hinnissy, is th' polite name f'r fracture iv th' skull.

"I was f'r sthrikin' off th' shackles iv th' slave, me la-ad. 'Twas thrue I didn't vote f'r it, bein' that I heerd Stephen A. Douglas say 'twas onconstitootional, an' in thim days I wud go to th' flure with anny man f'r th' constitootion. I'm still with it, but not sthrong. It's movin' too fast f'r me. But no matther. Annyhow I was f'r makin' th' black man free, an' though I shtud be th' south as a spoortin' proposition I was kind iv glad in me heart whin Gin'ral Ulyss S. Grant bate Gin'ral Lee an' th' rest iv th' Union officers captured Jeff Davis. I says to mesilf, 'Now,' I says, 'th' coon 'll have a chanst f'r his life,' says I, 'an' in due time we may injye him,' I says.

"An' sure enough it looked good f'r awhile, an' th' time come whin th' occas'nal dollar bill that wint acrost this bar on pay night wasn't good money onless it had th' name iv th' naygur on it. In thim days they was a young la-ad—a frind iv wan iv th' Donohue boys—that wint to th' public school up beyant, an' he was as bright a la-ad as ye'd want to see in a day's walk. Th' larnin' iv him wud sind Father Kelly back to his grammar. He cud spell to make a hare iv th' hedge schoolmasther, he was as quick at figures as th' iddycated pig they showed in th' tint las' week in Haley's vacant lot, and in joggerphy, asthronomy, algybbera, jommethry, chimisthry, physiojnomy, bassoophly an' fractions, I was often har-rd put mesilf to puzzle him. I heerd him gradyooate an' his composition was so fine very few cud make out what he meant.

"I met him on th' sthreet wan day afther he got out iv school. 'What ar-re ye goin' to do f'r ye'ersilf, Snowball,' says I—his name was Andhrew Jackson George Wash'n'ton Americus Caslateras Beresford Vanilla Hicks, but I called him 'Snowball,' him bein' as black as coal, d'ye see—I says to him: 'What ar-re ye goin' to do f'r ye'ersilf?' I says. 'I'm goin' to enther th' profission iv law,' he says, 'where be me acooman an' industhry I hope,' he says, 'f'r to rise to be a judge,' he says, 'a congrissman,' he says, 'a sinator,' he says, 'an' p'rhaps,' he says, 'a prisidint iv th' United States,' he says. 'They'se nawthin' to prevint,' he says. 'Divvle a thing,' says I. 'Whin we made ye free,' says I, 'we opened up all these opporchunities to ye,' says I. 'Go on,' says I, 'an' enjye th' wealth an' position conferred on ye be th' constitootion,' I says. 'On'y,' I says, 'don't be too free,' I says. 'Th' freedom iv th' likes iv ye is a good thing an' a little iv it goes a long way,' I says, 'an' if I ever hear iv ye bein' prisidint iv th' United States,' I says, 'I'll take me whitewashin' away fr'm ye'er father, ye excelsior hair, poached-egg eyed, projiny iv tar,' I says, f'r me Anglo-Saxon feelin' was sthrong in thim days.

"Well, I used to hear iv him afther that defindin' coons in th' polis coort, an' now an' thin bein' mintioned among th' scatthrin' in raypublican county con-vintions, an' thin he dhropped out iv sight. 'Twas years befure I see him again. Wan day I was walkin' up th' levee smokin' a good tin cint seegar whin a coon wearin' a suit iv clothes that looked like a stained glass window in th' house iv a Dutch brewer an' a pop bottle in th' fr-ront iv his shirt, steps up to me an' he says: 'How d'ye do, Mistah Dooley,' says he. 'Don't ye know me—Mistah Hicks?' he says. 'Snowball,' says I. 'Step inside this dureway,' says I, 'less Clancy, th' polisman on th' corner, takes me f'r an octoroon,' I says. 'What ar-re ye do-in'?' says I. 'How did ye enjye th' prisidincy?' says I. He laughed an' told me th' story iv his life. He wint to practisin' law an' found his on'y clients was coons, an' they had no assets but their vote at th' prim'ry. Besides a warrant f'r a moke was the same as a letther iv inthroduction to th' warden iv th' pinitinchry. Th' on'y thing left f'r th' lawyer to do was to move f'r a new thrile an' afther he'd got two or three he thought ol' things was th' best an' ye do well to lave bad enough alone. He got so sick iv chicken he cudden't live on his fees an' he quit th' law an' wint into journalism. He r-run 'Th' Colored Supplimint,' but it was a failure, th' taste iv th' public lanin' more to quadhroon publications, an' no man that owned a resthrant or theaytre or dhrygoods store'd put in an adver-tisemint f'r fear th' subscribers'd see it an' come ar-round. Thin he attimpted to go into pollytics, an' th' best he cud get was carryin' a bucket iv wather f'r a Lincoln Club. He thried to larn a thrade an' found th' on'y place a naygur can larn a thrade is in prison an' he can't wurruk at that without committin' burglary. He started to take up subscriptions f'r a sthrugglin' church an' found th' profission was overcrowded. 'Fin'ly,' says he, ''twas up to me to be a porther in a saloon or go into th' on'y business,' he says, 'in which me race has a chanst,' he says. 'What's that?' says I. 'Craps,' says he. 'I've opened a palachal imporyium,' he says, 'where,' he says, ''twud please me very much,' he says, 'me ol' abolitionist frind,' he says, 'if ye'd dhrop in some day,' he says, 'an' I'll roll th' sweet, white bones f'r ye,' he says. ''Tis th' hope iv me people,' he says. 'We have an even chanst at ivry other pursoot,' he says, 'but 'tis on'y in craps we have a shade th' best iv it,' he says.

"So there ye ar-re, Hinnissy. An' what's it goin' to come to, says ye? Faith, I don't know an' th' naygurs don't know, an' be hivins, I think if th' lady that wrote th' piece we used to see at th' Halsted Sthreet Opry House come back to earth, she wudden't know. I used to be all broke up about Uncle Tom, but cud I give him a job tindin' bar in this here liquor store? I freed th' slave,

Hinnissy, but, faith, I think 'twas like tur-rnin' him out iv a panthry into a cellar."

"Well, they got to take their chances," said Mr. Hennessy. "Ye can't do annything more f'r thim than make thim free."

"Ye can't," said Mr. Dooley; "on'y whin ye tell thim they're free they know we're on'y sthringin' thim."

TROUBLES OF A CANDIDATE

"I wisht th' campaign was over," said Mr. Dooley.

"I wisht it'd begin," said Mr. Hennessy. "I niver knew annything so dead. They ain't been so much as a black eye give or took in th' ward an' it's less thin two months to th' big day."

"'Twill liven up," said Mr. Dooley, "I begin to see signs iv th' good times comin' again. 'Twas on'y th' other day me frind Tiddy Rosenfelt opened th' battle mildly be insinuatin' that all dimmycrats was liars, horse thieves an' arnychists. 'Tis thrue he apologized f'r that be explainin' that he didn't mean all dimmycrats but on'y those that wudden't vote f'r Mack but I think he'll take th' copper off befure manny weeks. A ladin' dimmycratic rayformer has suggested that Mack though a good man f'r an idjiot is surrounded be th' vilest scoundhrels iver seen in public life since th' days iv Joolyus Cæsar. Th' Sicrety iv th' Threeasury has declared, that Mr. Bryan in sayin' that silver is not convartible be th' terms iv th' Slatthry bankin' law iv 1870, an' th' sicond clause iv th' threaty iv Gansville, has committed th' onpard'nable pollytical sin iv so consthructin' th' facts as to open up th' possibility iv wan not knowin' th' thrue position iv affairs, misundhersthandin' intirely. If he had him outside he'd call him a liar. Th' raypublicans have proved that Willum Jennings Bryan is a thraitor be th' letther written be Dr. Lem Stoggins, th' cillybrated anti-thought agytator iv Spooten Duyvil to Aggynaldoo in which he calls upon him to do nawthin' till he hears fr'm th' doc. Th' letther was sint through th' postal authorities an' as they have established no post-office in Aggynaldoo's hat they cudden't deliver it an' they opened it. Upon r-readin' th' letther Horace Plog iv White Horse, Minnesota, has wrote to Willum Jennings Bryan declarin' that if he (Plog) iver went to th' Ph'lippeens, which he wud've done but f'r th' way th' oats was sproutin' in th' stack, an' had been hit with a bullet he'd ixpict th' Coroner to hold Bryan to

th' gran' jury.   This was followed be th' publication iv a letther
fr'm Oscar L. Swub iv East Persepalis, Ohio, declarin' that his
sister heerd a cousin iv th' man that wash'd buggies in a livery
stable in Canton say Mack's hired man tol' him Mack'd be hanged
befure he'd withdraw th' ar-rmy fr'm Cuba.

"Oh, I guess th' campaign is doin' as well as cud be ixpicted.
I see be th' raypublican pa-apers that Andhrew Carnegie has
come out f'r Bryan an' has conthributed wan half iv his income
or five hundhred millyon dollars to th' campaign fund.   In th'
dimmycratic pa-apers I r-read that Chairman Jim Jones has
inthercipted a letther fr'm the Prince iv Wales to Mack congratu-
latin' him on his appintmint as gintleman-in-waitin' to th' queen.
A dillygation iv Mormons has started fr'm dimmycratic headquarthers to thank Mack f'r his manly stand in favor iv poly-gamy
an' th' raypublican comity has undher con-sideration a letther
fr'm long term criminals advisin' their colleagues at large to vote
f'r Willum Jennings Bryan, th' frind iv crime.

"In a few short weeks, Hinnissy, 'twill not be safe f'r ayether
iv the candydates to come out on th' fr-ront porch till th' waitin'
dillygations has been searched be a polisman.   'Tis th' divvle's
own time th' la-ads that r-runs f'r th' prisidincy has since that ol'
boy Burchard broke loose again' James G. Blaine.   Sinitor Jones
calls wan iv his thrusty hinchmen to his side, an' says he: 'Mike,
put on a pig-tail, an' a blue shirt an' take a dillygation iv Chinnymen out to Canton an' congratulate Mack on th' murdher iv
mission'ries in China.   An',' he says, 'ye might stop off at Cincinnati on th' way over an' arrange f'r a McKinley an' Rosenfelt
club to ilict th' British Consul its prisidint an' attack th' office iv
th' German newspaper,' he says.   Mark Hanna rings f'r his
sicrety an', says he: 'Have ye got off th' letther fr'm George Fred
Willums advisin' Aggynaldoo to pizen th' wells?'   'Yes sir.'
'An' th' secret communication fr'm Bryan found on an arnychist
at Pattherson askin' him to blow up th' White House?'   'It's in
th' hands iv th' tyepwriter.'   'Thin call up an employmint agency
an' have a dillygation iv Jesuites dhrop in at Lincoln, with a
message fr'm th' pope proposin' to bur-rn all Protestant churches
th' night befure iliction.'

"I tell ye, Hinnissy, th' candydate is kept movin'.   Whin he
sees a dilly-gation pikin' up th' lawn he must be r-ready.   He
makes a flyin' leap f'r th' chairman, seizes him by th' throat an'
says: 'I thank ye f'r th' kind sintimints ye have conveyed.   I am,

indeed, as ye have remarked, th' riprisintative iv th' party iv manhood, honor, courage, liberality an' American thraditions. Take that back to Jimmy Jones an' tell him to put it in his pipe an' smoke it.' With which he bounds into th' house an' locks the dure while th' baffled conspirators goes down to a costumer an' changes their disguise. If th' future prisidint hadn't been quick on th' dhraw he'd been committed to a policy iv sthranglin' all the girl babies at birth.

"No, 'tis no aisy job bein' a candydate, an' 'twud be no easy job if th' game iv photygraphs was th' on'y wan th' candydates had to play. Willum Jennings Bryan is photygraphed smilin' back at his smilin' corn fields, in a pair iv blue overalls with a scythe in his hand borrid fr'm th' company that's playin' 'Th' Ol' Homestead,' at th' Lincoln Gran' Opry House. Th' nex' day Mack is seen mendin' a rustic chair with a monkey wrench, Bryan has a pitcher took in th' act iv puttin' on a shirt marked with th' union label, an' they'se another photygraph iv Mack carryin' a scuttle iv coal up th' cellar stairs. An' did ye iver notice how much th' candydates looks alike, an' how much both iv thim looks like Lydia Pinkham? Thim wondherful boardhin'-house smiles that our gifted leaders wears, did ye iver see annythin' so entrancin'? Whin th' las' photygrapher has packed his ar-rms homeward I can see th' gr-reat men retirin' to their rooms an' lettin' their faces down f'r a few minyits befure puttin' thim up again in curl-pa-apers f'r th' nex' day display. Glory be, what a relief 'twill be f'r wan iv thim to raysume permanently th' savage or fam'ly breakfast face th' mornin' afther iliction! What a raylief 'twill be to no f'r sure that th' man at th' dure bell is on'y th' gas collector an' isn't loaded with a speech iv thanks in behalf iv th' Spanish Gover'mint! What a relief to snarl at wife an' frinds wanst more, to smoke a seegar with th' thrust magnate that owns th' cider facthry near th' station, to take ye'er nap in th' afthernoon undisthurbed be th' chirp iv th' snap-shot! 'Tis th' day afther iliction I'd like f'r to be a candydate, Hinnissy, no matther how it wint."

"An' what's become iv th' vice-prisidintial candydates?" Mr. Hennessy asked.

"Well," said Mr. Dooley, "Th' las' I heerd iv Adly, I didn't hear annythin', an' th' las' I heerd iv Tiddy he'd made application to th' naytional comity f'r th' use iv Mack as a soundin' board."

A BACHELOR'S LIFE

"It's always been a wondher to me," said Mr. Hennessy, "ye niver marrid."

"It's been a wondher to manny," Mr. Dooley replied haughtily. "Maybe if I'd been as aisy pleased as most—an' this is not sayin' annything again you an' ye'ers, Hinnissy, f'r ye got much th' best iv it—I might be th' father iv happy childher an' have money in th' bank awaitin' th' day whin th' intherest on th' morgedge fell due. 'Tis not f'r lack iv opporchunities I'm here alone, I tell ye that me bucko, f'r th' time was whin th' sound iv me feet'd bring more heads to th' windies iv Ar-rchey r-road thin'd bob up to see ye'er fun'ral go by. An' that's manny a wan."

"Ah, well," said Mr. Hennessy, "I was but jokin' ye." His tone mollified his friend, who went on: "To tell ye th' truth, Hinnissy, th' raison I niver got marrid was I niver cud pick a choice. I've th' makin' iv an ixcillint ol' Turk in me, to be sure, f'r I look on all the sect as iligeable f'r me hand an' I'm on'y resthrained fr'm r-rentin' Lincoln Park f'r a home an' askin' thim all to clave on'y to me, be me nachral modesty an' th' laws iv th' State iv Illinye. 'Twas always so with me an' I think it is so with most men that dies bachelors. Be r-readin' th' pa-apers ye'd think a bachelor was a man bor-rn with a depraved an' parvarse hathred iv wan iv our most cherished institootions, an' anti-expansionist d'ye mind. But 'tis no such thing. A bachelor's a man that wud extind his benificint rule over all th' female wurruld, fr'm th' snow-capped girls iv Alaska to th' sunny eileens iv th' Passyfic. A marrid man's a person with a limited affection—a protictionist an' anti-expansionist, a mugwump, be hivins. 'Tis th' bachelor that's keepin' alive th' rivrince f'r th' sect.

"Whin I was a young man, ye cud search fr'm wan end iv th' town to th' other f'r me akel with th' ladies. Ye niver see me in them days, but 'twas me had a rogue's eye an' a leg far beyant th' common r-run iv props. I cud dance with th' best iv thim, me voice was that sthrong 'twas impossible to hear annywan else whin I sung 'Th' Pretty Maid Milkin' th' Cow,' an' I was dhressed to kill on Sundahs. 'Twas thin I bought th' hat ye see me wear at th' picnic. 'Twas 'Good mornin', Misther Dooley, an' will ye come in an' have a cup iv tay,' an' 'How d'ye do, Misther Dooley, I didn't see ye at mass this mornin',' an' 'Martin, me boy, dhrop in an' take a hand at forty-fives. Th' young ladies has been askin' me ar-re ye dead.' I was th' pop'lar idol, ye might say, an' manny's th' black look I got over th' shouldher at picnic an' wake. But I minded thim little. If a bull again me come fr'm th' pope himsilf in thim days whin me heart was high, I'd tuck it in me pocket an' say: 'I'll r-read it whin I get time.'

"Well, I'd take one iv th' girls out in me horse an' buggy iv a Sundah an' I'd think she was th' finest in th' wurruld an' I'd be sayin' all kinds iv jokin' things to her about marredge licenses bein' marked down on account iv th' poor demand an' how th' parish priest was thinkin' iv bein' thransferred to a parish where th' folks was more kindly disposed to each other an' th' likes iv that, whin out iv th' corner iv me eye I'd see another girl go by, an' bless me if I cud keep th' lid iv me r-right eye still or hold me tongue fr'm such unfortchnit remarks as: 'That there Molly Heaney's th' fine girl, th' fine, sthrappin' girl, don't ye think so?' Well, ye know, afther that I might as well be dhrivin' an ice wagon as a pleasure rig; more thin wanst I near lost th' tip iv me nose in th' jamb iv th' dure thryin' to give an affictshionate farewell. An' so it wint on, till I got th' repytation iv a flirt an' a philandhrer f'r no raison at all, d'ye mind, but me widespread fondness. I like thim all, dark an' light, large an' small, young an' old, marrid an' single, widdied an' divorced, an' so I niver marrid annywan. But ye'll find me photygraft in some albums an' me bills in more thin wan livery stable.

"I think marrid men gets on th' best f'r they have a home an' fam'ly to lave in th' mornin' an' a home an' fam'ly to go back to at night; that makes thim wurruk. Some men's domestic throubles dhrives thim to dhrink, others to labor. Ye r-read about a man becomin' a millyonaire an' ye think he done it be his own exertions whin 'tis much again little 'twas th' fear iv comin' home impty handed an' dislike iv stayin' ar-round th' house all day that made him rich. Misther Standard Ile takes in millyons in a year but he might be playin' dominoes in an injine house if it wasn't f'r Mrs. Standard Ile. 'Tis th' thought iv that dear quiet lady at home, in her white cap with her ca'm motherly face, waitin' patiently f'r him with a bell-punch that injooces him to put a shtick iv dinnymite in somebody else's ile well an' bury his securities whin th' assissor comes ar-round. Near ivry man's property ought to be in wife's name an' most iv it is.

"But with a bachelor 'tis diff'rent. Ye an' I ar-re settin' here

together an' Clancy dhrops in.   Clancy's wife's away an' he's out
f'r a good time an' he comes to me f'r it.   A bachelor's f'r th'
enjymint of his marrid frinds' vacations.   Whin Clancy's wife's
at home an' I go to see him he r-runs th' pail out in a valise, an'
we take our criminal dhrink in th' woodshed.   Well, th' three iv
us sits here an' pass th' dhrink an' sing our songs iv glee till about
ilivin o'clock; thin ye begin to look over ye'er shouldher ivry time
ye hear a woman's voice an' fin'lly ye get up an' yawn an' dhrink
ivrything on th' table an' gallop home.   Clancy an' I raysume our
argymint on th' Chinese sityation an' afterwards we carol together,
me singin' th' chune an' him doin' a razor edge tinor.   Thin he
tells me how much he cares f'r me an' proposes to rassle me an'
weeps to think how bad he threats his wife an' begs me niver to
marry, f'r a bachelor's life's th' on'y wan, an' 'tis past two o'clock
whin I hook him on a frindly polisman an' sind him thrippin'—th'
polisman—down th' sthreet.   All r-right so far.   But in th'
mornin' another story.   If Clancy gets home an' finds his wife's
rayturned fr'm th' seaside or th' stock yards, or whereiver 'tis
she'se spint her vacation, they'se no r-rest f'r him in th' mornin'.
His head may sound in his ears like a automobill an' th' look iv an
egg may make his knees thremble, but he's got to be off to th'
blacksmith shop, an' hiven help his helper that mornin'.   So
Clancy's gettin' r-rich an' puttin' a coopoly on his house.

"But with me 'tis diff'rent.   Whin Phibbius Apollo as Hogan
calls th' sun, raises his head above th' gas house, I'm cuddled up in
me couch an' Morpus, gawd iv sleep, has a sthrangle holt on me.
Th' alarm clock begins to go off an' I've just sthrength enough to
raise up an' fire it through th' window.   Two hours afterward
I have a gleam iv human intillygince an' hook me watch out fr'm
undher th' pillow.   'It's eight o'clock,' says I.   'But is it eight in
th' mornin' or eight in th' evenin'?' says I.   'Faith, I dinnaw, an'
divvle a bit care I.   Eight's on'y a number,' says I.   'It riprisints
nawthin',' says I.   "They'se hours enough in th' day f'r a free
man.   I'll tur-rn over an' sleep till eight-wan and thin I'll
wake up refreshed,' I says.   'Tis ilivin o'clock whin me tired lids
part f'r good an' Casey has been here to pay me eight dollars an'
findin' me not up has gone away f'r another year.

"A marrid man gets th' money, Hinnissy, but a bachelor man
gets th' sleep.   Whin all me marrid frinds is off to wurruk
poundin' th' ongrateful sand an' wheelin' th' rebellyous slag, in
th' heat iv th' afthernoon, ye can see ye'er onfortchnit bachelor

frind perambulatin' up an' down th' shady side iv th' sthreet, with
an umbrelly over his head an' a wurrud iv cheer fr'm young an'
old to enliven his loneliness."

"But th' childher?" asked Mr. Hennessy slyly.

"Childher!" said Mr. Dooley. "Sure I have th' finest
fam'ly in th' city. Without scandal I'm th' father iv ivry child in
Ar-rchey r-road fr'm end to end."

"An' none iv ye'er own," said Mr. Hennessy.

"I wish to hell, Hinnissy," said Mr. Dooley savagely, "ye'd not
lean against that mirror, I don't want to have to tell ye again."

THE EDUCATION OF THE YOUNG

The troubled Mr. Hennessy had been telling Mr. Dooley
about the difficulty of making a choice of schools for Packy
Hennessy, who at the age of six was at the point where the family
must decide his career.

"'Tis a big question," said Mr. Dooley, "an' wan that seems to
be worryin' th' people more thin it used to whin ivry boy was
designed f'r th' priesthood, with a full undherstandin' be his
parents that th' chances was in favor iv a brick yard. Nowadays
they talk about th' edycation iv th' child befure they choose th'
name. 'Tis: 'Th' kid talks in his sleep. 'Tis th' fine lawyer
he'll make.' Or, 'Did ye notice him admirin' that photygraph?
He'll be a gr-reat journalist.' Or, 'Look at him fishin' in Uncle
Tim's watch pocket. We must thrain him f'r a banker.' Or,
'I'm afraid he'll niver be sthrong enough to wurruk. He must go
into th' church.' Befure he's baptized too, d'ye mind. 'Twill
not be long befure th' time comes whin th' soggarth'll christen th'
infant: 'Judge Pathrick Aloysius Hinnissy, iv th' Northern
District iv Illinye,' or 'Profissor P. Aloysius Hinnissy, LL.D.,
S.T.D., P.G.N., iv th' faculty iv Nothre Dame.' Th' innocent
child in his cradle, wondherin' what ails th' mist iv him an' where
he got such funny lookin' parents fr'm, has thim to blame that
brought him into th' wurruld if he dayvilops into a sicond story
man befure he's twinty-wan an' is took up be th' polis. Why
don't you lade Packy down to th' occylist an' have him fitted with
a pair iv eye-glasses? Why don't ye put goloshes on him, give
him a blue umbrelly an' call him a doctor at wanst an' be done with
it?

"To my mind, Hinnissy, we're wastin' too much time thinkin' iv th' future iv our young, an' thryin' to larn thim early what they oughtn't to know till they've growed up. We sind th' childher to school as if 'twas a summer garden where they go to be amused instead iv a pinitinchry where they're sint f'r th' original sin. Whin I was a la-ad I was put at me ah-bee abs, th' first day I set fut in th' school behind th' hedge an' me head was sore inside an' out befure I wint home. Now th' first thing we larn th' future Mark Hannas an' Jawn D. Gateses iv our naytion is waltzin', singin', an' cuttin' pitchers out iv a book. We'd be much betther teachin' thim th' strhangle hold, f'r that's what they need in life.

"I know what'll happen. Ye'll sind Packy to what th' Germans call a Kindygartin, an' 'tis a good thing f'r Germany, because all a German knows is what some wan tells him, an' his grajation papers is a certy-ficate that he don't need to think anny more. But we've inthrajooced it into this counthry, an' whin I was down seein' if I cud injooce Rafferty, th' Janitor iv th' Isaac Muggs Grammar School, f'r to vote f'r Riordan—an' he's goin' to—I dhropped in on Cassidy's daughter, Mary Ellen, an' see her kindygartnin'. Th' childher was settin' ar-round on th' flure an' some was moldin' dachshunds out iv mud an' wipin' their hands on their hair, an' some was carvin' figures iv a goat out iv paste-board an' some was singin' an' some was sleepin' an' a few was dancin' an' wan la-ad was pullin' another la-ad's hair. 'Why don't ye take th' coal shovel to that little barbaryan, Mary Ellen?' says I. 'We don't believe in corporeal punishment,' says she. 'School shud be made pleasant f'r th' childher,' she says. 'Th' child who's hair is bein' pulled is larnin' patience,' she says, 'an' th' child that's pullin' th' hair is discovrin' th' footility iv human indeavor,' says she. 'Well, oh, well,' says I, 'times has changed since I was a boy,' I says. 'Put thim through their exercises,' says I. 'Tommy,' says I, 'spell cat,' I says. 'Go to th' divvle,' says th' cheerub. 'Very smartly answered,' says Mary Ellen. 'Ye shud not ask thim to spell,' she says. 'They don't larn that till they get to colledge,' she says, 'an',' she says, 'sometimes not even thin,' she says. 'An' what do they larn?' says I. 'Rompin',' she says, 'an' dancin',' she says, 'an' indepindance iv speech, an' beauty songs, an' sweet thoughts, an' how to make home home-like,' she says. 'Well,' says I, 'I didn't take anny iv thim things at colledge, so ye needn't unblanket thim,' I says. 'I won't put

thim through anny exercise to-day,' I says. 'But whisper, Mary
Ellen,' says I, 'don't ye niver feel like bastin' th' seeraphims?'
'Th' teachin's iv Freebull and Pitzotly is conthrary to that,' she
says. 'But I'm goin' to be marrid an' lave th' school on Choosdah,
th' twinty-sicond iv Janooary,' she says, 'an' on Mondah, th'
twinty-first, I'm goin' to ask a few iv th' little darlin's to th' house
an',' she says, 'stew thim over a slow fire,' she says. Mary Ellen
is not a German, Hinnissy.

"Well, afther they have larned in school what they ar-re
licked f'r larnin' in th' back yard—that is squashin' mud with
their hands—they're conducted up through a channel iv free an'
beautiful thought till they're r-ready f'r colledge. Mamma
packs a few doylies an' tidies into son's bag, an' some silver to be
used in case iv throuble with th' landlord, an' th' la-ad throts off
to th' siminary. If he's not sthrong enough to look f'r high
honors as a middle weight pugilist he goes into th' thought departmint. Th' prisidint takes him into a Turkish room, gives
him a cigareet an' says: 'Me dear boy, what special branch iv
larnin' wud ye like to have studied f'r ye be our compitint pro-
fissors? We have a chair iv Beauty an' wan iv Puns an' wan iv
Pothry on th' Changin' Hues iv the Settin' Sun, an' wan on
Platonic Love, an' wan on Nonsense Rhymes, an' wan on Sweet
Thoughts, an' wan on How Green Grows th' Grass, an' wan on
th' Relation iv Ice to th' Greek Idee iv God,' he says. 'This is
all ye'll need to equip ye f'r th' perfect life, onless,' he says, 'ye
intind bein' a dintist, in which case,' he says, 'we won't think
much iv ye, but we have a good school where ye can larn that
disgraceful thrade,' he says. An' th' la-ad makes his choice, an'
ivry mornin' whin he's up in time he takes a whiff iv hasheesh an'
goes off to hear Profissor Maryanna tell him that 'if th' dates iv
human knowledge must be rejicted as subjictive, how much more
must they be subjicted as rejictive if, as I think, we keep our
thoughts fixed upon th' inanity iv th' finite in comparison with th'
onthinkable truth with th' ondivided an' onimaginable reality.
Boys ar-re ye with me?'

"That's at wan colledge—Th' Colledge iv Speechless Thought.
Thin there's th' Colledge iv Thoughtless Speech, where th' la-ad
is larned that th' best thing that can happen to annywan is to be
prisident iv a railroad consolidation. Th' head iv this colledge
believes in thrainin' young men f'r th' civic ideel, Father Kelly
tells me. Th' on'y thrainin' I know f'r th' civic ideel is to have an

alarm clock in ye'er room on iliction day. He believes 'young men shud be equipped with Courage, Discipline, an' Loftiness iv Purpose'; so I suppose Packy, if he wint there, wud listen to lectures fr'm th' Profissor iv Courage an' Erasmus H. Noddle, Doctor iv Loftiness iv Purpose. I loft, ye loft, he lofts. I've always felt we needed some wan to teach our young th' Courage they can't get walkin' home in th' dark, an' th' loftiness iv purpose that doesn't start with bein' hungry an' lookin' f'r wurruk. An' in th' colledge where these studies are taught, it's undhershtud that even betther thin gettin' th' civic ideel is bein' head iv a thrust. Th' on'y trouble with th' coorse is that whin Packy comes out loaded with loftiness iv purpose, all th' lofts is full iv men that had to figure it out on th' farm."

"I don't undherstand a wurrud iv what ye're sayin'," said Mr. Hennessy.

"No more do I," said Mr. Dooley. "But I believe 'tis as Father Kelly says: 'Childher shudden't be sint to school to larn, but to larn how to larn. I don't care what ye larn thim so long as 'tis onpleasant to thim.' 'Tis thrainin' they need, Hinnissy. That's all. I niver cud make use iv what I larned in colledge about thrigojoomethry an'—an'—grammar an' th' welts I got on th' skull fr'm the schoolmasther's cane I have nivver been able to turn to anny account in th' business, but 'twas th' bein' there and havin' to get things to heart without askin' th' meanin' iv thim an' goin' to school cold an' comin' home hungry, that made th' man iv me ye see befure ye."

"That's why th' good woman's throubled about Packy," said Hennessy.

"Go home," said Mr. Dooley.

CASUAL OBSERVATIONS

To most people a savage nation is wan that doesn't wear oncomf'rtable clothes.

Manny people'd rather be kilt at Newport thin at Bunker Hill.

If ye live enough befure thirty ye won't care to live at all afther fifty.

As Shakespere says, be thrue to ye'ersilf an' ye will not thin be false to ivry man.

Play actors, orators an' women ar-re a class be thimsilves.

Among men, Hinnissy, wet eye manes dhry heart.

Th' nearest anny man comes to a con-ciption iv his own death is lyin' back in a comfortable coffin with his ears cocked f'r th' flatthrin' remarks iv th' mourners.

A fanatic is a man that does what he thinks th' Lord wud do if He knew th' facts iv th' case.

A millionyaire—or man out iv debt—wanst tol' me his dhreams always took place in th' farm-house where he was bor-rn. He said th' dhreamin' part iv his life was th' on'y part that seemed real.

'Tis no job to find out who wrote an anonymous letter. Jus' look out iv th' window whin ye get it. 'Tis harder to do evil thin good be stealth.

A German's idee iv Hivin is painted blue an' has cast-iron dogs on th' lawn.

No man was iver so low as to have rayspict f'r his brother-in-law.

Th' modhren idee iv governmint is 'Snub th' people, buy th' people, jaw th' people.'

I wisht I was a German an' believed in machinery.

A vote on th' tallysheet is worth two in the box.

I care not who makes th' laws iv a nation if I can get out an injunction.

An Englishman appears resarved because he can't talk.

What China needs is a Chinese exclusion act.

All th' wurruld loves a lover—excipt sometimes th' wan that's all th' wurruld to him.

———

A nation with colonies is kept busy. Look at England! She's like wan iv th' Swiss bell-ringers.

———

Th' paramount issue f'r our side is th' wan th' other side doesn't like to have mintioned.

———

If ye put a beggar on horseback ye'll walk ye'ersilf.

———

It takes a sthrong man to be mean. A mean man is wan that has th' courage not to be gin'rous. Whin I give a tip 'tis not because I want to but because I'm afraid iv what th' waiter'll think. Russell Sage is wan iv Nature's noblemen.

———

An autocrat's a ruler that does what th' people wants an' takes th' blame f'r it. A constitootional ixicutive, Hinnissy, is a ruler that does as he dam pleases an' blames th' people.

———

'Tis as hard f'r a rich man to enther th' kingdom iv Hiven as it is f'r a poor man to get out iv Purgatory.

———

Evil communications corrupt good Ph'lippeens.

———

Ivry man has his superstitions. If I look at a new moon over me shoulder I get a crick in me neck.

———

Thrust ivrybody—but cut th' ca-ards.

———

If Rooshia wud shave we'd not be afraid iv her.

———

Some day th' Ph'lippeens 'll be known as th' Standard Isles iv th' Passyfic.

———

A woman's sinse iv humor is in her husband's name.

———

Most women ought niver to look back if they want a following.

———

If ye dhrink befure siven ye'll cry befure iliven.

A man that'd expict to thrain lobsters to fly in a year is called a loonytic; but a man that thinks men can be tur-rned into angels be an iliction is called a rayformer an' remains at large.

———

Th' throuble with most iv us, Hinnissy, is we swallow pollytical idees befure they're ripe an' they don't agree with us.

———

Dhressmakers' bills sinds women into lithrachoor an' men into an early decline.

———

A bur-rd undher a bonnet is worth two on th' crown.

———

People tell me to be frank, but how can I be whin I don't dare to know mesilf?

———

People that talk loud an' offind ye with their insolence are usu'lly shy men thryin' to get over their shyness. 'Tis th' quite, resarved, ca'm spoken man that's mashed on himsilf.

———

If men cud on'y enjye th' wealth an' position th' newspapers give thim whin they're undher arrest! Don't anny but prominent clubmen iver elope or embezzle?

———

Miditation is a gift con-fined to unknown philosophers an' cows. Others don't begin to think till they begin to talk or write.

———

A good manny people r-read th' ol' sayin' "Larceny is th' sincerest form iv flatthry."

———

'Tis a good thing th' fun'ral sermons ar-re not composed in th' confissional.

———

Most vigitaryans I iver see looked enough like their food to be classed as cannybals.

———

I don't see why anny man who believes in medicine wud shy at th' faith cure.

———

Miracles are laughed at be a nation that r-reads thirty millyon newspapers a day an' supports Wall sthreet.

All men are br-rave in comp'ny an' cow'rds alone, but some shows it clearer thin others.

———

I'd like to tell me frind Tiddy that they'se a strenuse life an' a sthrenuseless life.

———

I'd like to've been ar-round in th' times th' historical novelists writes about—but I wudden't like to be in th' life insurance business.

———

I wondher why porthrait painters look down on phrenologists.

———

Di-plomacy is a continyual game iv duck on th' rock—with France th' duck.

———

Whin we think we're makin' a gr-reat hit with th' wurruld we don't know what our own wives thinks iv us.

MR. DOOLEY'S OPINIONS

THE SUPREME COURT'S DECISIONS[1]

"I see," said Mr. Dooley, "th' supreme coort has decided th' constitution don't follow th' flag."

"Who said it did?" asked Mr. Hennessy.

"Some wan," said Mr. Dooley. "It happened a long time ago an' I don't raymimber clearly how it come up, but some fellow said that ivrywhere th' constitution wint, th' flag was sure to go. 'I don't believe wan wurrud iv it,' says th' other fellow. 'Ye can't make me think th' constitution is goin' thrapezin' around ivrywhere a young liftnant in th' ar-rmy takes it into his head to stick a flag pole. It's too old. It's a home-stayin' constitution with a blue coat with brass buttons onto it, an' it walks with a goold-headed cane. It's old an' it's feeble an' it prefers to set on th' front stoop an' amuse th' childher. It wudden't last a minyit in thim thropical climes. 'Twud get a pain in th' fourteenth amindmint an' die before th' doctors cud get ar-round to cut it out. No, sir, we'll keep it with us, an' threat it tenderly without too much hard wurruk, an' whin it plays out entirely we'll give it dacint buryal an' incorp'rate oursilves under th' laws iv Noo Jarsey. That's what we'll do,' says he. 'But,' says th' other, 'if it wants to thravel, why not lave it?' 'But it don't want to.' 'I say it does.' 'How'll we find out?' 'We'll ask th' supreme coort. They'll know what's good f'r it.'

"So it wint up to th' supreme coort. They'se wan thing about th' supreme coort, if ye lave annything to thim, ye lave it to thim. Ye don't get a check that entitles ye to call f'r it in an hour. The supreme coort iv th' United States ain't in anny hurry about

---

[1] In this well-known essay Dunne examines the decision of the Supreme Court in the so-called Insular Cases of 1901, a decision which in effect aided the cause of American expansion. Mr. Dooley's observation that "no matther whether th' constitution follows th' flag or not, th' supreme coort follows th' iliction returns" was widely quoted.

catchin' th' mails. It don't have to make th' las' car. I'd back
th' Aujitoroom again it anny day f'r a foot race. If ye're lookin'
f'r a game iv quick decisions an' base hits, ye've got to hire another
empire. It niver gives a decision till th' crowd has dispersed an'
th' players have packed their bats in th' bags an' started f'r home.

"F'r awhile ivrybody watched to see what th' supreme coort
wud do. I knew mesilf I felt I cudden't make another move in th'
game till I heerd fr'm thim. Buildin' op'rations was suspinded
an' we sthud wringin' our hands outside th' dure waitin' f'r
information fr'm th' bedside. 'What're they doin' now?'
'They just put th' argymints iv larned counsel in th' ice box an'
th' chief justice is in a corner writin' a pome. Brown J. an'
Harlan J. is discussin' th' condition iv th' Roman Empire befure
th' fire. Th' r-rest iv th' coort is considherin' th' question iv
whether they ought or ought not to wear ruchin' on their skirts an'
hopin' crinoline won't come in again. No decision to-day?'
An' so it wint f'r days, an' weeks an' months. Th' men that had
argyied that th' constitution ought to shadow th' flag to all th'
tough resorts on th' Passyfic coast an' th' men that argyied that
th' flag was so lively that no constitution cud follow it an' survive,
they died or lost their jobs or wint back to Salem an' were f'rgotten.
Expansionists contracted an' anti-expansionists blew up an' little
childher was born into th' wurruld an' grew to manhood an' niver
heerd iv Porther Ricky except whin some wan get a job there.
I'd about made up me mind to thry an' put th' thing out iv me
thoughts an' go back to wurruk when I woke up wan mornin' an'
see be th' pa-aper that th' Supreme Coort had warned th' constitution to lave th' flag alone an' tind to its own business.

"That's what th' pa-aper says, but I've r-read over th' decision
an' I don't see annything iv th' kind there. They'se not a wurrud
about th' flag an' not enough to tire ye about th' constitution.
'Tis a matther iv limons, Hinnissy, that th' Supreme Coort has
been settin' on f'r this gineration—a cargo iv limons sint fr'm
Porther Ricky to some Eyetalian in Philydelphy. Th' decision
was r-read be Brown J., him bein' th' las' justice to make up his
mind, an' ex-officio, as Hogan says, th' first to speak, afther a
crool an' bitther contest. Says Brown J.: 'Th' question here is
wan iv such gr-reat importance that we've been sthrugglin' over it
iver since ye see us las' an' on'y come to a decision (Fuller C. J.,
Gray J., Harlan J., Shiras J., McKenna J., White J., Brewer J., an'
Peckham J. dissentin' fr'm me an' each other) because iv th' hot

weather comin' on. Wash'n'ton is a dhreadful place in summer (Fuller C. J. dissentin'). Th' whole fabric iv our government is threatened, th' lives iv our people an' th' pro-gress iv civilization put to th' bad. Men ar-re excited. But why? We ar-re not. (Harlan J., "I am." Fuller C. J. dissentin', but not f'r th' same reason.) This thing must be settled wan way or th' other undher that dear ol' constitution be varchue iv which we are here an' ye ar-re there an' Congress is out West practicin' law. Now what does th' constitution say? We'll look it up thoroughly whin we get through with this case (th' rest iv th' coort dissentin'). In th' manetime we must be governed by th' ordnances iv th' Khan iv Beloochistan, th' laws iv Hinnery th' Eighth, th' opinyon iv Justice iv th' Peace Oscar Larson in th' case iv th' township iv Red Wing varsus Petersen, an' th' Dhred Scott decision. What do they say about limons? Nawthin' at all. Again we take th' Dhred Scott decision. This is wan iv th' worst I iver r-read. If I cudden't write a betther wan with blindhers on, I'd leap off th' bench. This horrible fluke iv a decision throws a gr-reat, an almost dazzlin' light on th' case. I will turn it off. (McKenna J. concurs, but thinks it ought to be blowed out.) But where was I? I must put on me specs. Oh, about th' limons. Well, th' decision iv th' Coort (th' others dissentin') is as follows: First, that th' Disthrict iv Columbya is a state; second, that it is not; third, that New York is a state; fourth, that it is a crown colony; fifth, that all states ar-re states an' all territories ar-re territories in th' eyes iv other powers, but Gawd knows what they ar-re at home. In th' case iv Hogan varsus Mullins, th' decision is he must paper th' barn. (Hinnery VIII, sixteen, six, four, eleven.) In Wiggins varsus et al. th' cow belonged. (Louis XIV, 90 in rem.) In E. P. Vigore varsus Ad Lib., the custody iv th' childher. I'll now fall back a furlong or two in me chair, while me larned but misguided collagues r-read th' Histhry iv Iceland to show ye how wrong I am. But mind ye, what I've said goes. I let thim talk because it exercises their throats, but ye've heard all th' decision on this limon case that'll get into th' fourth reader.' A voice fr'm th' audjeence, 'Do I get me money back?' Brown J.: 'Who ar-re ye?' Th' Voice: 'Th' man that ownded th' limons.' Brown J.: 'I don't know.' (Gray J., White J., dissentin' an' th' r-rest iv th' birds concurrin' but f'r entirely diff'rent reasons.)

"An' there ye have th' decision, Hinnissy, that's shaken th' intellicts iv th' nation to their very foundations, or will if they thry to read it. 'Tis all r-right. Look it over some time. 'Tis fine spoort if ye don't care f'r checkers. Some say it laves th' flag up in th' air an' some say that's where it laves th' constitution. Annyhow, something's in th' air. But there's wan thing I'm sure about."

"What's that?" asked Mr. Hennessy.

"That is," said Mr. Dooley, "no matther whether th' constitution follows th' flag or not, th' supreme coort follows th' iliction returns."

THANKSGIVING

"Whin I was a young man," said Mr. Dooley, "I often heerd Thanksgivin' day alooded to fr'm th' altar as a pagan fistival. Father Kelly don't think so. He says 'twas founded be th' Puritans to give thanks f'r bein' presarved fr'm th' Indyans, an' that we keep it to give thanks we are presarved fr'm th' Puritans. In th' beginnin', Hinnissy, 'twas a relijous fistival, like dividend day in th' synagogues. Ye see, th' Puritan fathers, whose dayscindants mostly live in Kansas now, had had such a divvle iv a time inthrajoocin' rellijon an' slavery among th' savage r-red men that they found huntin' th' wild cranberry in th' neighborhood iv Salem, Mass., that whin th' job was completed they set apart a day to thank th' Lord for his opporchune assistance in their wurruk iv rayformin' th' wurruld an' with a few frills added in th' way iv food th' custom's been kept up to this very day. In iv'ry city iv this fair land th' churches is open an' empty, the fleet anise seed bag is pursooed over th' smilin' potato patch an' th' groans iv th' dyin' resound fr'm manny a fut-ball field. We're givin' thanks that we're presarved fr'm hunger, fr'm thirst, fr'm free silver, fr'm war an' pestilence an' famine an' each other. But don't ye f'rget it, Hinnissy, 'tis none iv these things we really give thanks f'r. In our hearts we're grateful f'r on'y wan blessin' an' that's on Thanksgivin' day we get th' first good crack iv th' season at th' Turkey bur-rd an' his r-runnin' mate, ol' Uncle Cranberry Sauce. Ye bet ye.

"Annyhow, seein' that the iliction come out th' way it did an this counthry ain't goin' to be handed over to th' likes iv ye, we ought to cillybrate Thanksgivin' if necess'ry with achin' hearts. I'm always in favor iv givin' thanks—f'r annything. 'Tis a good habit to get into. 'Thank ye kindly,' is betther thin 'bad cess to ye,' annyhow. Even whin I sneeze I say: 'Gawd bless us kindly,' an' f'r th' slender blessin' iv livin' at all I say 'Praise be.' So we ought to be thankful. We have a big counthry an' 'tis growin' bigger an' we ought to be thankful f'r that, an' pray that it may stop growin' in width an' grow a little more in height. Th' farmer is thankful he has a good crop an' I'm thankful I'm not a farmer. Ye cud always find room f'r thanks that ye're not some wan else, if ye cud know how th' other fellow feels. A few days ago I wud've said that I'd like to be the Czar iv Rooshia but I wudden't trade places with him to-day if he'd throw in th' Kingdom of Boolgahrya to make th' thrade good. Crowned though he is, he lies on his back while a trained nurse pipes hot milk an' limon juice into him, while I go across th' sthreet an' hurl into me dimmycratic frame two furlongs iv corned beef an' a chain iv cabbage. Me timp'rature is normal save whin I'm asked f'r money. Me pulse bates sivinty to th' minyit an' though I have patches on me pantaloons, I've ne'er a wan on me intestines. (I touch wood to keep off bad luck.) No, I wudden't be th' Czar iv Rooshia. An' I wudden't be th' Impror Willum. I'm thankful I'm not th' Impror iv Chiny, whoiver he is or whereiver he is. I'm thankful I'm not John D. Rockyfellar, f'r I know I can't get his money an' he thinks he can get mine, an' I'll fool him. I'm thankful I ain't Prisident Tiddy, f'r whin me day's wurruk is done, I can close up th' shop, wind th' clock an' go to sleep. If th' stars an' moon don't shine, if th' sun don't come up, if th' weather is bad, if th' crops fail or th' banks bust or Hinnissy ain't ilicted director iv th' rollin' mills, no wan can blame me. I done me jooty. Ye can't come to me an say: 'Dooley, th' north star wasn't at wurruk last night—what have ye done with it?' Or 'Look here, Dooley, what ails ye sindin' rainy weather befure th' hay is cut?' 'No sir,' says I. 'I promised ye nawthin' but five cints worth iv flude exthract iv hell f'r fifteen cints an' ye got it. I'm not responsible f'r th' vagaries iv th' ilimints. If I was I'd be sellin' umbrellys, not rum,' I says. But th' prisidint can't escape it. He has to set up at night steerin' th' stars sthraight, hist th' sun at th' r-right moment, turn on th' hot an' cold fassit, have rain wan place, an' fr-rost another, salt mines with a four years' supply iv goold, thrap th' mickrobes as they fly through th' air an' see that tin dollars is akelly divided among wan hundherd men so that each man gits thirty dollars more thin anny other. If he can't do that he's lible to be arrested th' first pay day f'r obtainin' money be false pretences.   So I'm thankful I'm not him.

"But I'm always thankful f'r these things.   Be thankful f'r what ye have not, Hinnissy—'tis th' on'y safe rule.   If ye're on'y thankful f'r ye'er possissions ye'er supply won't last a day.   But if ye're thankful f'r what others have, an' ye have not, an' thankful ye haven't it, all th' wurruld conthributes to ye'er gratichood.   Ye set here like a poor box in th' back iv th' church an' iv'rybody dhrops in his bad money an' swells ye.

"But as I told ye, Hinnissy, afther all, th' Turkey bur-rd's th' rale cause iv Thanksgivin'.   He's th' naytional air.   Abolish th' Turkey an' ye desthroy th' tie that binds us as wan people.   We're wan race, hitched together be a gr-reat manny languages, a rellijon apiece, thraditions that don't agree with each other, akel opporchunities f'r th' rich an' poor, to continue bein' rich an' poor, an' a common barnyard food.   Whin iv'rybody in a nation eats th' same things that all th' others eats, ye can't break thim up.   Talk about th' dove iv peace!   Th' Turkey makes him look like a game cock.   Can I help ye, Mr. Hinnissy ?   White or dark ?   Th' leg, p'raps, or maybe th' part that goes over th'—"

"Some iv us," said Mr. Hennessy, gloomily, "some iv us will be atin' another kind iv bur-rd this fall."

"Ye're wrong there, me la-ad," said Mr. Dooley.   "Ye're wrong there.   Ye're wrong.   They'se no such thing as crow.   Thanksgivin' day comes too quick afther iliction.   We're all r-ready f'r th' blackest crow that ivver dimmycrat ate an' we have our noses in th' air.   An' thin we look down, an' lo an' behold! 'tis THANKSGIVIN' TURKEY."

THE CRUSADE AGAINST VICE[1]

"Vice," said Mr. Dooley, "is a creature of such heejous mien, as Hogan says, that th' more ye see it th' betther ye like it.   I'd be afraid to enther upon a crusade again vice f'r fear I might prefer it to th' varchous life iv a rayspictable liquor dealer.   But annyhow th' crusade has started, an' befure manny months I'll be lookin' undher th' table whin I set down to a peaceful game iv solytaire to see if a polisman in citizens' clothes ain't concealed there.

"Th' city iv Noo York, Hinnissy, sets th' fashion iv vice an' starts th' crusade again it.   Thin ivrybody else takes it up.

---

[1] Parkers: The Rev. Charles Henry Parkhurst, whose sermons against vice and corruption in New York City led to the Lexow Investigation (1894).

They'se crusades an' crusaders in ivry hamlet in th' land, an' places that is cursed with nawthin' worse thin pitchin' horseshoes sinds to th' neighborin' big city f'r a case iv vice to suppress. We're in th' mist iv a crusade now, an' there isn't a polisman in town who isn't thremblin' f'r his job.

"As a people, Hinnissy, we're th' greatest crusaders that iver was—f'r a short distance. On a quarther mile thrack we can crusade at a rate that wud make Hogan's frind, Godfrey th' Bullion look like a crab. But th' throuble is th' crusade don't last afther th' first sprint. Th' crusaders drops out iv th' procission to take a dhrink or put a little money on th' ace an' be th' time th' end iv th' line iv march is reached th' boss crusader is alone in th' job an' his former followers is hurlin' bricks at him fr'm th' windows iv policy shops. Th' boss crusader always gets th' double cross. If I wanted to sind me good name down to th' ginerations with Cap. Kidd an' Jesse James I'd lead a movement f'r th' suppression iv vice. I wud so.

"Ye see, Hinnissy, 'tis this way: th' la-ads ilicted to office an' put on th' polis foorce is in need iv a little loose change, an' th' on'y way they can get it is to be negotyatin' with vice. Tammany can't raise anny money on th' churches; it won't do f'r thim to raid a gints' furnishin' sthore f'r keepin' disorderly neckties in th' window. They've got to get th' money where it's comin' to thim an' 'tis on'y comin' to thim where th' law an' vile human nature has a sthrangle holt on each other. A polisman goes afther vice as an officer iv th' law an' comes away as a philosopher. Th' theery iv mesilf, Hogan, Croker, an' other larned men is that vice whin it's broke is a crime an' whin it's got a bank account is a necessity an' a luxury.

"Well, th' la-ads goes on usin' th' revised statues as a sandbag an' by an' by th' captain iv th' polis station gets to a pint where his steam yacht bumps into a canoe iv th' prisidint iv th' Standard Ile Comp'ny an' thin there's th' divvle to pay. It's been a dull summer annyhow an' people ar-re lookin' f'r a change an' a little divarsion, an' somebody who doesn't raymimber what happened to th' last man that led a crusade again vice, gets up an', says he: 'This here city is a verytable Sodom an' it must be cleaned out,' an' ivrybody takes a broom at it. Th' churches appints comities an' so does th' Stock Exchange an' th' Brewers' Society an' afther awhile other organizations jumps into th' fray, as Hogan says. Witnesses is summoned befure th' comity iv th' Amalgamated

Union iv Shell Wurrukers, th' S'ciety f'r th' Privintion iv Good Money, th' Ancient Ordher iv Send Men, th' Knights iv th' Round Table with th' slit in th' centhre; an' Spike McGlue th' burglar examines thim on vice they have met an' what ought to be done tow'rd keepin' th' polis in nights. Thin th' man that objects to canary bur-rds in windows, sthreet-music, vivysection, profanity, expensive fun'rals, open sthreet cars an' other vices, takes a hand an' ye can hear him as well as th' others. Vice is th' on'y thing talked iv at th' church socyables an' th' mothers' meetin's; 'tis raysolved be th' Insomnya Club that now's th' time to make a flyin' wedge again th' divvlish hurdy gurdy an' meetin's are called to burn th' polis in ile f'r not arrestin' th' criminals who sell vigitables at th' top iv their lungs. Some wan invints an anti-vice cocktail. Lectures is delivered to small bodies iv preachers on how to detect vice so that no wan can palm off countherfeit vice on thim an' make thim think 'tis good. Th' polis becomes active an' whin th' polis is active 'tis a good time f'r dacint men to wear marredge certy-ficates outside iv their coats. Hanyous monsthers is nailed in th' act iv histin' in a shell iv beer in a German Garden; husbands waits in th' polis station to be r-ready to bail out their wives whin they're arrested f'r shoppin' afther four o'clock; an' there's more joy over wan sinner rayturned to th' station thin f'r ninety an' nine that've rayformed.

"Th' boss crusader is havin' th' time iv his life all th' while. His pitcher is in th' papers ivry mornin' an' his sermons is a directhry iv places iv amusement. He says to himsilf, 'I am improvin' th' wurruld an' me name will go down to th' ginerations as th' greatest vice buster iv th' cinchry. Whin I get through they won't be enough crime left in this city to amuse a sthranger fr'm Hannybal, Missoury f'r twinty minyits,' he says. That's where he's wrong. Afther awhile people gets tired iv th' pastime. They want somewhere to go nights. Most people ain't vicious, Hinnissy, an' it takes vice to hunt vice. That accounts f'r polis-men. Besides th' horse show or th' football games or something else excitin' divarts their attintion an' wan day th' boss crusader finds that he's alone in Sodom. 'Vice ain't so bad afther all. I notice business was betther whin 'twas rampant,' says wan la-ad. 'Sure ye're right,' says another. 'I haven't sold a single pink shirt since that man Parkers closed th' faro games,' says he. 'Th' theaytre business ain't what it was whin they was more vice,' says another. 'This ain't no Connecticut village,' he says.

'An' 'tis no use thryin' to inthrajooce soomchury ligislation in this impeeryal American city,' he says, 'where people come pursooed be th' sheriff fr'm ivry corner iv th' wurruld,' he says. 'Ye can't make laws f'r this community that wud suit a New England village,' he says, 'where,' he says, 'th' people ar-re too uncivilizeu to be immoral,' he says. 'Vice,' he says, 'goes a long way tow'rd makin' life bearable,' he says. 'A little vice now an' thin is relished be th' best iv men,' he says. 'Who's this Parkers, anny-how, intherferin' with th' liberty iv th' individooal, an',' he says, 'makin' it hard to rent houses on th' side sthreets,' he says. 'I bet ye if ye invistigate ye'll find that he's no betther thin he shud be himsilf,' he says. An' th' best Parkers gets out iv it is to be able to escape fr'm town in a wig an' false whiskers. Thin th' captain iv th' polis that's been a spindin' his vacation in th' disthrict where a man has to be a Rocky Mountain sheep to be a polisman, returns to his old place, puts up his hat on th' rack an' says, 'Garrity, if annybody calls ye can tell him to put it in an anvelope an' leave it in me box. An' if ye've got a good man handy I wisht ye'd sind him over an' have him punch th' bishop's head. His grace is gettin' too gay.'

"An' there ye ar-re, Hinnissy. Th' crusade is over an' Vice is rampant again. I'm afraid, me la-ad, that th' frinds iv vice is too sthrong in this wurruld iv sin f'r th' frinds iv varchue. Th' good man, th' crusader, on'y wurruks at th' crusade wanst in five years, an' on'y whin he has time to spare fr'm his other jooties. 'Tis a pastime f'r him. But th' definse iv vice is a business with th' other la-ad an' he nails away at it, week days an' Sundays, holy days an' fish days, mornin', noon an' night."

"They ought to hang some iv thim pollyticians," said Mr. Hennessy angrily.

"Well," said Mr. Dooley, "I don't know. I don't expict to gather calla lillies in Hogan's turnip patch. Why shud I expict to pick bunches iv spotless statesmen f'rm th' gradooation class iv th' house iv correction."

THE NEW YORK CUSTOM HOUSE

"Hannigan's back," said Mr. Dooley.

"I didn't know he'd iver been away," said Mr. Hennessy.

"Oh, he has that," said Mr. Dooley. "He's been makin' what Hogan calls th' gran' tower. He's been to New York an' to

Cork an' he see his rilitives, an' now he's come home f'r to thry to get even. He had a gran' time, an' some day I'll get him in here an' have him tell ye about it."

"Did he bring annything back?" asked Mr. Hennessy.

"He started to," said Mr. Dooley. "Befure he left Queenstown he laid in a supply iv th' stimulant that's made th' Irish th' finest potes an' rivolutionists an' th' poorest bookkeepers in th' wurruld, an' a dozen or two iv blackthorn sticks f'r frinds iv his on th' polis. He had a most tumulchuse v'yage. There was a man played th' accorjeen all th' way acrost. Glad he was to see th' pleasant fields iv Noo Jarsey an' th' sthreet clanin' department's scows goin' out to sea, an' th' la-ad fr'm th' health boord comin' aboord an' askin' ivrybody did they have th' small pox an' was they convicts. There was a Rooshian on th' boat that'd been run out iv Rooshia because he cud r-read, an' people thought he was gettin' r-ready to peg something at th' Czar, an' Hannigan an' him got to be gr-reat frinds. As they shtud on th' deck, Hannigan banged him on th' back an' says he: 'Look,' he says with th' tears r-runnin' down his cheeks. He was wanst in th' ligislachure. 'Look,' he says, 'ye poor down-throdden serf,' he says. 'Behold, th' land iv freedom,' he says, 'where ivry man's as good as ivry other man,' he says, 'on'y th' other man don't know it,' he says. 'That flag which I can't see, but I know 'tis there,' he says, 'floats over no race iv slaves,' he says. 'Whin I shtep off th' boat,' he says, 'I'll put me box on me shouldher,' he says, 'an' I'll be as free as anny man alive,' he says, 'an' if e'er a sowl speaks to me, I'll give him a dhrink out iv th' bottle or a belt with th' blackthorn,' he says, 'an' little I care which it is,' he says. 'A smile f'r those that love ye, an' a punch f'r those that hate, as Tom Moore, th' pote, says,' he says. 'Land iv liberty,' he says, 'I salute ye,' he says, wavin' his hat at a soap facthry. 'Have ye declared yet?' says a man at his elbow. 'Declared what?' says Hannigan. 'Th' things ye have in th' box,' says th' man. 'I have not,' says Hannigan. 'Th' contints iv that crate is sacred between me an' mesilf,' he says. 'Well,' says th' man, 'Ye'd betther slide down th' companyion way or stairs to th' basement iv th' ship an' tell what ye know,' he says, 'or 'tis mindin' bar'ls at th' pinitinchry ye'll be this day week,' he says.

"Well, Hannigan is an Irish raypublican that does what he's told, so he wint downstairs an' there was a lot iv la-ads sittin' ar-round a table, an' says wan iv thim: 'What's ye'er name, Tim

Hannigan, an' ar-re ye a citizen iv this counthry?' 'Well, Glory be to th' saints!' says Hannigan, 'if that ain't Petie Casey, th' tailor's son. Well, how ar-re ye an' what ar-re ye doin' down here?' he says. 'I'm a customs inspictor,' says th' boy. ''Tis a good job,' says Hannigan. 'I thried f'r it wanst mesilf, but I jined th' wrong or-gan-ization,' he says. 'Step out an' have a dhrink,' he says. 'I've a bottle iv Irish whiskey in my thrunk that'd make ye think ye was swallowin' a pincushion,' he says. 'Sh-h,' says Petie Casey. 'Man alive, ye'll be in th' lock-up in another minyit if ye don't keep quite. That fellow behind ye is a mannyfacthrer iv Irish whiskey in Bleecker Sthreet an' he's hand in glove with th' administhration,' he says. 'Well, annyhow,' says Hannigan, 'I want to give ye a blackthorn shtick f'r ye'er father,' he says. 'Lord bless me sowl!' says th' boy. 'Ye'll lose me me job yet. That fellow with th' r-red hair is th' principal Rahway dealer in blackthorns. His name is Schmidt, an' he's sint down here f'r to see that th' infant industhries iv Rahway don't get th' worst iv it fr'm th' pauper labor iv Europe,' he says. With that, th' chief inspector come up an' says he: 'Misther Hannigan,' he says, 'On ye'er wurrud iv honor as an Irish gintleman an' an American citizen,' he says, 'have ye annything in that box that ye cud've paid more f'r in this counthry?' 'On me wurrud iv honor,' says Hannigan. 'I believe ye,' says th' chief. 'Swear him. Ye know th' solemnity iv an oath. Ye do solemnly swear be this an' be that that ye have not been lyin' all this time like th' knavish scoundhrel that ye wud be if ye did,' he says. 'I swear,' says Hannigan. 'That will suffice,' says th' chief. 'Ye look like an honest man, an' if ye're perjured ye'ersilf, ye'll go to jail,' he says. 'Ye're an American citizen an' ye wudden't lie,' he says. 'We believe ye an th' sicrety iv th' threeasury believes ye as much as we wud oursilves,' he says. 'Go down on th' dock an' be searched,' he says.

"Hannigan says he wint down on th' dock practisin' th' lock step, so he wudden't seem green whin they put him in f'r perjury. I won't tell ye what he see on th' dock. No, I won't, Hinnissy. 'Tisn't annything ye ought to know, onless ye're goin' into th' dhry goods business. Hannigan says they hadn't got half way to th' bottom iv th' thrunks an' there wasn't a woman fr'm th' boat that he'd dare to look in th' face. He tur-rned away with a blush an' see his wife an' childher standin' behind th' bars iv a fence an' he started f'r thim. 'Hol' on there,' says a polisman. 'Where are ye goin'?' he says. 'To see me wife, ye gom,' says Hannigan. 'Ye can't see her till we look at what ye've got in th' box,' says th' copper. 'Ye'er domestic jooties can wait ontil we see about th' others,' says he. 'Ye're a prisoner,' says he, 'till we prove that ye ought to be,' he says. With that Mrs. Hannigan calls out: 'Tim,' she says, 'Pah-pah,' she says. 'Ar-re ye undher arrest?' she says. 'An' ye promised me ye wudden't dhrink,' she says. 'What ar-re ye charged with?' she says. 'Threason,' says he. 'I wint away fr'm home,' he says. 'But that's no crime,' she says. 'Yes it is,' says he. 'I come back,' he says.

"With that another inspector come along an' he says: 'Open that thrunk,' he says. 'Cut th' rope,' he says. 'Boys, bring an axe an' lave us see what this smuggler has in th' box,' he says. 'What's this? A blackthorn cane! Confiscate it. A bottle iv whiskey. Put it aside f'r ividence. A coat! Miscreent! A pair iv pants! Ye perjured ruffyan! Don't ye know ye can get nearly as good a pair iv pants f'r twice th' money in this counthry? Three collars? Hyena! A bar iv soap. An' this man calls himself a pathrite! Where did ye get that thrunk? It looks foreign. I'll take it. Open ye'er mouth. I'll throuble ye f'r that back tooth. Me man,' he says, 'ye have taken a long chanst,' he says, 'but I won't be hard on ye. Ye'll need clothes,' he says. 'Here's me card,' he says. 'I'm an inspector iv customs on th' side, but th' govermint really hires me to riprisint Guldenheim an' Eckstein, shirt makers, be appintmint to th' cabinet, an' Higgins an' Co., authors iv th' Durable Pant. A good pant. If ye want annything in our line, call on our store. No throuble to take money.'

"Hannigan wint out an' found Honorya an' th' childher had gone off f'r to get a bondsman. Thin he tur-rned an' called out to th' inspector: 'Look here, you!' 'What is it?' says th' man. 'Ye missed something,' says Hannigan. 'I was tattooed in Cork,' he says. 'Stop that man,' says th' head iv a ladin' firm iv tattooers an' prisidint iv th' society f'r th' Protection iv American Art, If Such There Be. 'Stop him; he's smugglin' in foreign art!' he says. But Hannigan bate him to th' sthreet car. An' that was his welcome home.

"'Call me Hanniganoffski,' says he las' night. 'I'm goin' to Rooshia,' he says. 'F'r to be a slave iv th' Czar?' says I. 'Well,' says he, 'if I've got to be a slave,' he says, 'I'd rather be opprissed be th' Czar thin be a dealer in shirt waists,' he says. 'Th' Czar ain't so bad,' he says. 'He don't care what I wear undherneath,' he says."

"Oh, well, divvle mend Hannigan," said Mr. Hennessy. "It's little sympathy I have f'r him, gallivantin' off acrost th' ocean an' spindin' money he arned at home. Annyhow, Hannigan an' th' likes iv him is all raypublicans."

"That's why I can't make it out," said Mr. Dooley. "Why do they stick him up? Maybe th' sicrety iv th' threeasury is goin' in to what Hogan calls th' lingery business an' is gettin' information on th' fashions. But I wondher why they make thim swear to affidavits."

"'Tis wrong," said Mr. Hennessy. "We're an honest people."

"We are," said Mr. Dooley. "We are, but we don't know it."

YOUTH AND AGE[1]

"I see that Tiddy—" Mr. Dooley began.

"Don't be disrayspictful," said Mr. Hennessy.

"I'm not disrayspictful," said Mr. Dooley. "I'm affictionate. I'm familyar. But I'm not disrayspictful. I may be burned at th' stake f'r it. Whiniver annything happens in this counthry, a comity iv prom'nent business men, clargymen an' colledge professors meets an' raysolves to go out an' lynch a few familyar dimmycrats. I wondher why it is th' clargy is so much more excitable thin anny other people. Ye take a man with small side whiskers, a long coat an' a white choker, a man that wudden't harm a spider an' that floats like an Angel iv Peace, as Hogan says, over a mixed quartette choir, an' lave annything stirrin' happen an' he'll sind up th' premyums on fire insurance. Lave a bad man do a bad deed an' th' preachers is all f'r quartherin' ivrybody that can't recite th' thirty-nine articles on his head. If somebody starts a fire, they grab up a can iv karasene an' begin f'r to burn down th' block. 'Tis a good thing preachers don't go to Congress. Whin they're ca'm they'd wipe out all th' laws, an' whin they're excited they'd wipe out all th' popylation. They're niver two jumps fr'm th' thumbscrew. 'Tis quare th' best iv men at times shud feel like th' worst tow'rd those between.

"But annyhow, I see that Tiddy, Prisidint Tiddy—here's his

---

[1] Theodore Roosevelt became President just before his forty-third birthday.

health—is th' youngest prisidint we've iver had, an' some iv th' pa-apers ar-re wondherin' whether he's old enough f'r th' ray-sponsibilities iv th' office. He isn't afraid, but a good manny ar-re, that a man iv on'y forty-two or three, who hasn't lost a tooth, an' maybe has gained a few, a mere child, who ought to be playin' mibs or 'Run, sheep, run,' at Eyesther Bay, will not be able f'r to conduct th' business iv Gover'mint with th' proper amount iv infirmity. Some day whin th' cab'net hobbles in to submit a gr-reat quistion iv foreign policy, th' prisidint'll be out in th' back yard performin' at knock up an' catch with his sicrety. Whin he wants to see a foreign ambassadure, he won't sind f'r him an' rayceive him standin' up with wan hand on th' Monroe docthrine an' th' other on th' map iv our foreign possissions, but will pull his hat over his eyes an' go ar-round to Lord Ponsyfoot's house an' whistle or call out, 'Hee-oo-ee.' He'll have a high chair at th' table an' drink th' health iv his guests in milk an' wather; he'll outrage th' rools iv diplomacy be screamin' 'fen ivrythings' whin th' Chinese ministher calls, an' instead iv studyin' th' histhry iv our counthry, he'll be caught in a corner iv th' White House, peroosin' th' histhry iv Shorty in Sarch iv his Dad. I suppose we'll have th' usu'l diffyculties with him—makin' him comb his hair an' black th' heels iv his boots an' not put his elbows on th' table, an' not reach or pint, an' go to bed afther supper an' get up in time f'r breakfast, an' keep away fr'm th' wather an' cut out cigreets an' go back to his room an' thry behind th' ears. But what can ye expict fr'm a kid iv forty-two ?

"I wondher sometimes, Hinnissy, whin is a man old enough. I've seen th' age limit risin' iver since I wint into public life. Whin I was a young la-ad, a fellow wud come out iv colledge or th' rayform school or whatever was his alma mather, knock down th' first ol' man in his way an' leap to th' fr-ront. Ivry time school let out, some aged statesman wint back like Cincinnati to his farm an' was glad to get there safe. Ye cud mark th' pro-gress iv youth be th' wreck iv spectacles, goold-headed walkin' sticks, unrale teeth, an' pretinded hair. Th' sayin' was in thim days, ol' men f'r th' crossin', young men f'r th' cab. Whin ol' age discinded like a binidiction on a man's head, we put a green flag in his hand an' gave him a good steady job as assistant to an autymatic gate. Age is gr-reat, Hinnissy, as a flagman. It saves th' thrucks an' drays iv life fr'm gettin' in th' way iv th' locymotives. But it don't stop th' locymotives. They come too fast. Fifteen or twinty years hince, whin I become machure, I can tell ye ivrything nearly ye oughtn't to do but nawthin' ye ought to do.

"In th' ol' days, a man was a man whin he voted—at twinty-wan in Boston, at eighteen in th' sixth war-rd. I r-read in this pa-aper that 'twas even more so befure me time. Alexandher th' Gr-reat was on'y foorteen whin he conkered Boolgahrya, Cæsar was jus' fr'm business colledge whin he put Mark Antony out iv th' business. Frederick th' Gr-reat was in skirts whin he done whativer he done an' done it well. Fox an' Pitt, if I have th' names r-right, was in compound fractions whin they wint into th' council. Why, Hinnissy, I was hardly thirty-five whin I accipted th' prisidincy iv this establishment with all its foreign complications an' rivinoo problems! A man iv thirty was counted machure, a man iv forty was looked on as a patriarch an' whin a man got to be fifty, th' fam'ly put his chair in th' corner an' give him th' back bedroom. I had it all fixed to make me millyion at thirty an' retire. I don't raymimber now what happened to me between twinty-nine an' thirty-wan.

"But nowadays, be hivins, a man don't get started till he's too old to run. Th' race iv life has settled down to something between a limp an' a hobble. 'Tis th' ol' man's time. An orator is a boy orator as long as he can speak without th' aid iv a dintal surgeon; an acthor is a boy acthor until he's so old he can't play King Lear without puttin' a little iv th' bloom iv youth on his cheeks out iv th' youth jar; a statesman that can't raymimber what Bushrod Wash'nton thought about th' Alyen an' Sedition law belongs in th' nurs'ry. I look ar-round me at th' pitchers iv gr-reat men in th' pa-aper an' greatness manes white whiskers. There's no such thing as age. If Methuselah was alive, he'd be captain iv a football team. Whin a man gets to ninety, he's jus' beginnin' to feel sthrong enough f'r wurruk. Annybody that thries to do annything befure he's an oncomfortable risk f'r th' life insurance comp'ny is snubbed f'r youthful impertinence. 'A new lithry light has appeared on th' lithrachoor horizon. Although on'y eighty-two, his little story iv "An afthernoon with Prudy" shows gr-reat promise. We hope he will some day do something worthy iv him.' 'Keokuk H. Higbie has been ilicted prisidint iv th' G. O. an' L. system to take th' place iv Lamson N. Griggs who has become head coach iv th' Cintinaryan Athletic club. Mr. Higbie has had a meteeyoric career, havin' risen in less thin eighty years fr'm th' position iv brakeman to be head iv this gr-reat system. Youth must be sarved.' 'A vacancy is expicted in th' supreme coort. Misther Justice Colligan will cillybrate his wan hundherd an' fiftieth birthday nex' month an' it is ixpected he will retire. That august body becomes more an' more joovenile ivry year, an' there is danger it will lose th' rayspict iv th' naytion. Manny iv th' mimbers was not prisint whin th' constitution was signed an' don't know annything about it.'

"So it goes. Mind ye, Hinnissy, I don't object. 'Tis all r-right in me hand, f'r, though far fr'm decrepit, barrin' th' left leg, I'm old enough to look down on Prisidint Tiddy if I didn't look up to him. If I was as old as I am now whin I was as young as I was befure th' war, I'd be shy ivry time I see a man come into th' pasture with a bag an' an axe. They say rayspict f'r ol' age is gone out. That may be thrue, but if 'tis so, 'tis because us ol' la-ads is still doin' things on th' thrapeze. I don't want anny man's rayspict. It manes I don't count. So whin I come to think it over, I agree with th' pa-apers. Prisidint Tiddy is too young f'r th' office. What is needed is a man iv—well, a man iv my age. An' I don't know as I'm quite ripe enough. I'm goin' out now to roll me hoop."

"Go on with ye," said Mr. Hennessy. "Whin do ye think a man is old enough?"

"Well," said Mr. Dooley, "a man is old enough to vote whin he can vote, he's old enough to wurruk whin he can wurruk. An' he's old enough to be prisidint whin he becomes prisidint. If he ain't, 'twill age him."

OBSERVATIONS BY
MR. DOOLEY

SHERLOCK HOLMES

"Dorsey an' Dugan are havin' throuble," said Mr. Hennessy.

"What about?" asked Mr. Dooley.

"Dorsey," said Mr. Hennessy, "says Dugan stole his dog. They had a party at Dorsey's an' Dorsey heerd a noise in th' back yard an' wint out an' see Dugan makin' off with his bull tarryer."

"Ye say he see him do it?"

"Yis, he see him do it."

"Well," said Mr. Dooley, "'twud baffle th' injinooty iv a Sherlock Holmes."

"Who's Sherlock Holmes?"

"He's th' gr-reatest detictive that iver was in a story book. I've been r-readin' about him an' if I was a criminal, which I wud be if I had to wurruk f'r a livin', an' Sherlock Holmes got afther me, I'd go sthraight to th' station an' give mesilf up. I'd lay th' goods on th' desk an' say: 'Sargeant, put me down in th' hard cage. Sherlock Holmes has jus' see a man go by in a cab with a Newfoundland dog an' he knows I took th' spoons.' Ye see, he ain't th' ordh'nry fly cop like Mulcahy that always runs in th' Schmidt boy f'r ivry crime rayported fr'm stealin' a ham to forgin' a check in th' full knowledge that some day he'll get him f'r th' right thing. No, sir; he's an injanyous man that can put two an' two together an' make eight iv thim. He applies his brain to crime, d'ye mind, an' divvle th' crime, no matther how cunnin' it is, will escape him. We'll suppose, Hinnissy, that I'm Sherlock Holmes. I'm settin' here in me little parlor wearin' a dhressin' gown an' now an' thin pokin' mesilf full iv morpheen. Here we are. Ye come in. 'Good-mornin', Watson.'"

"I ain't Watson," said Mr. Hennessy. "I'm Hinnissy."

"Ah," said Mr. Dooley; "I thought I'd wring it fr'm ye. Perhaps ye'd like to know how I guessed ye had come in. 'Tis very simple. On'y a matther iv observation. I heerd ye'er step; I seen ye'er refliction in th' lookin' glass; ye spoke to me. I put these things together with me thrained faculty f'r observation an' deduction, d'ye mind. Says I to mesilf: 'This must be Hinnissy.' But mind ye, th' chain iv circumstances is not complete. It might be some wan disguised as ye. So says I to mesilf: 'I will throw this newcome, whoiver he is, off his guard, be callin' him be a sthrange name!' Ye wudden't feel complimented, Hinnissy, if ye knew who Watson is. Watson knows even less than ye do. He don't know annything, an' annything he knows is wrong. He has to look up his name in th' parish raygisther befure he can speak to himsilf. He's a gr-reat frind iv Sherlock Holmes an' if Sherlock Holmes iver loses him, he'll find him in th' nearest asylum f'r th' feeble-minded. But I surprised ye'er secret out iv ye. Thrown off ye'er guard be me innocent question, ye popped out 'I'm Hinnissy,' an' in a flash I guessed who ye were. Be th' same process iv raisonin' be deduction, I can tell ye that ye were home las' night in bed, that ye're on ye'er way to wurruk, an' that ye'er salary is two dollars a day. I know ye were at home las' night because ye ar're always at home between iliven an' sivin, bar Pathrick's night, an' ye'er wife hasn't been in lookin' f'r ye. I know ye're on ye'er way to wurruk because I heerd ye'er dinner pail jingle as ye stepped softly in. I know ye get two dollars a day because ye tol' me ye get three an' I deducted thirty-three an' wan third per cint f'r poetic license. 'Tis very simple. Ar-re those shoes ye have on ye'er feet? Be hivins, I thought so."

"Simple," said Mr. Hennessy, scornfully; "'tis foolish."

"Niver mind," said Mr. Dooley. "Pass th' dope, Watson. Now bein' full iv th' cillybrated Chow Sooey brand, I addhress me keen mind to th' discussion iv th' case iv Dorsey's dog. Watson, look out iv th' window an' see if that's a cab goin' by ringin' a gong. A throlley car? So much th' betther. Me observation tol' me it was not a balloon or a comet or a reindeer. Ye ar-re a gr-reat help to me, Watson. Pass th' dope. Was there a dog on th' car? No? That simplifies th' thing. I had an idee th' dog might have gone to wurruk. He was a bull-tarryer, ye say. D'ye know annything about his parents? Be Mulligan's Sloppy Weather out iv O'Hannigan's Diana iv th' Slough? Iv coorse. Was ayether iv thim seen in th' neighborhood th' night iv th' plant? No? Thin it is not, as manny might suppose, a case iv abduction. What were th' habits iv Dorsey's coyote? Was he a dog that dhrank? Did he go out iv nights? Was he payin' anny particular attintions to anny iv th' neighbors? Was he baffled in love? Ar-re his accounts sthraight? Had Dorsey said annything to him that wud've made him despondent? Ye say no. He led a dog's life but seemed to be happy. Thin 'tis plainly not a case iv suicide.

"I'm gettin' up close to th' criminals. Another shot iv th' mad mixture. Wait till I can find a place in th' ar-rm. There ye ar-re. Well, Watson, what d'ye make iv it?"

"If ye mane me, Dugan stole th' dog."

"Not so fast," said Mr. Dooley. "Like all men iv small minds ye make ye'ers up readily. Th' smaller th' mind, th' aisier 'tis made up. Ye'ers is like a blanket on th' flure befure th' fire. All ye have to do to make it up is to lave it. Mine is like a large double bed, an' afther I've been tossin' in it, 'tis no aisy job to make it up. I will puncture me tire with th' fav'rite flower iv Chinnytown an' go on. We know now that th' dog did not elope, that he didn't commit suicide an' that he was not kidnaped be his rayturnin' parents. So far so good. Now I'll tell ye who stole th' dog. Yisterdah afthernoon I see a suspicious lookin' man goin' down th' sthreet. I say he was suspicious lookin' because he was not disguised an' looked ivry wan in th' face. He had no dog with him. A damning circumstance, Watson, because whin he'd stolen th' dog he niver wud've taken it down near Dorsey's house. Ye wudden't notice these facts because ye'er mind while feeble is unthrained. His coat collar was turned up an' he was whistlin' to himsilf, a habit iv dog fanciers. As he wint be Hogan's house he did not look around or change his gait or otherwise do annything that wud indicate to an unthrained mind that there was annything wrong, facts in thimsilves that proved to me cultivated intilligence that he was guilty. I followed him in me mind's eye to his home an' there chained to th' bed leg is Dorsey's dog. Th' name iv th' criminal is P. X. O'Hannigan, an' he lives at twinty-wan hundhred an' ninety-nine South Halsted sthreet, top flat, rear, a plumber be pro-fission. Officer, arrest that man!"

"That's all right," said Mr. Hennessy; "but Dugan rayturned th' dog las' night."

"Oh, thin," said Mr. Dooley, calmly, "this is not a case f'r Sherlock Holmes but wan f'r th' polis. That's th' throuble, Hinnissy, with th' detective iv th' story. Nawthin' happens in rale life that's complicated enough f'r him. If th' Prisidint iv th' Epworth League was a safe-blower be night th' man that'd catch him'd be a la-ad with gr-reat powers iv observation an' thrained habits iv raisonin'. But crime, Hinnissy, is a pursoot iv th' simple-minded—that is, catchable crime is a pursoot iv th' simple-minded. Th' other kind, th' uncatchable kind that is took up be men iv intellect is called high fi-nance. I've known manny criminals in me time, an' some iv thim was fine men an' very happy in their home life, an' a more simple, pasth'ral people ye niver knew. Wan iv th' ablest bank robbers in th' counthry used to live near me—he ownded a flat buildin'—an' befure he'd turn in to bed afther rayturnin' fr'm his night's wurruk, he'd go out in th' shed an' chop th' wood. He always wint into th' house through a thransom f'r fear iv wakin' his wife who was a delicate woman an' a shop lifter. As I tell ye he was a man without guile, an' he wint about his jooties as modestly as ye go about ye'ers. I don't think in th' long run he made much more thin ye do. Wanst in a while, he'd get hold iv a good bunch iv money, but manny other times afther dhrillin' all night through a steel dure, all he'd find'd be a short crisp note fr'm th' prisidint iv th' bank. He was often discouraged, an' he tol' me wanst if he had an income iv forty dollars th' month, he'd retire fr'm business an' settle down on a farm.

"No, sir, criminals is th' simplest crathers in th' wide wide wurruld—innocent, sthraight-forward, dangerous people, that haven't sinse enough to be honest or prosperous. Th' extint iv their schamin' is to break a lock on a dure or sweep a handful iv change fr'm a counter or dhrill a hole in a safe or administher th' strong short arm to a tired man takin' home his load. There are no mysteryous crimes excipt thim that happens to be. Th' ordh'nry crook, Hinnissy, goes around ringin' a bell an' disthribut-in' hand-bills announcin' his business. He always breaks through a window instead iv goin' through an open dure, an' afther he's done annything that he thinks is commindable, he goes to a neighborin' liquor saloon, stands on th' pool table an' confides th' secret to ivrybody within sound iv his voice. That's why Mul-ligan is a betther detictive thin Sherlock Holmes or me. He can't put two an' two together an' he has no powers iv deduction, but he's a hard dhrinker an' a fine sleuth. Sherlock Holmes niver wud've caught that frind iv mine. Whin th' safe iv th' Ninth Rational Bank was blowed, he wud've put two an' two together an' arristed me. But me frind wint away lavin' a hat an' a pair iv cuffs marked with his name in th' safe, an' th' polis combined these discoveries with th' well-known fact that Muggins was a notoryous safe blower an' they took him in. They found him down th' sthreet thryin' to sell a bushel basket full iv Alley L stock. I told ye he was a simple man. He ralized his ambition f'r an agaracoolchral life. They give him th' care iv th' cows at Joliet."

"Did he rayform ?" asked Mr. Hennessy.

"No," said Mr. Dooley; "he escaped. An' th' way he got out wud baffle th' injinooty iv a Sherlock Holmes."

"How did he do it ?" asked Mr. Hennessy.

"He climbed over th' wall," said Mr. Dooley.

IMMIGRATION[1]

"Well, I see Congress has got to wurruk again," said Mr. Dooley.

"The Lord save us fr'm harm," said Mr. Hennessy.

"Yes, sir," said Mr. Dooley, "Congress has got to wurruk again, an' manny things that seems important to a Congressman 'll be brought up befure thim. 'Tis sthrange that what's a big thing to a man in Wash'nton, Hinnissy, don't seem much account to me. Divvle a bit do I care whether they dig th' Nicaragoon Canal or cross th' Isthmus in a balloon; or whether th' Monroe docthrine is enfoorced or whether it ain't; or whether th' thrusts is abolished as Teddy Rosenfelt wud like to have thim or encouraged to go on with their neefaryous but magnificent entherprises as th' Prisidint wud like; or whether th' water is poured into th' ditches to reclaim th' arid lands iv th' West or th' money f'r thim to fertilize th' arid pocket-books iv th' conthractors; or whether th' Injun is threated like a depindant an' miserable thribesman or like a free an' indepindant dog; or whether we restore th' merchant marine to th' ocean or whether we lave it to restore itsilf. None iv these here questions inthrests me, an' be me I mane you an' be you I

[1] Henry Cabot Lodge (1850–1924) was an advocate of restricted immigration, proposing a literacy test for immigrants in 1896.

mane ivrybody. What we want to know is, ar-re we goin' to have coal enough in th' hod whin th' cold snap comes; will th' plumbin' hold out, an' will th' job last.

"But they'se wan question that Congress is goin' to take up that you an' me are intherested in. As a pilgrim father that missed th' first boats, I must raise me claryon voice again' th' invasion iv this fair land be th' paupers an' arnychists iv effete Europe. Ye bet I must—because I'm here first. 'Twas diff'rent whin I was dashed high on th' stern an' rockbound coast. In thim days America was th' refuge iv th' oppressed iv all th' wurruld. They cud come over here an' do a good job iv oppressin' thimsilves. As I told ye I come a little late. Th' Rosenfelts an' th' Lodges bate me be at laste a boat lenth, an' be th' time I got here they was stern an' rockbound thimsilves. So I got a gloryous rayciption as soon as I was towed off th' rocks. Th' stars an' sthripes whispered a welcome in th' breeze an' a shovel was thrust into me hand an' I was pushed into a sthreet excyvatin' as though I'd been born here. Th' pilgrim father who bossed th' job was a fine ol' puritan be th' name iv Doherty, who come over in th' Mayflower about th' time iv th' potato rot in Wexford, an' he made me think they was a hole in th' breakwather iv th' haven iv refuge an' some iv th' wash iv th' seas iv opprission had got through. He was a stern an' rockbound la-ad himsilf, but I was a good hand at loose stones an' wan day—but I'll tell ye about that another time.

"Annyhow, I was rayceived with open arms that sometimes ended in a clinch. I was afraid I wasn't goin' to assimilate with th' airlyer pilgrim fathers an' th' instichoochions iv th' counthry, but I soon found that a long swing iv th' pick made me as good as another man an' it didn't require a gr-reat intellect, or sometimes anny at all, to vote th' dimmycrat ticket, an' befure I was here a month, I felt enough like a native born American to burn a witch. Wanst in a while a mob iv intilligint collajeens, whose grandfathers had bate me to th' dock, wud take a shy at me Pathrick's Day procission or burn down wan iv me churches, but they got tired iv that befure long; 'twas too much like wurruk.

"But as I tell ye, Hinnissy, 'tis diff'rent now. I don't know why 'tis diff'rent but 'tis diff'rent. 'Tis time we put our back again' th' open dure an' keep out th' savage horde. If that cousin iv ye'ers expects to cross, he'd betther tear f'r th' ship. In a few minyits th' gates 'll be down an' whin th' oppressed wurruld comes hikin' acrost to th' haven iv refuge, they'll do well to put a couplin' pin undher their hats, f'r th' Goddess iv Liberty 'll meet thim at th' dock with an axe in her hand. Congress is goin' to fix it. Me frind Shaughnessy says so. He was in yisterdah an' says he: ' 'Tis time we done something to make th' immigration laws sthronger,' says he. 'Thrue f'r ye, Miles Standish,' says I; 'but what wud ye do?' 'I'd keep out th' offscourin's iv Europe,' says he. 'Wud ye go back?' says I. 'Have ye'er joke,' says he. ' 'Tis not so seeryus as it was befure ye come,' says I. 'But what ar-re th' immygrants doin' that's roonous to us?' I says. 'Well,' says he, 'they're arnychists,' he says; 'they don't assymilate with th' counthry,' he says. 'Maybe th' counthry's digestion has gone wrong fr'm too much rich food,' says I; 'perhaps now if we'd lave off thryin' to digest Rockyfellar an' thry a simple diet like Schwartz-meister, we wudden't feel th' effects iv our vittels,' I says. 'Maybe if we'd season th' immygrants a little or cook thim thurly, they'd go down betther,' I says.

" ' 'They're arnychists, like Parsons,' he says. 'He wud've been an immygrant if Texas hadn't been admitted to th' Union,' I says. 'Or Snolgosh,' he says. 'Has Mitchigan seceded?' I says. 'Or Gittoo,' he says. 'Who come fr'm th' effete monarchies iv Chicago, west iv Ashland Av'noo,' I says. 'Or what's-his-name, Wilkes Booth,' he says. 'I don't know what he was —maybe a Boolgharyen,' says I. 'Well, annyhow,' says he, 'they're th' scum iv th' earth.' 'They may be that,' says I; 'but we used to think they was th' cream iv civilization,' I says. 'They're off th' top annyhow. I wanst believed 'twas th' best men iv Europe come here, th' la-ads that was too sthrong and indepindant to be kicked around be a boorgomasther at home an' wanted to dig out f'r a place where they cud get a chanst to make their way to th' money. I see their sons fightin' into politics an' their daughters tachin' young American idee how to shoot too high in th' public school, an' I thought they was all right. But I see I was wrong. Thim boys out there towin' wan heavy foot afther th' other to th' rowlin' mills is all arnychists. There's warrants out f'r all names endin' in 'inski, an' I think I'll board up me windows, f'r,' I says, 'if immygrants is as dangerous to this counthry as ye an' I an' other pilgrim fathers believe they are, they'se enough iv thim sneaked in already to make us aborigines about as infloointial as the prohibition vote in th' Twenty-ninth Ward. They'll dash again' our stern an' rock-bound coast till they bust it,' says I.

"'But I ain't so much afraid as ye ar-re. I'm not afraid iv me father an' I'm not afraid iv mesilf. An' I'm not afraid iv Schwartzmeister's father or Hinnery Cabin Lodge's grandfather. We all come over th' same way, an' if me ancestors were not what Hogan calls rigicides, 'twas not because they were not ready an' willin', on'y a king niver come their way. I don't believe in killin' kings, mesilf. I niver wud've sawed th' block off that curly-headed potintate that I see in th' pitchers down town, but, be hivins, Presarved Codfish Shaughnessy, if we'd begun a few years ago shuttin' out folks that wudden't mind handin' a bomb to a king, they wudden't be enough people in Mattsachoosetts to make a quorum f'r th' Anti-Impeeryal S'ciety,' says I. 'But what wud ye do with th' offscourin' iv Europe?' says he. 'I'd scour thim some more,' says I.

"An' so th' meetin' iv th' Plymouth Rock Assocyation come to an end. But if ye wud like to get it together, Deacon Hinnissy, to discuss th' immygration question, I'll sind out a hurry call f'r Schwartzmeister an' Mulcahey an' Ignacio Sbarbaro an' Nels Larsen an' Petrus Gooldvink, an' we 'll gather to-night at Fanneil-noviski Hall at th' corner iv Sheridan an' Sigel sthreets. All th' pilgrim fathers is rayquested f'r to bring interpreters."

"Well," said Mr. Hennessy, "divvle th' bit I care, on'y I'm here first, an' I ought to have th' right to keep th' bus fr'm bein' overcrowded."

"Well," said Mr. Dooley, "as a pilgrim father on me gran' nephew's side, I don't know but ye're right. An' they'se wan sure way to keep thim out."

"What's that?" asked Mr. Hennessy.

"Teach thim all about our instichoochions befure they come," said Mr. Dooley.

PRINCE HENRY'S VISIT[1]

"It's goin' to be gr-reat times f'r us Germans whin Prince Hinnery comes over," said Mr. Dooley.

"By th' way," said Mr. Hennessy with an air of polite curiosity, "what relation's he to th' impror iv Germany? Is he th' son or th' nevvew?"

---

[1] Heinrich Albert Wilhelm, brother of William II of Germany, visited the United States in 1882–1884 and 1902.

"He's nayther," said Mr. Dooley. "Th' impror has no sons that I iver heerd iv. If he had a son he'd be a steam injine. No, sir, this man is th' impror's brother Hinnery or Hans. I don't exactly know what th' usual jooties iv an impror's brother is. I know what an impror has to do. His wurruk's cut out f'r him. I cud fill th' job mesilf to me own satisfaction an' th' on'y wan an impror has to plaze is himsilf. Th' German impror frequently mintions another, but on'y in th' way iv politeness. I know what an impror's jooties is, but I don't know what an impror's brother has to do ex officio, as Hogan says. But this boy Hinnery or Hans has more wurruk thin a bartinder in a prohibition town. He's a kind iv travellin' agent f'r th' big la-ad. His bag is ready packed ivry night, he sleeps like a fireman with his pants in his boots beside his bed, an' they'se a thrap dure alongside th' cradle f'r him to slide down to th' first flure.

"He's no more thin got to sleep whin th' three iliven sounds on th' gong. In Hinnery leaps to th' pantaloons, down th' laddher he goes pullin' up his suspinders with wan hand an' puttin' on his hat with th' other an' off he is f'r Corea or Chiny or Booloochistan at a gallop. His brother stands at th' dure an' hollers farewell to him. 'Go, Hinnery,' he says. 'Go, me dear brother, to th' land iv perpetchooal sunshine an' knock in nails f'r to hang up th' German armor,' he says. 'Knock in th' nails, an' if ye happen to hit ye'ersilf on th' thumb, swear on'y be th' German Mike an' raymimber ye done it f'r me,' he says. 'I will remain at home an' conthrol th' rest iv th' wurruld with th' assistance iv that German Providence that has been as kind to us as we desarve an' that we look up to as our akel,' he says. An' Hinnery goes away. He travels o'er land an' sea, be fire an' flood an' field. He's th' ginooine flyin' Dutchman. His home is in his hat. He hasn't slept all night in a bed f'r tin years. 'Tis Hinnery this an' Hinnery that; Hinnery up th' Nile an' Hinnery to Injy; Hinnery here an' Hinnery there. Th' cuffs iv his shirts is made iv th' time cards iv railroads. Ivry time they'se a change in schedool he ordhers new shirts. He knows th' right iv way fr'm Berlin to Ballymachoo; he speaks all known languages, an' ivrywhere he goes he makes a frind or an inimy, which is th' same thing to th' Germans. He carries a sample case undher wan arm an' a gun undher th' other, an' if ye don't like Rhine wine perhaps ye'll take lead. On second considherations he won't shoot ye but he'll sell ye th' Krupp. They'se more where it come fr'm.

"I tell ye, Hinnissy, this Impror or Kaiser iv Germany is a smart man. I used to think 'twas not so. I thought he had things unaisy in his wheel-house. I mind whin he got th' job, ivrywan says: 'Look out f'r war. This wild man will be in that office f'r a year whin he'll just about declare fight with th' wurruld.' An' ivrybody framed up f'r him. But look ye what happened. 'Tis twenty years since he was swore in an' ne'er a fight has he had. Ivrybody else has been in throuble. A screw-maker iv a sindintary life has ploonged England into a war; me frinds th' Greeks that were considhered about akel to a flush iv anger over a raid on a push cart has mixed it up with th' Turks; th' Japs has been at war, an' th' Dagoes; our own peace-lovin' nation has been runnin' wan short an' wan serryal war, an' aven th' Chinese has got their dandher up, be hivins, but Willum, th' Middleweight Champeen, Willum th' Potsdam Game Chicken, Willum, th' Unterdenlin-den Cyclone, Willum has been ladin' th' ca'm an' prosperous life iv a delicatessen dealer undher a turner hall. He's had no fights. He niver will have anny fights. He'll go to his grave with th' repytation iv nayether winnin' nor losin' a battle, but iv takin' down more forfeits thin anny impror pugilist iv our time.

"What do I think iv him? Well, sir, I think he's not a fighter but a fight lover. Did ye iver see wan iv thim young men that always has a front seat at a scrap so near th' ring that whin th' second blows th' wather he gets what's left on his shirt front? Well, that's me frind Willum. He is a pathron iv spoort an' not a spoort. His ideel is war but he's a practical man. He has a season ticket to th' matches but he niver will put on the gloves. He's in the spoortin' goods business an' he usu'lly gets a percintage iv th' gate receipts. If he sees two nations bellowin' at each other th' assurances iv their distinguished considheration, he says: 'Boys, get together. 'Tis a good match. Ye're both afraid. Go in, uncle; go in, Boer.' He is all around th' ringside, encouragin' both sides. 'Stand up again' him there, Paul; rassle him to th' flure. Good f'r ye, uncle. A thrifle low, that wan, but all's fair in war. Defind ye'er indipindance, noble sons iv Teutonic blood. Exercise ye'er sov'reign rights, me English frinds.' If wan or th' other begins to weaken th' first bottle through th' ropes is Willum's. Whin annybody suggests a dhraw, he demands his money back. Nawthin' but a fight to a finish will do him. If ayether iv th' contestants is alive in th' ring at th' end, he congratulates him an' asks him if he heerd that German cheer in th' las' round.

"Oh, he's good. He'll do all right, that German man. In high di-plomacy, he's what in low di-plomacy wud be called a happy jollyer. But he knows that if a man's always slappin' ye on th' back, ye begin to think he's weak; so he first shakes his fist undher ye'er nose an' thin slaps ye on th' back. Sometimes he does both at th' same time. An' he's got th' thrue jollyer's way iv provin' to ye that he's ye'er frind alone an' th' deadly inimy iv all others. He's got th' Czar iv Rooshya hypnotized, th' King iv England hugged to a standstill, an' th' Impror iv Chiny in tears. An' he's made thim all think th' first thing annywan knows, he'll haul off an' swing on wan iv th' others.

"So, havin' fixed ivrything up in Europe, he cast his eyes on this counthry, an' says he: 'I think I'll have to dazzle thim furriners somewhat. They've got a round-headed man f'r prisidint that was born with spurs on his feet an' had a catridge-belt f'r a rattle, an' some day his goolash won't agree with him an' he'll call th' bluff I've been makin' these manny years. What'll I do to make thim me frinds so that 'twud be like settin' fire to their own house to attackt me? Be hivins, I've got it. They're a dimmycratic people. I'll sind thim a prince. They can't keep him away, an' whin he lands, th' German popylation'll come out an' get up schootzenfists f'r him an' me fellow impror acrost th' say'll see how manny iv them there ar-re, an' he'll think twict befure he makes faces at me. F'r, wanst a German, always a German be it iver so far,' he says. 'I'll sind thim Hinnery. Hinnery! Turn in th' alarm f'r Hinnery,' he says. Hinnery slides down th' pole an' th' Impror says: 'Brother, catch th' night boat f'r America an' pay a visit to whatever king they have there. Take along annywan ye like an' as manny thrunks as ye need, an' stay as long as ye plaze. Don't ring. Back th' dhray again' th' front dure an' hurl ye'ersilf into th' first bed room ye see. Act just as if ye was me,' he says. 'But I'm not invited,' says Hinnery. 'Write ye'er own invitation,' says Willum. 'Here's th' answer: "Fellow Potyntate, Ye'ers iv th' second instant askin' me brother Hinnery to spind a year with ye, not received. In reply will say that nawthin' cud give me gr-reater pleasure. He can stay as long as he plazes. Him an' his soot will not need more thin th' whole house, so ye can have th' barn to ye'ersilf. If ye have a brother, don't neglect to sind him over to see me. I know a good hotel at four a day, all included but candles, an' if he stands at th' front window, he can see me go by anny day. Ye'ers, Willum, Rex an' a shade more.'"

"So here comes Hinnery, an' we're goin' to give him a gloryous rayciption. Th' war vessels will be out to welcome him, th' prisidint will meet him at th' dock an' he will be threated to wan continyous round iv schutzenfists, turnd'yeminds, sangerbunds, katzenjammers, skats, an' other German fistivals. Th' aristocracy iv New York is practicin' Dutch an' th' Waldorf-Astorya will be festooned with dachshunds. He'll see more Germans an' more German Germans thin he iver see in Prooshya. An' I hope he'll have a good time."

"I wondher what Tiddy Rosenfelt thinks iv it?" asked Mr. Hennessy.

"Well, what wud ye think if ye'd had to intertain a German Prince unawares? Ye'd give him th' best ye'd got, ye'd dig up a bottle iv Knockimheimer down th' sthreet an' ye'd see that he got a noodle ivry time he reached. An' whin he wint away, ye'd go as far as th' dure with him an' pat him on th' back an' say: 'Good-bye, good-bye, Hinnery. Good-bye, Hans. Guten nobben, oof veedersayin, me boy. Good luck to ye. Look out f'r that shtep! There ye ar-re. Be careful iv th' gate. D'ye think ye can get home all right? I'd go as far as th' car with ye if I had me coat on. Well, good-bye lanksman. Raymimber me to ye'er brother. Tell him not to f'rget that little matther. Oh, of coorse, they'se no counthry in th' wurruld like Germany an' we're uncivilized an' rapacyous an' will get our heads knocked off if we go into a fight. Good-bye, mein frind.' An' whin ye'd shut th' dure on him, ye'd say: 'Well, what d'ye think iv that?'"

CUBA VS. BEET SUGAR[1]

"What's all this about Cubia an' th' Ph'lippeens?" asked Mr. Hennessy. "What's beet sugar?"

"Th' throuble about Cubia is that she's free; th' throuble about beet sugar is we're not; an' th' throuble about th' Ph'lippeens is th' Ph'lippeen throuble," said Mr. Dooley. "As rega-ards

---

[1] In 1902, when the Administration recommended that Cuban sugar be admitted at a reduced tariff rate, the proposal met strong opposition from protectionist forces.

Cubia, she's like a woman that th' whole neighborhood helps to divoorce fr'm a crool husband, but nivertheless a husband, an' a miserable home but a home, an' a small credit at th' grocery but a credit, an' thin whin she goes into th' dhressmakin' business, rayfuse to buy annything fr'm her because she's a divoorced woman. We freed Cubia but we didn't free annything she projooces. It wasn't her fault. We didn't think. We expicted that all we had to do was to go down to Sandago with a kinetoscope an' sthrike th' shackles fr'm th' slave an' she'd be comfortable even if she had no other protiction f'r her poor feet. We f'rgot about th' Beet. Most iv us niver thought about that beautiful but fragile flower excipt biled in conniction with pigs' feet or pickled in its own life juice. We didn't know that upon th' Beet hangs th' fate iv th' nation, th' hope iv th' future, th' permanence iv our instichoochions an' a lot iv other things akelly precious. Th' Beet is th' naytional anthem an', be hivins, it looks as though it might be th' naytional motto befure long.

"Well, Cubia got her freedom or something that wud look like th' same thing if she kept it out iv th' rain, but somehow or another it didn't suit her entirely. A sort iv cravin' come over her that it was hard to tell fr'm th' same feelin' iv vacancy that she knew whin she was opprissed be th' Hated Casteel. Hunger, Hinnissy, is about th' same thing in a raypublic as in a dispotism. They'se not much choice iv unhappiness between a hungry slave an' a hungry freeman. Cubia cudden't cuk or wear freedom. Ye can't make freedom into a stew an' ye can't cut a pair iv pants out iv it. It won't bile, fry, bake or fricassee. Ye can't take two pounds iv fresh creamery freedom, a pound iv north wind, a heapin' taycupfull iv naytional aspirations an' a sprinklin' iv bars fr'm th' naytional air, mix well, cuk over a hot fire an' sarve sthraight fr'm th' shtove; ye can't make a dish out iv that that wud nourish a tired freeman whin he comes home afther a hard day's wurruk lookin' f'r a job. So Cubia comes to us an' says she: 'Ye done well by us,' she says. 'Ye give us freedom,' says she, 'an' more thin enough to go round,' she says, 'an' now if ye plaze we'd like to thrade a little iv it back f'r a few groceries,' she says. 'We will wear wan shackle f'r a ham,' says she, 'an' we'll put on a full raygalia iv ball an' chain an' yoke an' fetters an' come-alongs f'r a square meal,' says she.

"That sounds raisonable enough an' bein' be nature a gin'rous people whin we don't think, we're about to help her disthress with whativer we have cold in th' panthry whin th' thought iv th' Beet crosses our minds. What will th' Beet say, th' red, th' juicy, th' sacchrine Beet, th' Beet iv our Fathers, th' Beet iv Plymouth Rock, Beet iv th' Pilgrim's Pride, Sweet Beet iv Liberty, iv thee I sing ? If we do annything f'r Cubia, down goes th' Beet, an' with th' Beet perishes our instichoochions. Th' constichoochion follows th' Beet ex propria vigore, as Hogan says. Th' juice iv th' Beet is th' life blood iv our nation. Whoiver touches a hair iv yon star spangled Beet, shoot him on th' spot. A bold Beet industhry a counthry's pride whin wanst desthroyed can niver be supplied. 'Beet sugar an' Liberty Now an' Foriver, wan an' insiprable'— Dan'l Webster. 'Thank Gawd I—I also—am a Beet'—th' same. 'Gover'mint iv th' Beet, by th' Beet an' f'r th' Beet shall not perish fr'm th' earth'—Abraham Lincoln. An' so, Hinnissy, we put th' pie back into th' ice-chest where we keep our honor an' ginerosity an' lock th' dure an' Cubia goes home, free an' hopeless. D'ye think so ? Well, I don't. Be hivins, Hinnissy, I think th' time has come whin we've got to say whether we're a nation iv Beets. I am no serf, but I'd rather be bent undher th' dispotism iv a Casteel thin undher th' tyranny iv a Beet. If I've got to be a slave, I'd rather be wan to a man, even a Spanish man, thin to a viggytable. If I'm goin' to be opprissed be a Beet, let it be fr'm th' inside not fr'm without. I'll choose me masther, Hinnissy, an' whin I do, 'twill not be that low-lyin', purple-complected, indygistible viggytable. I may bend me high head to th' egg-plant, th' potato, th' cabbage, th' squash, th' punkin, th' sparrow-grass, th' onion, th' spinach, th' rutabaga turnip, th' Fr-rench pea or th' parsnip, but 'twill niver be said iv me that I was subjygated be a Beet. No, sir. Betther death. I'm goin' to begin a war f'r freedom. I'm goin' to sthrike th' shackles fr'm a slave an' I'm him. I'm goin' to organize a rig'mint iv Rough Riders an' whin I stand on th' top iv San Joon hill with me soord in me hand an' me gleamin' specs on me nose, ye can mark th' end iv th' domina-tion iv th' Beet in th' western wurruld. F'r, Hinnissy, I tell ye what, if th' things I hear fr'm Wash'nton is thrue, that other war iv freedom stopped befure it was half done."

"An' what about th' Ph'lippeens ?" asked Mr. Hennessy.

"They'se nawthin' to say about th' Ph'lippeens," said Mr. Dooley, "excipt that th' throuble down there is all over."

"All over ?"

"All over."

HOME LIFE OF GENIUSES

"A woman ought to be careful who she marries," said Mr. Dooley.

"So ought a man," said Mr. Hennessy, with feeling.

"It don't make so much diff'rence about him," said Mr. Dooley. "Whin a man's marrid, he's a marrid man. That's all ye can say about him. Iv coorse, he thinks marredge is goin' to change th' whole current iv his bein', as Hogan says. But it doesn't. Afther he's been hooked up f'r a few months, he finds he was marrid befure, even if he wasn't, which is often th' case, d'ye mind. Th' first bride iv his bosom was th' Day's Wurruk, an' it can't be put off. They'se no groun's f'r dissolvin' that marredge, Hinnissy. Ye can't say to th' Day's Wurruk: 'Here, take this bunch iv alimony an' go on th' stage.' It turns up at breakfast about th' fourth month afther th' weddin' an' creates a scandal. Th' unforchnit man thries to shoo it off but it fixes him with its eye an' hauls him away fr'm the bacon an' eggs, while the lady opposite weeps and wondhers what he can see in annything so old an' homely. It says, 'Come with me, aroon,' an' he goes. An' afther that he spinds most iv his time an' often a good deal iv his money with th' enchantress. I tell ye what, Hinnissy, th' Day's Wurruk has broke up more happy homes thin comic opry. If th' coorts wud allow it, manny a woman cud get a divorce on th' groun's that her husband cared more f'r his Day's Wurruk thin he did f'r her. 'Hinnissy varsus Hinnissy; corryspondint, th' Day's Wurruk.' They'd be ividince that th' defindant was seen ridin' in a cab with th' corryspondint, that he took it to a picnic, that he wint to th' theaytre with it, that he talked about it in his sleep, an' that, lost to all sinse iv shame, he even escoorted it home with him an' inthrajooced it to his varchoos wife an' innocint childher. So it don't make much diff'rence who a man marries. If he has a job, he's safe.

"But with a woman 'tis diff'rent. Th' man puts down on'y part iv th' bet. Whin he's had enough iv th' convarsation that in Union Park undher th' threes med him think he was talkin' with an intellechool joyntess, all he has to do is to put on his coat, grab up his dinner pail an' go down to th' shops, to be happy though marrid. But a woman, I tell ye, bets all she has. A man don't have to marry but a woman does. Ol' maids an' clargymen do th' most good in th' wurruld an' we love thim f'r th' good they do.

But people, especially women, don't want to be loved that way. They want to be loved because people can't help lovin' thim no matther how bad they are. Th' story books that ye give ye'er daughter Honoria all tell her 'tis just as good not to be marrid. She reads about how kind Dorothy was to Lulu's childher an' she knows Dorothy was th' betther woman, but she wants to be Lulu. Her heart, an' a cold look in th' eye iv th' wurruld an' her Ma tell her to hurry up. Arly in life she looks f'r th' man iv her choice in th' tennis records; later she reads th' news fr'm th' militia encampmint; thin she studies th' socyal raygisther; further on she makes hersilf familyar with Bradsthreets' rayports, an' fin'lly she watches th' place where life presarvers are hangin'.

"Now, what kind iv a man ought a woman to marry? She oughtn't to marry a young man because she'll grow old quicker thin he will; she oughtn't to marry an old man because he'll be much older befure he's younger; she oughtn't to marry a poor man because he may become rich an' lose her; she oughtn't to marry a rich man because if he becomes poor, she can't lose him; she oughtn't to marry a man that knows more thin she does, because he'll niver fail to show it, an' she oughtn't to marry a man that knows less because he may niver catch up. But above all things she mustn't marry a janius. A flure-walker, perhaps; a janius niver.

"I tell ye this because I've been r-readin' a book Hogan give me, about th' divvle's own time a janius had with his fam'ly. A cap iv industhry may have throuble in his fam'ly till there isn't a whole piece iv chiny in th' cupboard, an' no wan will be the wiser f'r it but th' hired girl an' th' doctor that paints th' black eye. But ivrybody knows what happens in a janius' house. Th' janius always tells th' bartinder. Besides he has other janiuses callin' on him, an' 'tis th' business iv a janius to write about th' domestic throubles iv other janiuses so posterity'll know what a hard thing it is to be a janius. I've been readin' this book iv Hogan's an' as I tell ye, 'tis about th' misery a wretched woman inflicted on a pote's life.

"'Our hayro,' says th' author, 'at this peeryod conthracted an unforchnit alliance that was destined to cast a deep gloom over his career. At th' age iv fifty, afther a life devoted to th' pursoot iv such gayety as janiuses have always found niciss'ry to solace their avenin's, he marrid a young an' beautiful girl some thirty-two years his junior. This wretched crather had no appreciation iv

lithrachoor or lithry men.   She was frivolous an' light-minded an'
ividintly considhered that nawthin' was rally lithrachoor that
cudden't be thranslated into groceries.   Niver shall I f'rget th'
expression iv despair on th' face iv this godlike man as he came into
Casey's saloon wan starry July avenin' an' staggered into his
familyar seat, holdin' in his hand a bit iv soiled paper which he
tore into fragmints an' hurled into th' coal scuttle.   On that
crumpled parchmint findin' a sombre grave among th' disinterred
relics iv an age long past, to wit, th' cariboniferious or coal age,
was written th' iver-mim'rable pome: "Ode to Gin."   Our frind
had scribbled it hastily at th' dinner iv th' Betther-thin-Shakespere
Club, an' had attimpted to read it to his wife through th' keyhole
iv her bedroom dure an' met no response fr'm th' fillystein but a
pitcher iv wather through th' thransom.   Forchnitly he had
presarved a copy on his cuff an' th' gem was not lost to posterity.
But such was th' home life iv wan iv th' gr-reatest iv lithry
masters, a man indowed be nachure with all that shud make a
woman adore him as is proved be his tindher varses: "To Carrie,"
"To Maude," "To Flossie," "To Angebel," "To Queenie," an' so
foorth.   De Bonipoort in his cillybrated "Mimores," in which he
tells ivrything unpleasant he see or heerd in his frinds' houses,
gives a sthrikin' pitcher iv a scene that happened befure his eyes.
"Afther a few basins iv absceenthe in th' reev gosh," says he,
"Parnassy invited us home to dinner.   Sivral iv th' bum vivonts
was hard to wake up, but fin'lly we arrived at th' handsome cellar
where our gr-reat frind had installed his unworthy fam'ly.   Ivrything pinted to th' admirable taste iv th' thrue artist.   Th' tub,
th' washboard, th' biler singin' on th' fire, th' neighbor's washin'
dancin' on the clothes rack, were all in keepin' with th' best ideels
iv what a pote's home shud be.   Th' wife, a faded but still pretty
woman, welcomed us more or less, an' with th' assistance iv
sivral bottles iv paint we had brought with us, we was soon launched
on a feast iv raison an' a flow iv soul.   Unhappily befure th' ray-
past was con-cluded a mis'rable scene took place.   Amid cries iv
approval, Parnassy read his mim'rable pome intitled: 'I wisht
I nivir got marrid.'   Afther finishin' in a perfect roar of
applause, he happened to look up an' see his wife callously
rockin' th' baby.   With th' impetchosity so charackteristic iv th'
man, he broke a soup plate over her head an' burst into tears on
th' flure, where gentle sleep soon soothed th' pangs iv a weary
heart.   We left as quitely as we cud, considherin' th' way th'

chairs was placed, an' wanst undher th' stars comminted on th' ir'ny iv fate that condimned so great a man to so milancholy a distiny."

"'This,' says our author, 'was th' daily life iv th' hayro f'r tin years. In what purgatory will that infamous woman suffer if Hiven thinks as much iv janiuses as we think iv oursilves. Forchnitly th' pote was soon to be marcifully relieved. He left her an' she marrid a boorjawce with whom she led a life iv coarse happiness. It is sad to relate that some years afterward th' great pote, havin' called to make a short touch on th' woman f'r whom he had sacryficed so much, was unfeelingly kicked out iv th' boorjawce's plumbin' shop.'

"So, ye see, Hinnissy, why a woman oughtn't to marry a janius. She can't be cross or peevish or angry or jealous or frivolous or annything else a woman ought to be at times f'r fear it will get into th' ditchn'ry iv bio-graphy, an' she'll go down to histhry as a termygant. A termygant, Hinnissy, is a woman who's heerd talkin' to her husband after they've been marrid a year. Hogan says all janiuses was unhappily married. I guess that's thrue iv their wives, too. He says if ye hear iv a pote who got on with his fam'ly, scratch him fr'm ye'er public lib'ry list. An' there ye ar-re."

"Ye know a lot about marredge," said Mr. Hennessy.

"I do," said Mr. Dooley.

"Ye was niver marrid?"

"No," said Mr. Dooley. "No, I say, givin' three cheers. I know about marredge th' way an asthronomer knows about th' stars. I'm studyin' it through me glass all th' time."

"Ye're an asthronomer," said Mr. Hennessy; "but," he added, tapping himself lightly on the chest, "I'm a star."

"Go home," said Mr. Dooley crossly, "befure th' mornin' comes to put ye out."

REFORM ADMINISTRATION

"Why is it," asked Mr. Hennessy, "that a rayform adminis-thration always goes to th' bad?"

"I'll tell ye," said Mr. Dooley. "I tell ye ivrything an' I'll tell ye this. In th' first place 'tis a gr-reat mistake to think that annywan ra-aly wants to rayform. Ye niver heerd iv a man

rayformin' himsilf. He'll rayform other people gladly. He likes
to do it. But a healthy man'll niver rayform while he has th'
strenth. A man doesn't rayform till his will has been impaired
so he hasn't power to resist what th' pa-apers calls th' blandish-
ments iv th' timpter. An' that's thruer in politics thin annywhere else.

"But a rayformer don't see it. A rayformer thinks he was
ilicted because he was a rayformer, whin th' thruth iv th' matther
is he was ilicted because no wan knew him. Ye can always ilict a
man in this counthry on that platform. If I was runnin' f'r office,
I'd change me name, an' have printed on me cards: 'Give him a
chanst; he can't be worse.' He's ilicted because th' people don't
know him an' do know th' other la-ad; because Mrs. Casey's oldest
boy was clubbed be a polisman, because we cudden't get wather
above th' third story wan day, because th' sthreet car didn't stop
f'r us, because th' Flannigans bought a pianny, because we was
near run over be a mail wagon, because th' saloons are open
Sundah night, because they're not open all day, an' because we're
tired seein' th' same face at th' window whin we go down to pay th'
wather taxes. Th' rayformer don't know this. He thinks you
an' me, Hinnissy, has been watchin' his spotless career f'r twenty
years, that we've read all he had to say on th' evils iv pop'lar
sufferage befure th' Society f'r the Bewildermint iv th' Poor, an'
that we're achin' in ivry joint to have him dhrag us be th' hair iv
th' head fr'm th' flowin' bowl an' th' short card game, make good
citizens iv us an' sind us to th' pinitinchry. So th' minyit he gets
into th' job he begins a furyous attimpt to convart us into what
we've been thryin' not to be iver since we come into th' wurruld.

"In th' coorse iv th' twenty years that he spint attimptin' to get
office, he managed to poke a few warrum laws conthrollin' th'
pleasures iv th' poor into th' stachoo book, because no wan cared
about thim or because they made business betther f'r th' polis, an'
whin he's in office, he calls up th' Cap'n iv the polis an' says he:
'If these laws ar-re bad laws th' way to end thim is to enfoorce
thim.' Somebody told him that, Hinnissy. It isn't thrue, d'ye
mind. I don't care who said it, not if 'twas Willum Shakespere.
It isn't thrue. Laws ar-re made to throuble people an' th' more
throuble they make th' longer they stay on th' stachoo book.
But th' polis don't ast anny questions. Says they: 'They'll be less
money in th' job but we need some recreation,' an' that night a big
copper comes down th' sthreet, sees me settin' out on th' front

stoop with me countenance dhraped with a tin pail, fans me with his club an' runs me in. Th' woman nex' dure is locked up f'r sthringin' a clothes line on th' roof, Hannigan's boy Tim gets tin days f'r keepin' a goat, th' polis resarves are called out to protict th' vested rights iv property against th' haynyous pushcart man, th' stations is crowded with felons charged with maintainin' a hose conthrary to th' stachoos made an' provided, an' th' tindherline is all over town. A rayformer don't think annything has been accomplished if they'se a vacant bedroom in th' pinitinchry. His motto is 'Arrest that man.'

"Whin a rayformer is ilicted he promises ye a business administhration. Some people want that but I don't. Th' American business man is too fly. He's all right, d'ye mind. I don't say annything again' him. He is what Hogan calls th' boolwarks iv pro-gress, an' we cudden't get on without him even if his scales are a little too quick on th' dhrop. But he ought to be left to dale with his akels. 'Tis a shame to give him a place where he can put th' comether on millions iv people that has had no business thrainin' beyond occasionally handin' a piece iv debased money to a car conductor on a cold day. A reg'lar pollytician can't give away an alley without blushin', but a business man who is in pollytics jus' to see that th' civil sarvice law gets thurly enfoorced, will give Lincoln Park an' th' public libr'y to th' beef thrust, charge an admission price to th' lake front an' make it a felony f'r annywan to buy stove polish outside iv his store, an' have it all put down to public improvemints with a pitcher iv him in th' corner stone.

"Fortchnitly, Hinnissy, a rayformer is seldom a business man. He thinks he is, but business men know diff'rent. They know what he is. He thinks business an' honesty is th' same thing. He does, indeed. He's got thim mixed because they dhress alike. His idee is that all he has to do to make a business administhration is to have honest men ar-round him. Wrong. I'm not sayin', mind ye, that a man can't do good work an' be honest at th' same time. But whin I'm hirin' a la-ad I find out first whether he is onto his job, an' afther a few years I begin to suspect that he is honest, too. Manny a dishonest man can lay brick sthraight an' manny a man that wudden't steal ye'er spoons will break ye'er furniture. I don't want Father Kelly to hear me, but I'd rather have a competint man who wud steal if I give him a chanst, but I won't, do me plumbin' thin a person that wud scorn to help himsilf but didn't know how to wipe a joint. Ivry man ought to be honest to start with, but to give a man an office jus' because he's honest is like ilictin' him to Congress because he's a pathrite, because he don't bate his wife or because he always wears a right boot on th' right foot. A man ought to be honest to start with an' afther that he ought to be crafty. A pollytician who's on'y honest is jus' th' same as bein' out in a winther storm without anny clothes on.

"Another thing about rayform administhrations is they always think th' on'y man that ought to hold a job is a lawyer. Th' raison is that in th' coorse iv his thrainin' a lawyer larns enough about ivrything to make a good front on anny subject to annybody who doesn't know about it. So whin th' rayform administhration comes in th' mayor says: 'Who'll we make chief iv polis in place iv th' misguided ruffyan who has held th' job f'r twinty years?' 'Th' man f'r th' place,' says th' mayor's adviser, 'is Arthur Lightout,' he says. 'He's an ixcillent lawyer, Yale, '95, an' is well up on polis matthers. Las' year he read a paper on "The fine polis foorce iv London" befure th' annyal meetin' iv th' S'ciety f'r Ladin' th' Mulligan Fam'ly to a Betther an' Harder Life. Besides,' he says, 'he's been in th' milishy an' th' foorce needs a man who'll be afraid not to shoot in case iv public disturbance.' So Arthur takes hold iv th' constabulary an' in a year th' polis can all read Emerson an' th' burglars begin puttin' up laddhers an' block an' tackles befure eight A.M. An' so it is on ivry side. A lawyer has charge iv the city horse-shoein', another wan is clanin' th' sthreets, th' author iv 'Gasamagoo on torts' is thryin' to dispose iv th' ashes be throwin' thim in th' air on a windy day, an' th' bright boy that took th' silver ware f'r th' essay on *ne exeats* an' their relation to life is plannin' a uniform that will be sarviceable an' constitchoochinal f'r th' brave men that wurruks on th' city dumps. An' wan day th' main rayformer goes out expictin' to rayceive th' thanks iv th' community an' th' public that has jus' got out iv jail f'r lettin' th' wather run too long in th' bath tub rises up an' cries: 'Back to th' Univarsity Settlemint.' Th' man with th' di'mon' in his shirt front comes home an' pushes th' honest lawyers down th' steps, an' a dishonest horse shoer shoes th' city's horses well, an' a crooked plumber does th' city's plumbin' securely, an' a rascally polisman that may not be avarse to pickin' up a bet but will always find out whin Pathrolman Scanlan slept on his beat, takes hold iv th' polis

foorce, an' we raysume our nachral condition iv illagal merrimint.
An' th' rayformer spinds th' rest iv his life tellin' us where we are
wrong. He's good at that. On'y he don't undherstand that
people wud rather be wrong an' comfortable thin right in jail."

"I don't like a rayformer," said Mr. Hennessy.

"Or anny other raypublican," said Mr. Dooley.

NEWPORT

"About this time ivry year," said Mr. Dooley, "I go to Newport f'r th' summer."

"Ye go where?" asked Mr. Hennessy.

"I go to Newport," said Mr. Dooley, calmly, "in th' pa-apers.
Newport's always there. I may not find annything about th'
fire at th' yards or th' war in th' Ph'lippeens, but if Mrs. Rasther
opens a can iv salmon or pounds th' top off an egg, it's down in
black an' white be th' fearless hands iv th' iditor. 'Tis a gr-reat
joy bein' lithry an' knowin' how to read. Th' air is hot in Ar-
rchey Road; ye can see it. It looks an' feels like hot soup with
people floatin' around in it like viggytables. Th' smoke poors
fr'm th' chimbly iv th' rollin' mills an' comes right down on th'
sthreet an' jines us. People ar-re lyin' out iv doors with their
mouths open. They'se a gr-reat dale iv cholery infantum an' a
few deleeryam thremens. If I cudden't read I'd be hot about th'
weather an' things. But whin th' day is darkest an' I don't want
to see me best cukkin' frind, I takes me yacht at th' top iv page
eight an' goes sailin' off to Newport in me shirt sleeves with
twelve inches iv malt in th' hook iv me thumb, an' there I stay till
I want to come back an' rest.

"'Th' autymobill season has opened in deadly earnest. Manny
new machines is seen daily an' wan iv th' delights iv th' summer
colony is to go out iv an avenin' an' see th' farmers iv th' neighborhood pluckin' their horses fr'm th' top branches iv threes. Th'
younger Hankerbilt has atthracted much attintion be his acc'rate
ridin'. Th' other day he made a scoor iv eight fr'm a runnin'
start in tin minyits an' this is spite iv th' fact that he was obliged to
come back to th' last wan, a Swede named Olson, an' bump him
over again.

"'Misther Graball, th' Muskegon millionaire who got into
s'ciety las' year be dyin' his hair green an' givin' a dinner at

which all th' guests rayceived a lumber mill as sooveneers, has returned suddenly fr'm th' West an' his house party is over.

"'Little Aigrette Vandycooker has a tooth, her elder sister a markess, an' her mother a siparation.

"'Misther an' Mrs. Roger Smitherson an' frind ar-re spindin' th' summer at frind's house.'

"Gin'rally we lade a life iv quite an' iligant luxury. Wud ye like a line on me daily routine? Well, in th' mornin' a little spin in me fifty-horse-power 'Suffer-little-childher,' in th' afthernoon a whirl over th' green wathers iv th' bay in me goold-an'-ivory yacht, in th' avenin' dinner with a monkey or something akelly as good, at night a few leads out iv th' wrong hand, some hasty wur-ruds an' so to bed. Such is th' spoortin' life in Rhode Island, th' home iv Roger Williams an' others not so much. It grows tire-some afther awhile. I confess to ye, Algernon Hinnissy, that befure th' monkey was inthrajooced, I was sufferin' fr'm what Hogan calls onwee, which is th' same thing as ingrowin' money. I had got tired iv puttin' new storeys on me cottage an' ridin' up in th' ilivator fr'm th' settin' room on th' eighth flure to th' dinin' room on th' twinty-ninth, I didn't care about ayether thrap-shootin' or autymobillin', I felt like givin' a cawrnation dinner to th' poor iv th' village an' feedin' thim me polo ponies, I didn't care whether th' champagne bar'ls was kept iced, whether th' yacht was as long as th' wan ownded be th' Ginger Snap king nex' dure, whether I had three or tin millyon dollars in me pants pocket in th' mornin' or whether th' Poles in th' coal mine was sthrikin' f'r wan dollar an' forty-siven or wan dollar an' forty-eight cints a day. I was tired iv ivrything. Life had me be th' throat, th' black dog was on me back. I felt like suicide or wurruk. Thin come th' bright idee iv me young frind an' th' monkey saved me. He give me something to live f'r. Perhaps we too may be monkeys some day an' be amusin'. We don't talk half as loud or look half as foolish or get dhrunk half as quick, but give us a chanst. We're a young people an' th' monkeys is an old, old race. They've been Newportin' f'r cinchries. Sure that ol' la-ad who said man was descided fr'm monkeys knew what he was talkin' about. De-scinded, but how far?

"Now, don't go gettin' cross about th' rich, Hinnissy. Put up that dinnymite. Don't excite ye'ersilf about us folks in New-port. It's always been th' same way, Father Kelly tells me. Says he: 'If a man is wise, he gets rich an' if he gets rich, he gets foolish, or his wife does. That's what keeps th' money movin' around. What comes in at th' ticker goes out at th' wine agent. F'river an' iver people have been growin' rich, goin' down to some kind iv a Newport, makin' monkeys iv thimsilves an' goin' back to th' jungle. 'Tis a steady pro-cission. Aisy come, lazy go. In ivry little hamlet in this broad land, there's some man with a broad jaw an' th' encouragement iv a good woman, makin' ready to shove some other man off his steam yacht. At this very minyit whin I speak, me frind Jawn Grates has his eye on Hankerbilk's house. He wud swing a hammock in th' woodshed this year, but nex' he may have his feet up on th' bannister iv th' front stoop. Whin a captain iv industhry stops dhrinkin' at th' bar, he's near his finish. If he ain't caught in his own person, th' constable will get to his fam'ly. Ye read about th' union iv two gr-reat fortunes. A dollar meets another dollar, they are conganial, have sim'lar tastes, an' manny mutual frinds. They are marrid an' bring up a fam'ly iv pennies, dimes, thirty-cintses an' countherfeits. An' afther awhile, th' fam'ly passes out iv circylation. That's th' histhry iv it,' says Father Kelly. 'An',' says he, 'I'm glad there is a Newport,' he says. 'It's th' exhaust pipe,' he says. 'Without it we might blow up,' he says. 'It's th' hole in th' top iv th' kettle,' he says. 'I wish it was bigger,' he says."

"Oh, well," said Mr. Hennessy, "we are as th' Lord made us."

"No," said Mr. Dooley, "lave us be fair. Lave us take some iv th' blame oursilves."

MACHINERY

Mr. Dooley was reading from a paper. "'We live,' he says, 'in an age iv wondhers. Niver befure in th' histhry iv th' wurruld has such pro-gress been made.'

"Thrue wurruds an' often spoken. Even in me time things has changed. Whin I was a la-ad Long Jawn Wintworth cud lean his elbows on th' highest buildin' in this town. It took two months to come here fr'm Pittsburg on a limited raft an' a stage coach that run fr'm La Salle to Mrs. Murphy's hotel. They wasn't anny tillygraft that I can raymimber an' th' sthreet car was pulled be a mule an' dhruv be an engineer be th' name iv Mulligan. We thought we was a pro-grissive people. Ye bet we did. But look at us today. I go be Casey's house tonight an' there it is a fine storey-an'-a-half frame house with Casey settin' on th' dure shtep dhrinkin' out iv a pail. I go be Casey's house to-morrah an' it's a hole in th' groun'. I rayturn to Casey's house on Thursdah an' it's a fifty-eight storey buildin' with a morgedge onto it an' they're thinkin' iv takin' it down an' replacin' it with a modhren sthructure. Th' shoes that Corrigan th' cobbler wanst wurruked on f'r a week, hammerin' away like a woodpecker, is now tossed out be th' dozens fr'm th' mouth iv a masheen. A cow goes lowin' softly in to Armours an' comes out glue, beef, gelatine, fertylizer, celooloid, joolry, sofy cushions, hair restorer, washin' sody, soap, lithrachoor an' bed springs so quick that while aft she's still cow, for'ard she may be annything fr'm buttons to Pannyma hats. I can go fr'm Chicago to New York in twinty hours, but I don't have to, thank th' Lord. Thirty years ago we thought 'twas marvelous to be able to tillygraft a man in Saint Joe an' get an answer that night. Now, be wireless tillygraft ye can get an answer befure ye sind th' tillygram if they ain't careful. Me friend Macroni has done that. Be manes iv his wondher iv science a man on a ship in mid-ocean can sind a tillygram to a man on shore, if he has a confid'rate on board. That's all he needs. Be mechanical science an' thrust in th' op'rator annywan can set on th' shore iv Noofoundland an' chat with a frind in th' County Kerry.

"Yes, sir, mechanical science has made gr-reat sthrides. Whin I was a young man we used to think Hor'ce Greeley was th' gr-reatest livin' American. He was a gran' man, a gran' man with feathers beneath his chin an' specs on his nose like th' windows in a diver's hemlet. His pollyticks an' mine cudden't live in th' same neighborhood but he was a gran' man all th' same. We used to take th' Cleveland Plain Daler in thim days f'r raycreation an' th' New York Thrybune f'r exercise. 'Twas considhered a test iv a good natured dimmycrat if he cud read an article in th' Thrybune without havin' to do th' stations iv th' cross afterward f'r what he said. I almost did wanst but they was a line at th' end about a frind iv mine be th' name iv Andhrew Jackson an' I wint out an' broke up a Methodist prayer meetin'. He was th' boy that cud put it to ye so that if ye voted th' dimmy-crat tickit it was jus' th' same as demandin' a place in purgytory. Th' farmers wud plant annything fr'm a ruty baga to a congress-man on his advice. He niver had money enough to buy a hat but he cud go to th' sicrety iv th' threasury an' tell him who's pitcher to put on th' useful valentines we thrade f'r groceries.

"But if Hor'ce Greeley was alive today where'd he be? Settin' on three inches iv th' edge iv a chair in th' outside office iv me frind Pierpont Morgan waitin' f'r his turn. In th' line is th' Imp'ror iv Germany, th' new cook, th' prisidint iv a railroad, th' cap'n iv th' yacht, Rimbrandt th' painther, Jawn W. Grates, an' Hor'ce. Afther awhile th' boy at th' dure says: 'Ye're next, ol' party. Shtep lively f'r th' boss has had a Weehawken Peerooginy sawed off on him this mornin' an' he mustn't be kep' waitin'.' An' th' iditor goes in. 'Who ar-re ye?' says th' gr-reat man, givin' him wan iv thim piercin' looks that whin a man gets it he has to be sewed up at wanst. 'I'm ye'er iditor,' says Hor'ce. 'Which wan?' says Pierpont. 'Number two hundhred an' eight.' 'What's ye'er spishilty?' 'Tahriff an' th' improvemint iv th' wurruld,' says Hor'ce. 'See Perkins,' says Pierpont, an' th' intherview is over. Now what's made th' change? Mechanical Science, Hinnissy. Some wan made a masheen that puts steel billets within th' reach iv all. Hince Charlie Schwab.

"What's it done f'r th' wurruld? says ye. It's done ivrything. It's give us fast ships an' an autymatic hist f'r th' hod, an' small flats an' a taste iv solder in th' peaches. If annybody says th' wurruld ain't betther off thin it was, tell him that a masheen has been invinted that makes honey out iv pethrolyum. If he asts ye why they ain't anny Shakesperes today, say: 'No, but we no longer make sausages be hand.'

"'Tis pro-gress. We live in a cinchry iv pro-gress an' I thank th' Lord I've seen most iv it. Man an' boy I've lived pretty near through this wondherful age. If I was proud I cud say I seen more thin Julyus Cæsar iver see or cared to. An' here I am, I'll not say how old, still pushin' th' malt acrost th' counther at me thirsty counthrymen. All around me is th' refinemints iv mechanical janius. Instead iv broachin' th' beer kag with a club an' dhrawin' th' beer through a fassit as me Puritan forefathers done, I have that wondher iv invintive science th' beer pump. I cheat mesilf with a cash raygisther. I cut off th' end iv me good cigar with an injanyous device an' pull th' cork out iv a bottle with a conthrivance that wud've made that frind that Hogan boasts about, that ol' boy Archy Meeds, think they was witchcraft in th' house. Science has been a gr-reat blessin' to me. But amidst all these granjoors here am I th' same ol' antiquated combination iv bellows an' pump I always was. Not so good. Time has worn me out. Th' years like little boys with jackknives has carved their names in me top. Ivry day I have to write off something f'r deprecyation. 'Tis about time f'r whoiver owns me to wurruk me off on a thrust. Mechanical science has done ivrything f'r me but help me. I suppose I ought to feel supeeryor to me father. He niver see a high buildin' but he didn't want to. He cudden't come here in five days but he was a wise man an' if he cud've come in three he'd have stayed in th' County Roscommon.

"Th' pa-apers tells me that midical science has kept pace with th' hop-skip-an'-a-jump iv mechanical inginooty. Th' doctors has found th' mickrobe iv ivrything fr'm lumbago to love an' fr'm jandice to jealousy, but if a brick bounces on me head I'm crated up th' same as iv yore an' put away. Rockyfellar can make a pianny out iv a bar'l iv crude ile, but no wan has been able to make a blade iv hair grow on Rockyfellar. They was a doctor over in France that discovered a kind iv a thing that if 'twas pumped into ye wud make ye live till people got so tired iv seein' ye around they cud scream. He died th' nex' year iv premachure ol' age. They was another doctor cud insure whether th' nex' wan wud be a boy or a girl. All ye had to do was to decide wud it be Arthur or Ethel an' lave him know. He left a fam'ly iv unmarredgeable daughters.

"I sometimes wondher whether pro-gress is anny more thin a kind iv a shift. It's like a merry-go-round. We get up on a speckled wooden horse an' th' mechanical pianny plays a chune an' away we go, hollerin'. We think we're thravellin' like th' divvle but th' man that doesn't care about merry-go-rounds knows that we will come back where we were. We get out dizzy an' sick an' lay on th' grass an' gasp: 'Where am I? Is this th' meelin-yum?' An' he says: 'No, 'tis Ar-rchey Road.' Father Kelly says th' Agyptians done things we cudden't do an' th' Romans put up sky-scrapers an' aven th' Chinks had tillyphones an' phony-grafts.

"I've been up to th' top iv th' very highest buildin' in town, Hinnissy, an' I wasn't anny nearer Hivin thin if I was in th' sthreet. Th' stars was as far away as iver. An' down beneath is a lot iv us runnin' an' lapin' an' jumpin' about, pushin' each other over, haulin' little sthrips iv ir'n to pile up in little buildin's that ar-re called sky-scrapers but not be th' sky; wurrukin' night'an' day to make a masheen that'll carry us fr'm wan jack-rabbit colony to another an' yellin', 'Pro-gress!' Pro-gress, oho! I can see th' stars winkin' at each other an' sayin': 'Ain't they funny! Don't they think they're playin' hell!'

"No, sir, masheens ain't done much f'r man. I can't get up anny kind iv fam'ly inthrest f'r a steam dredge or a hydhraulic hist. I want to see sky-scrapin' men. But I won't. We're about th' same hight as we always was, th' same hight an' build, composed iv th' same inflammable an' perishyable mateeryal, an exthra hazardous risk, unimproved an' li'ble to collapse. We do make pro-gress but it's th' same kind Julyus Cæsar made an' ivry wan has made befure or since an' in this age iv masheenery we're still burrid be hand."

"What d'ye think iv th' man down in Pinnsylvanya who says th' Lord an' him is partners in a coal mine?" asked Mr. Hennessy, who wanted to change the subject.

"Has he divided th' profits?" asked Mr. Dooley.

SWEARING[1]

"Did ye see what th' prisidint said to th' throlley man that bumped him?" asked Mr. Dooley.

"I did not," said Mr. Hennessy. "What was it?"

"I can't tell ye till I get mad," said Mr. Dooley. "Lave us go into ixicutive sission. Whisper. That was it. Ha, ha. He give it to him sthraight. A good, honest, American blankety-blank. Rale language like father used to make whin he hit his thumb with th' hammer. No 'With ye'er lave' or 'By ye'er lave,' but a dacint 'Damn ye, sir,' an' a little more f'r th' sake iv imphasis.

"What else wud ye have him do? 'Twas nayether th' time nor th' occasion, as th' candydate said whin they ast him where he got his money, 'twas nayether th' time nor th' occasion f'r wurruds that wud be well rayceived at Chatauqua. A throlley car had pushed him an' diplomatic relations was suspinded. He was up on top iv a bus, hurryin' fr'm speech to speech an' thinkin' what to say next. 'Th' thrusts,' says he to himsilf, 'are heejous monsthers built up be th' inlightened intherprise iv th' men that have done so much to advance pro-gress in our beloved counthry,' he says. 'On wan hand I wud stamp thim undher fut; on th'

[1] Written on the occasion of President Theodore Roosevelt's first message to Congress.

other hand not so fast. What I want more thin th' bustin' iv th' thrusts is to see me fellow counthrymen happy an' continted. I wudden't have thim hate th' thrusts. Th' haggard face, th' droopin' eye, th' pallid complexion that marks th' inimy iv thrusts is not to me taste. Lave us be merry about it an' jovial an' affectionate. Lave us laugh an' sing th' octopus out iv existence. Betther blue but smilin' lips anny time thin a full coal scuttle an' a sour heart. As Hogan says, a happy peasanthry is th' hope iv th' state. So lave us warble ti-lire-a-lay—' Jus' thin Euclid Aristophanes Madden on th' quarther deck iv th' throlley car give a twisht to his brake an' th' chief ixicutive iv th' nation wint up in th' air with th' song on his lips. He wint up forty, some say, fifty feet. Sicrety Cortilloo says three hundherd an' fifty. Annyhow whin he come down he landed nachrally on his feet.

"Now, Hinnissy, no matther what a man may've been wan minyit befure he was hit be a throlley car, a minyit afther he's on'y a man. Th' throlley car plays no fav'rites. It bounces th' high an' th' low alike. It tears th' exalted fr'm their throne an' ilivates th' lowly. So whin th' prisidint got back to the earth he wasn't prisidint anny longer but Tiddy Rosenfelt, 180 pounds iv a man. An' he done accordin'ly. If it'd been Willum Jennings Bryan, he'd've ast th' throlley engineer was he a mimber iv th' Union. If he cud show a wurrukin' card he was entitled to bump anny wan. At worst Willum Jennings Bryan wud've written an article about him in th' *Commoner*, or if he felt unusually vindicative, maybe he'd sind it to him through th' mails. Whin Sicrety Cortilloo come to fr'm a dhream that he'd jus' rayfused a favor to Sinitor Tillman, he hauled out a little note book an' got ready to take down something that cud be put on th' transparencies two years fr'm now—something like—'No power on earth can stop American business entherprise.' But nawthin' that will iver be printed in th' first reader dhropped fr'm th' lips iv th' chief exicutive. With two jumps he was in th' throlley man's hair an' spoke as follows—No, I won't say it again. But I'll tell ye this much, a barn-boss that was standin' by an' heerd it, said he niver befure regretted his father hadn't sint him to Harvard.

"We know what Wash'nton said to his gin'rals an' what Grant said to Lee an' what Cleveland said to himsilf. They're in th' books. But engraved in th' hearts iv his counthrymen is what Rosenfelt said to th' throlley man. 'Twas good because 'twas so nachral. Most iv th' sayin's I've read in books sounds as though they was made be a patent inkybator. They go with a high hat an' a white tie. Ye can hear th' noise iv th' phonygraft. But this here jim of emotion an' thought come sthraight fr'm th' heart an' wint right to th' heart. That's wan reason I think a lot iv us likes Tiddy Rosenfelt that wudden't iver be suspected iv votin' f'r him. Whin he does anny talkin'—which he sometimes does—he talks at th' man in front iv him. Ye don't hear him hollerin' at posterity. Posterity don't begin to vote till afther th' polls close. So whin he wished to convey to th' throlley man th' sintimints iv his bosom, he done it in wurruds suited to th' crisis, as Hogan wud say. They do say his remarks singed th' hair off th' head iv th' unforchnit man.

"I don't believe in profanity, Hinnissy—not as a reg'lar thing. But it has its uses an' its place. F'r instance, it is issintial to some thrades. No man can be a printer without swearin'. 'Tis impossible. I mind wanst I wint to a printin' office where a frind iv mine be th' name iv Donovan held cases an' I heerd th' foreman say: 'What gintleman is setting A thirty?' he says. 'I am,' says a pale aristocrat with black whiskers who was atin' tobacco in th' rear iv th' room. 'Thin,' says th' foreman, 'ye blankety-blank blacksmith, get a move on ye. D'ye think this is a annyooal incyclopejee?' he says. Ivrybody swore at ivrybody else. Th' little boys runnin' around with type prattled innocent pro-fanity an' afther awhile th' iditor come in an' he swore more thin annybody else. But 'twas aisy to see he'd not larned th' thrade iv printer. He swore with th' enthusyasm an' inacc'racy iv an amachoor, though I mus' say, he had his good pints. I wisht I cud raymimber what it was he called th' Czar iv Rooshya f'r dyin' jus' as th' pa-aper was goin' to press. I cud've often used it since. But it's slipped me mind.

"Swearin' belongs to some thrades—like printin', brick-layin' an' plumbin'. It is no help at all, at all to tailors, shoe-makers, hair-dressers, dintists or authors. A surgeon needs it but a doctor niver. It is a great help in unloadin' a ship an' sailor men always swear—th' cap'n an' mate whin wurruk is goin' on an' th' men befure th' mast at meals. Sojers mus' swear. They'se no way out iv it. It's as much th' equipment iv a sojer as catridges. In vigorous spoort it is niciss'ry but niver at checkers or chess an' sildom at dominoes. Cowboys are com-pelled to use it. No wan cud rope a cow or cinch a pony without

swearin'. A sthrick bringin' up is th' same as havin' a wooden
leg on th' plains. Profanity shud be used sparingly if at all on
childher—especially girls—an' sildom on women, though I've
knowed an occasional domestic: 'Damn ye'er eyes' to wurruk
wondhers in reg-latin' a fam'ly. Women can't swear. They
have th' feelin' but not th' means. Westhern men swear betther
thin Eastern men though I mus' say th' mos' lib'ral swearers I
iver knew come fr'm Boston.

"But it don't do to use pro-fanity th' way ye wud ordin'ry
wurruds. No, sir. Ye've got to save it up an' invist it at th'
right time or get nawthin' fr'm it. It's betther thin a doctor
f'r a stubbed toe but it niver cured a broken leg. It's a kind iv a
first aid to th' injured. It seems to deaden th' pain. Women an'
childher cry or faint whin they're hurt. That's because they
haven't th' gift iv swearin'. But as I tell ye, they'se no good
wastin' it. Th' man that swears at ivrything has nawthin' to
say when rale throubles come. I hate to hear annywan spillin'
out th' valyable wurruds that he ought to save to be used whin
th' shtove-pipe comes down. Not that it shocks me. I'm a
dimmycrat. But I know th' foolish man is hurtin' himsilf. Put
a little pro-fanity by f'r rainy days, says I. Ye won't miss it an' at
th' end iv th' year whin ye renew ye'er lease ye'll be surprised to
find out how much ye have on hand. But if ye hurl it broadcast,
if ivry time ye open ye'er mouth a hot wan lapes out, th' time will
come whin ye'll want to say something scorchin' an' ye'll have
nawthin' to say that ye haven't said f'r fun. I'd as soon think iv
swearin' f'r pleasure as iv lindin' money f'r pleasure. They ain't
too much pro-fanity in th' wurruld. A good dale iv it has been
used up since th' coal sthrike begun. Th' govermint ought to
presarve it an' prevint annywan fr'm swearin' more thin was
niciss'ry f'r to support life.

"I niver knew Father Kelly to swear but wanst. 'Twas a little
wan, Hinnissy. Dhropped fr'm th' lips iv a polisman it wud've
sounded like a 'thank ye kindly.' But, be Hivins, whin I heerd
it I thought th' roof wud fall down on th' head iv Scanlan that
he was thryin' to show th' evil iv his ways. Melia Murdher,
but it was gran'! They was more varchue in that wan damn thin
in a fastin' prayer. Scanlan wint to wurruk th' nex' day an' he
hasn't tasted a dhrop since.

"But th' best thing about a little judicyous swearin' is that
it keeps th' temper. 'Twas intinded as a compromise between

runnin' away an' fightin'. Befure it was invinted they was on'y th' two ways out iv an argymint."

"But I've heerd ye say a man was swearin' mad," said Mr. Hennessy.

"He wasn't fightin' mad, thin," said Mr. Dooley.

RIGHTS AND PRIVILEGES OF WOMEN

"Woman's rights? What does a woman want iv rights whin she has priv'leges? Rights is th' last thing we get in this wurruld. They're th' nex' things to wrongs. They're wrongs tur-rned inside out. We have th' right to be sued f'r debt instead iv lettin' the bill run, which is a priv'lege. We have th' right to thrile be a jury iv our peers, a right to pay taxes an' a right to wurruk. None iv these things is anny good to me. They'se no fun in thim. All th' r-rights I injye I don't injye. I injye th' right to get money, but I niver have had anny money to spind. Th' constichooshion guarantees me th' right to life, but I die; to liberty, but if I thry bein' too free I'm locked up; an' to th' pursoot iv happiness, but happiness has th' right to run whin pursood, an' I've niver been able to three her yet. Here I am at iver-so-manny years iv age blown an' exhausted be th' chase, an' happiness is still able to do her hundhred yards in tin minyits flat whin I approach. I'd give all th' rights I read about for wan priv-lege. If I cud go to sleep th' minyit I go to bed I wudden't care who done me votin'.

"No, sir, a woman don't need rights. Th' pope, imprors, kings an' women have priv-leges; ordhin'ry men has rights. Ye niver hear iv th' Impror of Rooshya demandin' rights. He don't need thim in his wurruk. He gives thim, such as they ar-re, to th' moojiks, or whativer it is ye call thim. D'ye think anny wan wud make a gr-reat success be goin' to th' Czar an' sayin': 'Czar (or sire, as th' case may be), ye must be unhappy without th' sufferage. Ye must be achin' all over to go down to th' livry stable an' cast ye'er impeeral ballot f'r Oscaroviski K. Hickinski f'r school thrustee?' I think th' Czar wud reply: 'Gintlemen, ye do me too much honor. I mus' rayfuse. Th' manly art iv sufferage is wan iv th' most potint weepins iv th' freeman, but I'm not used to it, an' I wudden't know what to do with it. It might be loaded. I think I'll have to crawl along with me modest preerogatives iv collectin' th' taxes, dalin' life an' death to me subjicks, atin' free, dhrinkin' th' best an' livin' aisy. But ye shall have ye'er rights. Posieotofski, lade th' gintlemen out into th' coortyard an' give thim their rights as Rooshyan citizens. I think about twinty f'r each iv th' comity an' about a dozen exthry f'r the chairman. F'r wan iv th' rights guaranteed to his subjicks, be me sainted father, was a good latherin' ivry time it was comin' to thim.'

"An' so it is with women. They haven't th' right to vote, but they have th' priv'lege iv conthrollin' th' man ye ilict. They haven't th' right to make laws, but they have th' priv'lege iv breakin' thim, which is betther. They haven't th' right iv a fair thrile be a jury iv their peers; but they have th' priv'lege iv an unfair thrile be a jury iv their admirin' infeeryors. If I cud fly d'ye think I'd want to walk ?"

AVARICE AND GENEROSITY[1]

"I niver blame a man f'r bein' avaricyous in his ol' age. Whin a fellow gits so he has nawthin' else to injye, whin ivrybody calls him 'sir' or 'mister,' an' young people dodge him an' he sleeps afther dinner, an' folks say he's an ol' fool if he wears a buttonhole bokay an' his teeth is only tinants at will an' not permanent fixtures, 'tis no more thin nach'ral that he shud begin to look around him f'r a way iv keepin' a grip on human s'ciety. It don't take him long to see that th' on'y thing that's vin'rable in age is money an' he pro-ceeds to acquire anything that happens to be in sight, takin' it where he can find it, not where he wants it, which is th' way to accumylate a fortune. Money won't prolong life, but a few millyons judicyously placed in good banks an' occas'nally worn on th' person will rayjooce age. Poor ol' men are always older thin poor rich men. In th' almshouse a man is decrepit an' mournful-lookin' at sixty, but a millyonaire at sixty is jus' in th' prime iv life to a frindly eye, an' there are no others.

"It's aisier to th' ol' to grow rich thin it is to th' young. At makin' money a man iv sixty is miles ahead iv a la-ad iv twinty-five. Pollytics and bankin' is th' on'y two games where age has th' best iv it. Youth has betther things to attind to, an' more iv thim.

---

[1] Thomas L. Masson in *Our American Humorists* compares this essay with one written by Theophrastus in 300 B.C.

I don't blame a man f'r bein' stingy anny more thin I blame him f'r havin' a bad leg. Ye know th' doctors say that if ye don't use wan iv ye'er limbs f'r a year or so ye can niver use it again. So it is with gin'rosity. A man starts arly in life not bein' gin'rous. He says to himsilf: 'I wurruked f'r this thing an' if I give it away I lose it.' He ties up his gin'rosity in bandages so that th' blood can't circylate in it. It gets to be a superstition with him that he'll have bad luck if he iver does annything f'r annybody. An' so he rakes in an' puts his private mark with his teeth on all th' movable money in th' wurruld. But th' day comes whin he sees people around him gettin' a good dale iv injyement out iv gin'rosity an' somewan says: 'Why don't ye, too, be gin'rous? Come, ol' green goods, unbelt, loosen up, be gin'rous.' 'Gin'rous?' says he, 'what's that?' 'It's th' best spoort in th' wurruld. It's givin' things to people.' 'But I can't,' he says. 'I haven't annything to do it with,' he says. 'I don't know th' game. I haven't anny gin'rosity,' he says. 'But ye have,' says they. 'Ye have as much gin'rosity as annywan if ye'll only use it,' says they. 'Take it out iv th' plasther cast ye put it in an' 'twill look as good as new,' says they. An' he does it. He thries to use his gin'rosity, but all th' life is out iv it. It gives way undher him an' he falls down. He can't raise it fr'm th' groun'. It's ossyfied an' useless. I've seen manny a fellow that suffered fr'm ossyfied gin'rosity.

"Whin a man begins makin' money in his youth at annything but games iv chance, he niver can become gin'rous late in life. He may make a bluff at it. Some men are gin'rous with a crutch. Some men get the use of their gin'rosity back suddenly whin they ar-re in danger. Whin Clancy the miser was caught in a fire in th' Halsted Sthreet Palace hotel he howled fr'm a window: 'I'll give twinty dollars to annywan that'll take me down.' Cap'n Minehan put up a laddher an' climbed to him an' carrid him to the sthreet. Half-way down th' laddher th' brave rayscooer was seen to be chokin' his helpless burdhen. We discovered afther-wards that Clancy had thried to begin negotyations to rayjooce th' reward to five dollars. His gin'rosity had become suddenly pár'lyzed again.

"So if ye'd stay gin'rous to th' end niver lave ye'er gin'rosity idle too long. Don't run it ivry hour at th' top iv its speed, but fr'm day to day give it a little gintle exercise to keep it supple an' hearty an' in due time ye may injye it."

THE END OF THINGS

"The raison no wan is afraid iv Death, Hinnessy, is that no wan ra-ally undherstands it. If anny wan iver come to undherstand it he'd be scared to death. If they is anny such thing as a cow'rd, which I doubt, he's a man that comes nearer realizin' thin other men, how seeryous a matther it is to die. I talk about it, an' sometimes I think about it. But how do I think about it? It's me lyin' there in a fine shoot iv clothes an' listenin' to all th' nice things people are sayin' about me. I'm dead, mind ye, but I can hear a whisper in the furthest corner iv th' room. Ivry wan is askin' ivry wan else why did I die. 'It's a gr-reat loss to th' counthry,' says Hogan. 'It is,' says Donahue. 'He was a fine man,' says Clancy. 'As honest a man as iver dhrew th' breath iv life,' says Schwartzmeister. 'I hope he forgives us all th' harm we attimpted to do him,' says Donahue. 'I'd give annything to have him back,' says Clancy. 'He was this and that, th' life iv th' party, th' sowl iv honor, th' frind iv th' disthressed, th' boolwark iv th' constichoochion, a pathrite, a gintleman, a Christyan an' a scholard.' 'An' such a roguish way with him,' says th' Widow O'Brien.

"That's what I think, but if I judged fr'm expeeryence I'd know it'd be, 'It's a nice day f'r a dhrive to th' cimitry. Did he lave much?' No man is a hayro to his undertaker."

HYPOCRISY

"It must be a good thing to be good or ivrybody wudden't be pretendin' he was. But I don't think they'se anny such thing as hypocrisy in th' wurruld. They can't be. If ye'd turn on th' gas in th' darkest heart ye'd find it had a good raison for th' worst things it done, a good varchous raison, like needin' th' money or punishin' th' wicked or tachin' people a lesson to be more careful, or protectin' th' liberties iv mankind, or needin' the money."

HISTORY

"I know histhry isn't thrue, Hinnessy, because it ain't like what I see ivry day in Halsted Sthreet. If any wan comes along with a histhry iv Greece or Rome that'll show me th' people

fightin', gettin' dhrunk, makin' love, gettin' married, owin' th'
grocery man an' bein' without hard-coal, I'll believe they was a
Greece or Rome, but not befure. Historyans is like doctors.
They are always lookin' f'r symptoms. Those iv them that
writes about their own times examines th' tongue an' feels th'
pulse an' makes a wrong dygnosis. Th' other kind iv histhry is
a post-mortem examination. It tells ye what a counthry died iv.
But I'd like to know what it lived iv."

ENJOYMENT

"I don't think we injye other people's sufferin', Hinnessy.
It isn't acshally injyement. But we feel betther f'r it."

GRATITUDE

"Wan raison people ar-re not grateful is because they're
proud iv thimsilves an' they niver feel they get half what they
desarve. Another raison is they know ye've had all th' fun ye're
entitled to whin ye do annything f'r annybody. A man who expicts
gratichood is a usurer, an' if he's caught at it he loses th' loan
an' th' intherest."

DISSERTATIONS BY
MR. DOOLEY

THE PURSUIT OF RICHES

"Dear me, I wisht I had money," said Mr. Hennessy.

"So do I," said Mr. Dooley. "I need it."

"Ye wudden't get it fr'm me," said Mr. Hennessy.

"If I didn't," said Mr. Dooley, "'twould be because I was poor or tired. But what d'ye want money f'r? Supposin' I lost me head an' handed over all me accumylated wealth? What wud ye do with that gr-reat fortune? Befure ye had spint half iv it ye'd be so sick ye'd come to me an' hand me back th' remainin' eighteen dollars.

"A man has more fun wishin' f'r th' things he hasn't got thin injyin' th' things he has got. Life, Hinnissy, is like a Pullman dinin'-car: a fine bill iv fare but nawthin' to eat. Ye go in fresh an' hungry, tuck ye'er napkin in ye'er collar, an' square away at th' list iv groceries that th' black man hands ye. What'll ye have first? Ye think ye'd like to be famous, an' ye ordher a dish iv fame an' bid th' waither make it good an' hot. He's gone an age, an' whin he comes back ye'er appytite is departed. Ye taste th' ordher, an' says ye: 'Why, it's cold an' full iv broken glass.' 'That's th' way we always sarve Fame on this car,' says th' coon. 'Don't ye think ye'd like money f'r th' second coorse? Misther Rockyfellar over there has had forty-two helpin's,' says he. 'It don't seem to agree with him,' says ye, 'but ye may bring me some,' ye say. Away he goes, an' stays till ye're bald an' ye'er teeth fall out an' ye set dhrummin' on th' table an' lookin' out at th' scenery. By-an'-by he comes back with ye'er ordher, but jus' as he's goin' to hand it to ye Rockyfellar grabs th' plate. 'What kind iv a car is this?' says ye. 'Don't I get annything to eat?

Can't ye give me a little happiness ?' 'I wudden't ricommend th' happiness,' says th' waither. 'It's canned, an' it kilt th' las' man that thried it.' 'Well, gracious,' says ye. 'I've got to have something. Give me a little good health, an' I'll thry to make a meal out iv that.' 'Sorry, sir,' says th' black man, 'but we're all out iv good health. Besides,' he says, takin' ye gently be th' ar-rm, 'we're comin' into th' deepo an' ye'll have to get out,' he says.

"An' there ye ar-re. Ye'll niver get money onless ye fix th' waither and grab th' dishes away fr'm th' other passengers. An' ye won't do that. So ye'll niver be rich. No poor man iver will be. Wan iv th' sthrangest things about life is that th' poor, who need th' money th' most, ar-re th' very wans that niver have it. A poor man is a poor man, an' a rich man is a rich man. Ye're ayther born poor or rich. It don't make anny diff'rence whether or not ye have money to begin with. If ye're born to be rich ye'll be rich, an' if ye're born to be poor ye'll be poor. Th' buttons on ye'er vest tell th' story. Rich man, poor man, beggar man, rich man, or wurruds to that effect. I always find that I have ayether two buttons or six.

"A poor man is a man that rayfuses to cash in. Ye don't get annything f'r nawthin', an' to gather in a millyon iv thim beautiful green promises ye have to go down ivry day with something undher ye'er ar-rm to th' great pawn-shop. Whin Hogan wants four dollars he takes th' clock down to Moses. Whin Rocky-fellar wants tin millyon he puts up his peace iv mind or his health or something akelly valyable. If Hogan wud hock his priceless habit iv sleepin' late in th' mornin' he wud be able to tell th' time iv day whin he got up without goin' to th' corner dhrug-store.

"Look at McMullin. He's rowlin' in it. It bulges his pocket an' inflates his convarsation. Whin he looks at me I always feel that he's wondhrin' how much I'd bring at a forced sale. Well, McMullin an' I had th' same start, about forty yards behind scratch an' Vanderbilt to beat. They always put th' best man in anny race behind th' line. Befure McMullin gets through he'll pass Vanderbilt, carry away th' tape on his shoulders, an' run two or three times around th' thrack. But me an' him started th' same way. Th' on'y diff-rence was that he wud cash in an' I wudden't. Th' on'y thing I iver ixpicted to get money on was me dhream iv avarice. I always had that. I cud dhream iv money as hard as anny man ye iver see, an' can still. But I niver

thought iv wurrukin' f'r it. I've always looked on it as dis-
hon'rable to wurruk f'r money. I wurruk f'r exercise, an' I get
what th' lawyers call an honoraryium be dilutin' th' spirits. Th'
on'y way I iver expict to make a cint is to have it left to me
be a rich relation, an' I'm th' pluthycrat iv me fam'ly, or to stub
me toe on a gambler's roll or stop a runaway horse f'r Pierpont
Morgan. An' th' horse mustn't be runnin' too fast. He must be
jus' goin' to stop, on'y Morgan don't know it, havin' fainted.
Whin he comes to he finds me at th' bridle, modestly waitin' f'r
him to weep on me bosom. But as f'r scramblin' down-town
arly in th' mornin' an' buyin' chattel morgedges, I niver thought
iv it. I get up at siven o'clock. I wudden't get up at a quarther
to siven f'r all th' money I dhream about.

"I have a lot iv things ar-round here I cud cash in if I cared
f'r money. I have th' priceless gift iv laziness. It's made me
what I am, an' that's th' very first thing ivry rich man cashes in.
Th' millyionaires ye r-read about thryin' to give th' rest iv th'
wurruld a good time be runnin' over thim in autymobills all
started with a large stock iv indolence, which they cashed in.
Now, whin they cud enjoy it they can't buy it back. Thin I have
me good health. Ye can always get money on that. An' I have
me frinds; I refuse to cash thim in. I don't know that I cud get
much on thim, but if I wanted to be a millyionaire I'd tuck you
an' Hogan an' Donahue undher me ar-rm an' carry ye down to
Mose.

"McMullin did cash. He had no more laziness thin me, but
he cashed it in befure he was twinty-wan. He cashed in his good
health, a large stock iv fam'ly ties, th' affection iv his wife, th'
comforts iv home, an' wan frind afther another. Wanst in a
while, late in life, he'd thry to redeem a pledge, but he niver cud.
They wasn't annything in th' wurruld that McMullin wudden't
change f'r th' money. He cashed in his vote, his pathreetism, his
rellijon, his rilitives, and finally his hair. Ye heerd about him,
didn't ye? He's lost ivry hair on his head. They ain't a spear iv
vigitation left on him. He's as arid as th' desert iv Sahara. His
head looks like an iceberg in th' moonlight. He was in here th'
other day, bewailin' his fate. 'It's a gr-reat misfortune,' says he.
'What did ye get f'r it?' says I. 'That's th' throuble,' says he.
'Well, don't complain,' says I. 'Think what ye save in barber's
bills,' I says, an' he wint away, lookin' much cheered up.

"No, Hinnissy, you and I, me frind, was not cut out be

Provydence to be millyionaires. If ye had nawthin' but money
ye'd have nawthin' but money. Ye can't ate it, sleep it, dhrink it,
or carry it away with ye. Ye've got a lot iv things that McMullin
hasn't got. Annybody that goes down to Mose's won't see ye'er
peace iv mind hangin' in th' window as an unredeemed pledge.
An', annyhow, if ye're really in search iv a fortune perhaps I cud
help ye. Wud a dollar an' a half be anny use to ye?"

"Life is full iv disappointments," said Mr. Hennessy.

"It is," said Mr. Dooley, "if ye feel that way. It's thrue that
a good manny have thried it, an' none have come back f'r post-
gradjate coorse. But still it ain't so bad as a career f'r a young
man. Ye niver get what ye ordher, but it's pretty good if ye'er
appytite ain't keen an' ye care f'r th' scenery."

THE LABOR TROUBLES

"I see th' sthrike has been called off," said Mr. Hennessy.

"Which wan?" asked Mr. Dooley. "I can't keep thrack iv
thim. Somebody is sthrikin' all th' time. Wan day th' horse-
shoers are out, an' another day th' teamsters. Th' Brotherhood
iv Molasses Candy Pullers sthrikes, an' th' Amalgymated Union
iv Pickle Sorters quits in sympathy. Th' carpinter that has been
puttin' up a chicken coop f'r Hogan knocked off wurruk whin he
found that Hogan was shavin' himsilf without a card fr'm th'
Barbers' Union. Hogan fixed it with th' walkin' dillygate iv th'
barbers, an' th' carpinter quit wurruk because he found that
Hogan was wearin' a pair iv non-union pants. Hogan wint down-
town an' had his pants unionized an' come home to find that th'
carpinter had sthruck because Hogan's hens was layin' eggs without
th' union label. Hogan injooced th' hens to jine th' union. But
wan iv thim laid an egg two days in succission an' th' others
sthruck, th' rule iv th' union bein' that no hen shall lay more eggs
thin th' most reluctant hen in th' bunch.

"It's th' same ivrywhere. I haven't had a sandwich f'r a year
because ivry time I've asked f'r wan ayether th' butchers or th'
bakers has been out on sthrike. If I go down in a car in th'
mornin' it's eight to wan I walk back at night. A man I knew had
his uncle in th' house much longer than ayether iv thim had
intinded on account iv a sthrike iv th' Frindly Brotherhood iv
Morchuary Helpers. Afther they'd got a permit fr'm th' walkin'
dillygate an' th' remains was carrid away undher a profusyon iv

floral imblims with a union label on each iv thim, th' coortege was stopped at ivry corner be a picket, who first punched th' mourners an' thin examined their credintials. Me frind says to me: 'Uncle Bill wud've been proud. He was very fond iv long fun'rals, an' this was th' longest I iver attinded. It took eight hours, an' was much more riochous goin' out thin comin' back,' he says.

"It was diff'rent whin I was a young man, Hinnissy. In thim days Capital an' Labor were frindly, or Labor was. Capital was like a father to Labor, givin' it its boord an' lodgin's. Naye-ther intherfered with th' other. Capital wint on capitalizin', an' Labor wint on laborin'. In thim goolden days a wurrukin' man was an honest artisan. That's what he was proud to be called. Th' week befure iliction he had his pitcher in th' funny pa-apers. He wore a square paper cap an' a leather apron, an' he had his ar-rm ar-round Capital, a rosy binivolint old guy with a plug-hat an' eye-glasses. They were goin' to th' polls together to vote f'r simple old Capital.

"Capital an' Labor walked ar-rm in ar-rm instead iv havin' both hands free as at prisint. Capital was contint to be Capital, an' Labor was used to bein' Labor. Capital come ar-round an' felt th' ar-rm iv Labor wanst in a while, an' ivry year Mrs. Capital called on Mrs. Labor an' congratylated her on her score. Th' pride iv ivry artisan was to wurruk as long at his task as th' boss cud afford to pay th' gas bill. In return f'r his fidelity he got a turkey ivry year. At Chris'mas time Capital gathered his happy fam'ly around him, an' in th' prisince iv th' ladies iv th' neighbor-hood give thim a short oration. 'Me brave la-ads,' says he, 'we've had a good year. (Cheers.) I have made a millyon dollars. (Sinsation.) I atthribute this to me supeeryor skill, aided be ye'er arnest efforts at th' bench an' at th' forge. (Sobs.) Ye have done so well that we won't need so manny iv us as we did. (Long an' continyous cheerin'.) Those iv us who can do two men's wurruk will remain, an', if possible, do four. Our other faithful sarvants,' he says, 'can come back in th' spring,' he says, 'if alive,' he says. An' th' bold artysans tossed their paper caps in th' air an' give three cheers f'r Capital. They wurruked till ol' age crept on thim, and thin retired to live on th' wish-bones an' kind wurruds they had accumylated.

"Nowadays 'tis far diff'rent. Th' unions has desthroyed all individjool effort. Year be year th' hours iv th' misguided wurrukin' man has been cut down, till now it takes a split-second watch to time him as he goes through th' day's wurruk. I have a gintleman plasthrer frind who tells me he hasn't put in a full day in a year. He goes to his desk ivry mornin' at tin an' sthrikes punchooly at iliven. 'Th' wrongs iv th' wurrukin' men mus' be redhressed,' says he. 'Ar-re ye inthrested in thim?' says I. 'Ye niver looked betther in ye'er life,' says I. 'I niver felt betther,' he says. 'It's th' out-iv-dure life,' he says. 'I haven't missed a baseball game this summer,' he says. 'But,' he says, 'I need exercise. I wish Labor Day wud come around. Th' boys has choose me to carry a life-size model iv th' Masonic Temple in th' parade,' he says.

"If I was a wurrukin' man I'd sigh f'r th' good ol' days, whin Labor an' Capital were frinds. Those who lived through thim did. In thim times th' arrystocracy iv labor was th' la-ads who r-run th' railroad injines. They were a proud race. It was a boast to have wan iv thim in a fam'ly. They niver sthruck. 'Twas again' their rules. They conferred with Capital. Capital used to weep over thim. Ivry wanst in a while a railroad prisidint wud grow red in th' face an' burst into song about thim. They were a body that th' nation might well be proud iv. If he had a son who asked f'r no betther fate, he wud ask f'r no betther fate f'r him thin to be a Brotherhood iv Locymotive Ingineers. Ivry-body looked up to thim, an' they looked down on ivrybody, but mostly on th' bricklayers. Th' bricklayers were niver bulwarks iv th' constichoochion. They niver conferred with Capital. Th' polis always arrived just as th' conference was beginnin'. Their motto was a long life an' a merry wan; a brick in th' hand is worth two on th' wall. They sthruck ivry time they thought iv it. They sthruck on th' slightest provocation, an' whin they weren't provoked at all. If a band wint by they climbed down th' laddhers an' followed it, carryin' banners with th' wurruds: 'Give us bread or we starve,' an' walked till they were almost hungry. Ivry Saturdah night they held a dance to protest again' their wrongs. In th' summer-time th' wails iv th' oppressed bricklayers wint up fr'm countless picnics. They sthruck in sympathy with annybody. Th' union wint out as wan man because they was a rumor that th' superintindent iv th' rollin'-mills was not nice to his wife. Wanst they sthruck because Poland was not free.

"What was th' raysult? Their unraisoning demands fin'lly enraged Capital. To-day ye can go into a bricklayer's house an' niver see a capitalist but th' bricklayer himsilf. Forty years ago a bricklayer was certain iv twelve hours wurruk a day, or two hours more thin a convicted burglar. To-day he has practically nawthin' to do, an' won't do that. They ar-re out iv wurruk nearly all th' time an' at th' seashore. Jus' as often as ye read 'Newport colony fillin' up,' ye read, 'Bricklayers sthrike again.' Ye very sildom see a bricklayer nowadays in th' city. They live mostly in th' counthry, an' on'y come into town to be bribed to go to wurruk. It wud pay anny man who is buildin' a house to sind thim what money he has be mail an' go live in a tent.

"An' all this time, how about th' arrystocracy iv labor, th' knights iv th' throttle? Have they been deprived iv anny hours iv labor? On th' conthry, they have steadily increased, ontil to-day there is not a knight iv th' throttle who hasn't more hours iv wurruk in a day thin he can use in a week. In th' arly mornin', whin he takes his ir'n horse out iv th' stall, he meets th' onforchnit, misguided bricklayer comin' home in a cab fr'm a sthrike meetin'. Hardly a year passes that he can't say to his wife: 'Mother, I've had an increase.' 'In wages?' 'No, in hours.' It's th' old story iv th' ant an' th' grasshopper—th' ant that ye can step on an' th' grasshopper ye can't catch.

"Well, it's too bad that th' goolden days has passed, Hinnissy. Capital still pats Labor on th' back, but on'y with an axe. Labor rayfuses to be threated as a frind. It wants to be threated as an inimy. It thinks it gets more that way. They ar-re still a happy fam'ly, but it's more like an English fam'ly. They don't speak. What do I think iv it all? Ah, sure, I don't know. I belong to th' onforchnit middle class. I wurruk hard, an' I have no money. They come in here undher me hospital roof, an' I furnish thim with cards, checks, an' refreshmints. 'Let's play without a limit,' says Labor. 'It's Dooley's money.' 'Go as far as ye like with Dooley's money,' says Capital. 'What have ye got?' 'I've got a straight to Roosevelt,' says Labor. 'I've got ye beat,' says Capital. 'I've got a Supreme Court full of injunctions.' Manetime I've pawned me watch to pay f'r th' game, an' I have to go to th' joolry-store on th' corner to buy a pound iv beef or a scuttle iv coal. No wan iver sthrikes in sympathy with me."

"They ought to get together," said Mr. Hennessy.

"How cud they get anny closer together thin their prisint clinch?" asked Mr. Dooley. "They're so close together now that those that ar-re between thim ar-re crushed to death."

THE VICE-PRESIDENT[1]

"It's sthrange about th' vice-prisidincy," said Mr. Dooley. "Th' prisidincy is th' highest office in th' gift iv th' people. Th' vice-prisidincy is th' next highest an' th' lowest. It isn't a crime exactly. Ye can't be sint to jail f'r it, but it's a kind iv a disgrace. It's like writin' anonymous letters. At a convintion nearly all th' dillygates lave as soon as they've nommynated th' prisidint f'r fear wan iv thim will be nommynated f'r vice-prisidint. They offered it to me frind Joe Cannon, and th' language he used brought th' blush iv shame to th' cheeks iv a naygur dillygate fr'm Allybamy. They thried to hand it to Hinnery Cabin Lodge, an' he wept bitterly. They found a man fr'm Wisconsin, who was in dhrink, an' had almost nommynated him whin his wife came in an' dhragged him away fr'm timptation. Th' way they got Sinitor Fairbanks to accipt was be showin' him a pitcher iv our gr-reat an' noble prisidint thryin' to jump a horse over a six-foot fence. An' they on'y prevailed upon Hinnery Davis to take this almost onequalled honor be tellin' him that th' raison th' Sage iv Esoopus didn't speak earlier was because he has weak lungs.

"Why is it, I wondher, that ivrybody runs away fr'm a nommynation f'r vice-prisidint as if it was an indictment be th' gran' jury? It usen't to be so. I've hollered mesilf black in th' face f'r ol' man Thurman an' Hendricks iv Injyanny. In th' ol' days, whin th' boys had nommynated some unknown man fr'm New York f'r prisidint, they turned in an' nommynated a gr-reat an' well-known man fr'm th' West f'r vice-prisidint. Th' candydate f'r vice-prisidint was all iv th' ticket we iver see durin' a campaign. Th' la-ad they put up f'r prisidint stayed down East an' was niver allowed to open his mouth except in writin' befure witnesses, but th' candydate f'r vice-prisidint wint fr'm wan end iv th' counthry to th' other howlin' again' th' tariff an' other immortal issues, now dead. I niver voted f'r Grover Cleveland. I wudden't vote f'r him anny more thin he'd vote f'r me. I voted f'r old man Thurman an' Tom Hendricks an' Adly Stevenson befure he became a profissional vice-prisidint. They thought it was an honor, but if ye'd read their bio-graphies to-day ye'd find at th' end: 'Th' writer will pass over th' closin' years iv Mr. Thurman's

[1] Adly Stevenson: Adlai E. Stevenson, Vice-President, 1892–1896.

career hurriedly. It is enough to say iv this painful peryod that afther a lifetime iv devoted sarvice to his counthry th' statesman's declinin' days was clouded be a gr-reat sorrow. He become vice-prisidint iv th' United States. Oh, how much betther 'twere that we shud be sawed off arly be th' gr-reat reaper Death thin that a life iv honor shud end in ignomy.' It's a turr'ble thing.

"If ye say about a man that he's good prisidintial timber he'll buy ye a dhrink. If ye say he's good vice-prisidintial timber ye mane that he isn't good enough to be cut up into shingles, an' ye'd betther be careful.

"It's sthrange, too, because it's a good job. I think a man cud put in four years comfortably in th' place if he was a sound sleeper. What ar-re his jooties, says ye? Well, durin' th' campaign he has to do a good deal iv th' rough outside wurruk. Th' candydate f'r prisidint is at home pickin' out th' big wurruds in th' ditchnry an' firin' thim at us fr'm time to time. Th' candydate f'r th' vice-prisidincy is out in Ioway yellin' fr'm th' back iv a car or a dhray. He goes to all th' church fairs an' wakes an' appears at public meetin's between a cornet solo an' a glee club. He ought to be a man good at repartee. Our now honored (be some) prisidint had to retort with th' very hands that since have signed th' Pannyma Canal bill to a Colorado gintleman who accosted him with a scantling. An' I well raymimber another candydate, an' a gr-reat man, too, who replied to a gintleman in Shelbyville who made a rude remark be threatin' him as though he was an open fireplace. It was what Hogan calls a fine-cut an' incisive reply. Yes, sir, th' candydate f'r vice-prisidint has a busy time iv it durin' th' campaign, hoppin' fr'm town to town, speakin', shakin' hands with th' popylace who call him Hal or Charlie, dodgin' bricks, fightin' with his audjeence, an' diggin' up f'r th' fi-nance comity. He has to be an all-round man. He must be a good speaker, a pleasant man with th' ladies, a fair boxer an' rassler, something iv a liar, an' if he's a Raypublican campaignin' in Texas, an active sprinter. If he has all thim qualities, he may or may not rayceive a majority at th' polls, an' no wan will know whether they voted f'r him or not.

"Well, he's ilicted. Th' ilictors call on th' candydate f'r prisidint an' hand him th' office. They notify th' candydate f'r vice-prisidint through th' personal columns iv th' pa-apers: 'If th' tall, dark gintleman with hazel eyes, black coat an' white vest, who was nommynated at th' convintion f'r vice-prisidint, will

call at headquarters he will hear iv something to his advantage.'
So he buys a ticket an' hops to Wash'nton, where he gets a good
room suited to his station right above th' kitchen an' overlookin'
a wood-yard. Th' prisidint has to live where he is put, but th'
vice-prisidint is free to go annywhere he likes, where they are not
particklar. Th' Constitution provides that th' prisidint shall have
to put up with darky cookin', but th' vice-prisidint is permitted to
eat out. Ivry mornin' it is his business to call at th' White House
an' inquire afther th' prisidint's health. Whin told that th'
prisidint was niver betther he gives three cheers, an' departs
with a heavy heart.

"'Th' feelin' iv th' vice-prisidint about th' prisidint's well-
bein' is very deep. On rainy days he calls at th' White House
an' begs th' prisidint not to go out without his rubbers. He has
Mrs. Vice-Prisidint knit him a shawl to protect his throat again'
th' night air. If th' prisidint has a touch iv fever th' vice-prisidint
gets a touch iv fever himsilf. He has th' doctor on th' 'phone
durin' th' night. 'Doc, I hear th' prisidint is onwell,' he says.
'Cud I do annything f'r him—annything like dhrawin' his salary
or appintin' th' postmasther at Injynnapolis?' It is princip'lly,
Hinnissy, because iv th' vice-prisidint that most iv our prisidints
have enjoyed such rugged health. Th' vice-prisidint guards th'
prisidint, an' th' prisidint, afther sizin' up th' vice-prisidint,
con-cludes that it wud be betther f'r th' counthry if he shud live
yet awhile. 'D'ye know,' says th' prisidint to th' vice-prisidint,
'ivry time I see you I feel tin years younger?' 'Ye'er kind
wurruds,' says th' vice-prisidint, 'brings tears to me eyes. My
wife was sayin' on'y this mornin' how comfortable we ar-re in
our little flat.' Some vice-prisidints have been so anxious f'r th'
prisidint's safety that they've had to be warned off th' White
House grounds.

"Aside fr'm th' arjoos duties iv lookin' afther th' prisidint's
health, it is th' business iv th' vice-prisidint to preside over th'
deliberations iv th' Sinit. Ivry mornin' between ten an' twelve,
he swings his hammock in th' palachial Sinit chamber an' sinks
off into dhreamless sleep. He may be awakened by Sinitor
Tillman pokin' Sinitor Beveridge in th' eye. This is wan way th'
Sinit has iv deliberatin'. If so, th' vice-prisidint rises fr'm his
hammock an' says: 'Th' Sinitor will come to ordher.' 'He won't,'
says th' Sinitor. 'Oh, very well,' says th' presidin' officer;
'he won't,' an' dhrops off again. It is his jooty to rigorously

enforce th' rules iv th' Sinit. There ar-re none. Th' Sinit is ruled be courtesy, like th' longshoreman's union. Th' vice-prisidint is not expected to butt in much. It wud be a breach iv Sinitoryal courtesy f'r him to step down an' part th' Sinitor fr'm Texas an' th' Sinitor fr'm Injyanny in th' middle iv a debate undher a desk on whether Northern gintlemen ar-re more gintlemanly thin Southern gintlemen. I shuddent wondher if he thried to do it if he was taught his place with th' leg iv a chair. He isn't even called upon to give a decision. All that his grateful counthry demands fr'm th' man that she has ilivated to this proud position on th' toe iv her boot is that he shall keep his opinyons to himsilf. An' so he whiles away th' pleasant hours in th' beautiful city iv Wash'nton, an' whin he wakes up he is ayether in th' White House or in th' sthreet. I'll niver say annything again' th' vice-prisidincy. It is a good job, an' is richly deserved be ayether iv th' candydates. An', be Hivens, I'll go further an' say it richly desarves ayether iv thim."

THE AMERICAN FAMILY

"Is th' race dyin' out?" asked Mr. Dooley.

"Is it what?" replied Mr. Hennessy.

"Is it dyin' out?" said Mr. Dooley. "Th' ministhers an' me frind Dock Eliot iv Harvard say it is. Dock Eliot wud know diff'rent if he was a rale dock an' wint flying up Halsted Sthreet in a buggy, floggin' a white horse to be there on time. But he ain't, an' he's sure it's dyin' out. Childher ar-re disappearin' fr'm America. He took a squint at th' list iv Harvard gradjates th' other day, an' discovered that they had ivrything to make home happy but kids. Wanst th' wurruld was full iv little Harvards. Th' counthry swarmed with thim. Ye cud tell a Harvard man at wanst be a look at his feet. He had th' unmistakable cradle fut. It was no sthrange thing to see an ol' Harvard man comin' back to his almy mather pushin' a baby-carredge full iv twins an' ladin' a fam'ly that looked like an advertisemint in th' newspapers to show th' percintage iv purity iv bakin'-powdhers. Prisidint Eliot was often disturbed in a discoorse, pintin' out th' dangers iv th' counthry, be th' outcries iv th' progeny iv fair Harvard. Th' campus was full iv baby-carredges on commincemint day, an' specyal accomydations had to be took f'r nurses. In thim happy days some wan was always teethin' in a Harvard fam'ly. It looked as if ivinchooly th' wurruld wud be peopled with Harvard men, an' th' Chinese wud have to pass an Exclusion Act. But something has happened to Harvard. She is projoocin' no little rah-rahs to glad th' wurruld. Th' av'rage fam'ly iv th' Harvard gradjate an' th' jackass is practically th' same. Th' Harvard man iv th' prisint day is th' last iv his race. No artless prattle is heerd in his home.

"An' me frind Prisidint Eliot is sore about it, an' he has communicated th' sad fact to th' clargy. Nawthin' th' clargy likes so much as a sad fact. Lave wan iv me frinds iv th' clargy know that we're goin' to th' divvle in a new way an' he's happy. We used to take th' journey be covetin' our neighbor's ox or his ass or be disobeyin' our parents, but now we have no parents to disobey or they have no childher to disobey thim. Th' American people is becomin' as unfruitful as an ash-heap. We're no betther thin th' Fr-rinch. They say th' pleasin' squawk iv an infant hasn't been heerd in France since th' Franco-Prooshun war. Th' governmint offers prizes f'r families, but no wan claims thim. A Frinch gintleman who wint to Germany wanst has made a good deal iv money lecturin' on 'Wild Babies I have Met,' but ivry wan says he's a faker. Ye can't convince anny wan in France that there ar-re anny babies. We're goin' th' same way. Less thin three millyon babies was bor-rn in this counthry las' year. Think iv it, Hinnissy—less thin three millyon, hardly enough to consume wan-tenth iv th' output iv pins! It's a horrible thought. I don't blame ivry wan, fr'm Tiddy Rosenfelt down, f'r worryin' about it.

"What's th' cause, says ye? I don't know. I've been readin' th' newspapers, an' ivrybody's been tellin' why. Late marredges, arly marredges, no marredges, th' cost iv livin', th' luxuries iv th' day, th' tariff, th' thrusts, th' spots on th' sun, th' difficulty iv obtainin' implyemint, th' growth iv culture, th' pitcher-hat, an' so on. Ivrybody's got a raison, but none iv thim seems to meet th' bill. I've been lookin' at th' argymints pro an' con, an' I come to th' conclusion that th' race is dyin' out on'y in spots. Th' av'rage size iv th' fam'ly in Mitchigan Avnoo is .000001, but th' av'rage size iv th' fam'ly in Ar-rchey R-road is somewhat larger. Afther I r-read what Dock Eliot had to say I ast me frind Dock Grogan what he thought about it. He's a rale dock. He has a horse an' buggy. He's out so much at night that th' polis ar-re always stoppin' him, thinkin' he is a burglar. Th' dock has prepared some statistics f'r me, an' here they ar're: Number iv twins bor-rn in Ar-rchey Road fr'm Halsted Sthreet to Western Avnoo, fr'm Janooary wan to Janooary wan, 355 pairs; number iv thrips iv thriplets in th' same fiscal year, nine; number iv individjool voters, eighty-three thousan' nine hundherd an' forty-two; av'rage size iv fam'ly, fourteen; av'rage weight iv parents, wan hundherd an' eighty-five; av'rage size iv rooms, nine be eight; av'rage height iv ceilin', nine feet; av'rage wages, wan dollar sivinty-five; av'rage duration iv doctor's bills, two hundherd years.

"I took th' statistics to Father Kelly. He's an onprejudiced man, an' if th' race was dyin' out he wud have had a soundin'-boord in his pulpit long ago, so that whin he mintioned th' wurrud 'Hell,' ivry wan in th' congregation wud have thought he meant him or her. 'I think,' says Father Kelly, 'that Dock Grogan is a little wrong in his figures. He's boastin'. In this parrish I allow twelve births to wan marredge. It varies, iv coorse, bein' sometimes as low as nine, an' sometimes as high as fifteen. But twelve is about th' av'rage,' he says. 'If ye see Dock Eliot,' he says, 'ye can tell him th' race ain't dyin' out very bad in this here part iv the wurruld. On th' conthry. It ain't liable to, ayether,' he says, 'onless wages is raised,' he says. 'Th' poor ar-re becomin' richer in childher, an' th' rich poorer,' he says. ''Tis always th' way,' he says. 'Th' bigger th' house th' smaller th' fam'ly. Mitchigan Avnoo is always thinnin' out fr'm itsilf, an' growin' fr'm th' efforts iv Ar-rchey R-road. 'Tis a way Nature has iv gettin' even with th' rich an' pow'rful. Wan part iv town has nawthin' but money, an' another nawthin' but childher. A man with tin dollars a week will have tin childher, a man with wan hundherd dollars will have five, an' a man with a millyon will buy an autymobill. Ye can tell Schwartzmeister, with his thirteen little Hanses an' Helenas, that he don't have to throw no bombs to make room f'r his childher. Th' people over in Mitchigan Avnoo will do that thimsilves. Nature,' he says, 'is a wild dimmycrat,' he says.

"I guess he's right. I'm goin' to ask Dock Eliot, Tiddy Rosenfelt, an' all th' rest iv thim to come up Ar-rchey R-road some summer's afthernoon an' show thim th' way th' r-race is dyin' out. Th' front stoops is full iv childher; they block th' throlley-cars; they're shyin' bricks at th' polis, pullin' up coal-hole covers, playin' ring-around-th'-rosy, makin' paper dolls, goin' to Sundah-school, hurryin' with th' sprinklin'-pot to th' place at th' corner, an' indulgin' in other spoorts iv childhood. Pah-pah is settin' on th' steps, ma is lanin' out iv th' window gassin' with th' neighbors, an' a squad iv polis ar-re up at th' church, keepin' th' christenin' parties fr'm mobbin' Father Kelly while he inthrajooces wan thousan' little howlin' dimmycrats to Christyan s'ciety. No, sir, th' race, far fr'm dyin' out in Ar-rchey R-road, is runnin' aisy an' comin' sthrong."

"Ye ought to be ashamed to talk about such subjicks, ye, an ol' batch," said Mr. Hennessy. "It's a seeryous question."

"How many childher have ye?" asked Mr. Dooley.

"Lave me see," said Mr. Hennessy. "Wan, two, four, five, eight, siven, eight, tin—no, that's not right. Lave me see. Ah, yes, I f'rgot Terence. We have fourteen."

"If th' race iv Hinnissys dies out," said Mr. Dooley, "'twill be fr'm overcrowdin'."

AN INTERNATIONAL POLICE FORCE[1]

"I thought," said Mr. Dooley, "that whin me young frind th' Czar iv Rooshya got up that there Dutch polis coort f'r to settle th' backyard quarr'ls among th' nations iv th' earth, 'twud be th' end iv war f'r good an' all. It looked all right to me. Why not? If be anny chanst I get mesilf full iv misconduck an' go ar-round thryin' to collect me debts with a gun, an' camp out in somebody's house an' won't lave, th' polis take me down to Deerin' Sthreet station an' throw me in among th' little playmates iv th' criminal, an' in th' mornin' I'm befure me cousin th' chief justice, an' he confiscates th' gun an' sinds me up th' bullyvard f'r thirty days. Why not th' same thing f'r th' powers whin they go off on a tear? I thought I'd be readin' in th' pa-apers: 'Judge Oolenboff, at th' Hague coort, had a large docket yisterdah mornin'. Thirty mimbers iv th' notoryous Hapsburg fam'ly was sint up f'r varyous terms, an' th' polis think they have completely broke up th' gang. Th' King iv Spain was charged with non-support, but was dis-missed with a warnin'. Th' Impror iv Chiny was let off with a fine f'r maintainin' a dope jint, an' warrants was issued f'r th'

[1] The first Hague Conference in 1899 set up a Permanent Court of Arbitra-tion.

owners iv th' primises, the King of England an' th' Czar iv Rooshya. Th' Sultan iv Turkey, alias Hamid th' Hick, alias th' Turrible Turk, was charged with poly-gamy Th' coort give him th' alternative iv five more wives or thirty days. Whin these cases had been cleared away th' bailiff led into th' dock three notoryous charackters. Th' first was a large, heavy-set German, who proved to be Bill th' Bite, less known by his thrue name iv Willum H. J. E. I. K. L. M. N. O. P. Q. R. S. T., etc., Hohenzollern. By his side was an undhersized, little dark man, th' notoryous Emilio Casthro, a pro-fissyonal dead-beat an' embizzler, an' a stout party be th' name iv Albert Edward or Edwards, who is said be th' internaytional polis to be behind some iv th' biggest grafts that have been run through f'r th' last twinty years, though niver so far caught with th' goods on. Hohenzollern was accused iv assault with intint to kill, robbery, blackmail, carryin' concealed weepins, an' raysistin' an officer. Edward or Edwards was charged with maintainin' a fence f'r rayceivin' stolen property an' carryin' concealed weepins. Casthro was charged with vagrancy, maintainin' a disordherly house, an' fraud.

"'Th' attorney f'r th' pro-secution made out a sthrong case again' th' pris'ners. He said that Hohenzollern was a desprit charackter, who was constantly a menace to th' peace iv th' wurruld. He had no sympathy f'r Casthro, who was an idle, dangerous ruffyan, an' he hoped th' coort wud dale severely with him. He niver paid his debts, an' none iv th' neighbors' chickens was safe fr'm him. He was a low-down, worthless, mischief-makin' loafer. But Casthro's bad charackter did not excuse th' other pris'ners. It seems that Casthro, who niver paid annybody annything, owed a bill with th' well-known grocery firm iv Schwartzheim an' Hicks, which he rayfused to settle. Hearin' iv this, Hohenzollern an' Edward or Edwards con-spired together to go to Casthro's place undher pretinse iv collectin' th' bill an' throw Casthro out an' take possession iv his property. Hohenzollern was th' more vilent iv th' pair. He appeared, carryin' loaded revolvers, which he fired into th' windows iv Casthro's shop, smashed in th' dure, an' endangered th' lives iv manny innocint people. He was ar-rested afther a sthruggle, in which he severely injured wan iv th' internaytional polis foorce, an' was carried off in a hurry-up wagon. Edward or Edwards was caught in th' neighborhood. He pretinded to be an innocint spectator, but whin sarched was found to have loaded revolvers in his pocket, as well as an addhress to th' Christian nations iv th' wurruld justifyin' his conduck an' denouncin' his accomplice. Casthro was taken into custody on gin'ral principles. Th' prosecution asked that an example be made iv th' pris'ners.

"'Afther tistymony had been inthrojooced showin' th' bad charackter iv th' men in th' dock, Hohenzollern was put on th' stand to testify in his own definse. He swore that he had no inmity again' Casthro, but Schwartzheim iv Schwartzheim an' Hicks, was a German frind iv his, an' he wint down to see that no injustice was done him. "Did he ask ye to go?" ast th' coort. "No," says th' pris'ner, "but me pristige as a slugger wud be in danger if I didn't go over an' punch this here little naygur," he says. "Niver, niver shud it be said that a German citizen sha'n't be able to collect his debts annywhere but in Germany," he says. "Th' mailed fist," he says, "is iver raised f'r th' protiction—" "No more iv that," says th' judge. "This is a coort iv law. Hohenzollern, ye're a dangerous man. Ye're noisy, ritous, an' offinsive. I'm determined to make an example iv ye, an' I sintince ye to stay in Germany f'r th' rest iv ye'er nachral life, an' may th' Lord have mercy on ye'er sowl. As f'r ye, Edwards, ye're even worse. I will hold ye without bail ontil th' polis can collect all their ividence again' ye. Casthro, ye're discharged. Th' worst thing I cud think iv doin' to ye is to sind ye back to ye'er beautiful Vinzwala." Th' pris'ner Hohenzollern made a dimonsthration while bein' raymoved fr'm th' dock. It is undherstud that Edward or Edwards has offered to tell all he knows, an' promises to implicate siv'ral prominent parties.'

"That's th' way I thought 'twould be. Be Hivins, Hinnissy, I looked forward to th' day whin, if a king, impror, or czar started a rough-house, th' blue 'bus wud come clangin' through th' sthreets an' they'd be hauled off to Holland f'r thrile. I looked to see th' United States Sinit pulled ivry month or two, an' all th' officers iv th' navy fugitives fr'm justice. I thought th' coort wud have a kind iv a bridewell built, where they'd sind th' internaytional dhrunks an' disordhlies, an' where ye cud go anny day an' see Willum Hohenzollern cooperin' a bar'l, an' me frind Joe Chamberlain peggin' shoes, while gr-reat war iditors, corryspondints, statesmen, an' other disturbers iv th' peace walked around in lock-step, an' th' keeper iv th' jail showed ye a book filled with photygrafts iv th' mos' notoryous iv thim: 'Number two thousan' an' wan, Joe Chamberlain, profissional land-grabber, five years'; or 'Willum Hohenzollern, all-round ruffyan, life.'

"That wud be th' fine day whin th' wagon wud be backed up in fr-ront iv th' parlymints iv th' wurruld an' th' bull-pen wud be full iv internaytional grafters, get-rich-quick op'rators, an' sthrong-ar-rm men; whin th' Monroe docthrine wud be condimned as a public nuisance, an' South America wud be burned undher ordhers iv th' coort. But it hasn't come. The coort is there noddin' over th' docket jus' like a coort, while outside th' rowdies ar-re shootin' at each other, holdin' up Chinymen an' naygurs, pickin' pockets, blowin' safes, an' endangerin' th' lives iv dacint people. They'se a warrant out f'r Bill Hohenzollern, but they'se no wan to sarve it. He's on th' rampage, breakin' windows an' chasin' people over th' roofs, while Edward or Edwards stands around th' corner waitin' f'r th' goods to be delivered an' savin' his ammunytion to use it on his pal if they quarrel over th' divide. There's th' internaytional coort, ye say, but I say where ar-re th' polis? A coort's all r-right enough, but no coort's anny good onless it is backed up be a continted constabulary, its counthry's pride, as th' pote says. Th' Czar iv Rooshya didn't go far enough. Wan good copper with a hickory club is worth all th' judges between Amsterdam an' Rotterdam. I want to see th' day whin just as Bill Hohenzollern an' Edward or Edwards meets on th' corner an' prepares a raid on a laundry a big polisman will step out iv a dure an' say: 'I want ye, Bill, an' ye might as well come along quiet.' But I suppose it wud be just th' same thing as it is now in rale life."

"How's that?" asked Mr. Hennessy.

"All th' biggest crooks wud get on th' polis foorce," said Mr. Dooley.

THE CARNEGIE LIBRARIES

"Has Andhrew Carnaygie given ye a libry yet?" asked Mr. Dooley.

"Not that I know iv," said Mr. Hennessy.

"He will," said Mr. Dooley. "Ye'll not escape him. Befure he dies he hopes to crowd a libry on ivry man, woman, an' child in th' counthry. He's given thim to cities, towns, villages, an' whistlin' stations. They're tearin' down gas-houses an' poor-houses to put up libries. Befure another year, ivry house in

Pittsburg that ain't a blast-furnace will be a Carnaygie libry.
In some places all th' buildin's is libries. If ye write him f'r an
autygraft he sinds ye a libry. No beggar is iver turned impty-
handed fr'm th' dure. Th' pan-handler knocks an' asts f'r a
glass iv milk an' a roll. 'No, sir,' says Andhrew Carnaygie.
'I will not pauperize this onworthy man. Nawthin' is worse f'r
a beggar-man thin to make a pauper iv him. Yet it shall not be
said iv me that I give nawthin' to th' poor. Saunders, give him a
libry, an' if he still insists on a roll tell him to roll th' libry. F'r
I'm humorous as well as wise,' he says."

"Does he give th' books that go with it?" asked Mr. Hennessy.

"Books?" said Mr. Dooley. "What ar-re ye talkin' about?
D'ye know what a libry is? I suppose ye think it's a place where a
man can go, haul down wan iv his fav'rite authors fr'm th' shelf,
an' take a nap in it. That's not a Carnaygie libry. A Carnaygie
libry is a large, brown-stone, impenethrible buildin' with th' name
iv th' maker blown on th' dure. Libry, fr'm th' Greek wurruds,
libus, a book, an' ary, sildom—sildom a book. A Carnaygie libry
is archytechoor, not lithrachoor. Lithrachoor will be riprisinted.
Th' most cillybrated dead authors will be honored be havin' their
names painted on th' wall in distinguished comp'ny, as thus:
Andhrew Carnaygie, Shakespeare; Andhrew Carnaygie, Byron;
Andhrew Carnaygie, Bobby Burns; Andhrew Carnaygie, an' so on.
Ivry author is guaranteed a place next to pure readin' matther like
a bakin'-powdher advertisemint, so that whin a man comes along
that niver heerd iv Shakespeare he'll know he was somebody,
because there he is on th' wall. That's th' dead authors. Th'
live authors will stand outside an' wish they were dead.

"He's havin' gr-reat spoort with it. I r-read his speech th'
other day, whin he laid th' corner-stone iv th' libry at Pianola,
Ioway. Th' entire popylation iv this lithry cinter gathered to see
an' hear him. There was th' postmaster an' his wife, th' blacksmith an' his fam'ly, the station agent, mine host iv th' Farmers'
Exchange, an' some sthray live stock. 'Ladies an' gintlemen,'
says he. 'Modesty compels me to say nawthin' on this occasion,
but I am not to be bulldozed,' he says. 'I can't tell ye how much
pleasure I take in disthributin' monymints to th' humble name
around which has gathered so manny hon'rable associations with
mesilf. I have been a very busy little man all me life, but I like
hard wurruk, an' givin' away me money is th' hardest wurruk I
iver did. It fairly makes me teeth ache to part with it. But

there's wan consolation. I cheer mesilf with th' thought that no matther how much money I give it don't do anny particular person anny good. Th' worst thing ye can do f'r anny man is to do him good. I pass by th' organ-grinder on th' corner with a savage glare. I bate th' monkey on th' head whin he comes up smilin' to me window, an' hurl him down on his impecyoonyous owner. None iv me money goes into th' little tin cup. I cud kick a hospital, an' I lave Wall Sthreet to look afther th' widow an' th' orphan. Th' submerged tenth, thim that can't get hold iv a good chunk iv th' goods, I wud cut off fr'm th' rest iv th' wurruld an' prevint fr'm bearin' th' haughty name iv papa or th' still lovelier name iv ma. So far I've got on'y half me wish in this matther.

"'I don't want poverty an' crime to go on. I intind to stop it. But how? It's been holdin' its own f'r cinchries. Some iv th' gr-reatest iv former minds has undertook to prevint it an' has failed. They didn't know how. Modesty wud prevint me agin fr'm sayin' that I know how, but that's nayether here nor there. I do. Th' way to abolish poverty an' bust crime is to put up a brown-stone buildin' in ivry town in th' counthry with me name over it. That's th' way. I suppose th' raison it wasn't thried befure was that no man iver had such a name. 'Tis thrue me efforts is not apprecyated ivrywhere. I offer a city a libry, an' oftentimes it replies an' asks me f'r something to pay off th' school debt. I rayceive degraded pettyshuns fr'm so-called proud methropolises f'r a gas-house in place iv a libry. I pass thim by with scorn. All I ask iv a city in rayturn f'r a fifty-thousan'-dollar libry is that it shall raise wan millyon dollars to maintain th' buildin' an' keep me name shiny, an' if it won't do that much f'r lithrachoor, th' divvle take it, it's onworthy iv th' name iv an American city. What ivry community needs is taxes an' lithrachoor. I give them both. Three cheers f'r a libry an' a bonded debt! Lithrachoor, taxation, an' Andhrew Carnaygie, wan an' insiprable, now an' foriver! They'se nawthin' so good as a good book. It's betther thin food; it's betther thin money. I have made money an' books, an' I like me books betther thin me money. Others don't, but I do. With these few wurruds I will con-clude. Modesty wud prevint me fr'm sayin' more, but I have to catch a thrain, an' cannot go on. I stake ye to this libry, which ye will have as soon as ye raise th' money to keep it goin'. Stock it with useful readin', an' some day ye'er otherwise pauper an' criminal childher will come to know me name whin I am gone an' there's no wan left to tell it thim.'

"Whin th' historyan comes to write th' histhry iv th' West he'll say: 'Pianola, Ioway, was a prosperous town till th' failure iv th' corn crop in nineteen hundherd an' wan, an' th' Carnaygie libry in nineteen hundherd an' two. Th' govermint ast f'r thirty dollars to pave Main Sthreet with wooden blocks, but th' gr-reat philanthropist was firm, an' the libry was sawed off on th' town. Th' public schools, th' wurruk-house, th' wather wurruks, an' th' other penal instichoochions was at wanst closed, an' th' people begun to wurruk to support th' libry. In five years th' popylation had deserted th' town to escape taxation, an' now, as Mr. Carnaygie promised, poverty an' crime has been abolished in th' place, th' janitor iv th' buildin' bein' honest an' well paid.'

"Isn't it good f'r lithrachoor, says ye? Sure, I think not, Hinnissy. Libries niver encouraged lithrachoor anny more thin tombstones encourage livin'. No wan iver wrote annythin' because he was tol' that a hundherd years fr'm now his books might be taken down fr'm a shelf in a granite sepulcher an' some wan wud write 'Good' or 'This man is crazy' in th' margin. What lithrachoor needs is fillin' food. If Andhrew wud put a kitchen in th' libries an' build some bunks or even swing a few hammocks where livin' authors cud crawl in at night an' sleep while waitin' f'r this enlightened nation to wake up an' discover th' Shakespeares now on th' turf, he wud be givin' a rale boost to lithrachoor. With th' smoke curlin' fr'm th' chimbley, an' hundherds iv potes settin' aroun' a table loaded down with pancakes an' talkin' pothry an' prize-fightin', with hundherds iv other potes stacked up nately in th' sleepin'-rooms an' snorin' in wan gran' chorus, with their wives holdin' down good-payin' jobs as libraryans or cooks, an' their happy little childher playin' through th' marble corrydors, Andhrew Carnaygie wud not have lived in vain. Maybe that's th' on'y way he knows how to live. I don't believe in libries. They pauperize lithrachoor. I'm f'r helpin' th' boys that's now on th' job. I know a pote in Halsted Sthreet that wanst wrote a pome beginnin', 'All th' wealth iv Ind,' that he sold to a magazine f'r two dollars, payable on publycation. Lithrachoor don't need advancin'. What it needs is advances f'r th' lithrachoors. Ye can't shake down posterity f'r th' price.

"All th' same, I like Andhrew Carnaygie. Him an' me ar-re agreed on that point. I like him because he ain't shamed to give

publicly. Ye don't find him puttin' on false whiskers an' turnin'
up his coat-collar whin he goes out to be benivolent. No, sir.
Ivry time he dhrops a dollar it makes a noise like a waither fallin'
down-stairs with a tray iv dishes. He's givin' th' way we'd all
like to give. I niver put annything in th' poor-box, but I wud if
Father Kelly wud rig up like wan iv thim slot-machines, so that
whin I stuck in a nickel me name wud appear over th' altar in red
letthers. But whin I put a dollar in th' plate I get back about
two yards an' hurl it so hard that th' good man turns around to
see who done it. Do good be stealth, says I, but see that th'
burglar-alarm is set. Anny benivolent money I hand out I want
to talk about me. Him that giveth to th' poor, they say, lindeth
to th' Lord; but in these days we look f'r quick returns on our
invistmints. I like Andhrew Carnaygie, an', as he says, he puts
his whole soul into th' wurruk."

"What's he mane be that?" asked Mr. Hennessy.

"He manes," said Mr. Dooley, "that he's gin'rous. Ivry
time he gives a libry he gives himsilf away in a speech."

SENATORIAL COURTESY

"It's a question iv Sinitoryal courtesy. What's that? Well,
Hinnissy, ye see, there ain't anny rules in th' Sinit. Ivrybody
gets up whin he wants to, an' hollers about annything that comes
into his head. Whin Dorgan was in Wash'nton he wint to hear
th' debate on th' naval bill, an' a Sinitor was r-readin' the *Life iv
Napolyon* to another Sinitor who was asleep.

"Sinitoryal courtesy rules th' body. If ye let me talk I'll let
ye sleep. Th' presidin' officer can't come down with his hammer
an' bid wan iv thim vin'rable men, grim with thraditions, to chase
himsilf fr'm th' flure. In such a case it wud be parlyminthry f'r
th' grim Sinitor to heave an ink-well at th' presidin' officer.
Undher Sinitoryal courtesy it is proper an' even affable to call a
fellow-Sinitor a liar. It is th' hith iv courtesy to rush over an'
push his cigar down his throat, to take him be th' hair an' dhrag
him around th' room, or to slap him in th' eye on account iv a
diff'rence iv opinyon about collectors iv intarnal rivinue.
Southern Sinitors have been known to use a small case-knife in a
conthrovarsy. It is etiket to take off ye'er boots in th' heat iv
debate. It is courteous f'r a Sinitor to go to sleep an' swallow his

teeth while another Sinitor is makin' a speech.   But wanst a
Sinitor is on his feet it is th' hith iv misbehavior to stop him excipt
f'r th' purpose iv givin' him a poke in th' nose.   Afther a rough-
an'-tumble fight, th' Sinitor who previously had the flure can get
up fr'm it if able an' raysume his spectacles, his wig, an' his speech.
But while he has wan syllable left in his face he is th' monarch iv
all he surveys.

    "No rules f'r thim ol' boys.   Ye can say annything again'
thim, but if ye attack that palajeem iv our liberties, th' sacred right
to drool, they rally at wanst.   Me frind Sinitor Morgan knew this,
an' says he: 'Gintlemen, they'se a bill here I don't want to see
passed.   It's a mischeevous, foul, criminal bill.   I didn't inthrajooce it.   I don't wish to obsthruct it.   If anny wan says I do,
Sinitoryal courtesy will compel me to jam th' libel down his
throat with a stove-lifter.   I will on'y make a speech about it.
In th' year fourteen hundherd an' two—'   An' so he goes on.
He's been talkin' iver since, an' he's on'y got down to th' sixteenth
cinchry, where th' question broadens out.   No wan can stop him.
Th' air is full iv his wurruds.   Sinitors lave Wash'nton an' go
home an' spind a week with th' fam'ly an' come back, an' that
grim ol' vethran is still there, poorin' out moist an' numerous
language.   They'se no raison why he shouldn't talk f'river.   I
hope he will.   I don't care whether he does or not.   I haven't a
frind in th' Sinit.   As f'r th' Pannyma Canal, 'tis thirty to wan
I'll niver take a ride on it.   But that's Sinitoryal courtesy."

    "What's to be done about it?" asked Mr. Hennessy.

    "What do I do whin ye an' ye'er aged frinds stay here whin ye
ought to be home?" asked Mr. Dooley.

    "Ye tur-rn out th' gas," said Mr. Hennessy.

    "An' that's what I'd do with th' Sinit," said Mr. Dooley.

WAR

    "War is a fine thing.   Or, perhaps I'm wrong.   Annyhow,
it's a sthrange thing.   Here's th' Czar iv Rooshya, an' here's th'
Imp'ror iv Japan.   They have a diff'rence iv opinyon.   All right,
says I, lave thim fight it out.   It's a good, healthful exercise.
I'll arrange th' preliminaries, fix th' polis, an' be Hivens, I'll
ref'ree th' fight.   I make th' offer now.   Anny time anny two high-
spirited monarchs feel that their rile blood threatens to blow up

I'll arrange ivrything down to th' photygrafts. Whiniver th' boys are ready I'll find th' barn. An' th' offer also goes f'r sicrities iv state.

"But what happens? A couple iv stout, middle-aged gintlemen get into a conthrovarsy. Instead iv layin' their stove-pipe hats on th' table an' mixin' it up, they hurry home an' invite ivrybody in th' house to go out an' do their war-makin' f'r thim. They set up on th' roof an' encourage th' scrap. 'Go in there, Olaf!' 'Banzai, Hip Lung, ye're doin' well f'r me!' 'There goes wan iv me brave fellows. I'd almost send somethin' to his widow if I cud larn her name!'

"An' so it goes. Bill Ivanovitch is settin' at home with his wife an' forty small childher. He has done a good day's wurruk, an' his salary iv nine cents is jinglin' in his pocket. He sets at th' head iv th' table carvin' th' candle, an' just as he has disthributed th' portions among th' fam'ly an' kep' th' wick f'r himsilf, there's a knock at th' dure an' a man in a fur cap calls him away to thravel eight thousan' versts—a verst bein' Schwartzmeister's way iv describin' a mile on a Rooshyan railroad—an' fight f'r Gawd an' his czar.

"It's th' ol' firm. Whiniver I'm called on to fight f'r Gawd an' me counthry I'd like to be sure that th' senyor partner had been consulted. But Bill Ivanovitch puts on his coat, kisses th' fam'ly good-by, an' th' next his wife sees iv him is a pitcher iv th' old man an' a Jap he niver met befure locked in an endurin' embrace, an' both iv thim as dead as anny Mikado or Czar cud wish their most lile subjick. Th' Jap don't know what it's all about. In Japan he was a horse. There ar-re no rale horses in Japan. If there were th' people wud have more to eat. So th' citizens iv th' counthry harness thimsilves up an' haul th' wagons. All ye have to say to a Jap is 'Get ap,' an' he moves. So th' Mikado says, 'Get ap,' an' th' little fellow laves his fireside an' his wives an' fam'lies an' niver comes home no more. Th' best he gets whin he is kilt is a remark in th' news fr'm Tokyo that Gin'ral Odzoo's plans is wurrukin' fav'rably. That ought to make him feel good.

"Now, if I had me way, Hinnissy, I wudden't let th' common people fight at all. That's th' way it used to be. Whin wan iv th' old kings in Brian Boru's day had a spat with a neighbor both of thim ordhered hats at th' hardware store an' wint out an' pounded thim till their head ached. That's th' way it ought to be. Supposin' th' Czar iv Rooshya an' th' Mikado iv Japan fell out.

What wud be dacinter f'r thim thin to have a gintlemanly mix-up? Nick Romanoff, th' Rooshyan champeen, an' Mike Adoo, th' cillybrated Jap'nese jiu-jitsu bantam, come together las' night befure a crowd iv riprisintative spoorts in a barn on th' outskirts iv th' city. Th' Rooshyan was seconded be Faure, th' Frinch lightweight, an' Bill Honezollern, th' Prooshyan whirlwind. In th' Jap's corner was Al Guelph, who bate th' Llama iv Thibet las' week, an' Rosenfelt, th' American champeen, who has issued a defi to th' wurruld. Befure th' gong sounded th' Jap rushed over an' sthruck th' Rooshyan a heavy blow beneath th' belt. A claim iv foul was enthered but not allowed. At th' tap iv th' gong both boys wint at it hammer an' tongs, but it was soon apparent that th' Rooshyan, though heavier, was not in as good condition as his opponent. It was Walcott an' Choynski all over, on'y th' Rooshyan hung on with gr-reat courage. At th' end iv th' twentieth round, whin both boys were on th' ropes, th' ref'ree, th' well-known fight promotor, Misther Rothschild, declared th' bout a dhraw. Considherable bad blood was aroused be a claim be th' fighters that durin' th' battle they were robbed iv their clothes be their seconds. As a financial entherprise, th' fight was a frost. Th' box-office receipts did not akel th' rent iv th' barn an' thrainin' expinses, an' th' ref'ree decided, that as th' fight was a dhraw he was entitled to th' stakes.

"Wudden't it be fine? Who wudden't walk to Bloomington, Illinye, to see that sturdy but prudent warryor, th' King iv England, mixin' it up with th' Llama iv Thibet, or our own invincible champeen takin' on th' Imp'ror iv Germany? If they didn't like th' weepins they'd have me permission to use axes. I'd go further. I wudden't bar annybody fr'm fightin' who wanted to fight. If annybody felt th' martial spirit in time he wud have a chance to use it up. I'd have armies composed on'y iv officers. It wud be gr-reat. D'ye s'pose they'd iver get near enough to each other to hurt? They'd complain that th' throuble with th' long-distance guns was that they cudden't be made distant enough. Supposin' Gin'ral Kurypotkin had to do all th' fightin' f'r himsilf. It wud be betther f'r him, because thin he cud ordher an advance without bein' so crowded comin' back. Supposin', to gratify his heeryoic spirit, he had to ordher himsilf to carry a thrunk, a cook-stove, a shovel, a pickaxe, an ikon, an' a wurrud iv good cheer fr'm th' czar two hundherd miles over a clay road, an' if he did it successfully an' didn't spill annything he might hope to be punctured be a bayonet. An' s'pose Gin'ral Oyama had to walk barefooted acrost Manchuria an' subsist f'r four months be whettin' his beak on a cuttle-fish bone. How soon, d'ye think, there wud be a battle? War wud be wan continyous manoover, with wan iv thim manooverin' west an' th' other manooverin' east. They'd niver meet till years afther th' gloryous sthruggle."

"They'll niver do it," said Mr. Hennessy. "There have always been wars."

"An' fools," said Mr. Dooley.

"But wudden't ye defind ye'er own fireside?"

"I don't need to," said Mr. Dooley. "If I keep on coal enough, me fireside will make it too hot f'r anny wan that invades it."

CORPORAL PUNISHMENT

"I see," said Mr. Dooley, "that th' Prisidint is plannin' an attack on th' good old English custom iv wife-beatin'. He wants to inthrajooce th' other good old English instichoochion iv a whippin'-post."

"He's all right," said Mr. Hennessy. "I'd like to have th' job."

"So wud I," said Mr. Dooley. "If th' law iver goes through I'll run f'r sheriff an' promise to give back all me salary an' half what I get fr'm th' race-thracks. Not, mind ye, that wife-beatin' is much practised in this counthry. Slug-ye'er-spouse is an internaytional spoort that has niver become pop'lar on our side iv th' wather. An American lady is not th' person that anny man but a thrained athlete wud care to raise his hand again' save be way iv smoothin' her hair. Afther goin' to a school an' larnin' to box, throw th' shot, an' play right-guard on th' futball team, th' gentle crather has what Hogan calls an abundant stock iv repartee. In me life I've known on'y six haitchool wife-beaters. Two iv thim were lucky to beat their wives to th' sidewalk, an' I've rescued th' other four fr'm th' roof iv th' house with a ladder. But now an' thin I suppose an American gintleman, afther losin' three or four fights on his way home, does thry to make a repytation be swingin' on th' ex-heavy-weight champeen iv th' Siminary f'r Rayfined Females, an' if she can't put th' baby on th' flure in time to get to wurruk with th' loose parts iv th' stove, 'tis Thaydore's idee that she shud call a polisman an' have father taken down to th' jail an' heartily slapped.

"An' he's right. No gintleman shud wallop his wife, an' no gintleman wud. I'm in favor iv havin' wife-beaters whipped, an' I'll go further an' say that 'twud be a good thing to have ivry marrid man scoorged about wanst a month. As a bachelor man, who rules entirely be love, I've spint fifty years invistigatin' what Hogan calls th' martial state, an' I've come to th' con-clusion that ivry man uses vilence to his wife. He may not beat her with a table-leg, but he coerces her with his mind. He can put a savage remark to th' pint iv th' jaw with more lastin' effect thin a right hook. He may not dhrag her around be th' hair iv her head, but he dhrags her be her sympathies, her fears, an' her anxieties. As a last raycoorse he beats her be doin' things that make her pity him. An' th' ladies, Gawd bless thim, like it. Th' whippin'-post f'r wife-beaters won't be popylar with th' wife-beaters. In her heart ivry woman likes th' sthrong arm. Ye very sildom see th' wife iv an habitchool wife-beater lavin' him. Th' husband that gives his wife a vilet bokay is as apt to lose her as th' husband that gives her a vilet eye. Th' man that breaks th' furniture, tips over th' table, kicks th' dog, an' pegs th' lamp at th' lady iv his choice is seen no more often in our justly popylar divoorce coorts thin th' man who comes home arly to feed th' canary. Manny a skilful mandolin player has been onable to prevint his wife fr'm elopin' with a prize-fighter.

"No, you won't find anny malthreated ladies' names on th' petition f'r th' new govermint departmint. Th' Whippin' Postmasther-Gin'ral will have to look elsewhere f'r applause thin to th' downthrodden wives iv th' counthry. But th' departmint has come to stay; I hope, Hinnissy, to see its mission enlarged. I look forward to th' day whin there will be a govermint whippin'-post, with a large American flag at th' top iv it, in ivry American city. Afther awhile we can attind to th' wants iv th' rural com-munities. A fourth assistant whippin' postmasther-gin'ral will be sint to th' farmin' counthry, so that Cy an' Alick will get just as good a lammin' as Alphonso an' Augustus. He will carry a red, white an' blue post on his thravels, an' a special cat-o'-nine-tails, with th' arms iv th' United States an' th' motto, 'Love wan another,' engraved on th' handle. Th' whippin'-post will grow up to be wan iv th' foundations iv our govermint, like th' tariff. Whin annybody proposes to abolish it they will be met with th' cry: 'Let th' whippin'-post be rayformed be its frinds.' Th' frinds will build a bigger post an' put a few nails on th' lash. Ivinchooly people will quit goin' to Mt. Vernon an' make pilgrimages to Delaware, where th' whippin'-post has had such a fine moral effect. An' thin Addicks will be ilicted prisidint.

"Won't it be fine? Th' govermint gives us too little amusemint nowadays. Th' fav'rite pastime iv civilized man is crooly to other civilized man. Ye take a Southern gintleman, who has been accustomed to pathronize th' lynchin' iv naygurs. All other spoorts seem tame to him afthervard. He won't go to th' theaytre or th' circus, but pines at home till there's another black man to be burned. A warden iv a pinitinchry niver has anny fun out iv life afther he loses his job. Judges in civil coorts sometimes resign, but niver a hangin' judge in a criminal coort.

"Yes, sir, 'twill be a good thing f'r th' criminal an' a good thing f'r a spoort-lovin' public, but th' question that comes up in me mind is, Will it be a good thing f'r Uncle Sam an' a good thing f'r Sheriff Dooley. Th' only habit a man or a govermint ought to pray again' acquirin' is crooly. It's th' gr-reatest dissypation in th' wurruld. Ye can't swear off bein' crool wanst ye begin to make a practice iv it. Ye keep gettin' crooler an' crooler, till ye fin'lly think iv nawthin' but injurin' ye'er neighbor an' seein' him suffer. I mind wanst, whin I was a boy at home, a new schoolmasther come to th' hedge. He was a nice, quiet, near-sighted young fellow, an' he began be larrupin' on'y th' worst iv th' boys. But ye cud see in a minyit that he was injyin' th' pastime. At th' end iv th' month he was lickin' somebody all th' time. He used to get fairly dhrunk switchin' us. Glory be, it seems to me that I spint all me boyhood days on another boy's shoulders. He licked us f'r ivrything, an' annythin' an' nawthin' at all. It wasn't that it done us anny good, but it gave him pleasure. He's been dead an' gone these forty years, an' I bear him no ill-will, but if I iver r-run acrost his ghost I'll put a head on it.

"So it is with Uncle Sam: If he begins to lick wife-beaters, befure he's been at it long he won't have anny time f'r annythin' but th' whippin'-post. He'll be in his shirt-sleeves all day long, slashin' away at countherfeiters, illicit distillers, postal thieves, an' dimmycrats.

"No, Hinnissy, there ain't a hair's diff'rence between a blackguard who beats his wife an' a govermint that beats its childher. Ye can't cure corp'ral punishmint be makin' th' govermint th' biggest kind iv corp'ral punisher. Ye can't inflict corp'ral punishmint onless ye'er sthronger thin th' fellow ye punish, an' if ye ar-re sthronger ye ought to be ashamed iv ye'ersilf. Whiniver I hear iv a big six-fut school-teacher demandin' that he be allowed to whale a thirty-two-inch child I feel like askin' him up here to put on th' gloves with Jeffreys. Whin a govermint or a man raysorts to blows it shows they're ayether afraid or have lost their timpers. An' there ye ar-re."

"Spare th' rod an' spile th' child," said Mr. Hennessy.

"Yes," said Mr. Dooley, "but don't spare th' rod an' ye spile th' rod, th' child, an' th' child's father."

THE FOOD WE EAT[1]

"What have ye undher ye'er arm there?" demanded Mr. Dooley.

"I was takin' home a ham," said Mr. Hennessy.

"Clear out iv here with it," cried Mr. Dooley. "Take that thing outside—an' don't lave it where th' dog might get hold iv it. Th' idee iv ye'er bringin' it in here! Glory be, it makes me faint to think iv it. I'm afraid I'll have to go an' lay down."

"What ails ye?" asked Mr. Hennessy.

"What ails me?" said Mr. Dooley. "Haven't ye r-read about th' invistygation iv th' Stock Yards? It's a good thing f'r ye ye haven't. If ye knew what that ham—oh, th' horrid wurrud—was made iv ye'd go down to Rabbi Hirsch an' be baptized f'r a Jew.

"Ye may think 'tis th' innocint little last left leg iv a porker ye're inthrajoocin' into ye'er innocint fam'ly, but I tell ye, me boy, th' pig that that ham was cut fr'm has as manny legs to-day as iver he had. Why did ye waste ye'er good money on it? Why didn't ye get th' fam'ly into th' dining-room, shut th' windows, an' turn on th' gas? I'll be readin' in th' pa-aper to-morrah that wan Hinnissy took an overdose iv Unblemished Ham with suicidal intint an' died in gr-reat agony. Take it away! It's lible to blow up at anny minyit, scattherin' death an' desthruction in its train.

"Dear, oh dear, I haven't been able to ate annything more nourishin' thin a cucumber in a week. I'm grajally fadin' fr'm

---

[1] Dunne's reaction to Upton Sinclair's *The Jungle* (1906).

life. A little while ago no wan cud square away at a beefsteak
with betther grace thin mesilf. To-day th' wurrud resthrant
makes me green in th' face. How did it all come about? A
young fellow wrote a book. Th' divvle take him f'r writin' it.
Hogan says it's a grand book. It's wan iv th' gr-reatest books he
iver r-read. It almost made him commit suicide. Th' hero is a
Lithuanian, or as ye might say, Pollacky, who left th' barb'rous
land iv his birth an' come to this home iv opporchunity where
ivry man is th' equal iv ivry other man befure th' law if he isn't
careful. Our hero got a fancy job poling food products out iv a
catch-basin, an' was promoted to scrapin' pure leaf-lard off th'
flure iv th' glue facthry. But th' binifits iv our gloryous civilyza-
tion were wasted on this poor peasant. Instead iv bein' thankful
f'r what he got, an' lookin' forward to a day whin his opporchunity
wud arrive an', be merely stubbin' his toe, he might become rich
an' famous as a pop'lar soup, he grew cross an' unruly, bit his
boss, an' was sint to jail. But it all tur-rned out well in th' end.
Th' villain fell into a lard-tank an' was not seen again ontil he
tur-rned up at a fash'nable resthrant in New York. Our hero got
out iv jail an' was rewarded with a pleasant position as a porter iv
an arnychist hotel, an' all ended merry as a fun'ral bell.

"Ye'll see be this that 'tis a sweetly sintimintal little volume
to be r-read durin' Lent. It's had a grand success, an' I'm glad iv
it. I see be th' publishers' announcemints that 'tis th' gr-reatest
lithry hog-killin' in a peryod iv gin'ral lithry culture. If ye want
to rayjooce ye'er butcher's bills buy *Th' Jungle*. It shud be taken
between meals, an' is especially ricomminded to maiden ladies
contimplatin' their first ocean voyage.

"Well, sir, it put th' Prisidint in a tur-rble stew. Oh, Lawd,
why did I say that? Think iv—but I mustn't go on. Annyhow,
Tiddy was toying with a light breakfast an' idly turnin' over th'
pages iv th' new book with both hands. Suddenly he rose fr'm
th' table, an' cryin': 'I'm pizened,' begun throwin' sausages out
iv th' window. Th' ninth wan sthruck Sinitor Biv'ridge on th'
head an' made him a blond. It bounced off, exploded, an'
blew a leg off a secret-service agent, an' th' scatthred fragmints
desthroyed a handsome row iv ol' oak-trees. Sinitor Biv'ridge
rushed in, thinkin' that th' Prisidint was bein' assassynated be his
devoted followers in th' Sinit, an' discovered Tiddy engaged in a
hand-to-hand conflict with a potted ham. Th' Sinitor fr'm
Injyanny, with a few well-directed wurruds, put out th' fuse an'

rendered th' missile harmless. Since thin th' Prisidint, like th' rest iv us, has become a viggytaryan, an' th' diet has so changed his disposition that he is writin' a book called *Suffer in Silence*, didycated to Sinitor Aldrich. But befure doin' annything else, he selected an expert comity fr'm a neighborin' univarsity settle- mint to prepare a thorough, onbiased rayport that day on th' situation an' make sure it was no betther thin th' book said. Well, what th' experts discovered I won't tell ye. Suffice it to say, that whin th' report come in Congress decided to abolish all th' days iv th' week except Friday.

"I have r-read th' report, an' now, whin I'm asked to pass th' corned-beef, I pass. Oh dear, th' things I've consumed in days past. What is lard? Lard is annything that isn't good enough f'r an axle. What is potted ham? It is made in akel parts iv plasther iv Paris, sawdust, rope, an' incautious laborer. To what kingdom does canned chicken belong? It is a mineral. How is soup—Get me th' fan, Hinnissy.

"Thank ye. I'm betther now. Well, sir, th' packers ar-re gettin' r-ready to protect thimsilves again' *Th' Jungle*. It's on'y lately that these here gin'rous souls have give much attintion to lithrachoor. Th' on'y pens they felt an inthrest in was those that resthrained th' rectic cow. If they had a blind man in th' Health Departmint, a few competint frinds on th' Fedhral bench, an' Farmer Bill Lorimer to protect th' cattle inthrests iv th' Gr-reat West, they cared not who made th' novels iv our counthry. But Hogan says they'll have to add a novel facthry to their plant, an' in a few months ye'll be able to buy wan iv Nels Morris's pop-lar series warranted to be fr'm rale life, like th' pressed corned-beef.

"Hogan has wrote a sample f'r thim:

"'"Dear!" Ivan Ivanovitch was seated in th' consarvatory an' breakfast-room pro-vided be Schwartzchild & Sulsberger f'r all their employees. It was a pleasant scene that sthretched beneath th' broad windows iv his cosey villa. Th' air was redolent with th' aroma iv th' spring rendherin', an' beneath th' smoke iv th' May mornin' th' stately expanse iv Packin'town appeared more lovely than iver befure. On th' lawn a fountain played brine incessantly an' melojously on th' pickled pigs'-feet. A faint odor as iv peach blossoms come fr'm th' embalmin' plant where kine that have perished fr'm joy in th' long journey fr'm th' plains are thransformed into th' delicacies that show how an American sojer can die. Thousan's iv battle-fields are sthrewn with th' labels iv this justly pop'lar firm, an' a millyon heroes have risen fr'm their viands an' gone composedly to their doom. But to rayturn to our story. Th' scene, we say, was more beautiful thin wurruds can describe. Beyond th' hedge a physician was thryin' to make a cow show her tongue, while his assistant wint over th' crather with a stethoscope. Th' air was filled with th' joyous shouts iv dhrivers iv wagons heavily laden with ol' boots an' hats, arsenic, boric acid, bone-dust, sthricknine, sawdust, an' th' other ingree-jents iv th' most nourishing food f'r a sturdy people. It was a scene f'r th' eye to dote upon, but it brought no happiness to Ivan Ivanovitch. Yisterdah had been pay-day at th' yards an' little remained iv th' fourteen thousan' dollars that had been his portion. There was a soupcan iv anger in his voice as he laid down a copy iv th' *Ladies' Home Journal* an' said: "Dear!" Th' haughty beauty raised her head an' laid aside th' spoon with which she had been scrapin' th' life-givin' proosic acid fr'm th' Deer Island sausage. "Dear," said Ivanovitch, "if ye use so much iv th' comp'ny's peroxide on ye'er hair there will be none left f'r th' canned turkey." Befure she cud lift th' buttherine dish a cheery voice was heerd at th' dure, an' J. Ogden Cudahy bounded in. Ivanovitch flushed darkly, an' thin, as if a sudden determination had sthruck him, dhrew on his overhalls an' wint out to shampoo th' pigs. [Th' continyuation iv this thrillin' story will be found in th' next issue iv *Leaf Lard*. F'r sale at all dellycatessen-stores.]'

"An' there ye ar-re, Hinnissy. It's a turr'ble situation. Here am I an' here's all th' wurruld been stowin' away meat since th' days iv Nebudcud—what-ye-may-call-him. 'Tis th' pleasant hour iv dinner. We've been waitin' half an hour, pretindin' we were in no hurry, makin' convarsation, an' lookin' at th' clock. There is a commotion in th' back iv th' house, an' a cheery per-fume iv beefsteak an' onions comes through an open dure. Th' hired girl smilin' but triumphant flags us fr'm th' dinin'-room. Th' talk about th' weather stops at wanst. Th' story iv th' wondherful child on'y four years old that bit his brother is stowed away f'r future use. Th' comp'ny dashes out. There is some crowdin' at th' dure. 'Will ye sit there, Mrs. Casey?' 'Mrs. Hinnissy, squat down next to Mike.' 'Tom, d'ye stow ye'ersilf at th' end iv th' table, where ye can deal th' potatoes.' 'Ar-re ye all r-ready? Thin go.' There ar-re twinty good stories flyin' befure th' napkins ar-re well inside iv th' collar. Th' platter comes in smokin' like Vesuvyous. I begin to play me fav'rite

chune with a carvin'-knife on a steel whin Molly Donahue remarks:
'Have ye r-read about th' invistygations iv th' Stock Yards?'
I dhrop me knife. Tom Donahue clutches at his collar. Mrs.
Hinnissy says th' rooms seem close, an' we make a meal off
potatoes an' wathercress. Ivrybody goes home arly without
sayin' good-bye, an' th' next day Father Kelly has to patch up a
row between you an' ye'er wife. We ate no more together, an'
food bein' th' basis iv all frindship, frindship ceases. Christmas
is marked off th' calendar an' Lent lasts f'r three hundherd an'
sixty-five days a year.

"An', be Hivens, I can't stop with thinkin' iv th' way th'
food is got r-ready. Wanst I'm thurly sick I don't care how much
sicker I get, an' I go on wondherin' what food ra-aly is. An' that
way, says Hogan, starvation lies. Th' idee that a Polish gintleman has danced wan iv his graceful native waltzes on me beefsteak
is horrible to think, but it's on'y a shade worse thin th' thought
that this delicate morsel that makes me th' man I am was got be
th' assassynation iv a gentle animile that niver done me no harm
but look kindly at me. See th' little lamb friskin' in th' fields.
How beautiful an' innocint it is. Whin ye'er little Packy has been
a good boy ye call him ye'er little lamb, an' take him to see thim
skippin' in th' grass. 'Aren't they cunnin', Packy?' But look!
Who is this gr-reat ruffyanly man comin' acrost th' fields? An'
what is that horrid blade he holds in his hands? Is he goin' to
play with th' lamb? Oh, dhreadful sight. Take away th' little
boy, Hinnissy. Ye have ordhered a leg iv lamb f'r supper.

"Th' things we eat or used to eat! I'll not mintion anny iv
thim, but I'd like some pote to get up a list iv eatable names that
wud sound th' way they taste. It's askin' too much f'r us to be
happy whin we're stowin' away articles iv food with th' same titles
as our own machinery. 'But why not ate something else?' says
ye. Fish? I can't. I've hooked thim out iv th' wather.
Eggs? What is an egg? Don't answer. Let us go on. Milk?
Oh, goodness! Viggytables, thin? Well, if it's bad to take th'
life iv a cow or a pig, is it anny betther to cut off a tomato in th'
flower iv its youth or murdher a fam'ly iv baby pease in th'
cradle? I ate no more iv annything but a few snowballs in winter
an' a mouthful iv fresh air in th' summer-time.

"But let's stop thinkin' about it. It's a good thing not to
think long about annything—ye'ersilf, ye'er food, or ye'er here-
after. Th' story iv th' nourishmint we take is on'y half written in

Th' Jungle. If ye followed it fr'm th' cradle to th' grave, as ye might say—fr'm th' day Armour kicked it into a wheelbarrow, through varyous encounters, th' people it met, with their pictures while at wurruk, until it landed in th' care iv th' sthrange lady in th' kitchen—ye'd have a romance that wud make th' butcher haul down his sign. No, sir, I'm goin' to thry to fight it. If th' millyonaire has a gredge again' me he'll land me somehow. If he can't do me with sugar iv lead, he'll run me down with a throlley-car or smash me up in a railroad accident. I'll shut me eyes an' take me chance. Come into th' back room, cut me a slice iv th' ham, an' sind f'r th' priest."

"They ought to make thim ate their own meat," said Mr. Hennessy, warmly.

"I suggisted that," said Mr. Dooley, "but Hogan says they'd fall back on th' Constitution. He says th' Constitution f'rbids crool an' unusual punishmints."

NATIONAL HOUSECLEANING[1]

"It looks to me," said Mr. Hennessy, "as though this counthry was goin' to th' divvle."

"Put down that magazine," said Mr. Dooley. "Now d'ye feel betther? I thought so. But I can sympathize with ye. I've been readin' thim mesilf. Time was whin I sildom throubled thim. I wanted me fiction th' day it didn't happen, an' I cud buy that f'r a penny fr'm th' newsboy on th' corner. But wanst in a while some homefarin' wandhrer wud jettison wan in me place, an' I'd frequently glance through it an' find it in me lap whin I woke up. Th' magazines in thim days was very ca'ming to th' mind. Angabel an' Alfonso dashin' f'r a marredge license. Prom'nent lady authoressesses makin' pomes at th' moon. Now an' thin a scrap over whether Shakespeare was enthered in his own name or was a ringer, with th' long-shot players always again Shakespeare. But no wan hurt. Th' idee ye got fr'm these here publications was that life was wan glad, sweet song. If annything, ivrybody was too good to ivrybody else. Ye don't need to lock th' dure at night. Hang ye'er watch on th' knob. Why do polismen carry clubs? Answer, to knock th' roses off th' throlley-poles.

[1] Though Dunne's name is sometimes linked with those of the muckrakers, he himself was frequently highly critical of them. Idarem: Ida M. Tarbell.

They were good readin'.   I liked thim th' way I like a bottle iv
white pop now an' thin.

   "But now whin I pick me fav'rite magazine off th' flure,
what do I find ?   Ivrything has gone wrong.   Th' wurruld is
little betther thin a convict's camp.   Angabel an' Alfonso ar-re
about to get marrid whin it is discovered that she has a husband in
Ioway an' he has a wife in Wisconsin.   All th' pomes be th' lady
authoressesses that used to begin: 'Oh, moon, how fair!' now
begin: 'Oh, Ogden Armour, how awful!'   Shakespeare's on'y
mintioned as a crook.   Here ye ar-re.   Last edition.   Just out.
Full account iv th' Crimes iv Incalculated.   Did ye read Larsen
last month on 'Th' use iv Burglars as Burglar Alarums' ?   Good,
was it ?   Thin read th' horrible disclosures about th' way Jawn C.
Higgins got th' right to build a bay-window on his barber-shop at
iliven forty-two Kosciusko Avnoo, South Bennington, Arkansaw.
Read Wash'n'ton Bliffens's dhreadful assault on th' board iv
education iv Baraboo.   Read Idarem on Jawn D.; she's a lady,
but she's got th' punch.   Graft ivrywhere.   'Graft in th' Insurance
Comp'nies,' 'Graft in Congress,' 'Graft in th' Supreem Coort,'
'Graft be an Old Grafter,' 'Graft in Lithrachoor,' be Hinnery
James; 'Graft in Its Relations to th' Higher Life,' be Dock Eliot;
'Th' Homeeric Legend an' Graft; Its Cause an' Effect; Are They
th' Same ?   Yes and No,' be Norman Slapgood.

   "An' so it goes, Hinnissy, till I'm that blue, discouraged, an'
broken-hearted I cud go to th' edge iv th' wurruld an' jump off.
It's a wicked, wicked, horrible place, an' this here counthry is
about th' toughest spot in it.   Is there an honest man among us ?
If there is throw him out.   He's a spy.   Is there an institution that
isn't corrupt to its very foundations ?   Don't ye believe it.   It
on'y looks that way because our graft iditor hasn't got there on his
rounds yet.   Why, if Canada iver wants to increase her popylation
all she has to do is to sind a man in a balloon over th' United
States to yell: 'Stop thief!'   At th' sound iv th' wurruds sivinty
millyon men, women, an' little scoundhrelly childher wud
skedaddle f'r th' frontier, an' lave Jerome, Folk, an' Bob La
Follette to pull down th' blinds, close th' dure, an' hang out a sign:
'United States to rent.'   I don't thrust anny man anny more.
I niver did much, but now if I hear th' stealthy step iv me dearest
frind at th' dure I lock th' cash dhrawer.   I used to be nervous
about burglars, but now I'm afraid iv a night call fr'm th' Chief Justice iv th' Supreem Coort or th' prisidint iv th' First National Bank.

"It's slowly killin' me, Hinnissy, or it wud if I thought about it. I'm sorry George Wash'n'ton iver lived. Thomas Jefferson I hate. An' as f'r Adam, well, if that joker iver come into this place I'd— but I mustn't go on.

"Do I think it's all as bad as that? Well, Hinnissy, now that ye ask me, an' seein' that Chris'mas is comin' on, I've got to tell ye that this counthry, while wan iv th' worst in th' wurruld, is about as good as th' next if it ain't a shade betther. But we're wan iv th' gr-reatest people in th' wurruld to clean house, an' th' way we like best to clean th' house is to burn it down. We come home at night an' find that th' dure has been left open an' a few mosquitoes or life-insurance prisidints have got in, an' we say: 'This is turr'ble. We must get rid iv these here pests.' An' we take an axe to thim. We desthroy a lot iv furniture an' kill th' canary bird, th' cat, th' cuckoo clock, an' a lot iv other harmless insects, but we'll fin'lly land th' mosquitoes. If an Englishman found mosquitoes in his house he'd first thry to kill thim, an' whin he didn't succeed he'd say: 'What pleasant little humming-bur-rds they ar-re. Life wud be very lonesome without thim,' an he'd domesticate thim, larn thim to sing 'Gawd Save th' King,' an' call his house Mosquito Lodge. If these here inthrestin' life-insurance scandals had come up in Merry ol' England we'd niver hear iv thim, because all th' boys wud be in th' House iv Lords be this time, an' Lord Tontine wud sit hard on anny scheme to have him searched be a lawyer fr'm Brooklyn. But with this here nation iv ours somebody scents something wrong with th' scales at th' grocery-store an' whips out his gun, another man turns in a fire alarm, a third fellow sets fire to th' Presbyterian Church, a vigilance comity is formed an' hangs ivry foorth man; an' havin' started with Rockyfellar, who's tough an' don't mind bein' lynched, they fin'lly wind up with desthroyin' me because th' steam laundhry has sint me home somebody else's collars.

"It reminds me, Hinnissy, iv th' time I lived at a boardin'-house kept be a lady be th' name iv Doherty. She was a good woman, but her idee iv life was a combination iv pneumony an' love. She was niver still. Th' sight iv a spot on th' wall where a gintleman boorder had laid his head afther dinner would give her nervous prostration. She was always polishin', scrubbin', sweepin', airin'. She had a plumber in to look at th' dhrains twice a week. Fifty-two times a year there was a rivolution in th' house that wud've made th' Czar iv Rooshya want to go home to rest. An' yet th' house was niver really clean. It looked as if it was to us. It was so clean that I always was ashamed to go into it onless I'd shaved. But Mrs. Doherty said no; it was like a pig-pen. 'I don't know what to do,' says she. 'I'm worn out, an' it seems impossible to keep this house clean.' 'What is th' throuble with it?' says she. 'Madam,' says me frind Gallagher, 'wud ye have me tell ye?' he says. 'I wud,' says she. 'Well,' says he, 'th' throuble with this house is that it is occypied entirely be human bein's,' he says. 'If 'twas a vacant house,' he says, 'it cud aisily be kept clean,' he says.

"An' there ye ar-re, Hinnissy. Th' noise ye hear is not th' first gun iv a rivolution. It's on'y th' people iv th' United States batin' a carpet. Ye object to th' smell? That's nawthin'. We use sthrong disinfectants here. A Frinchman or an Englishman cleans house be sprinklin' th' walls with cologne; we chop a hole in th' flure an' pour in a kag iv chloride iv lime. Both are good ways. It depinds on how long ye intind to live in th' house. What were those shots? That's th' housekeeper killin' a couple iv cockroaches with a Hotchkiss gun. Who is that yellin'? That's our ol' frind High Fi-nance bein' compelled to take his annual bath. Th' housecleanin' season is in full swing, an' there's a good deal iv dust in th' air; but I want to say to thim neighbors iv ours, who're peekin' in an' makin' remarks about th' amount iv rubbish, that over in our part iv th' wurruld we don't sweep things undher th' sofa. Let thim put that in their pipes an' smoke it."

"I think th' counthry is goin' to th' divvle," said Mr. Hennessy, sadly.

"Hinnissy," said Mr. Dooley, "if that's so I congratylate th' wurruld."

"How's that?" asked Mr. Hennessy.

"Well," said Mr. Dooley, "f'r nearly forty years I've seen this counthry goin' to th' divvle, an' I got aboord late. An' if it's been goin' that long an' at that rate, an' has got no nearer thin it is this pleasant Chris'mas, thin th' divvle is a divvle iv a ways further off thin I feared."

A CATALOGUE OF SELECTED DOVER BOOKS
IN ALL FIELDS OF INTEREST

A CATALOGUE OF SELECTED DOVER BOOKS
IN ALL FIELDS OF INTEREST

WHAT IS SCIENCE?, *N. Campbell*
The role of experiment and measurement, the function of mathematics, the nature of scientific laws, the difference between laws and theories, the limitations of science, and many similarly provocative topics are treated clearly and without technicalities by an eminent scientist. "Still an excellent introduction to scientific philosophy," H. Margenau in *Physics Today*. "A first-rate primer . . . deserves a wide audience," *Scientific American*. 192pp. 5⅜ x 8.
60043-2 Paperbound $1.25

THE NATURE OF LIGHT AND COLOUR IN THE OPEN AIR, *M. Minnaert*
Why are shadows sometimes blue, sometimes green, or other colors depending on the light and surroundings? What causes mirages? Why do multiple suns and moons appear in the sky? Professor Minnaert explains these unusual phenomena and hundreds of others in simple, easy-to-understand terms based on optical laws and the properties of light and color. No mathematics is required but artists, scientists, students, and everyone fascinated by these "tricks" of nature will find thousands of useful and amazing pieces of information. Hundreds of observational experiments are suggested which require no special equipment. 200 illustrations; 42 photos. xvi + 362pp. 5⅜ x 8.
20196-1 Paperbound $2.00

THE STRANGE STORY OF THE QUANTUM, AN ACCOUNT FOR THE GENERAL READER OF THE GROWTH OF IDEAS UNDERLYING OUR PRESENT ATOMIC KNOWLEDGE, *B. Hoffmann*
Presents lucidly and expertly, with barest amount of mathematics, the problems and theories which led to modern quantum physics. Dr. Hoffmann begins with the closing years of the 19th century, when certain trifling discrepancies were noticed, and with illuminating analogies and examples takes you through the brilliant concepts of Planck, Einstein, Pauli, Broglie, Bohr, Schroedinger, Heisenberg, Dirac, Sommerfeld, Feynman, etc. This edition includes a new, long postscript carrying the story through 1958. "Of the books attempting an account of the history and contents of our modern atomic physics which have come to my attention, this is the best," H. Margenau, Yale University, in *American Journal of Physics*. 32 tables and line illustrations. Index. 275pp. 5⅜ x 8.
20518-5 Paperbound $2.00

GREAT IDEAS OF MODERN MATHEMATICS: THEIR NATURE AND USE, *Jagjit Singh*
Reader with only high school math will understand main mathematical ideas of modern physics, astronomy, genetics, psychology, evolution, etc. better than many who use them as tools, but comprehend little of their basic structure. Author uses his wide knowledge of non-mathematical fields in brilliant exposition of differential equations, matrices, group theory, logic, statistics, problems of mathematical foundations, imaginary numbers, vectors, etc. Original publication. 2 appendixes. 2 indexes. 65 ills. 322pp. 5⅜ x 8.
20587-8 Paperbound $2.25

THE MUSIC OF THE SPHERES: THE MATERIAL UNIVERSE — FROM ATOM TO QUASAR, SIMPLY EXPLAINED, *Guy Murchie*
Vast compendium of fact, modern concept and theory, observed and calculated data, historical background guides intelligent layman through the material universe. Brilliant exposition of earth's construction, explanations for moon's craters, atmospheric components of Venus and Mars (with data from recent fly-by's), sun spots, sequences of star birth and death, neighboring galaxies, contributions of Galileo, Tycho Brahe, Kepler, etc.; and (Vol. 2) construction of the atom (describing newly discovered sigma and xi subatomic particles), theories of sound, color and light, space and time, including relativity theory, quantum theory, wave theory, probability theory, work of Newton, Maxwell, Faraday, Einstein, de Broglie, etc. "Best presentation yet offered to the intelligent general reader," *Saturday Review*. Revised (1967). Index. 319 illustrations by the author. Total of xx + 644pp. 5⅜ x 8½.
21809-0, 21810-4 Two volume set, paperbound $5.00

FOUR LECTURES ON RELATIVITY AND SPACE, *Charles Proteus Steinmetz*
Lecture series, given by great mathematician and electrical engineer, generally considered one of the best popular-level expositions of special and general relativity theories and related questions. Steinmetz translates complex mathematical reasoning into language accessible to laymen through analogy, example and comparison. Among topics covered are relativity of motion, location, time; of mass; acceleration; 4-dimensional time-space; geometry of the gravitational field; curvature and bending of space; non-Euclidean geometry. Index. 40 illustrations. x + 142pp. 5⅜ x 8½.
61771-8 Paperbound $1.35

HOW TO KNOW THE WILD FLOWERS, *Mrs. William Starr Dana*
Classic nature book that has introduced thousands to wonders of American wild flowers. Color-season principle of organization is easy to use, even by those with no botanical training, and the genial, refreshing discussions of history, folklore, uses of over 1,000 native and escape flowers, foliage plants are informative as well as fun to read. Over 170 full-page plates, collected from several editions, may be colored in to make permanent records of finds. Revised to conform with 1950 edition of Gray's Manual of Botany. xlii + 438pp. 5⅜ x 8½.
20332-8 Paperbound $2.50

MANUAL OF THE TREES OF NORTH AMERICA, *Charles Sprague Sargent*
Still unsurpassed as most comprehensive, reliable study of North American tree characteristics, precise locations and distribution. By dean of American dendrologists. Every tree native to U.S., Canada, Alaska; 185 genera, 717 species, described in detail—leaves, flowers, fruit, winterbuds, bark, wood, growth habits, etc. plus discussion of varieties and local variants, immaturity variations. Over 100 keys, including unusual 11-page analytical key to genera, aid in identification. 783 clear illustrations of flowers, fruit, leaves. An unmatched permanent reference work for all nature lovers. Second enlarged (1926) edition. Synopsis of families. Analytical key to genera. Glossary of technical terms. Index. 783 illustrations, 1 map. Total of 982pp. 5⅜ x 8.
20277-1, 20278-X Two volume set, paperbound $6.00

It's Fun to Make Things From Scrap Materials,
Evelyn Glantz Hershoff
What use are empty spools, tin cans, bottle tops? What can be made from
rubber bands, clothes pins, paper clips, and buttons? This book provides
simply worded instructions and large diagrams showing you how to make
cookie cutters, toy trucks, paper turkeys, Halloween masks, telephone sets,
aprons, linoleum block- and spatter prints — in all 399 projects! Many are easy
enough for young children to figure out for themselves; some challenging
enough to entertain adults; all are remarkably ingenious ways to make things
from materials that cost pennies or less! Formerly "Scrap Fun for Everyone."
Index. 214 illustrations. 373pp. 5⅜ x 8½.   21251-3 Paperbound $1.75

Symbolic Logic and The Game of Logic, *Lewis Carroll*
"Symbolic Logic" is not concerned with modern symbolic logic, but is instead
a collection of over 380 problems posed with charm and imagination, using
the syllogism and a fascinating diagrammatic method of drawing conclusions.
In "The Game of Logic" Carroll's whimsical imagination devises a logical game
played with 2 diagrams and counters (included) to manipulate hundreds of
tricky syllogisms. The final section, "Hit or Miss" is a lagniappe of 101 additional puzzles in the delightful Carroll manner. Until this reprint edition,
both of these books were rarities costing up to $15 each. Symbolic Logic:
Index. xxxi + 199pp. The Game of Logic: 96pp. 2 vols. bound as one. 5⅜ x 8.
                                                                20492-8 Paperbound $2.50

Mathematical Puzzles of Sam Loyd, Part i
selected and edited by M. Gardner
Choice puzzles by the greatest American puzzle creator and innovator. Selected
from his famous collection, "Cyclopedia of Puzzles," they retain the unique
style and historical flavor of the originals. There are posers based on arithmetic,
algebra, probability, game theory, route tracing, topology, counter and sliding
block, operations research, geometrical dissection. Includes the famous "14-15"
puzzle which was a national craze, and his "Horse of a Different Color" which
sold millions of copies. 117 of his most ingenious puzzles in all. 120 line
drawings and diagrams. Solutions. Selected references. xx + 167pp. 5⅜ x 8.
                                                                20498-7 Paperbound $1.35

String Figures and How to Make Them, *Caroline Furness Jayne*
107 string figures plus variations selected from the best primitive and modern
examples developed by Navajo, Apache, pygmies of Africa, Eskimo, in Europe,
Australia, China, etc. The most readily understandable, easy-to-follow book in
English on perennially popular recreation. Crystal-clear exposition; step-by-
step diagrams. Everyone from kindergarten children to adults looking for
unusual diversion will be endlessly amused. Index. Bibliography. Introduction
by A. C. Haddon. 17 full-page plates, 960 illustrations. xxiii + 401pp. 5⅜ x 8½.
                                                                20152-X Paperbound $2.25

Paper Folding for Beginners, *W. D. Murray and F. J. Rigney*
A delightful introduction to the varied and entertaining Japanese art of
origami (paper folding), with a full, crystal-clear text that anticipates every
difficulty; over 275 clearly labeled diagrams of all important stages in creation.
You get results at each stage, since complex figures are logically developed
from simpler ones. 43 different pieces are explained: sailboats, frogs, roosters,
etc. 6 photographic plates. 279 diagrams. 95pp. 5⅜ x 8⅜.
                                                                20713-7 Paperbound $1.00

PRINCIPLES OF ART HISTORY,
H. Wölfflin
Analyzing such terms as "baroque," "classic," "neoclassic," "primitive,"
"picturesque," and 164 different works by artists like Botticelli, van Cleve,
Dürer, Hobbema, Holbein, Hals, Rembrandt, Titian, Brueghel, Vermeer, and
many others, the author establishes the classifications of art history and style
on a firm, concrete basis. This classic of art criticism shows what really
occurred between the 14th-century primitives and the sophistication of the
18th century in terms of basic attitudes and philosophies. "A remarkable
lesson in the art of seeing," *Sat. Rev. of Literature.* Translated from the 7th
German edition. 150 illustrations. 254pp. 6⅛ x 9¼. 20276-3 Paperbound $2.25

PRIMITIVE ART,
Franz Boas
This authoritative and exhaustive work by a great American anthropologist
covers the entire gamut of primitive art. Pottery, leatherwork, metal work,
stone work, wood, basketry, are treated in detail. Theories of primitive art,
historical depth in art history, technical virtuosity, unconscious levels of pat-
terning, symbolism, styles, literature, music, dance, etc. A must book for the
interested layman, the anthropologist, artist, handicrafter (hundreds of unusual motifs), and the historian. Over 900 illustrations (50 ceramic vessels,
12 totem poles, etc.). 376pp. 5⅜ x 8.   20025-6 Paperbound $2.50

THE GENTLEMAN AND CABINET MAKER'S DIRECTOR,
Thomas Chippendale
A reprint of the 1762 catalogue of furniture designs that went on to influence
generations of English and Colonial and Early Republic American furniture
makers. The 200 plates, most of them full-page sized, show Chippendale's
designs for French (Louis XV), Gothic, and Chinese-manner chairs, sofas,
canopy and dome beds, cornices, chamber organs, cabinets, shaving tables,
commodes, picture frames, frets, candle stands, chimney pieces, decorations, etc.
The drawings are all elegant and highly detailed; many include construction
diagrams and elevations. A supplement of 24 photographs shows surviving
pieces of original and Chippendale-style pieces of furniture. Brief biography
of Chippendale by N. I. Bienenstock, editor of *Furniture World.* Reproduced
from the 1762 edition. 200 plates, plus 19 photographic plates. vi + 249pp.
9⅛ x 12¼.   21601-2 Paperbound $3.50

AMERICAN ANTIQUE FURNITURE: A BOOK FOR AMATEURS,
Edgar G. Miller, Jr.
Standard introduction and practical guide to identification of valuable
American antique furniture. 2115 illustrations, mostly photographs taken by
the author in 148 private homes, are arranged in chronological order in extensive chapters on chairs, sofas, chests, desks, bedsteads, mirrors, tables, clocks,
and other articles. Focus is on furniture accessible to the collector, including
simpler pieces and a larger than usual coverage of Empire style. Introductory
chapters identify structural elements, characteristics of various styles, how to
avoid fakes, etc. "We are frequently asked to name some book on American
furniture that will meet the requirements of the novice collector, the beginning dealer, and . . . the general public. . . . We believe Mr. Miller's two
volumes more completely satisfy this specification than any other work,"
Antiques. Appendix. Index. Total of vi + 1106pp. 7⅞ x 10¾.
              21599-7, 21600-4 Two volume set, paperbound $7.50

THE BAD CHILD'S BOOK OF BEASTS, MORE BEASTS FOR WORSE CHILDREN, and A MORAL ALPHABET, *H. Belloc*
Hardly and anthology of humorous verse has appeared in the last 50 years without at least a couple of these famous nonsense verses. But one must see the entire volumes — with all the delightful original illustrations by Sir Basil Blackwood — to appreciate fully Belloc's charming and witty verses that play so subacidly on the platitudes of life and morals that beset his day — and ours. A great humor classic. Three books in one. Total of 157pp. 5⅜ x 8.
20749-8 Paperbound $1.00

THE DEVIL'S DICTIONARY, *Ambrose Bierce*
Sardonic and irreverent barbs puncturing the pomposities and absurdities of American politics, business, religion, literature, and arts, by the country's greatest satirist in the classic tradition. Epigrammatic as Shaw, piercing as Swift, American as Mark Twain, Will Rogers, and Fred Allen, Bierce will always remain the favorite of a small coterie of enthusiasts, and of writers and speakers whom he supplies with "some of the most gorgeous witticisms of the English language" (H. L. Mencken). Over 1000 entries in alphabetical order. 144pp. 5⅜ x 8.
20487-1 Paperbound $1.00

THE COMPLETE NONSENSE OF EDWARD LEAR.
This is the only complete edition of this master of gentle madness available at a popular price. *A Book of Nonsense, Nonsense Songs, More Nonsense Songs and Stories* in their entirety with all the old favorites that have delighted children and adults for years. The Dong With A Luminous Nose, The Jumblies, The Owl and the Pussycat, and hundreds of other bits of wonderful nonsense. 214 limericks, 3 sets of Nonsense Botany, 5 Nonsense Alphabets, 546 drawings by Lear himself, and much more. 320pp. 5⅜ x 8. 20167-8 Paperbound $1.75

THE WIT AND HUMOR OF OSCAR WILDE, *ed. by Alvin Redman*
Wilde at his most brilliant, in 1000 epigrams exposing weaknesses and hypocrisies of "civilized" society. Divided into 49 categories—sin, wealth, women, America, etc.—to aid writers, speakers. Includes excerpts from his trials, books, plays, criticism. Formerly "The Epigrams of Oscar Wilde." Introduction by Vyvyan Holland, Wilde's only living son. Introductory essay by editor. 260pp. 5⅜ x 8.
20602-5 Paperbound $1.50

A CHILD'S PRIMER OF NATURAL HISTORY, *Oliver Herford*
Scarcely an anthology of whimsy and humor has appeared in the last 50 years without a contribution from Oliver Herford. Yet the works from which these examples are drawn have been almost impossible to obtain! Here at last are Herford's improbable definitions of a menagerie of familiar and weird animals, each verse illustrated by the author's own drawings. 24 drawings in 2 colors; 24 additional drawings. vii + 95pp. 6½ x 6. 21647-0 Paperbound $1.00

THE BROWNIES: THEIR BOOK, *Palmer Cox*
The book that made the Brownies a household word. Generations of readers have enjoyed the antics, predicaments and adventures of these jovial sprites, who emerge from the forest at night to play or to come to the aid of a deserving human. Delightful illustrations by the author decorate nearly every page. 24 short verse tales with 266 illustrations. 155pp. 6⅝ x 9¼.
21265-3 Paperbound $1.50

THE PRINCIPLES OF PSYCHOLOGY,
William James
The full long-course, unabridged, of one of the great classics of Western literature and science. Wonderfully lucid descriptions of human mental activity, the stream of thought, consciousness, time perception, memory, imagination, emotions, reason, abnormal phenomena, and similar topics. Original contributions are integrated with the work of such men as Berkeley, Binet, Mills, Darwin, Hume, Kant, Royce, Schopenhauer, Spinoza, Locke, Descartes, Galton, Wundt, Lotze, Herbart, Fechner, and scores of others. All contrasting interpretations of mental phenomena are examined in detail—introspective analysis, philosophical interpretation, and experimental research. "A classic," *Journal of Consulting Psychology*. "The main lines are as valid as ever," *Psychoanalytical Quarterly*. "Standard reading ... a classic of interpretation," *Psychiatric Quarterly*. 94 illustrations. 1408pp. 5⅜ x 8.
20381-6, 20382-4 Two volume set, paperbound $6.00

VISUAL ILLUSIONS: THEIR CAUSES, CHARACTERISTICS AND APPLICATIONS,
M. Luckiesh
"Seeing is deceiving," asserts the author of this introduction to virtually every type of optical illusion known. The text both describes and explains the principles involved in color illusions, figure-ground, distance illusions, etc. 100 photographs, drawings and diagrams prove how easy it is to fool the sense: circles that aren't round, parallel lines that seem to bend, stationary figures that seem to move as you stare at them — illustration after illustration strains our credulity at what we see. Fascinating book from many points of view, from applications for artists, in camouflage, etc. to the psychology of vision. New introduction by William Ittleson, Dept. of Psychology, Queens College. Index. Bibliography. xxi + 252pp. 5⅜ x 8½. 21530-X Paperbound $1.50

FADS AND FALLACIES IN THE NAME OF SCIENCE,
Martin Gardner
This is the standard account of various cults, quack systems, and delusions which have masqueraded as science: hollow earth fanatics. Reich and orgone sex energy, dianetics, Atlantis, multiple moons, Forteanism, flying saucers, medical fallacies like iridiagnosis, zone therapy, etc. A new chapter has been added on Bridey Murphy, psionics, and other recent manifestations in this field. This is a fair, reasoned appraisal of eccentric theory which provides excellent inoculation against cleverly masked nonsense. "Should be read by everyone, scientist and non-scientist alike," R. T. Birge, Prof. Emeritus of Physics, Univ. of California; Former President, American Physical Society. Index. x + 365pp. 5⅜ x 8. 20394-8 Paperbound $2.00

ILLUSIONS AND DELUSIONS OF THE SUPERNATURAL AND THE OCCULT,
D. H. Rawcliffe
Holds up to rational examination hundreds of persistent delusions including crystal gazing, automatic writing, table turning, mediumistic trances, mental healing, stigmata, lycanthropy, live burial, the Indian Rope Trick, spiritualism, dowsing, telepathy, clairvoyance, ghosts, ESP, etc. The author explains and exposes the mental and physical deceptions involved, making this not only an exposé of supernatural phenomena, but a valuable exposition of characteristic types of abnormal psychology. Originally titled "The Psychology of the Occult." 14 illustrations. Index. 551pp. 5⅜ x 8. 20503-7 Paperbound $3.50

FAIRY TALE COLLECTIONS, *edited by Andrew Lang*
Andrew Lang's fairy tale collections make up the richest shelf-full of traditional children's stories anywhere available. Lang supervised the translation of stories from all over the world—familiar European tales collected by Grimm, animal stories from Negro Africa, myths of primitive Australia, stories from Russia, Hungary, Iceland, Japan, and many other countries. Lang's selection of translations are unusually high; many authorities consider that the most familiar tales find their best versions in these volumes. All collections are richly decorated and illustrated by H. J. Ford and other artists.

THE BLUE FAIRY BOOK. 37 stories. 138 illustrations. ix + 390pp. 5⅜ x 8½.
21437-0 Paperbound $1.95

THE GREEN FAIRY BOOK. 42 stories. 100 illustrations. xiii + 366pp. 5⅜ x 8½.
21439-7 Paperbound $1.75

THE BROWN FAIRY BOOK. 32 stories. 50 illustrations, 8 in color. xii + 350pp. 5⅜ x 8½.
21438-9 Paperbound $1.95

THE BEST TALES OF HOFFMANN, *edited by E. F. Bleiler*
10 stories by E. T. A. Hoffmann, one of the greatest of all writers of fantasy. The tales include "The Golden Flower Pot," "Automata," "A New Year's Eve Adventure," "Nutcracker and the King of Mice," "Sand-Man," and others. Vigorous characterizations of highly eccentric personalities, remarkably imaginative situations, and intensely fast pacing has made these tales popular all over the world for 150 years. Editor's introduction. 7 drawings by Hoffmann.
xxxiii + 419pp. 5⅜ x 8½.
21793-0 Paperbound $2.25

GHOST AND HORROR STORIES OF AMBROSE BIERCE,
edited by E. F. Bleiler
Morbid, eerie, horrifying tales of possessed poets, shabby aristocrats, revived corpses, and haunted malefactors. Widely acknowledged as the best of their kind between Poe and the moderns, reflecting their author's inner torment and bitter view of life. Includes "Damned Thing," "The Middle Toe of the Right Foot," "The Eyes of the Panther," "Visions of the Night," "Moxon's Master," and over a dozen others. Editor's introduction. xxii + 199pp. 5⅜ x 8½.
20767-6 Paperbound $1.50

THREE GOTHIC NOVELS, *edited by E. F. Bleiler*
Originators of the still popular Gothic novel form, influential in ushering in early 19th-century Romanticism. Horace Walpole's *Castle of Otranto*, William Beckford's *Vathek*, John Polidori's *The Vampyre*, and a *Fragment* by Lord Byron are enjoyable as exciting reading or as documents in the history of English literature. Editor's introduction. xi + 291pp. 5⅜ x 8½.
21232-7 Paperbound $2.00

BEST GHOST STORIES OF LEFANU, *edited by E. F. Bleiler*
Though admired by such critics as V. S. Pritchett, Charles Dickens and Henry James, ghost stories by the Irish novelist Joseph Sheridan LeFanu have never become as widely known as his detective fiction. About half of the 16 stories in this collection have never before been available in America. Collection includes "Carmilla" (perhaps the best vampire story ever written), "The Haunted Baronet," "The Fortunes of Sir Robert Ardagh," and the classic "Green Tea." Editor's introduction. 7 contemporary illustrations. Portrait of LeFanu. xii + 467pp. 5⅜ x 8.
20415-4 Paperbound $2.50

EASY-TO-DO ENTERTAINMENTS AND DIVERSIONS WITH COINS, CARDS, STRING, PAPER AND MATCHES, *R. M. Abraham*
Over 300 tricks, games and puzzles will provide young readers with absorbing fun. Sections on card games; paper-folding; tricks with coins, matches and pieces of string; games for the agile; toy-making from common household objects; mathematical recreations; and 50 miscellaneous pastimes. Anyone in charge of groups of youngsters, including hard-pressed parents, and in need of suggestions on how to keep children sensibly amused and quietly content will find this book indispensable. Clear, simple text, copious number of delightful line drawings and illustrative diagrams. Originally titled "Winter Nights' Entertainments." Introduction by Lord Baden Powell. 329 illustrations. v + 186pp. 5⅜ x 8½.   20921-0 Paperbound $1.00

AN INTRODUCTION TO CHESS MOVES AND TACTICS SIMPLY EXPLAINED, *Leonard Barden*
Beginner's introduction to the royal game. Names, possible moves of the pieces, definitions of essential terms, how games are won, etc. explained in 30-odd pages. With this background you'll be able to sit right down and play. Balance of book teaches strategy — openings, middle game, typical endgame play, and suggestions for improving your game. A sample game is fully analyzed. True middle-level introduction, teaching you all the essentials without oversimplifying or losing you in a maze of detail. 58 figures. 102pp. 5⅜ x 8½.   21210-6 Paperbound $1.25

LASKER'S MANUAL OF CHESS, *Dr. Emanuel Lasker*
Probably the greatest chess player of modern times, Dr. Emanuel Lasker held the world championship 28 years, independent of passing schools or fashions. This unmatched study of the game, chiefly for intermediate to skilled players, analyzes basic methods, combinations, position play, the aesthetics of chess, dozens of different openings, etc., with constant reference to great modern games. Contains a brilliant exposition of Steinitz's important theories. Introduction by Fred Reinfeld. Tables of Lasker's tournament record. 3 indices. 308 diagrams. 1 photograph. xxx + 349pp. 5⅜ x 8.20640-8Paperbound $2.50

COMBINATIONS: THE HEART OF CHESS, *Irving Chernev*
Step-by-step from simple combinations to complex, this book, by a well-known chess writer, shows you the intricacies of pins, counter-pins, knight forks, and smothered mates. Other chapters show alternate lines of play to those taken in actual championship games; boomerang combinations; classic examples of brilliant combination play by Nimzovich, Rubinstein, Tarrasch, Botvinnik, Alekhine and Capablanca. Index. 356 diagrams. ix + 245pp. 5⅜ x 8½.   21744-2 Paperbound $2.00

HOW TO SOLVE CHESS PROBLEMS, *K. S. Howard*
Full of practical suggestions for the fan or the beginner — who knows only the moves of the chessmen. Contains preliminary section and 58 two-move, 46 three-move, and 8 four-move problems composed by 27 outstanding American problem creators in the last 30 years. Explanation of all terms and exhaustive index. "Just what is wanted for the student," Brian Harley. 112 problems, solutions. vi + 171pp. 5⅜ x 8.   20748-X Paperbound $1.50

SOCIAL THOUGHT FROM LORE TO SCIENCE,
H. E. Barnes and H. Becker
An immense survey of sociological thought and ways of viewing, studying, planning, and reforming society from earliest times to the present. Includes thought on society of preliterate peoples, ancient non-Western cultures, and every great movement in Europe, America, and modern Japan. Analyzes hundreds of great thinkers: Plato, Augustine, Bodin, Vico, Montesquieu, Herder, Comte, Marx, etc. Weighs the contributions of utopians, sophists, fascists and communists; economists, jurists, philosophers, ecclesiastics, and every 19th and 20th century school of scientific sociology, anthropology, and social psychology throughout the world. Combines topical, chronological, and regional approaches, treating the evolution of social thought as a process rather than as a series of mere topics. "Impressive accuracy, competence, and discrimination . . . easily the best single survey," *Nation.* Thoroughly revised, with new material up to 1960. 2 indexes. Over 2200 bibliographical notes. Three volume set. Total of 1586pp. 5⅜ x 8.

20901-6, 20902-4, 20903-2 Three volume set, paperbound $9.00

A HISTORY OF HISTORICAL WRITING, *Harry Elmer Barnes*
Virtually the only adequate survey of the whole course of historical writing in a single volume. Surveys developments from the beginnings of historiography in the ancient Near East and the Classical World, up through the Cold War. Covers major historians in detail, shows interrelationship with cultural background, makes clear individual contributions, evaluates and estimates importance; also enormously rich upon minor authors and thinkers who are usually passed over. Packed with scholarship and learning, clear, easily written. Indispensable to every student of history. Revised and enlarged up to 1961. Index and bibliography. xv + 442pp. 5⅜ x 8½.

20104-X Paperbound $2.75

JOHANN SEBASTIAN BACH, *Philipp Spitta*
The complete and unabridged text of the definitive study of Bach. Written some 70 years ago, it is still unsurpassed for its coverage of nearly all aspects of Bach's life and work. There could hardly be a finer non-technical introduction to Bach's music than the detailed, lucid analyses which Spitta provides for hundreds of individual pieces. 26 solid pages are devoted to the B minor mass, for example, and 30 pages to the glorious St. Matthew Passion. This monumental set also includes a major analysis of the music of the 18th century: Buxtehude, Pachelbel, etc. "Unchallenged as the last word on one of the supreme geniuses of music," John Barkham, *Saturday Review Syndicate.* Total of 1819pp. Heavy cloth binding. 5⅜ x 8.

22278-0, 22279-9 Two volume set, clothbound $15.00

BEETHOVEN AND HIS NINE SYMPHONIES, *George Grove*
In this modern middle-level classic of musicology Grove not only analyzes all nine of Beethoven's symphonies very thoroughly in terms of their musical structure, but also discusses the circumstances under which they were written, Beethoven's stylistic development, and much other background material. This is an extremely rich book, yet very easily followed; it is highly recommended to anyone seriously interested in music. Over 250 musical passages. Index. viii + 407pp. 5⅜ x 8.

20334-4 Paperbound $2.25

THREE SCIENCE FICTION NOVELS,
John Taine
Acknowledged by many as the best SF writer of the 1920's, Taine (under the name Eric Temple Bell) was also a Professor of Mathematics of considerable renown. Reprinted here are *The Time Stream*, generally considered Taine's best, *The Greatest Game*, a biological-fiction novel, and *The Purple Sapphire*, involving a supercivilization of the past. Taine's stories tie fantastic narratives to frameworks of original and logical scientific concepts. Speculation is often profound on such questions as the nature of time, concept of entropy, cyclical universes, etc. 4 contemporary illustrations. v + 532pp. 5⅜ x 8⅜.
21180-0 Paperbound $2.50

SEVEN SCIENCE FICTION NOVELS,
H. G. Wells
Full unabridged texts of 7 science-fiction novels of the master. Ranging from biology, physics, chemistry, astronomy, to sociology and other studies, Mr. Wells extrapolates whole worlds of strange and intriguing character. "One will have to go far to match this for entertainment, excitement, and sheer pleasure . . ."*New York Times*. Contents: The Time Machine, The Island of Dr. Moreau, The First Men in the Moon, The Invisible Man, The War of the Worlds, The Food of the Gods, In The Days of the Comet. 1015pp. 5⅜ x 8.
20264-X Clothbound $5.00

28 SCIENCE FICTION STORIES OF H. G. WELLS.
Two full, unabridged novels, *Men Like Gods* and *Star Begotten*, plus 26 short stories by the master science-fiction writer of all time! Stories of space, time, invention, exploration, futuristic adventure. Partial contents: *The Country of the Blind, In the Abyss, The Crystal Egg, The Man Who Could Work Miracles, A Story of Days to Come, The Empire of the Ants, The Magic Shop, The Valley of the Spiders, A Story of the Stone Age, Under the Knife, Sea Raiders*, etc. An indispensable collection for the library of anyone interested in science fiction adventure. 928pp. 5⅜ x 8.
20265-8 Clothbound $5.00

THREE MARTIAN NOVELS,
Edgar Rice Burroughs
Complete, unabridged reprinting, in one volume, of Thuvia, Maid of Mars; Chessmen of Mars; The Master Mind of Mars. Hours of science-fiction adventure by a modern master storyteller. Reset in large clear type for easy reading. 16 illustrations by J. Allen St. John. vi + 499pp. 5⅜ x 8½.
20039-6 Paperbound $2.50

AN INTELLECTUAL AND CULTURAL HISTORY OF THE WESTERN WORLD,
Harry Elmer Barnes
Monumental 3-volume survey of intellectual development of Europe from primitive cultures to the present day. Every significant product of human intellect traced through history: art, literature, mathematics, physical sciences, medicine, music, technology, social sciences, religions, jurisprudence, education, etc. Presentation is lucid and specific, analyzing in detail specific discoveries, theories, literary works, and so on. Revised (1965) by recognized scholars in specialized fields under the direction of Prof. Barnes. Revised bibliography. Indexes. 24 illustrations. Total of xxix + 1318pp.
21275-0, 21276-9, 21277-7 Three volume set, paperbound $8.25

HEAR ME TALKIN' TO YA, *edited by Nat Shapiro and Nat Hentoff*
In their own words, Louis Armstrong, King Oliver, Fletcher Henderson, Bunk
Johnson, Bix Beiderbecke, Billy Holiday, Fats Waller, Jelly Roll Morton,
Duke Ellington, and many others comment on the origins of jazz in New
Orleans and its growth in Chicago's South Side, Kansas City's jam sessions,
Depression Harlem, and the modernism of the West Coast schools. Taken
from taped conversations, letters, magazine articles, other first-hand sources.
Editors' introduction. xvi + 429pp. 5⅜ x 8½.   21726-4 Paperbound $2.00

THE JOURNAL OF HENRY D. THOREAU
A 25-year record by the great American observer and critic, as complete a
record of a great man's inner life as is anywhere available. Thoreau's Journals
served him as raw material for his formal pieces, as a place where he could
develop his ideas, as an outlet for his interests in wild life and plants, in
writing as an art, in classics of literature, Walt Whitman and other contemporaries, in politics, slavery, individual's relation to the State, etc. The
Journals present a portrait of a remarkable man, and are an observant social
history. Unabridged republication of 1906 edition, Bradford Torrey and
Francis H. Allen, editors. Illustrations. Total of 1888pp. 8⅜ x 12¼.
20312-3, 20313-1 Two volume set, clothbound $30.00

A SHAKESPEARIAN GRAMMAR, *E. A. Abbott*
Basic reference to Shakespeare and his contemporaries, explaining through
thousands of quotations from Shakespeare, Jonson, Beaumont and Fletcher,
North's *Plutarch* and other sources the grammatical usage differing from the
modern. First published in 1870 and written by a scholar who spent much of
his life isolating principles of Elizabethan language, the book is unlikely ever
to be superseded. Indexes. xxiv + 511pp. 5⅜ x 8½. 21582-2 Paperbound $3.00

FOLK-LORE OF SHAKESPEARE, *T. F. Thistelton Dyer*
Classic study, drawing from Shakespeare a large body of references to supernatural beliefs, terminology of falconry and hunting, games and sports, good
luck charms, marriage customs, folk medicines, superstitions about plants,
animals, birds, argot of the underworld, sexual slang of London, proverbs,
drinking customs, weather lore, and much else. From full compilation comes
a mirror of the 17th-century popular mind. Index. ix + 526pp. 5⅜ x 8½.
21614-4 Paperbound $2.75

THE NEW VARIORUM SHAKESPEARE, *edited by H. H. Furness*
By far the richest editions of the plays ever produced in any country or
language. Each volume contains complete text (usually First Folio) of the
play, all variants in Quarto and other Folio texts, editorial changes by every
major editor to Furness's own time (1900), footnotes to obscure references or
language, extensive quotes from literature of Shakespearian criticism, essays
on plot sources (often reprinting sources in full), and much more.

HAMLET, *edited by H. H. Furness*
Total of xxvi + 905pp. 5⅜ x 8½.
21004-9, 21005-7 Two volume set, paperbound $5.25

TWELFTH NIGHT, *edited by H. H. Furness*
Index. xxii + 434pp. 5⅜ x 8½.   21189-4 Paperbound $2.75

LA BOHEME BY GIACOMO PUCCINI,
translated and introduced by Ellen H. Bleiler
Complete handbook for the operagoer, with everything needed for full enjoy-
ment except the musical score itself. Complete Italian libretto, with new,
modern English line-by-line translation—the only libretto printing all repeats;
biography of Puccini; the librettists; background to the opera, Murger's La
Boheme, etc.; circumstances of composition and performances; plot summary;
and pictorial section of 73 illustrations showing Puccini, famous singers and
performances, etc. Large clear type for easy reading. 124pp. 5⅜ x 8½.
20404-9 Paperbound $1.25

ANTONIO STRADIVARI: HIS LIFE AND WORK (1644-1737),
W. Henry Hill, Arthur F. Hill, and Alfred E. Hill
Still the only book that really delves into life and art of the incomparable
Italian craftsman, maker of the finest musical instruments in the world today.
The authors, expert violin-makers themselves, discuss Stradivari's ancestry, his
construction and finishing techniques, distinguished characteristics of many
of his instruments and their locations. Included, too, is story of introduction
of his instruments into France, England, first revelation of their supreme
merit, and information on his labels, number of instruments made, prices,
mystery of ingredients of his varnish, tone of pre-1684 Stradivari violin and
changes between 1684 and 1690. An extremely interesting, informative account
for all music lovers, from craftsman to concert-goer. Republication of original
(1902) edition. New introduction by Sydney Beck, Head of Rare Book and
Manuscript Collections, Music Division, New York Public Library. Analytical
index by Rembert Wurlitzer. Appendixes. 68 illustrations. 30 full-page plates.
4 in color. xxvi + 315pp. 5⅜ x 8½. 20425-1 Paperbound $2.25

MUSICAL AUTOGRAPHS FROM MONTEVERDI TO HINDEMITH,
Emanuel Winternitz
For beauty, for intrinsic interest, for perspective on the composer's personality,
for subtleties of phrasing, shading, emphasis indicated in the autograph but
suppressed in the printed score, the mss. of musical composition are fascinating
documents which repay close study in many different ways. This 2-volume
work reprints facsimiles of mss. by virtually every major composer, and many
minor figures—196 examples in all. A full text points out what can be learned
from mss., analyzes each sample. Index. Bibliography. 18 figures. 196 plates.
Total of 170pp. of text. 7⅞ x 10¾.
21312-9, 21313-7 Two volume set, paperbound $5.00

J. S. BACH,
Albert Schweitzer
One of the few great full-length studies of Bach's life and work, and the
study upon which Schweitzer's renown as a musicologist rests. On first appearance (1911), revolutionized Bach performance. The only writer on Bach to
be musicologist, performing musician, and student of history, theology and
philosophy, Schweitzer contributes particularly full sections on history of German Protestant church music, theories on motivic pictorial representations
in vocal music, and practical suggestions for performance. Translated by
Ernest Newman. Indexes. 5 illustrations. 650 musical examples. Total of xix
+ 928pp. 5⅜ x 8½. 21631-4, 21632-2 Two volume set, paperbound $4.50

THE METHODS OF ETHICS, *Henry Sidgwick*
Propounding no organized system of its own, study subjects every major methodological approach to ethics to rigorous, objective analysis. Study discusses and relates ethical thought of Plato, Aristotle, Bentham, Clarke, Butler, Hobbes, Hume, Mill, Spencer, Kant, and dozens of others. Sidgwick retains conclusions from each system which follow from ethical premises, rejecting the faulty. Considered by many in the field to be among the most important treatises on ethical philosophy. Appendix. Index. xlvii + 528pp. 5⅜ x 8½.
21608-X Paperbound $2.50

TEUTONIC MYTHOLOGY, *Jakob Grimm*
A milestone in Western culture; the work which established on a modern basis the study of history of religions and comparative religions. 4-volume work assembles and interprets everything available on religious and folkloristic beliefs of Germanic people (including Scandinavians, Anglo-Saxons, etc.). Assembling material from such sources as Tacitus, surviving Old Norse and Icelandic texts, archeological remains, folktales, surviving superstitions, comparative traditions, linguistic analysis, etc. Grimm explores pagan deities, heroes, folklore of nature, religious practices, and every other area of pagan German belief. To this day, the unrivaled, definitive, exhaustive study. Translated by J. S. Stallybrass from 4th (1883) German edition. Indexes. Total of lxxvii + 1887pp. 5⅜ x 8½.
21602-0, 21603-9, 21604-7, 21605-5 Four volume set, paperbound $11.00

THE I CHING, *translated by James Legge*
Called "The Book of Changes" in English, this is one of the Five Classics edited by Confucius, basic and central to Chinese thought. Explains perhaps the most complex system of divination known, founded on the theory that all things happening at any one time have characteristic features which can be isolated and related. Significant in Oriental studies, in history of religions and philosophy, and also to Jungian psychoanalysis and other areas of modern European thought. Index. Appendixes. 6 plates. xxi + 448pp. 5⅜ x 8½.
21062-6 Paperbound $2.75

HISTORY OF ANCIENT PHILOSOPHY, *W. Windelband*
One of the clearest, most accurate comprehensive surveys of Greek and Roman philosophy. Discusses ancient philosophy in general, intellectual life in Greece in the 7th and 6th centuries B.C., Thales, Anaximander, Anaximenes, Heraclitus, the Eleatics, Empedocles, Anaxagoras, Leucippus, the Pythagoreans, the Sophists, Socrates, Democritus (20 pages), Plato (50 pages), Aristotle (70 pages), the Peripatetics, Stoics, Epicureans, Sceptics, Neo-platonists, Christian Apologists, etc. 2nd German edition translated by H. E. Cushman. xv + 393pp. 5⅜ x 8.
20357-3 Paperbound $2.25

THE PALACE OF PLEASURE, *William Painter*
Elizabethan versions of Italian and French novels from *The Decameron*, Cinthio, Straparola, Queen Margaret of Navarre, and other continental sources — the very work that provided Shakespeare and dozens of his contemporaries with many of their plots and sub-plots and, therefore, justly considered one of the most influential books in all English literature. It is also a book that any reader will still enjoy. Total of cviii + 1,224pp.
21691-8, 21692-6, 21693-4 Three volume set, paperbound $6.75

THE WONDERFUL WIZARD OF OZ, *L. F. Baum*
All the original W. W. Denslow illustrations in full color—as much a part of "The Wizard" as Tenniel's drawings are of "Alice in Wonderland." "The Wizard" is still America's best-loved fairy tale, in which, as the author expresses it, "The wonderment and joy are retained and the heartaches and nightmares left out." Now today's young readers can enjoy every word and wonderful picture of the original book. New introduction by Martin Gardner. A Baum bibliography. 23 full-page color plates. viii + 268pp. 5⅜ x 8.
20691-2 Paperbound $1.95

THE MARVELOUS LAND OF OZ, *L. F. Baum*
This is the equally enchanting sequel to the "Wizard," continuing the adventures of the Scarecrow and the Tin Woodman. The hero this time is a little boy named Tip, and all the delightful Oz magic is still present. This is the Oz book with the Animated Saw-Horse, the Woggle-Bug, and Jack Pumpkinhead. All the original John R. Neill illustrations, 10 in full color. 287pp. 5⅜ x 8.
20692-0 Paperbound $1.75

ALICE'S ADVENTURES UNDER GROUND, *Lewis Carroll*
The original *Alice in Wonderland*, hand-lettered and illustrated by Carroll himself, and originally presented as a Christmas gift to a child-friend. Adults as well as children will enjoy this charming volume, reproduced faithfully in this Dover edition. While the story is essentially the same, there are slight changes, and Carroll's spritely drawings present an intriguing alternative to the famous Tenniel illustrations. One of the most popular books in Dover's catalogue. Introduction by Martin Gardner. 38 illustrations. 128pp. 5⅜ x 8½.
21482-6 Paperbound $1.00

THE NURSERY "ALICE," *Lewis Carroll*
While most of us consider *Alice in Wonderland* a story for children of all ages, Carroll himself felt it was beyond younger children. He therefore provided this simplified version, illustrated with the famous Tenniel drawings enlarged and colored in delicate tints, for children aged "from Nought to Five." Dover's edition of this now rare classic is a faithful copy of the 1889 printing, including 20 illustrations by Tenniel, and front and back covers reproduced in full color. Introduction by Martin Gardner. xxiii + 67pp. 6⅛ x 9¼.
21610-1 Paperbound $1.75

THE STORY OF KING ARTHUR AND HIS KNIGHTS, *Howard Pyle*
A fast-paced, exciting retelling of the best known Arthurian legends for young readers by one of America's best story tellers and illustrators. The sword Excalibur, wooing of Guinevere, Merlin and his downfall, adventures of Sir Pellias and Gawaine, and others. The pen and ink illustrations are vividly imagined and wonderfully drawn. 41 illustrations. xviii + 313pp. 6⅛ x 9¼.
21445-1 Paperbound $2.00

Prices subject to change without notice.

Available at your book dealer or write for free catalogue to Dept. Adsci, Dover Publications, Inc., 180 Varick St., N.Y., N.Y. 10014. Dover publishes more than 150 books each year on science, elementary and advanced mathematics, biology, music, art, literary history, social sciences and other areas.